THE
GOOD
PRODUCE
GUIDE2011

THE
GOOD
PRODUCE
GUIDE 2011

ROSE PRINCE

hardie grant books

The Good Produce Guide 2011 by Rose Prince

First published in 2011 by Hardie Grant Books

Hardie Grant Books London
Dudley House, North Suite
34–35 Southampton Street
London WC2E 7HF
www.hardiegrant.co.uk

Hardie Grant Books (Australia)
85 High Street, Prahran, Victoria, Australia 3181
www.hardiegrant.com.au

British Library Cataloguing-in-Publication Data. A catalogue record
for this book is available from the British Library.

ISBN 978-1-74270-046-5

Design by Geoff Borin (www.geoffborin.com)
Cover design by Susan St Louis
Cover image © Sharyn Cairns

Typeset by SX Composing DTP, Rayleigh, Essex SS6 7XF

Printed in the UK by CPI William Clowes Beccles NR34 7TL

10 9 8 7 6 5 4 3 2 1

About Rose Prince

Rose Prince is a food columnist on the *Daily Telegraph* and for the *Telegraph Magazine* and contributes to the *Daily Mail* and the *Independent on Sunday*. She has been writing campaigning articles about food and farming for over 10 years, travelling all over the world in pursuit of great producers. For her previous column on the *Daily Telegraph*, Shop Local, she travelled to 70 UK market towns and cities, studying regional food shops and producers. She is the author of four books, *The New English Kitchen* (2005), which champions economical ways to cook with better quality ingredients; *The Savvy Shopper* (2006), an ethical food guide; and *The New English Table* (2008), an encyclopedia of diverse British ingredients; and *Kitchenella*, a book of feminine recipes. In 2009 and 2010 she was one of the judges of the BBC Radio 4 Food and Farming Awards, and *Vogue* magazine listed her as one of Britain's 30 most inspirational women. She lives in London and Dorset with her husband Dominic and two children.

www.roseprince.co.uk

Contents

How to find your way around

The Good Produce Guide 2011

Welcome to *The Good Produce Guide 2011*. The guide is organised into 10 chapters arranged alphabetically by region: East of England, London, Midlands, North East and Yorkshire, North West, Northern Ireland, Scotland, South East, South West and Wales. Within each chapter, the entries are arranged into different types of food produce, for example Dairy, and places to buy food, such as Farm Shops and Food Markets.

● Entries are alphabetical along the same lines as a telephone directory. If you are looking for W. G. Smith, for example, look under S; for John Smith Butchers, look under J; for The Cheeseboard, look under C.

● Each entry gives you the web address, phone number, postal address with postcode and opening times. Some companies or producers have no website. Where a company trades only online there are no opening times. Occasionally opening times are so seasonally variable or irregular, we've suggested readers phone before visiting.

● Following the regional chapters there is a seasonal food calendar (which shows you when to buy great UK produce at its best); a list of major UK food festivals; a list of useful websites and addresses; and a list of useful publications.

● There are two indexes at the back of the book; one which is by trades, and the other which is an alphabetical list of all the producers and suppliers mentioned.

● Finally, there is a feedback form. This Guide is published annually so we'd like to know what you think of the food producers and suppliers we've included and to hear of any that you think should appear here next year.

▼ IMPORTANT INFORMATION AT A GLANCE

 Telephone number

 Address

 Opening times

 Goods can be sent via mail order/home delivery

 You can order goods online

 You can order goods over the phone to have them delivered or to collect

 There is a customer box scheme

 You can pick your own fruit or vegetables

 Cash or cheque only (no cards)

SCOTLAND

NORTHERN
IRELAND

NORTH
EAST
AND
YORKSHIRE

NORTH
WEST

MIDLANDS

WALES

EAST OF
ENGLAND

LONDON

SOUTH EAST

SOUTH WEST

Counties in England are divided into these regions:

East of England Bedfordshire, Cambridgeshire, Essex, Hertfordshire, Norfolk, Suffolk

London Within the M25

Midlands Birmingham (and West Midlands), Derbyshire, Herefordshire, Leicestershire, Lincolnshire, Northamptonshire, Nottinghamshire, Rutland, Shropshire, Staffordshire, Warwickshire, Worcestershire

North East and Yorkshire Cleveland, Co Durham, Humberside, Northumberland, North Yorkshire, South Yorkshire, Tyne & Wear, West Yorkshire

North West Cheshire, Cumbria, Greater Manchester, Lancashire, Merseyside

South East Berkshire, Buckinghamshire, East Sussex, Hampshire, Isle of Wight, Kent, Oxfordshire, Surrey, West Sussex

South West Cornwall, Devon, Dorset, Gloucestershire, Somerset, Wiltshire

Introduction

This is the second edition of the *Good Produce Guide*, updated and with dozens of interesting new entries. It is essentially a guide that shows where to buy food, but it will not direct you to a supermarket chain. At the heart of the guide is an independent spirit. The shops, markets and food producers featured inside are independent businesses, many of them family run and 'small' when compared to the retailing giants that prevail on every British high street. Those few that are not independent show overwhelming support for other independent food producers. Entries are chosen independently, too, by me and a small team of likeminded people.

The guide charges no fees to the entries – they are in the book simply because I like the food they sell and I believe they offer an invaluable service to British shoppers. Criteria for entry into this guide can be summed up in two words: honesty and talent. I want the entries in this book to be the kind of businesses that open their doors for inspection and some hard questioning and – equally importantly – to be people that make delicious things we'd all like to eat.

This time you will find a very different *Good Produce Guide* to the first, the major change being that the guide is now laid out in a regional format. It is now much easier to find a market or farm shop, butcher or pick-your-own in your area. This change was made in response to reader feedback from the first edition – and I think it makes the book even more useful. I love the new version because I can take a copy with me when travelling (or keep one permanently in the car) and find a good place to buy food wherever I am in the UK. Or, if I want to buy authentic, regional specialities, I can simply refer to the relevant section of the book.

For those who holiday in the UK, renting accommodation and/or catering for themselves, the new 2011 guide will tell you where to find the nearest farmers' markets, and on which day and what time. It will point you to the best local butcher, beekeeper or baker. It will help you find a glass of tangy, cloudy English apple juice, pick your own strawberries, find the freshest, sustainably caught fish and sample the wonders of British game – or just buy good, honestly produced, groceries for every day. Instead of going to a branch of the supermarket chain you use at home, you can have a real holiday and try local foods made by local people who, I promise, will give you a warm welcome.

The new 2011 guide has 180 new entries. As well as adding exciting new people that have recently opened or for some reason were not on my radar, I have tried to increase the number of entries in areas that seem a little 'thin' on good food produce – but that is not to say I add a new entry for the sake of it. The more the better however, and I hope that readers will make use of the feedback form at the back of the book and tell me of any new finds, or places that I have missed. I will then investigate, and we will make sure we visit or sample their food.

Sadly I have removed a few entries that had been in the 2010 guide. Some producers have retired, others closed down, unable to continue operating in the present financial climate. I sincerely hope their exclusion is temporary. In rare cases there were entries that no longer met our criteria – again, I hope their exclusion is short-term. Do be aware that the guide goes to print some time before it is on sale and it is impossible to be 100 per cent up to date – so please forgive any errors. Once again I am always happy to hear your thoughts – even the grumpy type!

I believe this guide has a great future. I shamelessly promote this possibility because while it means much to me, there are over 1100 people in this book that could bene-fit; a whole mini-economy that matters. Without them, life would be dull. With good food produce, every day brings the excitement of a great meal.

Rose Prince
2011

The best producers of 2011

This year I thought I would highlight the establishments who have gone that extra mile to produce something truly outstanding. Here are my top 10 must-visit producers for 2011 – these talented people, in my opinion, are selling some of the most delicious food in Britain.

Best Farm Shop
Dart's Farm Shop, Devon (page 301)
Runner-up
Loch Arthur Farm Shop, Dumfries and Galloway (page 218)

Best Food Market
Bristol Slow Food Market, Bristol (page 316)
Runner-up
Brixton Market, London (page 42)

Best Deli or Specialist
Melrose and Morgan, London (page 62)
Runner-up
Lawson's Delicatessen, Suffolk (page 12)

Best Butcher
M. Moen & Sons, London (page 80)
Runner-up
John Robinson & Son, Hampshire (page 262)

Best Baker or Confectioner
Long Crichel Bakery, Dorset (page 341)
Runner-up
Welbeck Bakehouse, Nottinghamshire (page 140)

Best Dairy Producer
Stichelton Dairy, Nottinghamshire (page 145)
Runner-up
Daylesford Organic Farm Shop, Gloucestershire (page 301)

Best Fishmonger
Matthew Stevens & Son, Cornwall (page 354)
Runner-up
The Whitby Catch, North Yorkshire (page 176)

Best Grower / Greengrocer
Buttervilla, Cornwall (page 360)
Runner-up
Woodlands Farm Organic Box Scheme, Lincolnshire (page 149)

Best Drinks Producer
The Orchard Pig, Somerset (page 369)
Runner-up
The Rare Tea Company, London (page 115)

East of England

▼ FARM SHOPS

Blackwells Farm Produce ✪

www.blackwellsfarmproduce.co.uk
☎ 01376 562500
✉ Herons Farm, Colne Road,
Coggeshall, Essex **CO6 1TQ**
🕐 Mon–Fri 8am–6pm;
Sat 8am–4pm; Sun 10am–3pm

Nineteen-year-old Phoebe Robinson, who has been a great help in the compilation of this year's guide cannot praise this farm shop highly enough – she lives nearby. The Blackwell family have been farming at Herons Farm since the '30s and in 2008 started their farm shop. It has gone down a storm with locals. Much of the produce is sourced within a 20-mile radius. They have an on-site bakery; the lamb, beef and game is particularly noteworthy; and they sell rare-breed meats, vegetables, fruit, wines, cider and beer. They also take home-delivery orders via the internet or by telephone. Apart from Phoebe I have had other complimentary reports and would welcome more observations.

Calcott Hall Farm Shop

www.calcotthall.com
☎ 01277 264164
✉ Ongar Road, Brentwood, Essex
CM15 9HS
🕐 Tues–Sat 8.30am–5.30pm;
Sun 10am–2pm

Andrew and Janet McTurk grow a vast range of vegetables and fruit, and sell a number of great foods from East Anglia. The couple have been here for over 35 years, and began selling potatoes and sweetcorn from crates in 1974. In 1983 they renovated an old Essex barn to house today's shop. Minimal pesticides are used, and varieties are chosen for flavour and not yield. Expect to find (season permitting) various potatoes, asparagus, strawberries, blackcurrants, squash, kohl rabi, purple sprouting broccoli, kale, carrots, beetroot and much more. A finalist in The National Farmers' Retail & Markets Association (FARMA) awards, 2010.

Christmas Hill Farm Shop

www.christmashill.co.uk/farmshop
☎ 01842 861144
✉ Station Road, Lakenheath,
Brandon, Suffolk **IP27 9AB**
🕐 Tues–Sat 9am–5.30pm;
Sun 10am–4pm

Housed in a former cowshed and dairy, a farm shop selling the farm's own rare-breed beef and lamb plus local pork, chicken and game. Beef is hung for four weeks; all meat is from animals that are slow grown and naturally fed. Mutton is sometimes on offer but call in advance – with the meat sold here being mostly rare breed, it is subject to availability.

Farmcafé & Foodmarket

www.farmcafe.co.uk
01728 747717
Farm Café and Foodmarket,
Main Road (A12), Marlesford,
Woodbridge, Suffolk **IP13 0AG**
Mon–Sun 7am–6pm

If only every A road in the UK boasted a place like this.
The café serves full English breakfasts and bacon rolls made
only from local ingredients, and the shop sells the pick of
Suffolk produce, which is some pick as this is a region with
a rich diversity of great farm producers and independent
entrepreneurs. Bread is from Woodbridge (marked if
'today's' or 'yesterday's'), milk is from local dairy Marybelle,
there are chickens from Sutton Hoo, black pudding from
Clarke's butchery, Pinneys of Alford smoked fish, Suffolk
Gold cheese and locally grown blueberries.

Farrowby Farm ⊙ ⊛

www.farrowbyfarm.co.uk
01462 733700
New Inn Road, Hinxworth,
Hertfordshire **SG7 5EY**
Mon–Tues, Thurs–Sun 10am–4pm

A small but appealing farm shop, run by Tim and Beverley
Burrows on their Hinxworth smallholding, specialising in
poultry. The welfare of the hens is not in question – these birds
are downright spoilt and seem to command the place as they
perch along the car park fence. Beside the shop is a café, and
the Burrows have thoughtfully fenced in the garden, keeping
the fat hens at bay and making a haven for visiting small
children. Venison casserole and rabbit stew was on the menu
on the day of my visit. There's also fresh duck and guinea fowl
on sale, free-range eggs, plus pork from their own pigs –
traditional breeds crossed with a large white boar. You can
also buy honey from an apiary in Much Haddon, cold-pressed
rapeseed oil from Suffolk, and flour from Glebe Farm Mill.
Make sure you order turkeys for Christmas well in advance.

Garden Friends Farm Shop

www.gardenfriendsvegetablebox.
com
01480 210383
Top Farm, The Lane, Wyboston,
Bedfordshire **MK44 3AS**

This shop sells a host of food from their surrounding area.
They have also just started a farm shop but for more details
visit their website, which I have to say is woefully out of date.
They do deliveries locally of their veg boxes. At the farm shop
local lamb, beef, chicken and pork is available, as well as
cheese, breads and honey. I would really welcome some
further comments on this shop. Although they are trying
really hard I am not sure yet about their business model.

Good Food Growers, Middleton Farm Shop

jack.rosenthal@btinternet.com
01728 648253
Reckford Farm, Middleton,
Saxmundham, Suffolk **IP17 3NS**
Summer Mon–Sat 9am–5pm;
Sun 10am–5pm; **Winter** Tues–Sun
10am–5pm

Jack Rosenthal's exemplary farm shop acts as an outlet for nearby producers of asparagus in season, soft and orchard fruit, cheeses, fish, honey, meat and bread. Much of the produce is grown on neighbouring farms with the aim of bringing the producer and consumer closer together. The second branch is called Reckford Farm shop and is located on Westleton Road, Middleton, Saxmundham, Suffolk IP17 3NS (Tel: 01728 643253).

Highways

www.highwaysonline.co.uk
01379 898357
Finningham Road, Rickinghall,
Diss, Norfolk **IP22 1LP**
Mon–Fri 9am–6pm;
Sat pm; Sun am

Farmers Philip and Glynis Brown specialise in home-reared, rare-breed Gloucester Old Spot pork, slow reared on the farm, plus home-reared lamb and Norfolk Bronze turkey (seasonal). Butchery is on site and you can buy at local farmers' markets (contact for times and details).

La Hogue Farm Shop & Delicatessen

www.lahogue.co.uk
01638 751128
La Hogue Farm, Chippenham,
Ely, Cambridgeshire **CB7 5PZ**
Tues–Fri 10am–6pm;
Sat 9am–5.30pm; Sun 10am–4pm

The success of this farm shop with its in-house butchery and astonishing range must be put down in part to the dearth of high-street food shopping in Newmarket (though it does still have some decent butchers). Chris and Jo Reeks claim to sell an astonishing 3000 products, making it an essential one-stop shop for locals. Highlights in the shop are the free-range eggs laid by traditional hen breeds on nearby Top Farm, Stoberry potted shrimps made in Newmarket by John and Barbara Rimmer, the Suffolk chickens, home-made stock from Exning and goose fat from local producer George Munn. There is also a wide range of ready-to-heat meals made with natural ingredients by Cook, a company in the south of England who have their own shops and supply many farm shops. There's also a good wine shop next door.

Martins Farm

01263 861 241
Melton Road, Hindolveston,
Norfolk **NR20 5DB**

Drop by the Jason family's farm and pick up amazing home-grown fruit and vegetables, or dip into the freezer for pork and chicken, reared on the farm. Farm gate sales – there is an honesty box, so make sure to take cash.

The Oak Tree Low Carbon Farm

www.the-oak-tree.co.uk
07954 289490
The Oak Tree, Playford Lane,
Rushmere, St Andrew, Ipswich,
Suffolk **IP5 1DW**

Seasonal vegetables from an exemplary farm with, as the name suggests, an exceptionally low sooty footprint. Vegetables are delivered locally by bike, and everything on the farm that can be recycled will be. Produce is fantastic, locals rave about it, and the next stage will be expansion into free-range hens' eggs. Local delivery available.

Pecks Farm Shop ○◎ ◑◐

www.pecksfarmshop.co.uk
01525 211859
Stockwell Farm, Eggington,
Leighton Buzzard, Bedfordshire
LU7 9PA
Mon–Sat 9am–6pm;
Sun 10am–3pm

The Pecks are dairy farmers who opened their farm shop in 2002 when the milk price dropped, leaving them with an unworkable income. The shop, housed in an airy barn, now sells a great range of locally grown vegetables. On the day of my visit there were cauliflowers on sale in not one, but four different colours – purple, green, yellow and white! The Pecks focus on quality, and not just on organic for the sake of it, so they prefer to sell produce that has not travelled far to the shop and that is as fresh as possible. Bread is baked every day and there is produce from the family's own Eggington Dairy, including milk, yoghurt, cream and butter. Sausages, bacon and pies are bought in from local firm Woburn Country Foods and pies are made by the Lime Tree Pantry. You will also find a few deli items, such as olive oil, olives and cheese.

Phil Truin Poultry

01284 828344
Elmwood Farm, Daking Lane,
Felsham, Bury St Edmunds, Suffolk
IP30 0QW
Opening times vary, please call
ahead.

For over 30 years Phil and his team have been rearing chickens 'the hard way, the slow way, the traditional way', and he is passionate about his product. Over the festive season he also stocks bronze turkeys and geese. The result of the birds' free-range, naturally fed and relaxed lives is a tender, juicy meat that is packed with flavour, and a skin that crisps up wonderfully. As it is a working farm, it is best to call ahead and check that the shop is open – although there is usually a friendly face around who will happily serve a passer-by.

Swafield Farm Shop

www.taverntasty.co.uk
☎ 01692 405 444
✉ The Street, Swafield, North Walsingham, Norfolk **NR28 0RQ**
🕐 Mon–Fri 7.30am–5pm; Sat 7.30am–1.30pm

The home-reared pork on sale in this good farm shop is from the farm's own delightful, British lop-eared pigs, and there are other rare-breed meats including Saddleback, Gloucestershire Old Spot, Large Black and Tamworth. It is the only Rare Breeds Survival Trust accredited butcher in Norfolk. The pigs are slow reared on a totally natural diet. Twenty or so varieties of sausage are made on the farm as well as pies – the pork and pickle pie is a BBC Oliver Magazine award winner. This is pork lovers' paradise, no doubt about it.

Walsingham Farms Shop ✔

www.walsinghamfarmsshop.co.uk
☎ 01328 821877
✉ Guild Street, Walsingham, Norfolk **NR22 6BU**
🕐 Tues–Fri 9am–6pm; Sat 9am–5pm; Sun 10am–4pm

This is a very popular, well-reviewed farm shop in the medieval pilgrimage village of Little Walsingham, run by the Walsingham Estate in conjunction with its tenant farmers. It sells excellent, locally sourced fresh meat (the beef is reared less than one mile away), with poultry and game all butchered on site by Clive and Dan, the shop's in-house butchers. Ready-made dishes including pies, pâtés, stews and puddings are made in the shop's kitchen every day. There are free-range hen, goose, duck and quail eggs from David and Helen Perowne at nearby Top Farm, Great Snoring and game from the Walsingham Estate. Delicious artisan cheeses (made by Catherine Temple at Wighton and Ellie Betts of Ferndale Farm, Little Barningham), Norfolk ham, sausages and bacon, a range of fresh fish and shellfish (smoked fish, too), plus cakes, jams and pickles make this one of the best-stocked shops I have found. Even the imported products are carefully sourced, including olive oils from local importers Casa de L'Oli, and Fairtrade bananas. The second branch is called Norfolk Lavender Farm and is located in Caley Hill, Heacham, King's Lynn, Norfolk PE31 7JE (tel: 01485 570384)

Wiveton Hall ◑ ◉

www.wivetonhall.co.uk
☎ 01263 740525
✉ Wiveton Hall, Holt, Norfolk
NR25 7TE
🕐 Mon–Sun 9.30am–5pm

Fruit and vegetables available here in season include asparagus, broad beans, tomatoes, squash, strawberries, raspberries, gooseberries, globe artichokes and blackcurrants. You can also buy the farm's own honey, free-range eggs, free-range pork and Gloucestershire Old Spot bacon. Next door there is a café headed by Alison Yetman, which continues to get rave reviews.

FOOD MARKETS ▼

Beccles Farmers' Market ◉

www.becclesfarmersmarket.co.uk
☎ 01502 476240
✉ Beccles Heliport, Ellough Airfield, Beccles, Suffolk **NR34 7UH**
🕐 **Monthly,** 1st and 3rd Sat 9am–1pm

A good-sized 'one-stop' market with about 30 stalls selling fresh meat, including plenty of Suffolk pork and hams, game birds, venison and poultry (including organic). There are also fresh and smoked fish from the Suffolk Coast, locally produced milk, yoghurt, cheese, fresh just-dug vegetables, artisan bread, home-made cakes and pies, plus free-range hen and duck eggs.

Ely Farmers' Market ◉

☎ 01353 650080
✉ Market Square, Ely, Cambridgeshire **CB7 4LS**
🕐 **Twice monthly,** 2nd and 4th Sat 8.30am–2pm

Traditional as well as exotic produce, such as ostrich meat, can be found at over 25 stalls at this popular market. Typical foodie items, such as cakes, jams, meats, organic breads, free-range eggs, fruit and vegetables can be found alongside chilli plants and local real ale and herbal remedies.

Eye Country Market ◉

www.country-markets.co.uk
☎ 01246 261508
✉ Eye Town Hall, Broad Street, Eye, Suffolk **IP23 7AF**
🕐 **Weekly,** Wed 10–11am

By way of an introduction to Country Markets (formerly the Women's Institute or WI markets), you could not do better than visit this one in Eye. These are not conventional markets with stalls piled with vast quantities of food. You are more likely to find an individual who has plucked a few greens from the garden, and who will just as happily barter with another stallholder as they would sell their produce. One rule with country markets is to arrive bang on time. Blink and you will miss the produce, which can sell out fast. The quality and freshness can be fantastic, however, and well worth the effort. (The only thing I take issue with is the prevalence of margarine used in cakes.) Country markets are especially good for people who live alone as they are great places to buy natural, ready-made dishes such as shepherd's pie, perfect if you do not feel like cooking. The Eye Market, incidentally, was a finalist in the 2009 BBC Radio 4 Food & Farming Awards Best Market category. See the website to find your nearest market.

Fakenham Farmers' Market £

www.fakenhamfarmersmarket. co.uk

☎ 01328 862702

✉ Market Square, Fakenham, Norfolk **NR21 9BE**

🕐 Monthly, 4th Sat 8.30am–12pm

On the fourth Saturday of every month, the lovely town of Fakenham hosts a farmers' market whose producers bring some of the great produce grown or harvested from Norfolk's fertile land and coast. Loyal locals describe this market as literally bulging with good things, ranging from Tavern Tasty Meats to Stuart Oetzman's excellent bread and pork pies at the Metfield Bakery stall. There are specialist egg stalls, hand-made cheeses, poultry, beef and game, plus a cornucopia of fruit and veg stalls, including organic. The market sells out quickly mind, so arrive early. Look for cheeses made by H Temples, free-range chicken from Rory Watson, game from Garner & Sons, kippers from Norfolk Kipper House and soft fruit from the Dickie family.

Lavenham Farmers' Market £

☎ 07704 627973

✉ Lavenham Village Hall, Church Street, Lavenham, Sudbury, Suffolk **CO10 9QT**

🕐 Monthly, 4th Sat 10am–1pm

As always in Suffolk, there is no shortage of good produce. Look out for heather honey from Rita Heath, blueberries in season from Jo Garden, fresh produce from Fox's of Colchester and freshly cut English flowers grown by Claire Congdon at Capel St Mary. This is the area for good pork, bacon and hams (check out Clavering Pigs' stall), free-range Christmas turkeys and geese, Red Poll beef and potatoes. If you just want to eat and not shop, stop by for some Chinese at One Tan Van, sip a coffee and nibble a cake at the Farmers' Market Café or buy an ice cream from Major Miles and his Ice Cream Machine.

Needham Farmers' Market

01502 476240
Alder Carr Farm, Creeting
St Mary, Ipswich, Suffolk **IP6 8LX**
Monthly, 3rd Sat 9am–1pm

You'll find fresh meat from the numerous and wonderful Suffolk farms where pork, cured hams and sausages are typical of the region, plus artisan bread, vegetables, Jersey cream, soft fruit grown at Alder Carr Farm (see page 33) and delicious Alder Tree fruit ice cream (see page 27). Look out also for the amazing Suffolk beef, in particular the local breed, Red Poll, grazed on the ancient heathlands that lead up to the coast. This is a special region for small-scale food production, so this is an especially exciting market to visit.

DELIS AND SPECIALISTS ▼

Al Amin

www.alamin.wserve.co.uk
01223 576396
100A–102A Mill Road,
Cambridge **CB1 2BD**
Mon–Sat 9am–7.30pm;
Sun 10am–7pm

Abdul Arain not only runs a wonderful community shop in this vibrant high street in the centre of Cambridge, but he sells a seemingly endless range of quality Asian ingredients. The pickles are a notch above the usual generic brands; the breads provide an economical wrap for all the curries and daals that you can make with other authentic ingredients, fresh and store cupboard, that are also sold in the shop. A proper bazaar that is fun to visit and – if you are a student –a great place to buy affordable staples, both Asian and European. Parents of undergraduates, please give them this address.

Arjuna Wholefoods

www.arjunawholefoods.co.uk
01223 364845
12 Mill Road, Cambridge
CB1 2AD
Mon–Sat 9.30am–6pm

A workers cooperative selling organic vegetables (any that are local are clearly highlighted) and wholefoods. This is a shop strong on ethical sourcing that is also good value for money. There is also a range of ready-made foods, cooked upstairs by vegetarian caterers Mouth Music, which includes olive breads, pasta salads, pizza and hummus.

Bakers & Larners ⊙ @ ⊘

www.bakersandlarners.co.uk

☎ 01263 712244

✉ 8–12 Market Place, Holt, Norfolk **NR25 6BW**

🕐 Mon–Sat 8.30am–5pm

A food hall in a department store that has been likened to London's Fortnum & Mason, but situated in a Norfolk market town. The range can only be described as ample, with a staggering number of lines (why is this oddly off-putting?), some of which are available online. The shop also owns a farm for finishing (fattening) livestock destined for its own butchery counter. This is impressive, but other aspects are lacking. Among the broad range of cheeses are almost no British artisans, yet an awful lot of continental types. Time to get into the 21st century.

Byfords Deli

www.byfords.org.uk

☎ 01263 714816

✉ 1–3 Shirehall Plain, Holt, Norfolk **NR25 6BG**

🕐 Mon–Sun 8am–8pm

Iain and Clair Wilson's deli is part of a Georgian townhouse in Holt that is also a B&B and a café. Specialising in ready-to-eat picnics, takeaway food and teas, the deli sells some beautifully crafted cakes, pastries, tarts and reheatable meals. Ingredients are locally sourced with beef coming from the nearby Stody Estate, shellfish from Morston and a range of cheeses all made close by (look out for Binham Blue and the excellent Suffolk Gold). You can also order pizza, tailor-made to contain your favourite toppings, or bring in your own serving dish and have it filled with a fish pie. The shop is particularly popular with local holidaymakers in self-catering accommodation who also need a holiday from cooking.

Cho Mee Chinese and Malaysian Food Specialists ⊘

☎ 01223 354399

✉ 108–110 Mill Road, Cambridge **CB1 2BD**

🕐 Mon–Sat 10am–7pm; Sun 10am–6pm

For south-east Asian specialities, head into this packed little shop, selling nutty hot-curry pastes from Thailand and Malaysia. There is every type of rice, noodle, dried exotic fungi, coconut milk and cream, and dozens of zesty sauces to add to stir-fries and barbecued meat or fish. They also sell very fresh vegetables for south-east Asian dishes.

Cley Smokehouse @ ⬠

www.cleysmokehouse.com
☎ 01263 740282
✉ High Street, Cley, Holt, Norfolk
NR25 7RF

In business for 30 years and still going strong, they have a thriving business. They endeavour to source locally and everything is prepared and smoked on-site. There's a wide range, too: they are best known for smoked prawns and kippers, and have delicacies such as buckling and hot smoked herring with the roes left intact inside the cavity. They also sell a selection of cured and smoked meat as well as pâtés.

Emmett's of Peasenhall ⬠

www.emmettsham.co.uk
☎ 01728 660250
✉ Peasenhall, Saxmundham,
Suffolk **IP17 2HJ**
🕐 Mon–Fri 8.30am–5.30pm;
Sat 8.30am–5pm

Mark Thomas's hams and bacon in this exciting former village shop are legendary. Made from locally sourced Suffolk pork, they are salted, cured and smoked on the premises. There's also a well-chosen range of superior Spanish cured pork, a magnificent display of olives marinating in huge jars, local cheeses, vinegars and wines. Observing the history of the shop, Thomas also sells newspapers, books, magazines and sweets.

The Food Company ⬠ @ ⬠

www.thefoodcompany.co.uk
☎ 01206 214000
✉ 86 London Road, Marks Tey,
Colchester, Essex **CO6 1ED**
🕐 Mon–Thurs 8.30am–5.30pm;
Fri–Sat 8.30am–6pm;
Sun 10am–4pm

An out-of-town food hall run by Leslie and Marc Linch, with an on-site bakery, a butchery selling locally sourced meat, fish provided by The Trawlerman, sourced from reputable fishermen and, of course, Colchester oysters. Vegetables are delivered from local farms or from the wholesale market. If you do not want to cook, there are ready-made foods containing locally sourced ingredients, plus good pies, tarts and an overgenerous offering of more than 150 cheeses. This is no small space, now occupying 10,000 square feet and housing a 60-seater restaurant. Succeeding in its original plan to take on the local supermarkets – The Food Company win on quality and make a great effort to keep prices competitive.

Green's

☎ 01621 854727
✉ 74 High Street Maldon, Essex
CM9 5ET
🕐 Mon–Sat 9am–5pm

A locally owned traditional grocer's, stocking locally grown produce and a select range of dried goods. Organic vegetables are clearly marked and are grown at Sarah Green Organics in nearby Tillingham, ensuring that stock is always fresh and seasonal. They also stock specialist coffees, locally grown and milled flour, and chutneys. Friendly and welcoming, the staff run this well-appointed shop with care and clearly feel strongly about the provenance and quality of their goods, a sentiment that they pass on to their regular and passing customers alike.

Halsey's Delicatessen and Tearooms

www.halseysdeli.co.uk
☎ 01462 432023
✉ 11 Market Place, Hitchin,
Hertfordshire **SG5 1DR**
🕐 Mon–Sat 8am–5pm

A much-loved deli, specialist food shop and café run by an enthusiastic couple. With Hitchin's thriving street market around the corner, the town has an admirable, independent high street culture, topped by this place that has a very loyal following. Vegetables are from local farms (it is veg-growing country), and even the mileage is marked on the boxes to show you just how local everything is. Every day there is a hot, roast joint of meat, slices of which go into hot sandwiches to eat in or take out. Free-range eggs are sourced in Bedfordshire, sausages are handmade by one of Hitchin's own butchers and local farmhouse cheeses are a speciality – try one of six versions of Wobbly Bottom goats' cheese (did the name have to be quite so hilarious?).

Humble Pie

www.humble-pie.com
☎ 01328 738 581
✉ Market Place, Burnham Market,
Norfolk **PE31 8HF**
🕐 Mon–Fri 9.30am–1pm,
2pm–5pm; Sat 9am–1pm,
2pm–4.45pm

In the summer, the queue for this little shop stretches down the street, as holidaymakers drop by to stock up on local Norfolk produce. Wonderful jams, chutneys, marmalades, cakes and biscuits are home-made in small batches, and the shop also buys in from some good suppliers nearby – look out for bread from the excellent Metfield Bakery. Local cheese is also sold, though subject to availability.

Lawson's Delicatessen

www.lawsonsdelicatessen.co.uk
🕿 01728 454052
✉ 138 High Street, Aldeburgh,
Suffolk **IP15 5AQ**
🕒 Mon–Sat 9am–5pm;
Sun 10am–2pm

It is the combination of a well-edited larder shop and a great, relaxed, but perfectly judged style of home-cooking that makes Claire Bruce-Clayton's and Richard Lawson's shop so special. In its smallish space you will find some great pies (Claire won Pie of Pies at the Aldeburgh Food Festival in 2009 – I was a judge, making assessments from a blind tasting; I made a second visit in 2010, and loved Lawson's all over again.) Other than pies, you can buy terrines and hams, and order food to take and heat at home from a huge and well-chosen menu. Almost all will contain locally sourced ingredients. The shop is big on Christmas, so ask for a catalogue.

Limoncello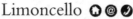

www.limoncello.co.uk
🕿 01223 507036
✉ 212 Mill Road, Cambridge,
Cambridgeshire **CB1 3NF**
🕒 Mon–Fri 9am–6.30pm;
Sat 9am–6pm; Sun 9am–3pm

Steve Turvill's continental (mainly Italian) deli on cheerful Mill Road is a treasure trove of great foods. Selling everything from artisan-made salami, mortadella and proscuitto to hand-made pecorino cheese from Sardinia and Sicilian canoli (cream-filled pastries). There are also the usual handy things to keep in the cupboard: canned and bottled tomatoes and passata, dried pasta, polenta meal and semolina, as well as good quality anchovies, olive oils and vinegars. If you do not live near a good Italian store, Turvill can send you the food you need via mail order – see the website for details.

Origin8

www.origin8delicafes.com
🕿 01223 354434
✉ 62 St Andrew's Street, Cambridge
CB2 3BZ
🕒 Mon–Sat 8am–6pm;
Sun 11am–5.30pm

Seasonal, traditional food from East Anglia – from jams to cheeses, wild game to ready-made meals – sold in a modern-looking city shop that aims to champion local produce in style. Good pork pies, bread baked in Cambridge, shorthorn beef and Oxford Sandy and Black pork, free-range chicken and duck eggs, and much more. There's a catering service, too, and a range of 'working lunch boxes'. In 2010 Origin8 won best local food retailer at the *Telegraph Magazine* Shop Awards.

Purely Pesto ○ @

www.purelypesto.co.uk
☎ 07725 638289
✉ Unit 1, The Reckford Farm Shop,
Leiston Road, Middleton, Suffolk
IP17 1SJ
🕐 Mon–Sat, 7am–1pm, 2–5pm

Ready-made pesto sauces usually lack decent oil, balance of flavour or texture and freshness. I am not sure what the secret is here, but the range of pesto sauces made by this youthful team in Suffolk tastes as if just made, and you can see the workmanship. I was especially impressed by one of the basil pestos that had large gratings of cheese in it, which contrasts perfectly with its finely ground herb leaves. Nice – and useful – food. See the website for stockists throughout the country. Good handmade soups available, too.

Richardson's Smokehouse ○

www.richardsonssmokehouse.co.uk
☎ 01394 450103
✉ Baker's Lane, Orford, Suffolk
IP12 2LH
🕐 Mon–Tues 10am–4pm; Wed
10am–2pm; Thurs-Sun 10am–4pm

For over two generations there has been a smokehouse in Orford owned by the Richardson family. Starting small, with locally caught mackerel, the demand for quality smoked meats, cheeses and other delicacies caused the business to grow and expand its range. The smoking itself involves Suffolk oak, salt and nothing else but a little heat – no preservatives or colourings. The smoked garlic bulbs are a heady mix of woody aromas and piquant garlic bite. There is also a kitchen on site that creates fabulous pâtés and fishcakes from the home-smoked goods, as well as selling home-cured hams, gammon and a variety of locally made sausages. For a real treat during the season, they smoke widgeon, pheasant and mallard. Mail order is also available.

River Farm Smokery ○ @ ⊘

www.riverfarmsmokery.co.uk
☎ 01223 811382
✉ Wilbraham Road, Bottisham,
Cambridgeshire **CB25 9BU**
🕐 Tues–Fri 10am–5.30pm;
Sat 10am–3pm

A wet fish shop and smokehouse near Newmarket, with three 'kilns' busy smoking everything that swims, flies or simply exists: from hams to haddock, cheese to olives. On the wet fish side they try, where possible, to buy fish from a sustainable source and during the season should have line-caught mackerel regularly on the counter.

Stark Naked Foods

www.starknakedfoods.co.uk
☎ 01379 870010
✉ Chestnuts Farm, Eye, Suffolk
IP23 7HL

A producer situated in Suffolk that grows and processes its own herbs and makes fabulous pesto. The herbs themselves travel only 15 minutes from the herb house, which has been growing herbs since 1899. They are then washed in spring water and blended – it is a simple process, using ingredients of the highest standard. Rocket, coriander and chilli, basil, tarragon, mint, chive, dill and sun-dried tomato, and watercress and spinach make up their pesto range at the moment, but they are always developing new flavours. The pesto tastes fresh and flavoursome, a far cry from the additive-ridden, acidic offerings of other manufacturers; it is a great addition to any recipe, or delicious with crusty bread. See their website for local stockists or email to place an order.

Stiffkey Stores ✅

www.stiffkeystores.com
☎ 01328 830489
✉ The Old Coach House,
Wells Road, Stiffkey, Norfolk
NR23 1QH
🕐 Mon–Tues, Thurs–Sat 8.30am–5pm; Wed 8.30am–12.30pm; Sun 9am–12.30pm

A charming and go-ahead village shop, run by a young pair Andy Griffin and Alice Burnet, that has expanded into selling lovely cakes (brownies, cupcakes, lemon syrup cake, earl grey cake), tea, coffee, locally grown vegetables and fruit, and hand-made bread. There's also meat and fish in the freezer. Griffin and Burnet originally came to the village for a holiday, but never left.

Thai Food Online ❶ @ ✅

www.thai-food-online.co.uk
☎ 01582 478149
✉ Unit 7, Thames Industrial Estate, Dunstable, Bedfordshire **LU6 3HL**

If you do not live near a Thai food shop and want to buy everything you need to make hot and sour curries, fishcakes, noodle dishes and soups, you can get it all from this efficient service via their information-packed website. There's just about everything: green, red and yellow curry pastes; fresh vegetables; spices and aromatic herbs from Thailand (including galangal, lemon grass, Thai basil, chillies and yard beans); rice and wheat flour noodles, jasmine rice and rice pancakes; and coconut milk, cream or powder.

Wells Deli

www.wellsdeli.co.uk
☎ 01328 711 171
✉ 15 The Quay, Wells-next-to-the-Sea, Norfolk **NR23 1AH**
🕐 Mon–Sat 9am–5pm;
Sun 10am–4pm

A nice little shop selling an imaginative, carefully chosen range of food – including local cheeses made by Ellie Betts and Mrs Temple, Lakenham creamery ice cream and Holkham venison, plus useful continental and British deli foods. Great for families looking for specialities while on holiday in Norfolk, and pretty good for locals, too.

▼ BUTCHERS

Allens ⊘

☎ 01986 872132
✉ 2 Market Place, Halesworth, Suffolk **IP19 8BA**
🕐 Mon, Wed, Fri 6am–5pm;
Thurs 6am–4pm; Sat 6am–3pm

Kevin Allen is a butcher with a strong local sourcing policy, tapping into Suffolk's wealth of great producers. His beef is three-weeks' hung (minimum) and is Aberdeen Angus from farmer John Flat at Ilketshall All Saints; lamb is a Dorset Cross reared by Di Herwin; and pork is from both Diss and Woodbridge. Allen cures some of his own bacon and buys the rest from Bramfield Meats, where Charlie Mills' treacle cure is famous.

Andrew Northrop Butchers ⊘

☎ 01223 345779
✉ 114 Mill Road, Cambridge **CB1 2BQ**
🕐 Mon–Sat 7.30am–5.30pm

This is a great city butcher's shop in a busy high street, full of great food shopping, run by Andrew Northrop and a team of very helpful staff. The beef, lamb and pork are sourced from nearby Cottenham. There is the strangely named, but good quality free-range Diaper Poultry, chickens from Essex poulterer Label Anglais and Powter's sausages from Newmarket. All the bacon is dry-cured, and there's a wealth of cheap cuts on sale – something good for less well-off student cooks, perhaps.

Arthur Howell

www.arthurhowell.com
☎ 01328 738230
✉ The Green, Burnham Market,
King's Lynn, Norfolk **PE31 8HE**
🕐 Mon–Sat 8am–5pm

An old-fashioned butcher's shop dedicated to sourcing locally: game birds and venison from the Holkham Park shoot; free-range, Norfolk born-and-bred beef and lamb; free-range hen's eggs from Richard Amies in Cromer; quail eggs from Mrs Flemming 'down the road'; plus seasonal goose and duck eggs from David Perowne at Snoring. There's also lovely bacon, which comes from the Binham smokehouse, and a range of fresh fruit and vegetables.

Bluebell Woods Wild Venison ⚘ @ ✦

www.wildvenison.co.uk
☎ 01502 733501
✉ 2 Rose Cottages, The Common,
Somerleyton, Lowestoft, Suffolk
NR32 5QJ

Mark Burrage runs an online butchery specialising in wild venison, selling a range of cuts including haunch steaks, loin medallions, fillet, silverside and rolled haunch. He also makes some good venison sausages. The meat is sourced from deer that are naturally wild, not parkland or farmed, but it is all traceable.

Briston Aberdeen Angus

☎ 01263 862734
✉ Hawthorn Farm, High Road,
Briston, Norfolk **NR24 2JQ**
🕐 Thurs, Fri 9am–5pm

An exemplary model of a beef farm with its own butchery, producing beef from grass- and silage-fed Aberdeen Angus cattle. Well-hung and neatly cut – the quality is terrific and the beef is good value for money, too.

K. W. Clarke ✦

www.kwclarke.co.uk
☎ 01986 784222
✉ Low Road, Bramfield,
Halesworth, Suffolk **IP19 9JH**
🕐 Mon–Fri 8am–5pm;
Sat 8am–1pm

Jeremy and Michael Thickitt buy animals from local farms, which have then been slaughtered nearby, and they personally supervise the hanging and cutting. They sell organic beef from Peter Fielden's herd of Red Poll cattle (a local Suffolk breed), lamb from Heveningham, Gloucester Old Spot and Saddleback pork, turkeys (in season) from Peter Potts farm and free-range eggs from Barsham.

J. R. Creasey

01728 660219
The Causeway, Peasenhall,
Suffolk **IP17 2HU**
Tues–Sat 8am–1pm, 2–5.30pm

A good butchers in a large village that also boasts a superior village shop (Emmett's, see page 11). Here you can buy beef from a herd of the gorgeous local breed, Red Poll, at Harleston, lamb from Hevaningham, and Blythburgh free-range pork. Specialities include salt beef and tongue.

M.V. Crump

01462 742255
3 Mill Street, Ashwell, Baldock,
Hertfordshire **SG7 5LY**
Tues–Wed 8am–5.30pm;
Thurs 8am–5.30pm; Sat 7am–1pm

If butchers could get prizes for interior design, this one would be top of the list. A lovely old shop, whitewashed until gleaming with a spotless workshop at the back where you can see handsome gammons and bacon sides going through various processes. But Crumps has a strong ethos, too, buying locally where possible. The butcher actually pointed out two Highland cattle in a field across the road, which were due to be hanging in his shop one day soon. If he does not buy from the area immediately around him, he sources meat from Suffolk and Norfolk and buys eggs from Franklin's lovely poultry and egg farm in Thorncote, not far away in Bedfordshire (see page 19). Fresh wet fish is also available and honey from Ashwell's own beekeeper, Stuart Greenbank.

Eric Tennant

01638 661530
11 The Rookery, Newmarket,
Suffolk **CB8 8EQ**
Mon, Tues, Thurs,
Fri 7am–5pm; Wed 7am–4pm;
Sat 6am–5pm

Eric's butcher's shop is a favourite among the racing fraternity in Newmarket, with many trainers' wives swearing by the meat, which he sources locally in Suffolk. He's also the sole stockist in the town of Musk's sausages, since Musk's closed their shop (see page 22).

Five Winds Farm Smokehouse and Butchery

www.fivewindsfarm.com

☎ 01394 461481

✉ The Rail Station, Melton, Woodbridge, Suffolk **IP12 2PS**

🕐 Mon–Sat 7.30am–5.30pm

A handily positioned butchers beside the station at Woodbridge, also housing a smokehouse producing the excellent bacon and hams you expect to find in Suffolk. Both are dry-cured first before the smoke treatment and the streaky cooks to a crisp, if that is how you like it. Game is sourced from local keepers in Wantisden, and free-range chickens are from a farm in Wharton. Most beef is from Granton-on-Spey, but there is some local beef sourced through Suffolk Meat Traders.

Frank Wright & Son ⊘

www.frankwrightandson.co.uk

☎ 01206 573688

✉ 43 Crouch Street, Colchester, Essex **CO3 3EN**

🕐 Mon–Fri 8am–4.45pm; Sat 8am–3.30pm

Established in 1926 by Frank Wright and family, but now run by Adrian Blake, this is a truly traditional butcher's shop where the emphasis is on British breeds. Look out for boned and stuffed legs of Romney Marsh lamb, crown roasts, dressed fillets of beef, beef olives (rolled and stuffed escalopes) and some unusual items including wild boar and venison. Suffolk gammons are also available, along with hams and terrines, and some lovely treacle-cured bacon. Local honey is also on the counter.

Franklins Free Range Poultry & Game 🏠 @ ⊘

www.franklinsfarm.co.uk

☎ 01767 627644

✉ Trumpetons Farm, Thorncote Green, Sandy, Bedford **SG19 1PU**

🕐 Tues–Thurs 9am–5pm; Fri 9am–6pm; Sat 9am–3pm

A farm, with a shop on site, that is a pleasure to see. Every field is filled with happy free-ranging chickens, ducks and (close to the season) turkeys and geese. John Franklin slaughters the poultry on the farm in a small abattoir where there is minimum stress. The birds are hung, non-eviscerated, for a period to flavour the meat – a deeply traditional touch – then dry-plucked so the skin is crisp after cooking. He also produces eggs on the farm and sells pork, lamb and game. At Christmas this remarkable place really comes into its own, selling a vast number of festive birds and boneless, three bird roasts – a boned goose, stuffed with a turkey and a pheasant. He makes his own Thorncote Bangers using locally produced Gloucester Old Spot pork, plus turkey and game sausages.

S. J. Frederick and Sons ○ ◎ ◐

www.sjfrederick.co.uk
☎ 01279 792460
✉ The Farm Office, Temple Farm, Roydon, Harlow, Essex **CM19 5LW**

This is an online shop selling British-reared, 'French-style' Label Anglais poultry. These birds are free-range and have long, muscular legs and slightly elongated breastbones carrying slightly less, but wonderfully flavoursome meat. The special reserve has more breast meat. Turkeys are available during the Christmas period. Label Anglais-branded poultry is also available in various butcher's shops, including several branches of Wyndham House Poultry in London – see website for locations of stockists.

Great Bircham Foods ◎ ○

www.greatbirchamfoods.co.uk
☎ 01485 542 219
✉ West Newton, Sandringham, Kings Lynn, Norfolk **PE31 6AY**
🕐 Mon–Fri 8am–4pm; Sat 8am–2pm

Great Bircham hand selects produce from the Royal Sandringham and surrounding estates in North Norfolk and gathers them together to be expertly butchered and sold in the 'Village Store'. Free-range pork, Red Poll beef and Dorper lamb are all sold in various cuts and are also available in mail-order 'meat boxes'. Hung for a minimum of three weeks, this establishment does not rush its butchery and the result is a beautifully deep colour to the beef. The quality of the meat is clear to see and the obvious experience of the team handling the produce is a real bonus.

F. Harris & Son ◐

☎ 01234 353351
✉ 113 Castle Road, Bedford
MK40 3QX
🕐 Mon–Fri 8am–5.30pm; Sat 8am–4pm

Michael Harris's family have had a butcher's shop in Bedford for three generations, selling great quality fresh meat sourced from Suffolk farms where the animals are reared naturally. He dry-cures his own bacon, prepares hams, makes sausages on the premises and sells free-range chickens and eggs.

K. G. Hutson

01502 722104
23 Market Place, Southwold,
Suffolk **IP18 6ED**
Mon–Sat 8am–4.30pm

Here you will find Suffolk Red Poll beef from Uggeshall and locally sourced lamb and ducks from Jack Reeve in Harleston (a nice change from Gressingham, a large duck producer who seems to supply every other butcher in the area). In season you will find partridge, mallard and pheasant from local shoots and there are free-range eggs from Havenfield Farm in Diss. At Christmas, this is the place to buy a Kelly Bronze turkey reared in Harleston.

Lane Farm Country Foods ⓞ ✿

www.lanefarm.co.uk
01379 384593
Lane Farm, Brundish, Suffolk
IP13 8BW
Mon–Fri 9am–4pm

Ian and Sue Whitehead rear their own pigs naturally and sell joints of fresh meat, plus mince and cubed pork for casseroles, as well as cured hams (the Brundish hams are delicious) and wonderful dry-cured bacon. They have also pioneered an Italian-style salami under the Suffolk Salami brand (telephone for stockists). The result is impressive: a lovely fresh pork flavour seasoned with herbs (the pork and fennel is wonderful) with yeasty overtones from the casing.

Lingers Butchers Ltd ✿

www.lingersbutchers.com
01234 353390
1 St Cuthbert's Street, Bedford
MK40 3JB
Tues–Thurs 8am–5pm;
Fri 8am–5.30pm; Sat 7.30am–5pm

Christopher Hubbard sources lamb, free-range chickens and pork from Northamptonshire. He is something of a sausage specialist, selling about 10 varieties at any one time, all made on the premises. He makes his own pies, too, but buys in the dry-cured bacon from an expert locally.

P. A. Mobbs & Sons ✿

01986 798340
White House Farm, Cratfield,
Halesworth, Suffolk **IP19 0QF**

A lovely farm in Suffolk run by the Mobbs family, who are third-generation turkey farmers. They rear turkeys slowly on home-grown GM-free grain and let them roam in grassy paddocks. They are then processed on the farm and hung non-eviscerated for flavour; these birds have an extra gamey flavour, but a good one. Order and collect or phone for stockists in the Suffolk area. Turkeys range from 4–9 kg.

Musk's ⊙ @ ⊘

www.musks.com
☎ 01638 662626
✉ 4 Goodwin Business Park,
Newmarket, Suffolk **CB8 7SQ**

A famous sausage-maker on the outskirts of Newmarket, Musk's was established in 1884 and is still making bangers to a traditional recipe that includes locally sourced pork, fresh breadcrumbs and a good pinch of white pepper. There is a gluten-free sausage, which is highly recommended, plus chipolatas, and pork and leek. Musk's sell their sausages to quite a few outlets – call or see the website for stockists.

Neaves of Debenham ⊙ ⊘

www.neavesofdebenham.co.uk
☎ 01728 860240
✉ 21 Cross Green, Debenham,
Suffolk **IP14 6RW**
🕐 Mon, Wed–Fri 7.30am–1pm,
2–5pm; Tues, Sat 7.30am–1pm

The home of Debenham-cured bacon, hand-made sausages, whole gammons and hams. A decent local butcher, recommended by Suffolk residents, but I'd like to know more. Please let me know what you think.

Peter J. Dale ⊘

www.pjdale.co.uk
☎ 020 8979 3800
✉ 27 Bridge Road, East Moseley,
Surrey **KT8 9EU**
🕐 Tues–Wed 7am–5pm;
Thurs–Fri 7am–7pm;
Sat 6am–3pm

It is really heartening when an urban butcher surrounded by supermarkets can thrive: Dale's has bucked the trend and is doing exactly that. Just across the road from Hampton Court Palace (whose catering outlets they supply with meat), it is possible to buy slow-grown Gloucester Old Spot pork from Marks Hall Estate in Essex. Salt marsh lamb from Romney Marsh is also available.

Powters ⊙ @ ⊘

www.powters.co.uk
☎ 01638 662418
✉ Wellington Street, Newmarket,
Suffolk **CB8 0HT**
🕐 Mon–Fri 8am–5pm;
Sat 7am–4pm

Powters is a traditional butcher's shop in the centre of town, where you can buy Newmarket sausages and choose from a range of fresh meat, including well-hung Aberdeen Angus, salt marsh lamb, and Gloucester Old Spot pork. They also sell meat accredited by the Rare Breeds Survival Trust, the excellent organisation that has done so much to protect Britain's meat breeds. Cooked meats, sausage rolls, bacons and hams are also available, along with poultry from Suffolk.

Ruse & Sons

01787 378 227
Hall Street, Sudbury, Suffolk
CO10 9JF
Mon–Fri 8am–1pm,
2pm–5.30pm; Sat 8am–5.30pm

This is a real old-fashioned butcher's shop that closes for lunch during the week between 1pm and 2pm. The Ruse family has run the business for more than 150 years and current incumbent Oliver Ruse intends to keep going until he drops. Some locals say that the prices are high but all the reports that I have had suggest that these are justified. As well as fabulous pork, beef and lamb they also have home-cured bacon and a good range of delicatessen foods. Highly recommended by well-heeled locals.

Salter's Family Butchers ✪

www.saltersfamilybutchers.co.uk
01728 452758
107–109 High Street,
Aldeburgh, Suffolk **IP15 5AR**
Mon, Wed 7am–1pm; Tues,
Thurs, Fri 7am–5pm;
Sat 7am–4pm

Richard Emsden's outstanding shop is a paean to local Suffolk produce. All meat, which comes from a number of small farm suppliers, is sourced and slaughtered locally. Look out for Alde Valley lamb from Great Glemham Farms, Blythborough pork, Sutton Hoo free-range chickens (see below), Mobbs turkeys (in season – see page 21) and game birds from local shoots. He makes five varieties of sausage, buys bacon from Bramfield Meats (Charlie Mills' brilliant, local, medium-sized wholesaler specialising in regional meat), and sells a few other Suffolk specials – Marybelle Milk (see page 29), Maple Farm organic vegetables (see page 35) and honey from Graham Owston. The perfect butcher.

Sutton Hoo Free Range and Organic Poultry

01394 386797
Kennel Farm, Woodbridge,
Suffolk **IP13 6JX**
Mon–Sat 7am–1pm, 2–5pm

Belinda Nash's poultry is reared as it used to be – slow-grown on a natural diet and free to roam on ancient grassland on a farm that has worked hard to create a perfect wild habitat for the foraging hens. The proof is in the meat, which has a well-exercised muscle texture and plenty of flavour. Some are reared in a free-range system and the rest in a certified organic system. The feed for the free-range birds is conventionally farmed grains, but is still additive-free. These chickens are widely available in the east – call to find out your nearest stockist.

Tavern Tasty Meats ♠ ∅

www.taverntasty.co.uk
☎ 01692 405444
✉ Farm Store, Swalfield, Nr
Walsham, Norfolk **NR28 0RQ**
🕐 Mon–Fri 7.30am–5pm;
Sat 7.30am–1pm

Roger Human started Tavern Tasty Meats 10 years ago in an unlicensed pub! White Park Beef comes from Swanton Morley, Longhorns from Fakenham, and Human himself keeps a herd of Southdown Shetland and Whiteface Woodland lamb. He supplies local butchers and other small shops with his meat, and his pies are raved about by locals. Tavern also sells British lop-eared pigs, but it's unfortunate that the pigs come all the way from Cornwall. Couldn't someone be convinced to rear them locally?

The Wild Meat Company ♠ @ ∅

www.wildmeat.co.uk
☎ 01728 663211
✉ Lime Tree Farm, Blaxhall,
Woodbridge, Suffolk **IP12 2DY**

Robert Gooch and Paul Denny's game birds and venison are from local Suffolk shoots, expertly dressed and oven-ready, alongside an ingenious range of game roulades and ballotines. The party roast is a boned pheasant, inside a boned chicken, inside a boned goose, all with layers of orange and thyme stuffing. Two-bird ballotines might be a partridge inside a pheasant or a quail with pigeon. Roulades include layered pheasant and wild duck fillets with stuffing rolled in streaky bacon. A great idea and a delicious introduction for novices. Order via the website.

A. Willsher & Son ∅

☎ 01206 210365
✉ 87 London Road, Marks Tey,
Colchester, Essex **CO6 1EB**
🕐 Mon–Fri 7.30am–5.30pm;
Sat 7.30am–4pm

Willshers sells a good range of traditionally reared meat, including traditional (pure bred) Aberdeen Angus, Red Poll (a Suffolk variety), White Park, traditional Hereford, Blythburgh Suffolk pork, Gloucester Old Spot pork, Romney Marsh lamb, 'primitive' Hogget breeds and free-range chicken from Layer de la Haye. A number of beef breeds are slow-matured for tenderness and flavour. There's game in season and home-made sausages (try the pork and cracked pepper), and great bacon (old-fashioned oak-smoked or treacle-cured). Pop in for the home-made pork scratchings, if nothing else.

Wimpole Home Farm

www.wimpole.org
☎ 01223 206000
✉ Wimpole Estate, Arrington, Royston, Cambridgeshire **SG8 0BW**
🕐 Sat–Wed 11am–4pm (seasonal opening times apply, see website)

Lamb, hogget and mutton from the White Faced Woodland breed, which can be seen grazing on the ancient pastures of this historic estate owned by the National Trust. The farm has an interesting history, set up over 200 years ago as an experimental 'model farm'. Some of the old thatched buildings are still intact. Try this mature and lovely meat – the flavour of the mutton is extremely intense and good. It has been a multiple winner of the National Trust's Fine Farm Produce awards.

BAKERS AND CONFECTIONERS ▼

The Cake Shop

☎ 01394 382515
✉ The Thoroughfare, Woodbridge, Suffolk **IP12 1AA**
🕐 Mon–Fri 7am–4.30pm; Sat 7am–3.30pm

This is an old-fashioned bakery into retro-innovation – making bread the slow way, yet it is not a trendy sourdough emporium. There are a few flavoured breads, such as one made with apricot and walnut. I liked the Pia-do, a ring of rolls that you can tear apart, made with olive oil, sun-dried tomatoes and mixed peppers. There's also organic spelt and honey and Suffolk Trencher bread (four flours, seven seeds).

Days of Ashwell ●

☎ 01462 742112
✉ 61 High Street, Ashwell, Baldock, Hertfordshire **SG7 5NP**
🕐 Mon–Sat 7.30am–4pm

Here is an old-fashioned baker baking lovely crusty loaves on the premises. Expect split tins, bloomers and 100 per cent wholemeal; plus rolls, cheese straws, hot cross buns and delicious Victoria sponges. Just as likeable are their blue and white striped paper bags, reminiscent of another age.

Dozen

www.dozenbakery.co.uk
☎ 01603 764798
✉ 107 Gloucester Street, Norwich **NR2 2DY**
🕐 Mon–Sat 8.00am–4pm

A real old-fashioned bakery, selling a broad range of favourites made the slow, traditional way: soft white rolls with a dusting of flour; a variety of sourdough breads including baguettes, fruited loaves, 'pippin kernel' and plain whites; earthy, worthy wholemeal loaves; plus good old bloomers, cobs and sandwich tins. You can order online for home delivery on www.welovelocalfood.co.uk.

Grooms Bakery

www.groomsbakery.co.uk
01328 738289
Grooms Bakery, Market Place, Burnham Market, Kings Lynn, Norfolk **PE31 8HD**
Mon–Sat 8am–4.30pm

Properly local bread, made with Norfolk flour milled from local wheat at Heygates Mill in Downham Market. James and Annie Groom's shop is a traditional-style bakery (white sandwich tins, bloomers, etc) rather than an artisan-crafted sourdough emporium, but it is a lovely small-scale bakers and the locals love it.

Gunns Bakery

www.gunns-bakery.co.uk
01767 680434
Gunns Bakery, 8 Market Square, Sandy, Bedfordshire **SG19 1HU**
Mon–Sat 6.30am–5.30pm

This is a great traditional bakers selling doughnuts bursting with cream and jam, sticky buns, and lots of sugar-topped fancies. If this is not your type of thing, however, there are some very well-made tin and bloomer-style breads made with British flour (some of the brown flour is milled locally at Bromham Mill). The meat and veg in the pies and pastries is locally sourced and you can even experience the 'Bedfordshire clanger' – a suet pudding roll with gammon and potato in one end and apple in the other, which was once the sustenance of farm workers.

Letheringsett Watermill

www.letheringsettwatermill.co.uk
01263 713153
Riverside Road, Letheringsett, Holt, Norfolk **NR25 7YD**
Summer Mon–Fri 10am–5pm; Sat 9am–1pm **Winter** Mon–Fri 9am–4pm; Sat 9am–1pm

A watermill built in 1802 that was restored by Mike and Marion Thurlow in the '80s. Despite it being a tourist honey pot, offering all sorts of flour-milling attractions, it also has a shop selling the various flours for bread and cake-making, including flour milled from the historic and healthy grain spelt, plus cereals and wholefoods.

Alder Tree Ltd Ⓨ

www.alder-tree.co.uk
☎ 01449 721220
✉ Alder Carr Farm, Needham
Market, Ipswich, Suffolk **IP6 8LX**
🕐 Tues–Sat 9am–4pm;
Sun 10am–4pm

Usually when ice cream is made on a farm it is because it is a dairy farm, but in this case it is the soft fruit grown by the Hardingham family that is the important factor. You can come here to buy fruit or pick your own, but also to buy the fruit cream ice, so-called because there is more fruit than anything else in the pot. It is also, uniquely, free from any additives such as fillers and gums. It is shocking how many 'artisan' ice cream-makers use skimmed milk, etc. The business is now run by Stephany (Nick and Joan Hardingham's savvy daughter) and you can buy the ice creams in a number of outlets (contact for stockists).

The Cambridge Cheese Company

☎ 01223 328672
✉ 4 All Saints Passage, Cambridge
CB2 3LS
🕐 Mon–Fri 10am–6pm;
Sat 9am–5pm

Paul Sutton Adam and David Wilshire sell a comprehensive list of artisan cheeses including several that are locally produced, such as Cambridge Gunburner, a cheddar-style matured for three years, and Nelson's Glory, a soft French-style goats' cheese rolled in ash. They are champions of Cambridgeshire honey farmers and give £1 on the price of each jar sold to Wildlife Charities. Their chutneys also star – in particular one made from windfalls and wild fruits, gathered from the gardens of their friends. A lovely shop.

The Cheese Kitchen ❶ @ ∅

www.thecheesekitchen.co.uk
☎ 01234 217325
✉ 108 Castle Road, Bedford
MK40 3QR
🕐 Mon–Sat 7.30am–5.30pm;
Sun 9am–4pm

A speciality cheese shop, packed with handmade British cheeses that are chosen seasonally so always the best are in stock. Many are made with unpasteurised milk, giving the cheese an extra edge when it comes to flavour. Cheeses to look out for are Stinking Bishop (a washed rind cheese from Gloucestershire) and Berkswell (a pecorino type made in the Midlands). If there is a cheese you are looking for and they have not got it, they will do their best to get it in. Continental cheeses are also on sale.

The Domini Dairy

www.dominidairy.co.uk
01359 221333
Village Farm, Market Weston,
Diss, Norfolk **IP22 2NZ**

A small, mixed farm with an impeccable traditional, organically certified dairy, processing milk from the farm's own herd of delightful Jersey cows. Locals adore their golden-tinted milk, which is available in nearby shops – contact for stockists.

Hamish Johnston ○ @ ○

www.hamishjohnston.com
01728 621544
Unit 6, Ore Trading Estate,
Woodbridge Road, Framlingham,
Suffolk **IP13 9LL**
Mon–Sat 9am–6pm

Hamish Johnston will be familiar to residents of Battersea, south-west London, where they have a retail outlet stocked with a huge number of artisan cheeses (see page 94). But residents in the Newmarket area, near Framlingham, can buy direct from the warehouse. It is not a shop exactly, but you will not be turned away unless perhaps you want just a tiny slice. They stock a decent list of Suffolk cheeses, including Hawkstone (who make amazing Cheshire-style cheeses), Buxlow Pagel and Suffolk Gold, but they also sell other excellent British and continental cheeses, too.

Lakenham Creamery

www.lakenhamcreamery.co.uk
01603 620970
2 Trafalgar Street, Norwich,
Norfolk **NR1 3HN**
Mon–Tues, Thurs–Fri 6am–1pm,
2–5pm; Sat 6am–1pm, 2–4pm

If Suffolk's Alder Tree is the best, additive-free fruit ice cream, Lakenham in Norfolk make the finest what I call traditional 'English' ice cream, subtly flavoured and rich. It is also totally additive-free. Why can't all ice creams be like this? It comes down to cost, of course. The Lackenham ices are made with milk and / or cream sourced from a small cooperative of eight Norfolk dairies. After the eggs and other natural flavouring ingredients have been added (vanilla, chocolate, strawberry, pistachio, Alphonse mango, passion fruit, butterscotch, maple walnut, coffee and many more) the mix is left to 'age' overnight then frozen down in the morning. The flavour of the finished ice cream is mellow and ripe – an old-fashioned taste of childhood ice cream (the good stuff, that is). Contact for stockists, which can be found far and wide.

Marybelle Milk

www.marybelle.co.uk

☎ 01986 784658

✉ The Clink, Walpole, Halesworth,
Suffolk **IP19 9AU**

Once upon a time, the Strachan family were dairy farmers who made no profit selling their milk to one of the large UK dairy conglomerates. They decided to break away and install their own bottling plant and market their milk under the name Marybelle. They sell it for no more than a supermarket would charge and it has therefore been adopted by a huge number of retailers in Suffolk, both independent shops and chains, who prefer to sell a local product. They have a sister company, Suffolk Meadow, that produces excellent cream, yoghurt and ice cream. A great company run by inspirational hard-working farmers, deserving of success. Contact for stockists or look out for the milk when shopping in Suffolk.

Mrs Temples Cheese

☎ 01328 820224

✉ Copys Green farm, Wighton,
Wells-Next-The-Sea, Norfolk
NR23 1NY

Catharine and Stephen Temples's determination to produce Norfolk cheese using Norfolk energy is admirable. Stephen was named most energy-efficient farmer 2009 in Britain. Specialising in Binham Blue cheese and other Norfolk cheeses, the products are available in farm shops and delis throughout East Anglia and beyond. The cheese is made with freshly churned milk, taken just minutes earlier from the cow. They have their own herd of Holstein-Friesian and Brown Swiss cattle. To make the cheese they use hot water and electricity generated using green energy arising from the anaerobic digestion of the cow waste and the residual whey from cheesemaking here on the farm. Contact for mail orders.

Norfolk Farmhouse Ice Cream

www.norfolkfarmhouseicecream.
co.uk

☎ 01362 638116

✉ Pound Farm, North Tuddenham,
East Dereham, Norfolk **NR20 3DA**

Using milk from their own cows, and eggs from their own free-range chickens, the staff source all their key ingredients within a mile of the production kitchen. Where possible, they use local fruits and avoid using any preservatives or colourings. Their blackcurrant ice cream, made with locally picked berries, is a stunning purple colour and tastes amazing. For the more adventurous customer they offer a range of tasty alcoholic sorbets featuring champagne, whisky and beer. Larger orders can be made ahead of time and picked up from the shop, or you can specify a flavour you would like to eat and they will do their best to make it up for you. The team here clearly care about what they do and create a fine product.

Rodwell Farm Dairy

www.rodwellfarmdairy.co.uk
☎ 01473 830192
✉ Rodwell Farm, Baylham,
Nr Needham Market, Suffolk **IP6 8JW**
🕐 Mon–Sat 9am–6pm

The Richards family has had a dairy in Suffolk for over 75 years; they have been making cheese since June 2006, using traditional methods and unpasteurised milk from their own dairy cows. The various cheeses are named after river meadows on the farm: Hawkston is a crumbly cheese with a pleasant acidity and a fresh taste; Shipcord is similar to alpine cheeses in texture and its deep flavour will stay on the palate much longer. There is also a smoked and an extra mature Shipcord available for customers who enjoy a stronger taste. This is a great example of a dairy farm that has diversified and created a wonderful product, while retaining a sense of tradition and locality.

Suffolk Farmhouse Cheeses

www.suffolkcheese.co.uk
☎ 01449 710458
✉ Whitegate Farm, Norwich Road,
Creeting St Mary, Suffolk **IP6 8PG**
🕐 Thurs 10am–3pm; Fri 4–6pm;
Sat 3–5pm

Jason and Katharine Salisbury began making cheese on their farm using milk from their own small herd of Guernsey cows in 2004. In an area where there are hundreds of small producers, but relatively little artisan farmhouse cheese-making, they are pioneers. The Suffolk Gold cheese indeed glisters, has a wonderful, sweet, ripe buttery flavour and has been a hit with locals. Suffolk Blue is – to my mind – slightly less successful, but do try it because cheese appreciation is subjective. Occasionally the Salisburys make other 'seasonal' cheeses, a Brie type and also cream cheese. Pay their farm shop a visit – check the opening hours, which are limited – and buy yoghurt, milk, butter and cream, too. If you can't visit, contact them for stockists.

The Company Shed ⊙⊘⊕

⊚ 01206 382700
✉ 129 Coast Road, West Mersea
Island, Colchester, Essex **CO5 8PA**
🕑 Tues–Sat 9am–5pm;
Sun 10am–5pm

Tucked away among the salt marshes of West Mersea Island in Essex is The Company Shed, a fishmongers and oyster farm, revitalising traditional farming methods brought to England by the Romans. This local family business was established 15 years ago by Richard and Heather Hayward. The house speciality is the flat native oyster (available September to April) grown from seed distributed on the bed of the Thames Estuary. You can sit down and eat fish here or buy fish to take home, including the oysters, lobster or any other that has been landed that day.

R.W. & J.A. Davies Fish Merchants

⊚ 01263 512727
✉ 7 Garden Street, Cromer, Norfolk
NR27 9HN
🕑 Tues 9.30am–4pm;
Wed 9am–2pm;
Thurs–Sat 8.30am–4pm

The Davies have their own boat that supplies their shop just a short distance from the sea at Cromer, guaranteeing some stunningly fresh fish. Locals describe both the fish and the service here as excellent, and you can expect to find lovely wild bass, rock oysters, fresh prawns when in season, mussels, Dover soles, squid and, of course, the famous Cromer crabs.

Gurney's Fish Shop ⊙⊘

www.gurneysfishshop.co.uk
⊚ 01328 738967
✉ Market Place, Burnham Market,
Norfolk **PE31 8HF**
🕑 **May–Oct** Mon–Sun 9am–5pm;
Nov–Apr Mon–Sat 9am–4pm

Burnham Market has a butcher, baker and fishmonger, and this is one of the best. On the day I visited, Mike Gurney had locally caught sea trout and mullet, oysters from Thornham, home-made fishcakes and a range of locally grown salads. An uplifting place.

MidNorfolk Smokehouse ⊙

www.midnorfolksmokehouse.co.uk
⊚ 01362 820 702
✉ Jubilee Hall Farm, Cranworth,
Norfolk **IP25 7SM**
🕑 Mon–Fri 9am–6pm;
Sat 9am–4pm

The name here is a bit misleading because there is a sister business run from the same premises by the same family selling wet fish. Called The Wet Fish Shop they sell a wide variety of locally caught fish – sea bass, Cromer crab, lobster and shellfish to name a few. Then there is the on-site smokery, which sells a range of smoked salmon and smoked salmon pâtés. Frozen fish is also available and the company visit several farmers' markets in the locality and will take along pre-ordered fish if you ring them with a day or two's notice. Home delivery also available. Consult the website or ring them.

The North Norfolk Fish Company

www.northnorfolkfish.co.uk
☎ 01263 711913
✉ 8 Old Stable Yard, Holt, Norfolk **NR25 6BN**
🕐 Tues–Sat 9am–5pm

John Griffin has been selling locally sourced Lowestoft fish from his small shop tucked behind the high street for 10 years. He also buys from Iceland and Ireland and puts a premium on quality – the fish I saw were superb. The wonderful display is worth a visit just to see it. His wife makes mayonnaises and sauces. They also offer catering services for parties and run demonstrations and workshops.

Pinneys of Orford 🏠 @ 🌱

www.pinneysoforford.co.uk
☎ 01394 450277
✉ Market Hill, Orford, Woodbridge, Suffolk **IP12 2LH**
🕐 Mon–Sat 10am–4.30pm; Sun 10am–4pm

William (Bill) and Janet Pinney run a fish shop on the quayside at Orford selling fish brought in by their own boats that fish in the North Sea and oysters farmed by the family at Butley Creek. They also have a smokehouse and sell all the products via mail order, including salmon, eel, trout, mackerel and some non-fishy things such as bacon and duck. If you'd rather not cook but still feel like having a fish supper, visit their restaurant, the Butley Orford Oysterage, on the market square.

W. J. Weston Fishmonger

www.westonsofblakeney.co.uk
☎ 01263 741112
✉ 5a Westgate Street, Blakeney, Norfolk **NR25 7NQ**
🕐 Mon–Fri 9.30am–4.30pm; Sat 9.30am–5pm; Sun 10am–4pm

Fishmonger Willy Weston has his own fishing boat, The *Leeson Lady*, and brings in local species such as mussels, crabs and lobster, all of which are guaranteed to be absolutely fresh. Scallops, Dover sole, squid and samphire (a succulent beach weed delicious to eat with fish) are also regular finds. The shop makes its own fishcakes, fish pies, sauces and a range of soups that include a good chowder. They will put together a seafood platter and will even cater for a party or an event using their mobile van. Weston's van can also be found in the National Trust car park at Morston – see website for details.

VEGETABLES AND FRUIT ▼

Alder Carr Farm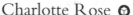

www.aldercarrfarm.co.uk
☎ 01449 720820
✉ Creeting St Mary, Ipswich, Suffolk
IP6 8LX
🕐 Tues–Sat 9am–4.30pm;
Sun 10am–4pm

The Hardingham family grow soft fruit, operating a pick-your-own during the growing season and selling the range in a farm shop that is open throughout the year, also selling seasonal vegetables grown on the farm. A few other local fresh foods are available and the farm hosts a regular farmers' market (see website for details). You can also come here to buy Alder Tree 'fruit cream ice' – so-called because there is more fruit than anything else in the pot. Made with added double cream, this ice cream is, uniquely, free from any additives such as fillers and gums. It is shocking how many 'artisan' ice cream-makers use skimmed milk and so on. (See page 27.)

Charlotte Rose

☎ 01462 743462
✉ 31 High Street, Ashwell,
Hertfordshire **SG7 5NP**
🕐 Mon–Fri 8am–5.30pm;
Sat 8am–1pm

Charlotte Snowden is really a florist (and one of the most enthusiastic and delightful shopkeepers I met on my travels), but she also sells locally grown vegetables, marking each box with the name of the grower, the farm and the mileage it has travelled. Expect to find purple sprouting broccoli from Flitwick, purple and green curly kale from Langford and sprouts from Caldecote. She specialises in produce that isn't always found in supermarkets, such as cobnuts, Fenn celery and chestnuts at Christmas. It is worth mentioning that she sells locally grown flowers, too.

Crapes Fruit Farm ⚘ ⊘

01206 212375
Aldham, Nr Colchester, Essex
CO6 3RR
Mon–Sat 9am–5pm

Andrew Tann is a third-generation fruit farmer. His grandfather started on the 12 acres of Crapes in 1922. He grows over 150 varieties of apples, which are available from the beginning of August to the end of March. Two of his favourites are Essex varieties the D'arcy Spice and Laxton's Fortune. He has a farm shop, but he also sells locally (contact for stockists) and can send fruit via mail order. Keep in mind that knobbly fruit makes great juice. There are many home-juicers who love Tann's apples. Try some for yourself and get juicing!

Drove Orchards ⚘ @ ⊘ ⚘

www.droveorchards.com
01485 525652
Thornham, Hunstanton, Norfolk
PE36 6LS
Mon–Sun 10am–5pm

This pick-your-own, farm shop and deli combined works well. They grow over 150 different varieties of apple (including Worcester Pearmain and Peasgood Nonesuch), originating from East Anglia. Apple, pear and quince juice is made on site, in season. They also grow 5 varieties of plum, 10 types of pears, as well as strawberries and raspberries, red, white and blackcurrants, gooseberries, jostaberries, walnuts, hazelnuts, artichokes and the whole range of seasonally available vegetables and salads. There's also a local fishmonger on site at weekends. Seasonal opening times tend to vary, so do check on the website.

Geoff Platt ⚘ ⊘ ⚘

01728 830362
43 High Street, Leiston, Suffolk
IP16 4EL
Mon–Sat 7am–5pm

Geoff Platt is a traditional greengrocer selling mainly seasonal vegetables, fruit and flowers, all locally sourced. Situated in the heart of Britain's vegetable-growing country, you can expect always to find Suffolk-grown potatoes and onions (there are a lot of them!), but also rarer items such as blueberries, and interesting orchard fruit varieties such as Worcester apples and William pears.

High House Fruit Farm ⦿ € ⓨ

www.high-house.co.uk
☎ 01394 450263
✉ Sudbourne, Woodbridge,
Suffolk **IP12 2BL**
🕐 Mon–Sun 9am–5pm

This is a brilliant family-run fruit farm, situated in an Area of Outstanding Natural Beauty on Suffolk's coast, looking out over the marshes of the River Alde. Land that is not in fruit production is grazed by sheep and cattle and managed under an Environmentally Sensitive Area scheme, and the farm is a haven for a variety of wildlife. Buy rhubarb and asparagus, soft fruit from June onwards (they even grow cherries); orchard fruits begin in mid-summer (apricots and plums), then the apples are gathered in the autumn. Varieties include Cox, Russet, Discovery, James Grieve, Worcester, Blenheim Orange, Charles Ross, Ribston Pippin and Bramley. Juices and loganberry jam are also available.

Lathcoats Farm ⓨ

www.eapples.co.uk
☎ 01245 353021
✉ Beehive Lane, Galleywood,
Chelmsford, Essex **CM2 8LX**
🕐 Mon–Thu 9am–5pm;
Fri 9am–6pm; Sun 10am–4pm

The farm's own apples are on sale here, including some less familiar types such as Essex's own Chelmsford Wonder, Queen, D'arcy Spice and Cornish Gilliflower, and there are plums and soft fruit – nice to see boysenberries for a change. The farm also makes single variety juices.

Maple Farm Kelsale ⦿ ⊙

www.maplefarmkelsale.co.uk
☎ 01728 652000
✉ Maple Farm Kelsale,
Saxmundham, Suffolk **IP17 2PL**

The Kendall family grow vegetable and cereal crops on their Soil Association-certified organic farm in Suffolk, operate a box scheme and supply over a dozen local shops with fresh produce and home-milled flour. They also keep hens and bees – you can order the eggs or honey (see page 36) with your box. William Kendall, incidentally, started the Covent Garden Soup Company and is a director of Green & Blacks, the organic chocolate success story. He and his wife Miranda have put much back, not only into this farm, but also the local Suffolk 'food economy', jointly running the local annual Aldeburgh Food Festival. If you live in the area, I strongly recommend you try one of their organic veg boxes or seek out the produce in nearby shops – see the website for a list of stockists.

Super Green

📞 01234 352155
✉ 113 Castle Road, Bedford
MK40 3RF
🕐 Mon–Fri 9am–5pm;
Sat 9am–4pm

On the day of my visit I bought locally grown hazelnuts, chillies grown by Edible Ornamentals near Bedford, and other perfectly fresh vegetables from Bedfordshire's great market gardens in Great Barford, Blunham, Bromham and Flitwick. This is a very nice small shop on a good high street with other independent food shops.

Whitnell's £

📞 01206 571326
✉ 99 Crouch Street, Colchester,
Essex **CO3 3HA**
🕐 Mon–Sat 8am–5pm

John Whitnell's shop has been on the same site for 70 years. He sells his own produce from his market garden, plus some nice regional specials including Fenland celery, beetroot, broccoli, peas, broad beans, apples, onions and plenty of locally grown potatoes.

Whitwell Watercress £

📞 01438 871232
✉ Nine Wells Watercress Farm,
Lillybottom Road, Whitwell,
Nr Hitchin, Hertfordshire
SG4 8JP
🕐 Mon–Sun 7am–6pm

While most watercress farms must rely on water diverted from a nearby river, Derek Sansom's farm is unique in that it is served by the water that bubbles up from nine underground natural springs. He has an obvious advantage of being able to guarantee the water is absolutely clean and safe. You can buy from the farm gate during the height of the season (March to June, then September to around Christmas), putting the money in a secure box fixed to the farmhouse wall.

▼ HONEY

Sophia's Very Delicious Suffolk Honey

www.maplefarmkelsale.co.uk
📞 01728 652000
✉ Maple Farm, Kelsale,
Saxmundham, Suffolk **IP17 2PL**

Maple Farm is near the food haven of Saxmundham in Suffolk and specialises in home-produced honey that is collected from Sophia's Wood, an area of ancient woodland on the farm. Generally the honey is smooth and pale, and easy to spread. Locals maintain that a spoonful a day keeps the hay fever at bay. Of course there is no scientific evidence to support this, but the honey is delicious nonetheless. It's available to collect from the farm on Fridays (see website) or at Woodbridge Farmers' Market and Snape Maltings.

DRINKS ▼

Aspall

www.aspall.co.uk
☎ 01728 860510
✉ The Cyder House, Aspall Hall, Debenham, Suffolk **IP14 6PD**

The Chevallier family has lived at Aspall Hall Farm in the parish of Aspall in Suffolk since 1702. In 1725, Clement Chevallier inherited Aspall from his cousin and set about making cider. Today, the business is owned and managed by the eighth generation of the Chevallier family. Aspall has won a raft of awards and, although mass market by many standards, I am a fan. They do cider vinegars and apple juice, too, mainly blends. Available at many outlets nationwide.

James White ○

www.jameswhite.co.uk
☎ 01473 890111
✉ James White Drinks, White's Fruit Farm, Helmingham Road, Ashbocking, Suffolk **IP6 9JS**

Lawrence Mallinson was one of the founders of the New Covent Garden Soup Company that was such a hit in the '80s. He bought James White at the end of the '80s as a freshly pressed apple juice company. It has since expanded to include a delicious Bloody Mary base, Big Tom, and beetroot juice (a new juice phenomenon that has been proved to lower blood pressure), plus a plethora of delicious single fruit juices. The company was awarded a well-deserved Royal Warrant for Big Tom in 2002. They sell to a range of small retailers, farm shops, garden centres and the like. James White is an innovative business with superior products that are really worth searching out. See website for stockists.

Paddy and Scott's ○ @

www.paddyandscotts.co.uk

☎ 0844 4778586

✉ Yew Tree Courtyard, Earl Soham, Woodbridge, Suffolk **IP13 7SG**

I know this company well and am very impressed. They have researched their product well and all the coffee I have tasted has been excellent. They also adhere to Fairtrade principles when it comes to buying the coffee from the farmers, so you can drink it with a clear conscience. Choose from at least 20 coffees, all slow-roasted to get the maximum flavour and guaranteeing that it will be free from any 'burnt taste'. They have an online shop or you can contact them to find your nearest stockist. Recently I have tried more varieties of P&S's coffee – they get better and better.

Park Fruit Farm ○ ◑ ⓟ

www.parkfruitfarm.co.uk

☎ 01255 674621

✉ Pork Lane, Great Holland, Nr Frinton-on-Sea, Essex **CO13 0ES**

🕐 Jul–Dec Mon–Sat 9am–5pm; Sun 10am–4pm

Owner Stephen Elsworth farms 12 acres of fruit, 7 acres of which are planted with apples. Unusual varieties such as Kidd's Orange Red and Blenheim Orange are available. His apple juice is generally made with outgrades (misshapen apples) of a mixture of Cox's, Russets and the rarer varieties. The juice is unpasteurised and pressed twice a week in small batches so freshness is guaranteed. Every batch of Elsworth's juice is different. It keeps for five days and up to two weeks if refrigerated.

Purely Organic ○ @ ◑

www.purely-organic.co.uk

☎ 01728 726510

✉ The Technology Centre, Station Road, Framlingham, Suffolk **IP13 9EZ**

A tea only company, selling a variety of ethically sourced teas that are both organic and Fairtrade certified. Black and green teas are available as well as herbal infusions, notably a very soothing camomile made from flowers that are, it is claimed, picked early so have maximum strength. The single estate Ceylon teas are from the Greenfield Estate in Sri Lanka's Uva Highlands. Growing nearly 6000 ft above sea level, the estate has a strong policy of both social and environmental responsibility.

London

▼ FARM SHOPS

Chegworth Farm Shop

www.chegworth.com

020 7229 3016

221 Kensington Church Street,
London **W8 7LX**

Mon–Wed 8am–8pm;
Thurs–Sat 8am–9pm; Sun 9am–6pm

Chegworth farm shop is unexpectedly located in Notting Hill selling produce from the family-run farm in Kent. They are famous for their fruit juices, which are made from their 30,000 apple and pear trees, including rare varieties, which are all organic and certified by the Soil Association. Juices include pure apple and pear and blends using their own berries, blackcurrants and rhubarb. All manner of seasonal fruit and veg can be found at this rustic shop together with dairy products, bread, eggs and tempting pastries. Also visit one of the 10 farmers' markets they sell from every week – see website for details.

Franklins Farm Shop

www.franklinsrestaurant.com/
farmshop

020 8693 3992

155 Lordship Lane, London
SE22 8HX

Mon–Sat 9am–6pm;
Sun 10am–5pm

Franklins is a beloved neighbourhood restaurant serving British grub. In 2008 they opened a farm shop next door selling the best of British. Native oysters, parsley root, UK cheeses, artisan cakes, home-made soups and sauces are sold along with fresh fruit and vegetables from farms in Kent – 95 per cent of the produce is sourced from around the UK. Discover Heirloom tomatoes, multicoloured aubergines and sweet Romano peppers.

Spitalfields City Farm

www.spitalfieldscityfarm.org

020 7247 8762

Buxton Street, London **E1 5AR**

Tues–Sun 10am–4.30pm

Spitalfields City Farm is the nearest city farm to the square mile, spread over 1.3 acres and is a registered charity. The farm rears rare-breed animals and has a range of activities, including cookery lessons and a young farmers' club for children. An affordable selection of seasonal vegetables is grown by local volunteers and sold within the shop. Fresh eggs and garden accessories are also available.

Acton Farmers' Market £

www.actonmarket.com
☎ 020 8993 9605
✉ The Mount, King Street, London
W3 9NW
🕐 **Weekly**, Sat 9am–1pm

There is a market almost every day in this venue, but on Saturdays it is transformed into a farmers' market featuring 20 stalls run by producers who make and grow food in or near London. The Acton farmers' market is the place to go for naturally reared meat and game, fresh fish, bread from West London bakeries and cut flowers. Look out, especially, for the ethnic foodstalls, sausages made by Parson's Nose, and local grower Stone Apples. The locals are impressed and speak highly of this market.

Bermondsey Farmers' Market £

www.lfm.org.uk
☎ 020 7833 0338
✉ Bermondsey Square, London
SE1 3UN
🕐 **Weekly**, Sat 10am–2pm

This is a new, smaller farmers' market, doing a good job especially as it's in close proximity to the larger and well-attended Borough Market just down the road. Visitors to this farmers' market are impressed. Expect to find Whiteys Fish, game from the South Downs, fruit, salad, herbs and vegetables (locals who go there say there are more organic producers than any other local market in London), bread and cooked foods. Look out for Ted's (excellent) veg, and meat from Galileo Farm.

Blackheath Farmers' Market £

www.lfm.org.uk
☎ 020 7833 0338
✉ Blackheath Rail Station Car Park,
2 Blackheath Village, London
SE3 0ZH
🕐 **Weekly**, Sun 10am–2pm

Regulars recommend arriving early at this small, high quality market, this year celebrating its 10th year, where brisk trade sees producers selling out fast. Like all the London farmers' markets it is an excellent place to come and do your weekly organic or locally grown vegetable shop, buy organic sausages, artisan breads and cakes, plus cheeses made just outside London (there is a producer here selling goats' and ewes' milk cheese that is very popular).

Borough Market

www.boroughmarket.org.uk

☏ 020 7407 1002

✉ 8 Southwark Street, London
SE1 1TL

🕐 Thurs 11am–5pm; Fri 12–6pm;
Sat 8am–5pm

Now the most famous food market in London, situated on an ancient market site under the railway tracks near London Bridge station, Borough has been transformed from a typical vegetable and salad market to a huge gourmet food market selling just about everything. It would take too long to list the number of stalls here. Some have been established a long time such as the pork butcher Sillfield Farm (see page 196), The Ginger Pig (see page 77) butchery, and Brindisa (who sell Spanish artisan foods). There are permanent stalls, but on Fridays and Saturdays the place fills with dozens of small producers. Among the best is Fern Verrow (see page 147), a stall selling outstanding biodynamically-grown vegetables, Furness Fish (see page 210), where you can find peeled, cooked brown shrimps and fresh wet fish, Topolski (very good artisan-made Polish sausages) and Portuguese foods from Rainha Santa (see page 66). Borough is not strong on local produce, and cannot be described as the greenest of markets, but the quality is great.

Brixton Farmers' Market

www.lfm.org.uk

☏ 020 7833 0338

✉ Brixton Station Road, Brixton,
London **SW9 8JX**

🕐 Weekly, Sun 10am–2pm

A new and thriving market with a growing following, where you can buy produce sourced from farms and food producers within a 100-mile radius of London. Most comes from much nearer, however. Expect to find fish from the south coast, organic fruit and vegetables, Somerset cheddar, free-range meat and poultry, game in season and artisan bread from a London bakery. The Norfolk Horn Lamb is also well worth seeking out.

Brixton Market £

www.brixtonmarket.net

☏ 020 7833 0338

✉ Electric Avenue, Brixton,
London **SW9 8JX**

🕐 Mon–Sat 10am–6pm (**Market
arcades**); Mon–Sat 8am–6pm
(**Street traders**)

The most exciting, alarming, vibrant tropical foods market in London, with over 80 street traders and dozens of shops inside the market arcades, all jostling for sales and patronised by a large number of enthusiastic traditional cooks. You will witness fishmongers getting a thorough dressing down for charging too much, and butchers selling every cut (and I mean *every* bit of the animal). There are stalls selling giant, live African snails and some fabulous fresh produce stalls selling pumpkin, yams, the hottest Scotch bonnet chillies, bunches of fresh herbs and loads of exotic fruit. There is now a new European element to the market: look out for Rosie's Deli Café (see page 67) and the now famous Franco Manca Pizzeria.

Broadway Market 💷

www.broadwaymarket.co.uk
☎ 020 7833 0338
✉ Broadway Market, Hackney
E8 4QJ
🕐 **Weekly**, Sat 9am–5pm

Just off London Fields lies Broadway Market. This street has had a market since the 1890s,when barrow boys sold everything from bacon to beans. Today there are 80 stallholders with a selection of good, affordable food. Organic beef, apples from orchards in Kent, fish from the south coast and regional cheeses are sold; plus fruit and vegetables, bread and cakes and other meats. The fashion and art stalls are also worth checking out.

Covent Garden Real Food Market 💷

www.coventgardenlondonuk.com
☎ 0870 780 5001
✉ Covent Garden Piazza, London
WC2E 8RF
🕐 **Weekly**, Thurs 11am–7pm

Bringing food shopping back to its old home at Covent Garden in the West End of London (not to be confused with the wholesale market at Vauxhall), these markets – which can be random so call beforehand or check the website if you are not local – feature some good, small-scale food producers and have a jolly atmosphere. Regular stallholders include S. J. Frederick (see page 20), selling delicious Label Anglais free-range chickens; Spore Boys exotic mushrooms; Neal's Yard Dairy (see page 96), selling the finest perfectly matured artisan cheeses; plus various cake and confectionery companies.

Ealing Farmers' Market

www.lfm.org.uk
☎ 020 7833 0338
✉ Leeland Rd, West Ealing, London
W13 9HH
🕐 **Weekly**, Sat 9am–1pm

I have friends who shop here and really rate this weekly market, which has a good number of stalls selling organic or locally grown vegetables, plus one stall, Perry Court Farm, selling biodynamic vegetables (basically an even more rigorous form of organic that works totally with nature, the lunar cycle, etc). There are producers here from the south-east area selling free-range poultry and naturally reared beef, pork and lamb. You can also buy honey harvested from hives actually kept in Ealing – few foods are more local than that, and seafood from Handpicked Shellfish Company.

Exmouth Market 🏃

www.exmouth-market.com
☎ 020 7527 3830
✉ Exmouth Market, London
EC1R 4QE
🕐 Thurs–Sat 11am–6pm

There is a small market on this old street from Monday to Saturday, but the best days are at the end of the week when there are more stalls selling both food and ready-made foods to take away. My sister and brother-in-law, Sam and Sam Clark, are the chefs who run Moro, a popular restaurant on this street and I am happy to blow their trumpet and credit them with having instigated the good food culture that now prevails. They often have a stall selling their paella cooked traditionally in huge open pans. Another stall does a fabulous hog roast, another home-made curries. There are also stalls selling artisan cheeses, bread, cakes, fresh vegetables and much more.

Islington Farmers' Market 🏃

www.lfm.org.uk
☎ 020 7833 0338
✉ Chapel Market (between Penton St and Baron St) western end, London **N1 9PZ**
🕐 **Weekly**, Sun 10am–2pm

This was the first farmers' market to open up in London, but has since moved to a new venue. Produce is mostly sourced from farms and producers working within a 100-mile radius of the capital, and there is exceptional quality here. There is the usual fantastic organic produce, stalls selling naturally reared meat and poultry, artisan breads and much more. It is not one of my local markets, but regulars speak highly of it and since it will soon be celebrating 13 years, the market must be doing something right.

Liverpool Street Farmers' Market

www.lfm.org.uk
☎ 020 7833 0338
✉ Devonshire Square, by Liverpool
Street Station, London **EC2M 4WQ**
🕐 Monthly, 1st Wed 8am–3pm

This is a great place for City workers to pick up lunch or ingredients for dinner. Hand-picked shellfish from Dorset, Parson's Nose free-range hog roast, award-winning cheeses, fruit and vegetables from Kent, and pies, cakes and breads from some of London's top bakers can be found here on a monthly basis.

Marylebone Farmers' Market

www.lfm.org.uk
☎ 020 7833 0338
✉ Cramer Street Car Park,
Marylebone High Street, London
W1U 4EA
🕐 Weekly, Sun 10am–2pm

I know this farmers' market, which has been open since 2003, quite well and love the scale of it, the diversity of the food producers selling here and the area itself. Marylebone has undergone a great high-street revival under the auspices of the Howard de Walden Estates who have encouraged independent retailers to open up shops in the area. The large size of this market makes it more competitive and keeps prices fair. There are at least four vegetable stalls, great poultry, apples from Kent orchards, produce from a tomato farm on the Isle of Wight, French *traiteur* food, fresh fish from the south-east coast and much more.

Northcote Road

www.welovenorthcoteroad.com
☎ 020 8871 6384
✉ Northcote Road, Battersea,
London **SW11 6QB**
🕐 Mon–Sat 9am–5pm

This pretty high -street market comes into its own on Friday and Saturday, when you can browse the stalls or pop into local shops such as Dove's butchers, Gail's Bakery, Salumeria Napoli and Dandelion Wholefoods, which are all great. There is also a well-stocked kitchen shop selling every gadget and pan. The market is not extensive, but there are two good fruit and vegetable stalls selling very fresh produce bought at wholesale markets. There is also an excellent (and popular) fish van, a bakery selling a vast range of handmade loaves, plus warm pizza and focaccia that you can eat as you wander up and down. I prefer Fridays at the market – the numbers can be overwhelming on Saturdays.

Notting Hill Gate Farmers' Market

www.lfm.org.uk
☎ 020 7833 0338
✉ Kensington Place, Notting Hill
Gate, London **W8 7PR**
🕐 Weekly, Sat 9am–1pm

Given that this farmers' market is held weekly in affluent
Notting Hill Gate, its success is not a huge surprise. There
are some great producers here, however, all working within
100 miles of the capital. Among the stalls, expect to find
handmade loaves and rolls from Flourish bakery and organic
vegetables from Sunnyfields organic farm. Fruit juices, wet
fish and naturally reared meat are also available.

The Partridges Food Market

www.partridges.co.uk/
foodmarket
☎ 020 7730 0651
✉ Duke of York Square,
King's Road, London **SW3 4LY**
🕐 Weekly, Sat 10am–4pm

Open since October 2005, this food market has become
extraordinarily popular and the queues – not surprisingly in
London – for the ready-made hot food, are legendary. There
are about 150 producers, selling a wide range from handmade Polish sausages by Topolski, to inspired, and rather
worthy, raw food made by Rainforest Creations. There are
some very good organic vegetables from Eostre Organics
and Secretts Farm (see page 253). All the other artisan foods
are represented, though some of the quality could go up a
notch. Great to see the Maldon Oyster van here, however.

Pimlico Road Farmers' Market 💷

www.lfm.org.uk
☎ 020 7833 0338
✉ Orange Square, corner of Pimlico
Road and Ebury Street, London
SW1W 8LP
🕐 Weekly, Sat 9am–1pm

Not Pimlico really, but much smarter Belgravia, so expect
to rub shoulders with the banking fraternity and – unless
it is my imagination – pay higher prices. I have shelled out
£20 for a single chicken and comparatively more for organic
pork. I have also noticed vegetable stalls selling produce that
has been picked days before and refrigerated – we can all
buy that stuff in supermarkets. There is good bread from
Flour Power City (see page 86), free-range turkey joints all
year round from Manor Farm Game, Chegworth apples and
buffalo cheese. Recent visits to the market show some
improvement all round; fewer 'professionals' and more
freshness.

Portobello Market

www.portobellovillage.com

☎ 020 7833 0338

✉ Portobello Road, London
W11 1AN

🕐 Mon–Wed 9am–6pm;
Thurs 9am–1pm; Fri–Sat 9am–7pm

I have a soft spot for this busy, touristy west London market. When I was cooking for the café at the Blenheim Crescent cookery bookshop, Books for Cooks, in 1992, I did most of my shopping on the market, especially for vegetables. You have to fight your way through crowds and head for the middle section of the market, but the produce is mainly top quality and the prices competitive. Open every day, things crank up a notch or two at the end of the week when a wider range of food is on offer. Keep your nerve and take it easy. Do not let the chaos get to you and you will enjoy this traditional London market. My teenage daughter loves the fashion stalls, which are, incidentally, located under the Westway.

Slow Food Southbank Markets

www.slowfood.org.uk

☎ 020 7099 1132

✉ Southbank Centre, Belvedere
Road, London **SE1 8XX**

🕐 Check website for details

Slow Food's London division organise good local and speciality produce markets that are held in the Southbank Centre, London. The markets are fairly random but if you check the Slow Food UK website regularly you will find forthcoming dates well in advance. Keep an eye out especially when preparing for Christmas as there is usually a special market at this time. There are over 30 stalls, all selling food with an emphasis on sustainability and artisan skills. You can expect to find fish from the south coast, such as hand-dived scallops from Shellseekers or native oysters from Richard Hayward on Mersea Island.

You might find artisan breads made by London baker Flour Power City (see page 86), naturally reared meat from Northfield Farm, or fruit and vegetables from Ash Green Organics. There are often a number of stalls selling artisan foods form France, Italy, Spain and Portugal. This is a moveable feast, but one worth keeping up with.

South Kensington £

www.lfm.org.uk

📞 020 7833 0338

✉ Bute Street, London **SW7 3EX**

🕐 Weekly, Sat 9am–1pm

A new and well-edited market with just a few essential stores, including three superb vegetable stalls, a great home-made soup stall and another selling venison from the South Downs. King of the stalls, however, is the fish stall from Christchurch in Dorset. Run by Les Lawrence, the produce is quiveringly fresh and includes oysters from Poole Harbour, Dover soles, clams and mussels – I once bought live Signal crayfish here, sourced by Les from a Hampshire trout lake. The French and Spanish residents of South Ken are going mad for Les's stall and large queues form early on. If you put your email address on his mailing list – he will email you on Friday night to let you know what he will bring the next day (christchurchfish@live.co.uk).

Spitalfields Fine Food Market

www.visitspitalfields.com

✉ Crispin Place, Spitalfields, London **E1 6DT**

🕐 Thurs, Fri and Sun 10am–5pm

Odd that this market does not open on Saturdays in the newly 'created' Crispin Place in the old Spitalfields Market building. But never mind, the food you can buy here is a great asset for London residents and visitors alike. Fresh meat, fish, artisan bread, vegetables and a wealth of home-made foods and deli specialities.

Stoke Newington Organic Market £

www.growingcommunities.org

📞 020 7502 7588

✉ William Patten School, Stoke Newington Church Street, London **N16 0NX**

🕐 Weekly, Sat 10am–2.30pm

This is the only all-organic weekly farmers' market in the UK, with 23 farmers and producers selling outstanding organic, biodynamic or wild produce from within 100 miles of Hackney. Stalls at the market include Say It With Herbs, a fresh herb company run by farmer Sheila Poole from Harpenden; fish from Channel Fish (landed by *Our Betty*, a boat fishing off the Sussex coast); organic vegetables from Ripple Farm; biodynamic vegetables from Perry Court Farm (see page 293); organic pork and lamb from Muck & Magic; organic salad grown by Adrian Izzard in Cambridgeshire; breads from Natures Bakehouse ready-made Creole food from Global Fusion; and fresh milk, yoghurt and cheese from Higher Allam buffalo farm. Most admirably of all, this is one of the first farmers' markets in London to accept Healthy Start vouchers for fresh vegetables, fruit and milk. These vouchers are issued free to families on low incomes (see www.healthystart.nhs.uk).

Swiss Cottage Farmers' Market £

www.lfm.org.uk
☎ 020 7833 0338
✉ Eton Avenue, London **NW3 3EU**
🕐 **Weekly**, Wed 10am–4pm

With most London farmers' markets opening on the weekends, it is great to find a place open mid-week where you can buy just-picked vegetables, plus herbs and salad that are all bouncy and fresh. There are also breads from Flour Power City (see page 84), handmade goats' cheeses from Sussex and some decent, naturally made, 'global' take-away foods for shoppers who do not feel like cooking.

Twickenham Farmers' Market £

www.lfm.org.uk
☎ 020 7833 0338
✉ Holly Road Car Park, Holly Road, Twickenham, Middlesex **TW1 4HF**
🕐 **Weekly**, Sat 9am–1pm

A good farmers' market established a decade ago, popular with locals who champion the quality of the organic and home-grown produce and good quality naturally reared meat. Special mention is made of the honey stall featuring honey made by a beekeeper in Twickenham itself. It is said that if you eat honey made in the area where you live and work, you will not be so susceptible to allergy / hay fever triggered by local pollen. A good reason in itself to attend this market.

Walthamstow Farmers' Market £

www.lfm.org.uk
☎ 020 7833 0338
✉ Town Square, Selbourne Walk Shopping Centre, Walthamstow, London **E17 7JY**
🕐 **Weekly**, Sun 10am–2pm

Checking through the long list of producers that attend this weekly east London market, I can assure you that you will find good food here. From Lincolnshire Poacher cheese (a big hearted, raw-milk cheddar-type cheese) to Allam Wood Buffalo products; bread from the Harvest Bakery to Miss Stoneham's preserves and cherries from Dallaways Farm (in summer). Not all attend every week, but there will always be naturally reared meat, poultry, fish and locally grown vegetables on sale.

Whitecross Street Market 🉐

www.whitecrossstreet.co.uk
☎ 020 7527 1761
✉ Whitecross Street, Islington
EC1Y 8QJ
🕐 Thurs–Fri 11am–5pm

First begun in the 17th century, today the specialist food market has been instrumental in revitalizing the area. It is famous for its range of international cuisine serving hot food to take away – aromatic curries from Sawadee and the Roast of Sharwood's 'manwiches' (slabs of ciabatta stuffed with slices of herby hog roast) – plus a host of other stalls serving dishes from around the world. There is much local produce on offer, too, including Italian 'Gastronomical' cheeses and Netty Poskitts' luxury fairy cakes, packaged in egg cartons.

Wimbledon Park Farmers' Market 🉐

www.lfm.org.uk
☎ 020 7833 0338
✉ Wimbledon Park First School,
Havana Road, London **SW19 8EJ**
🕐 **Weekly**, Sat 9am–1pm

Beloved of its regulars, this 10-year-old market thrives on a good variety of traders selling fresh, naturally produced food. Expect to find free-range poultry, pork, lamb and beef, organic vegetables, handmade breads and pastries, and tomato products, including decent natural ketchup, sauce, juice and roasted tomatoes infused with herbs and garlic.

▼ DELIS AND SPECIALISTS

T. Adamou & Sons 🉐🉐

☎ 020 8994 0752
✉ 124–126 Chiswick High Road,
London **W4 1PU**
🕐 Tues–Sat 9.45am–6.30pm;
Sun 10am–2pm

This family-run Greek deli in Turnham Green may have opened in 1959, but it is still popular and the service has remained personal and helpful. Fresh fruit, vegetables, lovely bunches of herbs, parmesan cut straight from the wheel, quince paste, De Cecco pasta and Italian risotto rice are available alongside Greek specialities such as vine leaves and Greek wines.

Andreas Michli

020 8802 0188
405–411 St Ann's Road,
London **N15 3JL**
Mon–Sat 10am–7pm;
Sun 11am–4pm

An acclaimed Greek-Cypriot shop, selling favourite vegetables for use in Greek dishes: aubergines, sweet onions, tomatoes, beans, plus fresh horta cultivated on Michli's own Hertfordshire farm. This is a kind of nourishing chicory that the Greeks believe, probably with good reason, has extraordinary nutritional qualities and which is often eaten in the autumn with the new season's peppery extra virgin olive oil. Pulses and live snails are also available in the shop, plus lovely ceramic pots to cook it all in.

The Barnsbury Grocer ○

www.thebarnsburygrocer.co.uk
0207 607 7222
237 Liverpool Road, London
N1 1LX
Mon–Fri 8am–8pm;
Sat 9am–6pm; Sun 10am–4pm

This shop opened five years ago. It is always amazing to me that there are still people out there who, even in the face of overwhelming, crushing competition from the supermarkets are willing to have a go and who succeed, too. This shop has become invaluable to the local community. It has an extensive cheese selection and a good charcuterie counter offering a variety of meats that change on a weekly basis. Many of the products stocked are organic and there is a good selection of wines as well. Takeaways and sandwiches are reportedly good and all are made in kitchens on the premises. Mail orders available.

Beamish & McGlue @ ○

www.beamishandmcglue.com
020 8761 8099
461 Norwood Road, London
SE27 0BW
Mon–Fri 9am–7pm;
Sat 9.30am–5.30pm;
Sun 10am–4pm

A much-loved deli in an area that locals otherwise describe as a food desert (though please let me know if there are other shops we should know about in this part of south London). Selling a wide range of local produce and ready-made foods, and serving delicious lunches at tables outside and in, this shop has a real community feel, as well as food of the highest standard. Lately they have begun serving coffee in reusable takeaway cups and stocking handmade ice lollies – a very family-friendly shop.

Bluebird Epicerie 🍴

www.danddlondon.com/
restaurants/bluebird_epicerie

☎ 020 7559 1140

✉ 350 King's Road, London
SW3 5UU

🕐 Mon–Fri 8am–8pm;
Sat 9am–7pm; Sun 9am–5pm

This two-storey shop began, as the name suggests, as an epicerie (or grocery), but the ground floor has become more focused on selling snacks, presumably because the location / lack of parking / clientele make it the wrong place to put a one-stop (albeit very upmarket) shop. You can buy good bread and croissants, plenty of store cupboard items, some charcuterie, cheeses and other dairy foods and ready-made, *traiteur*-type foods, plus wine downstairs.

Brindisa Shop 🍴 @

www.brindisa.com

☎ 020 7407 1036

✉ The Floral Hall, Stoney Street,
London **SE1 9AF**

🕐 Tues–Thurs 10am–5.30pm;
Fri 10am–6pm; Sat 8.30am–4pm

Whether you are visiting the Brindisa Shop or Borough Market, their close proximity make it easy to enjoy both foodie destinations. Brindisa is famed for its imported profusion of the finest Spanish foods and ingredients. Their ham counter serves hand-carved hams from all over Spain, each one offering a different flavour depending on the region, how the pig was reared and curing conditions. Their cheeses range from the crumbly salty Manchegos, to island cows' milk cheeses with paprika and olive oil, to goats' cheese from the southern mountains. Other store cupboard items include spices, herbs, paella rice, olive oils as well as fresh items such as olives, salt cod, chorizos and morcilla (a Spanish blood sausage). Also visit Casa and Tierra Brindisa restaurants in Kensington, Soho and Borough Market to try their Spanish dishes. See the website for details.

Brook's Counter & Table 🍴

www.counterandtable.com

☎ 020 7602 0664

✉ 140 Shepherd's Bush Road,
London **W6 7PB**

🕐 Mon–Fri 8am–7pm;
Sat 8am–6pm; Sun 9am–5pm

A cheerful deli-café run by Jo Cooke and Leander Faucet. These two young mothers have made their shop a haven for young families, as well as a place to buy home-made baby food and other food items such as olive oils, tea, coffee, cheeses and olives. Saturday is bread day when there is a large range of artisan loaves on offer, and every day is scooped ice cream day, offering Roskilly's ices.

Bushwacker Wholefoods

020 8748 2061

132 King Street, Hammersmith, London **W6 0QU**

Mon, Wed–Sat 10am–6pm; Tues 11am–6pm

A recommended wholefoods shop established 28 years ago, a near record on a London high street so they must be doing something right. On sale is a full range of grains, pulses, rice, nuts and seeds, organic cereals, muesli mixes, fruit juices and baking ingredients, plus fresh organic fruit and vegetables sourced directly from farms.

I. Camisa & Son @⌂

www.camisa.co.uk

020 7437 7610

61 Old Compton Street, London **W1V 5PN**

Mon–Sat 9am–6pm

Soho's other great Italian specialist food shop, after Lina Stores (see page 61), compliments the latter but has a totally different atmosphere. Enter this tiny place to stand shoulder to shoulder with eager cooks, shopping for some of the best ingredients. Food is stacked floor to ceiling, packed on to some very old-fashioned shop fittings, or sitting like museum pieces in glass-fronted drawers. The salami and ham are especially good, cotechino (fat-cured pork sausages that you poach in liquid and eat with little brown lentils) feature big (literally) in the crammed window. Fresh pasta and gnocchi are popular, too, and you can get dizzy choosing from dozens of different dried pasta asciutta shapes. Like Lina Stores, I. Camisa is excellent value for money. Home delivery available.

The Corner Café

020 8487 1200

1 Broadway, Barnes, London **SW13 0NY**

Mon–Fri 7.30am–5pm; Sat 9am–5pm; Sun 9am–4pm

A sweet deli, packed with good things, especially the cakes and brownies, which are baked on site. Adored by locals, who can come in and place special orders, asking for their favourite dishes, which cook Anita will prepare. Worth a visit, even for a cup of tea.

Daylesford Café and Store ⊕ @ ✪

www.daylesfordorganic.com

☎ 020 7881 8060

✉ 44b Pimlico Road, London
SW1W 8LP

🕐 Mon–Sat 8am–7pm;
Sun 10am–4pm

Daylesford has repeated its success in the Cotswolds (see page 301) with this store in central London selling much of the same produce in a smaller space. Organic meat, game and poultry; dairy foods including some outstanding cheeses made in the Cotswold dairy; bread, patisserie and savoury tarts from Daylesford's own bakery; ready-cooked foods to take home; plenty of grocery items; stunningly displayed seasonal vegetables and fruit; and a gorgeous café for light meals through the day. Expect big queues for tables on Saturday when the Pimlico Farmers' Market (see page 46) is in full swing outside the door. Daylesford has a third major shop in Westbourne Grove, Notting Hill. See website for details of other outlets in the UK.

Earth Natural Foods ⊕ ✪

www.earthnaturalfoods.co.uk

☎ 0207 482 2211

✉ 200 Kentish Town Road, London
NW5 2AE

🕐 Mon–Sat 8.30am–7pm

This is a real north London shop catering for vegans and vegetarians – it has a great reputation locally and they certainly try hard, with a variety of goods. A large selection of organic fruit and veg is complemented by bread, local London honey, home-made takeaways and artisan cheeses. They have a good selection of organic wines and Champagnes and also stock dried fruits, nuts and oils as well as the more down-to-earth eco household goods. Will deliver – contact for details.

East Dulwich Deli ✪

☎ 020 8693 2525

✉ 15 / 17 Lordship Lane, London
SE22 8EW

🕐 Mon–Thurs 9am–6pm;
Fri 9am–7pm; Sat 8.30am–6pm;
Sun 10am–4pm

A big high-ceilinged deli, where tall shelves are crammed with foods from all over Europe. Confectionery is a speciality – children love this shop. The fresh counter sells Italian and British cured meats and bread from an affiliated bakery Born and Bread – try the sourdough. Otherwise there are the usual, useful dried pasta ascuitta, oils, vinegar, anti-pasti, preserves and drinks. The chocolate fudge brownies are locally famous.

Frog On The Green

http://web.mac.com/designunited
1/iWeb/frogonthegreen.com

☎ 020 7732 2525

✉ 119 Consort Road, London
SW15 3RU

🕐 Mon–Sat 9am–7pm;
Sun 9am–6pm

If cured meats, cheese, fairly priced organic milk, sourdoughs and fabulous home-made cakes are what you enjoy then this deli is the place to go. Striving to promote a healthier lifestyle it stocks a range of organic, ethical and seasonal produce. They sell food from good-quality recognised suppliers, such as cheese from Neal's Yard, oats and flour from the Watermill in Cumbria and St Peter's ale. Localism, however, is also at the heart of the shop – they source food where they can from local allotments and are supplied with local honey. Home-made ready meals with a Greek and Mediterranean twist are also available.

R. Garcia and Sons ◉

www.garciacafe.co.uk

☎ 020 7221 6119

✉ 246 Portobello Road, London
W11 1LL

🕐 Mon–Sun 10am–6pm

R. Garcia and Sons is one of the largest Spanish supermarkets and delis in London. The shop is always busy, with their large charcuterie counter displaying the common and more unusual selection of meats, chorizos and jamon serrano, and an impressive cheese selection including Manchego, Mahan, Cabralles and Tetilla. Smoked paprika, marcona almonds and an excellent range of sherries can also be found with big-branded biscuits, dulce de leche, paellera pans, quince paste, cartons of Sangria and bottles of Manzanilla. They also have a good tapas bar next door.

Gastronomia Italia ◎ ◉

☎ 020 7834 2767

✉ 8 Upper Tachbrook Street,
Pimlico, London **SW1V 1SN**

🕐 Mon–Fri 9am–6pm;
Sat 9am–5pm

Unlike those gloomy delis housing dusty jars on shelves, Salvatore Di Bartolo's shop bursts with Italian specialities, both fresh and for the store cupboard. Stock up with the best Italian branded staples such as pasta, rice, antipasti and canned tomatoes, then buy fresh cheeses, mortadella, salami or take home a Bonifanti Pandoro, a slow-leavened plain cake. Locals rave about the pizzas, which they sell either whole or by the slice.

Gennaro Delicatessen ⛺ @ 🔥

www.italianfoodexpress.co.uk
☎ 020 8852 1370
✉ 23 Lewis Grove, London
SE13 6BG
🕐 Mon–Sat 9am–6pm

Antonio and Elena Nigro took over the running of this Italian deli in 2004. Their shop and now their website offer every conceivable Italian provision that can be delivered directly to your front door. Fresh and dried pastas, jars of sauces, parmigiano reggiano, pecorino and mozzarella cheese, olive oils, fresh bread, biscuits, Sicilian sea salt, cooking sausage and charcuterie, and even Italian coffee, beers and waters can be found, plus hundreds of other items. Check out their Sicilian own-brand olive oil as well.

German Deli ⛺ @ 🔥

www.germandeli.co.uk
☎ 020 7387 0000
✉ 3 Park Street, London
SE1 9AB
🕐 Mon–Fri 10am–7pm;
Sat 9am–5pm

Offering a wide range of foods and delicatessen items that would meet the needs of any homesick German, along with a comprehensive website citing even more products including jars of smoked fish, soft cheeses, smoked sausages, spreadable salamis, Black Forest ham, fetter Speck (back bacon with rind), plus sourdough rye and wheat bread, Rosinenbrot (sweet currant bread) and Streuselkuchen (crumble cake) from their bakery. Also visit their stall at Borough Market (see page 42) on Fridays and Saturdays.

A. Gold

☎ 020 7247 2487
✉ 42 Brushfield Street, London
E1 6AG
🕐 Mon–Fri 11am–8pm;
Sat 11am–6pm; Sun 10am–6pm

This is probably the most charming deli in London. Like something out of a Dickens novel, this green-fronted small treasure specialises entirely in British produce using traditional recipes and the best ingredients. The wood-panelled Georgian house, which was converted into a shop, is stacked with the perfect selection of cured meats, fish, jams, chutneys, sweets, biscuits, smelly cheeses, fruit cordials, sloe gin, home-made Scotch eggs and pork pies. It is hard to step into this time warp and leave empty handed – even their fresh marshmallows and sugared mice are tempting.

Greensmith's

www.greensmithsfood.co.uk

☎ 020 7921 2970

✉ 27 Lower Marsh, London
SE1 7RG

🕐 Mon–Fri 8am–8pm;
Sat 8am–6pm

A new grocery in a small high street near Waterloo Station that has brought five better-than-good London retailers together, all under one roof in a single shop. Meat is from rare breeds and supplied by The Ginger Pig (see page 77); bread is from The Old Post Office Bakery (see page 89) and fruit and vegetables are from Solstice in New Covent Garden market in Vauxhall. There is also wine and coffee from Waterloo Wine and Antica Coffee respectively. Locals tell me they are thrilled to have this shop in a market street that once heaved with vegetable stalls, but now boasts only one or two. Given the cost of rent and rates in London, I think this is a great idea and could inspire other small independent shops to get together in a similar enterprise.

The Grocer on Kings @ ✿

www.thegroceron.com

☎ 020 7351 5544

✉ 184a King's Road, London
SW3 5XP

🕐 Mon–Fri 8.30am–7pm;
Sat 9am–6pm; Sun 10am–6pm

This top-ranking, ready-made food specialist sells meals (nicely packed in bags) that you would expect to get in a decent restaurant, made from quality raw materials. Prices reflect this, but they are good value. The line is more or less Mediterranean – risottos, tagines, braises with wine and simple puds such as orchard fruit poached in wine. Added to this are groceries, artisan bread, cakes and croissants, giant meringues, dried pasta, preserves, chocolates, drinks and smoothies, Spanish piquillo peppers and dressings. See website for details of branches.

H. Gunton Ltd ✿ @ ✿

www.guntons.co.uk

☎ 01206 572200

✉ 81–83 Crouch Street, Colchester,
Essex CO3 3EZ

🕐 Mon–Sat 8.30am–5pm

There has been a grocery store here for 70 years hand-roasting coffee and selling cheese along with a great range of groceries. Gunton's has entered the 21st century with a flourish, offering artisan-made Cheddar from Quickes Dairy in Newton St Cyres and specialist foods from all over East Anglia, including proper English jam from Wilkin & Sons in Tiptree, Essex, damson cheese from Cooperas Wood Farm in Harwich and bread from the Colchester Blackberry Bakery.

Gusto & Relish

www.gustoandrelish.co.uk
020 8878 2005
56 White Hart Lane, Barnes, London **SW13 OPZ**
Mon–Fri 10am–6.30pm; Sat 9am–6pm; Sun 9am–1pm

This deli combines the best of British produce, carefully sourced from smaller producers, with select goods from the continent to create an eclectic and attractive range. As well as a fine selection of dried goods, hand-picked oils and vinegars sit alongside a tempting selection of cheeses and charcuterie – and attentive staff will happily advise you on the perfect combinations. Even more attractive are the puddings on offer – the Chocolate Nemesis is wonderfully indulgent – and their selection of wines is also good. The shop is warm and generous – and feels as though it is stocked with a food lover's favourites.

The Ham & Cheese Co.

www.thehamandcheeseco.co.uk
01428 645 958
98 Druid St, Southwark, London **SE1 2HQ**
Fri 11am–6pm; Sat 9am–4pm

The team of four at The Ham & Cheese Co. have scoured France and Italy, seeking out individuals who preserve traditional methods of production and animal husbandry. The importance of these traditional methods is reflected in the superior product at the end of the process. Although imported, the team regularly visit their producers and there is a good dialogue between the two areas of the business. Their outstanding mozzarella, made by hand in southern Italy, is soft, salty and fresh tasting. Charcuterie from the Basque Country takes pride of place on the stall at Borough Market (the best place to find The Ham & Cheese Co. on a Friday and Saturday) and rightly so – the free-range, rare-breed chorizo is fantastic.

Harrods Food Hall ○ @ ⦸

www.harrods.com
020 7730 1234
87–135 Brompton Road, Knightsbridge, London **SW1X 7XL**
Mon–Sat 10am–8pm; Sun 11.30am–6pm

Harrods has everything. That is what we were brought up to believe and, while the food hall has evolved into something much more of a self-service market than it was in my youth (when you could only be served by men in boaters), it is still fabulous. The architecture is amazing and the meat and fish hall, in particular, is a gem. Just go to gaze at the fresh fish display, or the beautifully dressed game. Wander among the counters in the chocolate department, or catch a whiff of hundreds of perfectly kept cheeses. Does it still have everything? Well, I often turn to Harrods when I need something unusual for a food photographic shoot, such as a piece of crystallised lemon peel, palm sugar, frozen gooseberries out of season, a few baby octopus, a brace of teal. They always (or almost always) have it. The downside is the crowd, most of whom are milling about for a gawp. You can hardly blame them. The store changed hands in 2010, and we will wait to see if it will alter what is offered in the historic food hall.

Here Organic Foods ✅

020 7351 4321
125 Sydney Street, London
SW3 6NR
Mon–Sat 9.30am–8pm;
Sun 10am–6.30pm

An organic and wholefood supermarket that has established a good reputation for freshness with an extensive range of organic vegetables, salad, fruit and meat. It also sells a huge store cupboard selection with all the best brands, making this a good place to stock up on pulses, breakfast cereals, home-baking ingredients, cans of tomatoes and fruit juices. There is a wall of freezer cabinets containing sustainably caught fish, vegetables and meat. Organic supermarkets do demonstrate, however, what a lot of ready-made and snack-food tat the sector manufactures. You would think that committed greens would do more food preparation and cooking from scratch.

Hubbub @ ⬡

www.hubbubdeliveries.co.uk
0207 354 5511
8 Blackstock Mews, London
N4 2BT
Mon–Fri 9am–5pm

This isn't so much a shop or producer but a facility that I think is well worth inclusion. Hubbub is a very innovative delivery service. Whilst the supermarkets put more onus on home deliveries, the independent shops are in danger of missing out. But Hubbub allows customers to shop locally online from a variety of suppliers and have everything delivered in one go. Suppliers include butcher Frank Godfrey, La Fromagerie, Saponara deli, deli Ottolenghi and many more. Sadly it is a service that is only available in north London at the moment but the more people who sign up the farther afield the company hope to expand its network. A great idea that really needs supporting.

Iberica ○ ○

www.ibericalondon.com
☎ 020 7636 8650
✉ 195 Great Portland Street,
London **W1W 5PS**
🕐 Mon–Sat 11.30am–7pm

A beautiful, large deli attached to a tapas bar in central
London, where you can buy wafer-thin slices of the famous
Iberico ham made from Spanish acorn-fed pigs.
The flavour is nutty and autumnal, the texture buttery and
rich. But the ham is only the start of an impressive list of
Spanish artisnal foods sold in this shop. There is cecina, an air-
dried smoked beef, venison chorizo, Catalan fuet and
cheaper hams from Serrano. Spain's great hard cheeses –
nicely chalky Manchego, pungent Mahon and rich Cabrales –
are also on offer, along with some delicious canned fish. I love
the bonito pâté with capers on bread seasoned with the best
extra virgin olive oil. Sweet things include a lovely soft turron,
which tastes like a combination of halva and nougat.

Le Pescalou ○

☎ 020 7352 1717
✉ 359 Fulham Road, London
SW10 9TW
🕐 Mon–Sat 8am–8pm;
Sun 10am–7pm

The large number of French residents in this area of London
keep this deli busy. Selling fresh fish – good quality though
little information about provenance – a range of beautiful
but definitely not British fruits and vegetables (including
white truffles when in season), charcuterie and preserves –
this is a shop to go to when you are looking for that elusive
French ingredient: marron purée, duck fat, fromage blanc
and ready-rolled butter pastry – or specialities and treats
such as 'Lu' raspberry wafers (something I associate with
childhood), jars of cornichons and olives, or cans of grated
celeriac and flageolets. I can't resist the guilty pleasure of
shopping at Le Pescalou. Local delivery available.

Leila's Shop

☎ 020 7729 9789
✉ 17 Calvert Avenue, London
E2 7JP
🕐 Mon–Sat 10am–6pm;
Sun 10am–5pm

A quirky shop and café, very popular with Shoreditch
residents who come here for European specialities, fresh
vegetables – appealingly displayed on shelves outside the
red-brick shop front – plus free-range eggs and home-made
foods to rave about. A cool place, typical of this area of
London, and fun to browse in.

Lina Stores

www.linastores.co.uk
☎ 020 7434 3977
✉ 18 Brewer Street, London
W1F 0SH
🕐 Mon–Fri 9am–6.30pm;
Sat 9am–5.30pm

I have been shopping in this wonderful, authentically Italian store run by the Filippi family for 30 years. I remember buying the freshly handmade raviolis for my (future) husband's supper when we first met, so I have much to thank Lina Stores for! In 2010 the shop closed briefly for refurbishment, to the shock of its many customers. As this guide went to press, the reopening was imminent so I cannot report on the new look. Giovanni and Rosa's family are still in charge – Gabriella and Tony are overseeing the changes, but they assure me that the improvements will not change the character. Fresh pasta is a speciality, made on the premises, plus good cheeses, salami, prosciutto, breads and dried porcini, as well as sauces to eat everything with. New to the shop is freshly brewed coffee, home-made Italian cakes and a few tables where you can sit and fall in love with the shop – all over again. Local delivery available.

Macfarlanes Deli ⊘

☎ 020 8673 5373
✉ 48 Abbeville Road, London
SW4 9NF
🕐 Mon–Fri 10am–7pm;
Sat 9am–6pm; Sun 10am–5pm

A family-owned and run neighbourhood deli with shelves stacked with quality food items – bacon and ham from a farm in Dorset, loose chocolates by Exquisite (a small Belgian producer), free-range eggs, Scottish specialities, organic baby food, freshly baked bread and a large range of British and French farmhouse cheeses that Mr MacFarlane is more than happy to guide you through, using his passion and knowledge for cheese.

Manicomio ⊘

www.manicomio.co.uk
☎ 020 7730 3366
✉ 85 Duke of York Square, London
SW3 4LY
🕐 Mon–Fri 8am–7pm;
Sat 10am–7pm; Sun 10am–6pm

This is a very fine delicatessen selling Italian-sourced specialist food. You'll find good pasta, risotto, gnocchi, rice, sauces, salads, roasted vegetables in oil, anchovies, air-dried ham, salami, oils, cheeses, cakes and pastries – not a huge range, but one chosen with care. Most of the premises is given over to a busy café, where, I have to say, I have had disappointing coffee in what is otherwise an exceptionally good place.

Marsh Ruby ✪

www.marshruby.com
☎ 020 7620 0593
✉ 30 Lower Marsh, Waterloo,
London **SE1 7RG**
🕓 Mon–Fri 11.30am–3pm

A remarkable curry café and ready-made food shop, which makes a virtue of sourcing fresh ingredients from British farms and other raw materials from sustainable sources, setting a great example to other Asian food shops. All the chicken is free-range and farmed in Gloucestershire; the basmati rice and daal are organic; vegetables are organic when possible; and all spices are freshly ground on site.

Melrose and Morgan ✪

www.melroseandmorgan.co.uk
☎ 020 7722 0011
✉ 42 Gloucester Avenue, London
NW1 8JD
🕓 Mon–Fri 8am–7pm;
Sat 8am–6pm; Sun 9am–5pm

This smart grocery shop benefits from an in-house kitchen enabling customers to eat in or take away freshly prepared dishes such as butternut squash, red onion and curd cheese tart, coq au vin with rice or marinated beetroot and quinoa salad. In-house pastry chefs make wonderful-looking cakes, tarts, biscuits and savoury tarts. Small artisan producers from around the UK supply the organic and free-range meat and poultry, dairy items, fresh bread, handmade chocolates, wines, oils and fresh fruit and vegetables. Packaging is kept to a minimum, recycled products are used when possible and an electric van makes the deliveries. This year, Melrose and Morgan opened a new store in Oriel Place, Hampstead. See website for details.

Merchant Gourmet ⊕ @ ✪

www.merchant-gourmet.com
☎ 020 7635 4096
✉ 2 Rollins Street, London
SE15 1EW
🕓 Mon–Fri 8am–8pm;
Sat 9am–8pm; Sun 10am–6pm

This long-established specialist food company sells some key ingredients, which I hate my kitchen to be without. Lovers of genuine green Puy lentils, Carmargue red rice, sweet chestnuts from France (peeled and cooked), goose fat in cans (to make the crispest roast potatoes), soft 'mis-cuit' plums from Agen and sunblush tomatoes are just a few of the deli items that you can buy here. Order online and they will post a hamper to your home.

Mortimer & Bennett ○ @ ◐

www.mortimerandbennett.co.uk
☎ 020 8995 4145
✉ 33 Turnham Green Terrace,
London **W4 1RG**
🕐 Mon–Fri 8.30am–6pm;
Sat 8.30am–5.30pm

Dan Mortimer and Di Bennett's aim in 1991 was to offer quality food. Their intent hasn't changed and today you can find hundreds of foody products from around the world. Whether you are looking for a gift of panettone from Turin or wild rose jam, or you need gelatine leaves or Italian '00' flour, or perhaps you fancy some Perail cheese from the Pyrenees, Mortimer & Bennett can meet your needs.

The Mount Street Deli

www.themountstreetdeli.co.uk
☎ 020 7499 6843
✉ 100 Mount Street, London
W1K 2TG
🕐 Mon–Fri 8am–7pm;
Sat 9am–6pm

You can only marvel as you walk into this utterly beautifully designed grocery, part of the Caprice group of restaurants and filled with rare and special foods. Hannah Gutteridge was brought in to get things started, and threw herself into finding the special things sold here, many of them from Slow Food presidia (artisan producer groups): Italian honeys gathered from bees that have visited every blossom imaginable; lardo di Colonatta, a cured herbed pork fat sliced very thin and eaten on hot bread. Plus superb farmhouse cheese, bestselling sausage rolls, chocolates, teas, breads, sweets and extraordinary oils. Not cheap, but very stylish. Stop for a light lunch, and make a trip of it.

Natural Kitchen ○ ◐

www.thenaturalkitchen.com
☎ 020 7486 8065
✉ 77 / 78 Marylebone High Street,
London **W1U 5JX**
🕐 Mon–Fri 8am–8pm;
Sat 9am–8pm; Sun 10am–6pm

A large and glamorous deli on Marylebone's lively high street, which combines a café with a food shop selling natural, fresh ingredients and ready-to-eat foods. There's artisan bread, fresh herbs and vegetables, cheeses and fresh meat from the shop's own butchery. There is the usual urban, food-in-a-dash fare – smoothies, wraps, cheese tarts and patisserie – and a rather ubiquitous Mediterranean thread to it all that mimics far too many London delis. Base elements are sound, though, and there is another branch in the City (see website for details). They will deliver in London and you can phone orders to collect. A second branch is now open in New Fetter Lane, London EC4. A limited range of foodstuffs is available to order online.

The Nutcase ◐

☎ 020 8743 0336
✉ 352 Uxbridge Road, London
W12 7LL
🕐 Mon–Sat 10am–9pm;
Sun 10am–5pm

A few streets down from Shepherd's Bush Market is The Nutcase. As the name suggests, it sells every sort of nut there is. Some are dry-roasted on the premises, and containers teeming with salted nuts, chilli nuts, toffee nuts, chocolate nuts, honey almonds, Iranian pistachios, etc, fill this small shop. Also specialising in Arabic sweets and fruits, baklava and Turkish jellies can be bought, plus freshly ground coffee from North Africa.

The Oil Merchant ◐ @ ◐

www.oilmerchant.co.uk
☎ 020 8740 1335
✉ 5 Goldhawk Mews, London
W12 8PA
🕐 Mon–Fri 9am–5pm;
Sat 9am–1pm

Charles Carey was the first of the specialist olive oil suppliers to bring the really top-class single estate oils from Italy, France and Spain to the UK. Among his reliable oils, available for home delivery, are the many delicious varieties made in Tuscany by Marina Collonna and some great Spanish oils from Marques de Valdueza.

Panzer's Delicatessen ◐ @ ◐

www.panzers.co.uk
☎ 020 7722 1496
✉ 13–19 Circus Road, London
NW8 6PB
🕐 Mon–Fri 8am–7pm;
Sat 8am–6pm; Sun 8am–2pm

Panzer's reminds me of Dr Who's Tardis in that it succeeds in packing the equivalent content of Harrods Food Hall into a space that is a fraction of the size. A delicatessen in the true sense of the word, it sells just about everything – and the quality is awesome. Hand-sliced smoked salmon, along with charcuterie and artisan cheeses in abundance, and if you need specialist foods from the USA, South Africa, Mexico, Japan, Morocco or Greece, it is all here. The fruit and vegetable display is unbelievably varied and fresh – I have to admit that I come here if I need great-looking figs in January for food photography. It has a huge and devoted following in north London, but on the understanding that if you are going to run a shop with such high standards of freshness, prices will err on the high side.

Partridges ⊕ @ ⊘

www.partridges.co.uk
☎ 020 7730 0651
✉ 2–5 Duke of York Square,
London **SW3 4LY**
🕐 Mon–Sun 8am–10pm

This old established store moved premises a few years ago to this new development on the old Duke of York Barracks, which also houses the Saatchi gallery. It is a big shop and café; the cheese and cooked meat counter is huge, and the range wide, though not all is in peak condition all the time (as is often the case with larger food halls). But there is very little that Partridges does not sell, from fresh meat to ready-made puddings, teas, sweet things, frozen vegetables, wines and beer. There is an increasing emphasis on Fairtrade and eco-friendly foods, and there is a café at the back.

Persepolis

www.foratasteofpersia.co.uk
☎ 020 7639 8007
✉ 30 Peckham High Street, London
SE15 5DP
🕐 Mon–Sun 10.35am–9pm

Sally Butcher owns and runs this treasure trove of Iranian foods, selling a wide choice including breads that are as flat and fluid as old linen sheets, a huge range of nuts and fruits, rose and orange water (to make sweet syrup to drizzle on pastry), yoghurt, fresh ewes' milk cheeses, olives, pickled peppers and a hoard of other good things. The added bonus is Sally herself, who will help with cooking advice (she is also a food writer) and guide you through the myriad ingredients she sells.

Power Snacks ⊕ @ ⊘

www.consciousfood.co.uk
☎ 0845 233 5000
✉ 28 Edithna Street, London
SW9 9JP
🕐 Mon–Tues, Thurs–Fri 6am–1pm, 2–5pm; Sat 6am–1pm, 2–4pm

A new and unusual range of biscuits and snacks made from unfamiliar grains such as millet, sorghum, soya and brown rice. Sourced in India, they may not be to everyone's taste, but I can assure you they soon grow on you. Biscuits are wafer thin and come in unfamiliar, peculiar hues (dark brown, 'greige'), but do not be put off. These are interesting flavours and a fascinating baking project. I'd love to know what you think of them.

Rainha Santa Portuguese Foods

www.rainhasanta.co.uk
020 7733 1222
Unit 31, Mahatma Gandhi
Industrial Estate, Milkwood Road,
London **SE24 0JF**
Mon–Fri 9am–5.30pm

Tim Clements spent his childhood in Portugal where his father had bought the preserving factory making the famous Elvas plum. He now sells these (in season) and other specialities such as Salpicao do Tavor (pork underbelly cured in garlic and pimiento) and Quiejo Puro dee Ovelha (an unusual cheese made from sheep and goats milk). The marmalades and honeys are also outstanding.

Raoul's Deli

www.raoulsgourmet.com
020 7289 7313
13 Clifton Road, London
W9 1SZ
Mon–Sat 8.30am–11pm;
Sun 9am–11pm

Believe it or not, Francis Bacon was the person to kick start this successful fine food deli and two cafés. Geraldine Leventis was urged by her artist friend to open a restaurant back in the mid '80s and on finding the existing Raoul's in the heart of Little Venice she took the project on. Today the food store sells ready meals, such as their vegetarian casserole pots-to-go, bottles of their own olive oil from groves in the Peloponnese, herbs and spices, breads from Princi (the Milanese luxury patisserie), plus much, much more. And in the summer months pick up one of their jute picnic bags filled with your choice of dishes.

Romeo Jones

www.romeojones.co.uk
020 8299 1900
80 Dulwich Village, London
SE21 7AJ
Mon–Fri 8am–6pm;
Sat–Sun 9am–6pm

A small yet delightful café-deli on a pretty street selling a well-edited range (dictated in part by space). Cured meat (prosciutto, cooked ham, salami, pancetta and bacon) is top class, fresh meats are brought from a Somerset farm where all livestock is naturally reared and there is a well-chosen stock of farmhouse cheeses. You will always find something new and rare to try, such as amazing flower honey from Italy, handmade chocolates, delicious antipasti or an unusual cake to eat in with a cup of tea or take home. Patrick Belton and Amanda Page are the friendly and enthusiastic proprietors – of a shop that everyone would like to have within walking distance.

Rosie's Deli Café

www.rosiesdelicafe.com

☎ 07807 505397

✉ 14e Market Row, Brixton Market, London **SW9 8JX**

🕐 Mon–Sat 9.30am–5.30pm

Rosie Lovell opened her shop in Brixton's predominantly African Caribbean market three years ago and it has become a favourite with locals who want to stop to buy deli food or eat a rustic sandwich washed down with good coffee. The market (see page 42) is gradually gaining a balance of European-style stalls and café-restaurants, which is no bad thing, though I have always loved the atmosphere (live giant African snails crawling down its halls being the exception). All at Rosie's is home-made using the best ingredients and some crafty imagination. She describes her shop as a deli with a twist, and she has certainly succeeded in this brave venture.

The Rosslyn Delicatessen ❶ @ ❷

www.delirosslyn.co.uk

☎ 020 7794 9210

✉ 56 Rosslyn Hill, London **NW3 1ND**

🕐 Mon–Sat 8.30am–8.30pm; Sun 8.30am–8pm

Helen Sherman opened Rosslyn's over 15 years ago to bring the world's finest products to her local community. Stocking a huge range of goods sourced from around the world, including charcuterie, pasta and sauces, rice and pulses, cheese, cakes and biscuits, jams and marmalades, this large deli can also make bespoke hampers to suit your needs, packed into blue and white striped canvas bags. Visit their website to view the items that can be delivered to your door.

Salumeria Napoli

✉ 69 Northcote Road, London **SW11 1NP**

🕐 Mon–Sat 9am–6pm

A friendly Neapolitan Italian grocery, selling all the favourite cooking ingredients you could need. Beloved brands of risotto rice, pasta, oils, polenta flour, canned and bottled vegetables, salami, ham and anchovies. In the glass-fronted fridge cabinet are fresh pasta and ravioli, pesto, mozzarella, parmesan and antipasti. Typical, traditional and tremendous.

Saponara Delicatessen

☎ 0207 226 2771
✉ 23 Prebend Street, Islington,
London **N1 8PF**
🕐 Mon–Thurs 8am–6.30pm;
Fri–Sat 8am–10pm

This place has a personal and local feel; it is run by a couple of charming Italians, the Saponara brothers, who certainly know their stuff. A variety of cured meats, smoked hams, cheeses and freshly made pasta, including beef ricotta and tortellini with beef mushrooms. They specialise in various pecorinos, from the exotic truffle-infused to the plainer, fully matured variety. They also sell a smoked buffalo mozzarella, delicious Italian pepper sausages and salads to take away.

Savoria ❁ @ ✦

www.savoria.co.uk
☎ 020 7993 4170
✉ 2 Painters Mews, London
SE16 3XT
🕐 Tues–Fri 5am–5pm;
Mon and Sat 4pm–5pm

This is one of the very best online retailers of Italian specialities, invaluable if you love to cover a table in high-grade antipasti, but live nowhere near an Italian deli. All is artisan-produced, sourced by Eric and Guiseppe from specialists all over Italy. You'll find the finest cured meats, including rare breeds, bottarga (air-dried mullet eggs), braesaola (marinated air-dried beef), the finest rare Vialone Nano rice for risotto, oils, salami, all sorts of cheeses, cantuccini (twice-baked sweet biscuits), pannettone and panforte. It is more a question of what can't you buy?

Selfridges Food Hall ❁ @ ✦

www.selfridges.co.uk
☎ 020 7629 1234
✉ 400 Oxford Street, London
W1A 1AB
🕐 Mon–Wed 10am–7pm;
Thurs–Fri 10am–8pm; Sat 9am–7pm;
Sun 12am–6pm

My earliest experiences of Selfridges was when my mother used to buy pickled herrings and German frankfurters from there, saying they were the best. My siblings and I wolfed down the frankfurters, but were not so mad about the herrings. Selfridges, bigger, with more branches and slightly more vulgar as the years go by, still boasts a good food hall. I recommend Jack O'Shea's butchery counter (see page 78), and also the fresh vegetables, which, while sometimes murderously expensive, are very fresh. Try also Hix smoked salmon – smoked on the store's roof! There is almost nothing they do not sell, from Spanish Iberica ham, to sashimi fish, to artisan bread and cheese, to an excellent range of Kosher foods. See website for branches.

Sonny's Food Shop

www.sonnys.co.uk
☎ 020 8741 8451
✉ 92 Church Road, Barnes, London
SW13 ODA
🕐 Mon–Sat 10am–6pm

A deli-specialist food shop with a long-held good reputation and a favourite among residents in Barnes. Fresh foods include unusual varieties of vegetables, such as borlotti beans, glorious la ratte potatoes and figs; there's a range of naturally reared meat available – but calling in advance to pre-order is recommended. Fresh fish includes Loch Duart salmon, fresh scallops and sea bass; there's artisan Poliane bread and Campo Filene pasta, some gorgeously pretty cakes and chocolates, and much, much more. If you are making a special trip, perhaps book a table at the restaurant next door.

The Spice Shop ✿ @ ✿

www.thespiceshop.co.uk
☎ 0207 221 4448
✉ 1 Blenheim Crescent, London
W11 2EE
🕐 Tues–Sat 9.30am–6pm;
Sun 11am–4pm

Birgit Erath's famous spice shop began life as a stall in Portobello Market, just metres from where the permanent location is now. The tiny shop crams over 2500 products on to its shelves and small tables inside and outside the front door. Birgit blends and mixes her own herb and spice recipes to sell among any and every herb and spice you can imagine – ajowan, barberries, wasabi paste, barbecue seasoning, Bloody Mary mix, black lava salt, diamond and Fleur de Sel salt, to name but a few. Of the curry blends, Kita Kat – with fennel, nigella, turmeric and ginger – is my absolute favourite.

Sri Thai ✿ ✿

☎ 020 7602 0621
✉ 56 Shepherds Bush Road,
London **W6 7PH**
🕐 Mon–Sun 9.30am–7.30pm

One of the best Thai supermarkets in the UK, Sri Thai stocks the usual brands of spices, curry ingredients, rice and noodles, but in the fridge you will find a large range of handmade curry pastes and there is a fresh, ready-to-eat dish made daily that you can take away. Fresh vegetables and spices / herbs are mainly imported, but until the UK farmers grow lemongrass (which apparently is possible) these treats must be air-freighted.

Sundrica

www.sundrica.co.uk
☎ 020 8748 6776
✉ 7 Beadon Road, Hammersmith, London **W6 0EA**
🕐 Mon–Fri 7am–8am; Sat 9am–6pm

A deli-food hall, literally stuffed with a vast number of foods, most from Italy, France and Spain, including over 30 salami, dozens of cheeses, various prosciutto and serrano hams, chorizo, filleticho (air-dried loin of pork), preserves and pickles, home-made chicken liver terrine and, of course, more olive oil than anyone could possibly ever want. Cakes are made on-site and include chocolate and pear, apple cake, brownies and cheesecake.

Taj Stores

www.tajstores.co.uk
☎ 020 7377 0061
✉ 112 Brick Lane, London **E1 6RL**
🕐 Daily 9am–9pm

More than a deli, this Bangladeshi grocer was founded in 1936. Still in it's original location, Taj Stores sells an extensive range of fresh fruit and vegetables (including unusual leaf and stem vegetables such as lata and danga), halal meat, exotic herbs and spices, and Bangladeshi fish. Freshly prepared foods are also available, including naan and pita breads, samosas and exotic sweets, as well as pulses, grains and spices. Hundreds of foody items from China, Thailand, Japan, Jamaica and Lebanon are also on offer.

Tom's Deli ✿

www.tomsdelilondon.co.uk
☎ 020 7221 8818
✉ 226 Westbourne Grove, London **W11 2RH**
🕐 Mon–Fri 8am–7.30pm; Sat 8am–6.30pm; Sun 8.30am–6.30pm

Tom's was started by Tom Conran, son of Terence, and is a popular deli and café rolled into one. Upstairs is the first-come-first-served café serving dishes such as eggs benedict with parma ham, various sandwiches, and sweet and savoury tarts. Downstairs is the deli full of everything from organic olives, British cheeses and artisan breads to charcuterie, meats and jams.

Tray Gourmet Ltd ✿✿

www.traygourmet.co.uk
☎ 020 7352 7676
✉ 240 Fulham Road, London **SW10 9NA**
🕐 Mon–Sat 8.30am–5.30pm

A French grocery with all the typical favourites, beginning with a number of AOC artisan-made cheeses. The owner Nicolas Dreyfus is a specialist and has installed a genuine,

Gibrat cheese fridge complete with slate counter to keep the cheeses in perfect nick. There's also charcuterie and duck liver terrines, cornichon pickles, patisserie and baguettes, packets of lentils de puy and Ebly (durum) wheat, Lu biscuits, sloppy French conserves and Orangina drinks. Classic.

Trinity Stores

www.trinitystores.co.uk
020 8673 3773
5–6 Balham Station Road, London **SW12 9SG**
Mon–Fri 9am–8pm; Sat 9.30am–5.30pm; Sun 10am–5pm

This is a truly well-planned shop, its shelves stacked with great produce though the team are careful not to overstuff with too many jams and oils. There are good home-made cakes and ready-to-eat salads and other dishes behind the counter, great coffee, fresh meat, organic vegetables (you can collect a box each week), chocolates, artisan breads and cheeses. A handful of tables make this a peaceful place to sit and sip coffee while you contemplate what to cook with your purchases, the first line of your novel or how much you really love your children even though they behaved so badly at breakfast. A lovely deli with a bohemian feel.

Union Market

www.unionmarket.co.uk
020 7386 2470
472 Fulham Road, London
SW6 1BY
Mon–Wed 8am–8pm; (7am for Bakery Café); Thurs–Fri 8am–8pm; Sat 8am–8pm; Sun 12–6pm

Union Market is where big business becomes an ethical investor. It is a company that I'm including because although it's not yet established at time of writing, it will be at the time of publication. Backed by some rather rich, very passionate food people, this new grocery promises it will sell a wealth of ethically sourced British food, including naturally reared meat, poultry, seasonal vegetables and numerous sundries. Newly opened and located in handsome premises in the old Fulham Broadway tube station, this is a significant opening in London and I wish Union Market well. It has great potential and a good philosophy. Please visit and let me know what you think.

Unpackaged

www.beunpackaged.com

020 7713 8368

42 Amwell Street, London
EC1R 1XT

Mon–Fri 10am–7pm;
Sat 9am–6pm; Sun 10am–4pm

Catherine Conway founded Unpackaged in 2006 to encourage customers to come in with their own containers and to fill them with whatever is needed. Choose from organic dry goods, such as flour, rice, oats, couscous, organic dried fruits, nuts and seeds; various vinegars and oils, such as balsamic and rapeseed. Even environmentally friendly household cleaners are available, plus beers, wines, spices, tea and coffee, cakes, biscuits, cheeses from Neal's Yard (see page 96), jams, chutneys, fresh dairy products and juices. Remember you can use whatever container you like – one devoted customer puts lentils in old water bottles.

Valentina Fine Foods

www.valentinafinefoods.com

020 8392 9127

Valentina Sheen, 210 Upper
Richmond Road West, East Sheen,
London **SW14 8AH**

Mon–Sun 8am–10pm

This fine Italian deli is named after the daughter of one of the founding families. The Zoccolas and Arcaris left their home in Monte Cassino, Italy in 1958 and moved to England. They brought with them to London their love of traditional cooking and set up the delicatessen, which would remind them of their local essential shops from home. Today, the third-generation family members Fabio, Antonio, Marco and Carmine offer fresh hams and salamis such as felino, fiocco and Milano. There is also a wonderful selection of creamy Italian cheeses on offer such as Cacio Cavallo, Fontina, Bel Paese and many more. Fresh antipasti, a selection of store cupboard essentials, as well as special cooked goods from the finest ingredients in their own kitchen are also available. Online orders available at sheen@valentinafinefoods.com

Vallebona

www.vallebona.co.uk

0208 944 5665

Unit 14, 59 Weir Road,
Wimbledon, London **SW19 8UG**

Tues–Fri 5am–5pm;
Mon and Sat 4pm–5pm

The Vallebona family offer that little bit more than most Italian delis, from Sardinian goat or venison prosciutto to cured wild boar fillet, herb-wrapped cheeses from the Dolomites to grey mullet bottarga (air-dried roe to grate over pasta) – an eclectic and exciting list of specialities sold from the wholesale warehouse in Wimbledon. Antipasti include jars of cardoons and creamed pecorino cheese, and there are various sauces for pasta including walnut, classic pesto, and a lovely passata pomodoro. Bulk buys make better value for money – well worth a visit if you are throwing a party or have a crowd for Christmas and would rather not cook.

Verde & Company Ltd

www.verde-and-company-ltd.co.uk

☎ 020 7247 1924

✉ 40 Brushfield Street, London **E1 6AG**

🕐 Mon–Fri 10am–7pm; Sat-Sun 10am–5pm

Next door to A. Gold (see page 56) is this similar establishment with as much charm. Wicker baskets filled with fresh fruit, vegetables, herbs and flowers are stacked on shelves outside the old shop front. Inside, large polished meat slicers sit behind the front counter ready for use, wooden shelves hold home-made chutneys and foie gras, and there is a large selection of Pierre Marcolini chocolates to choose from, kept safe in a large glass case. All produce is sourced from small family-run businesses. There's a menu of salads and sandwiches to eat in or take away.

Villandry ❷

www.villandry.com

☎ 020 7631 3131

✉ 170 Great Portland Street, London **W1W 5QB**

🕐 Mon–Sat 8am–10pm; Sun 9am–4pm

The Great Portland Street location is home to the flagship store that consists of different areas: the smart French restaurant, serving the likes of chicken paillard with wild rocket or asparagus risotto with truffled pecorino; a charcuterie and bar that serves a more casual breakfast, lunch or evening meal; and the food store that is packed full of artisanal, seasonal products sourced from the finest independent producers. The in-house bakery churns out fresh breads and pastries daily and many of their cheeses and meats are sourced from the continent. A rotisserie and salad-and-sandwich bar offer a great grab-and-go menu.

The Yard ❍❷

www.theyardfoods.co.uk

☎ 020 7924 1199

✉ 70 Chatham Road, corner of Northcote Road, London **SW11 6HG**

🕐 Mon–Sat 10am–9pm; Sun 2pm–8pm

Aimple but good shop, selling natural, home-made and ethically produced food, which doubles as a pizza bakery offering local delivery. It has taken over a year to develop this new business, much of it looking for the right produce. Fresh meat is naturally reared and sourced from Kent; organic vegetables, herbs, fruit, milk and eggs are from Langridge Organics; and there are store cupboard essentials from Brighton's excellent Infinity Foods. A new shop – and we hope one that will do well. Local delivery available: see website.

▼ BUTCHERS

Allens of Mayfair ⊕ @ ⊘

www.allensofmayfair.co.uk

☎ 020 7499 5831

✉ 117 Mount Street, London **W1K 3LA**

🕐 Mon–Fri 6am–6pm; Sat 6am–2pm

Allens, in the heart of Mayfair, is the oldest butcher in Britain – 120 years old and still serving customers from its original site. Stepping in to this shop is like stepping back in time with its Victorian tiled walls, an octagonal butcher's block as centre piece and huge sides of marbled beef hanging in the windows. The very best in pork, beef, lamb, poultry and game is on offer, however David House (co-owner with Justin Preston and master butcher) likes to encourage his customers to try more unusual cuts such as thin rib of beef for barbecues or scrag end of lamb for hotpots. A newly updated website has a useful interactive guide to choosing cuts of meat to fit a recipe or budget before you buy the cuts online. For the real meat-lover you can book a butchery class that takes place in-house every Wednesday.

Baldwins ⊘

www.baldwinsfoods.com

☎ 020 8340 5934

✉ 469 Green Lanes, London **N4 1AJ**

🕐 Mon–Sat 8am–6pm; Sun 8am–4pm

Baldwin customers can expect to find over 20 varieties of home-made sausages (flavours ranging from pork and fennel, and leek and chilli, to a blend of pork and beef laced with paprika), all types of game (from pheasant to quail), plus wild boar and venison, as well as deli items, such as Hungarian salamis, hams and cheeses. For the heartier consumer offal is available – lungs, tripe, liver, kidneys, pigs' ears and trotters.

The Butcher & Grill

www.thebutcherandgrill.com
020 7924 3999
39–41 Parkgate Road, Battersea,
London **SW11 4NP**
Mon–Sat 8am–9pm;
Sun 8.30am–4pm

There was local celebration when this much-needed butcher's shop, deli and café opened up near Battersea Park (the area is something of a food desert). Dominic Ford has a team of enthusiastic, skilled staff and they sell top-drawer meat. The display of roasting joints on a Saturday morning brings tears to the eyes of meat-lovers. Beef is sourced from Highfields Farm in East Sussex. Pork, sausages, veal, offal, poultry and game are also available alongside home-cooked meats, pies and pâtés, and the shop has recently been expanded, stocking many more products. There is also a good selection of artisan bread, baked locally. There's a second branch in Wimbledon.

Chadwick's Butchers

www.chadwicksbutchers.co.uk
020 8772 1895
208 Balham High Rd, Balham,
London **SW12 9BS**
Mon–Fri 9am–5pm;
Sat 9am–5.30pm; Sun 10am–3pm

Chadwick's was established six years ago and the owners decided not to focus on profit and quantity, but rather on care and quality. Their suppliers share their passion for food and stock the shop with a real taste of the British Isles as well as offering more exotic products from Tuscany and France. Friendly, knowledgeable staff are on hand in the shop, willing to offer advice, recommendations and information on provenance. Chadwick's is much more than a standard high-street butchers, offering both fantastic range and quality, but neither has the staff lost sight of the basics that underpin an excellent meat counter.

City Meat ◐

020 7352 9894
421 Kings Road, London
SW10 0LR
Mon–Sat 8.30am–6pm

A Portuguese butcher's shop run by the most charming and knowledgeable staff who know everything about both British and continental butchery. The veal and pork meatballs, spiced up with sweet pepper, are a favourite among locals. There are good, leggy, Label Anglais French-style chickens, game birds in season, and excellent well-hung beef. You can also buy ready-cooked foods – the rabbit stew is lovely, if it is on the counter – and there is a range of good charcuterie, free-range eggs, bags of pulses, cans of beans, Italian pasta and various deli items. At the time of writing, the shop owners were hoping for the Kensington and Chelsea congestion charge to be abolished. They warned they might otherwise close down.

A. Dove & Son ✿

☎ 020 7223 5191
✉ 71 Northcote Road, Clapham, London **SW11 6PJ**
🕐 Mon 8am–4pm; Tues–Sat 8am–5.30pm

Bob Dove has been selling good quality naturally reared meat on this pretty Battersea street since 1889. He prides himself on knowing all his farmers and those involved in supplying his meat, which is all British sourced. He is assisted by chef Jo Hopwood, who makes a range of preservative- and additive-free soups and stews, which are sold frozen.

English Meat ✿✿

www.englishmeat.co.uk
☎ 0845 500 5440

Dan Oaley and Robert Laughton set up this online butcher in 2008 with an aim to deliver the finest organic English meats directly to customer's doors. Rare-breed meat is butchered in Suffolk and then distributed from their warehouse in SW19. Suffolk Black Faced sheep are milk- and grass-fed, organic-certified and are available in traditional cuts or as a quarter, half or whole butchered lamb. Their Large Black pigs have been reared outdoors on organic vegetables and cereal-stock feed. Their Red Poll cattle are reared on grass and rolled barley in summer, hay and steamed barley in the winter. Handmade sausages in natural casings are produced by a family butcher in Long Melford, Suffolk. Call to place your order. They will deliver within the M25.

Frank Godfrey Ltd ✿@✿

www.fgodfrey.co.uk
☎ 020 7226 2425
✉ 7 Highbury Park, London **N5 1QJ**
🕐 Mon–Fri 8am–6pm; Sat 8am–5pm

Christopher Godfrey is the fifth generation to run this family butcher in the heart of Islington. Long gone are the days when the Godfreys could graze their cattle in Clissold Park, but today his two shops retain a traditional atmosphere selling free-range meats sourced from farms ensuring all aspects of animal husbandry and diet are met to the highest standards. Beef is matured on the bone for 28 days; the

British pork is from Plantation Pigs, a farm less than 40 miles from the city centre; lamb has grazed on green pastures around the UK; and chickens are selected from quality farms. The slow-growing Label Anglais breed is a bestseller.

The Ginger Pig ✪

www.thegingerpig.co.uk
☎ 020 7935 7788
✉ 8–10 Moxon Street,
Marylebone, London **W1U 4EW**
🕐 Mon–Thurs 9am–6pm;
Fri–Sat 9am–6.30pm;
Sun 10am–2pm

Tim Wilson has other branches in London (in Borough Market, Waterloo and Hackney – see website), but most of the meat hails from his farms in Yorkshire, where he specialises in traditional breeds, preferring the superior flavour and fat content of the Tamworth pig with its distinctive ginger hair. Lamb, mutton, veal and good beef are also available in both British and continental cuts. But, as the name suggests, this is a specialist pork butcher and at Marylebone the gifted English 'charcutier' Paul Hughes heads a team producing everything from delicate terrines to some deliciously rough-hewn pork pies. If you live in Yorkshire, you can buy from the farm gate in Levisham, near Pickering, if you call in advance on 01751 460242.

The Hampstead Butcher & Providore

www.hampsteadbutcher.com
☎ 020 7794 9210
✉ 56 Rosslyn Hill, Hampstead,
London **NW3 1ND**
🕐 Mon–Wed 9am–6pm;
Thurs 9am–8pm; Fri–Sat 9am–7pm;
Sun 9am–6pm

Jim Matthews and Guy Bossom run this elegant shop in the centre of Hampstead with their team of butchers, deli specialists and chefs. The butchers offer traditional cuts of free-range beef, pork and lamb, as well as free-range poultry. The development kitchen underneath the shop produces a wide variety of freshly prepared goods such as sausages, pies, terrines, pâtés, soups, hams and chutneys. Seasonal tastings occur regularly and are a great way to get to know the shop's variety of produce. Their cheese counter features the best of British, as well as some continental, cheesemaking skills. Well appointed and friendly, this is a wonderful place to pick up a tasty treat.

Hussey Butchers ⊘

www.husseyswappinglane.co.uk
☎ 020 7488 3686
✉ 64 Wapping Lane, London
E1W 2RL
🕐 Mon–Fri 7am–6pm;
Sat 7am–5pm

A traditional family butcher offering a multitude of choice – all manner of English poultry (chicken, free-range ducks and geese, guinea fowl, poussin, quail and corn-fed chicken), Scotch beef, English free-range pork from Plantation Pigs in Surrey, Dutch veal, Scottish venison and game when in season. Specialities include home-cured salt meats, 10 varieties of sausages filled in natural casings and barbecue items for the summer.

Jack O'Shea ⬆ @ ⊘

www.jackoshea.com
☎ 020 7318 3727
✉ Selfridges Food Hall,
400 Oxford Street, London
W1A 1AB
🕐 Mon–Wed 9.30am–8pm;
Thurs–Sat 9.30am–9pm;
Sun 12–6pm

Jack O'Shea's passion for quality can be seen on his meat counter at Selfridges (see page 68). The focus is on beef that comes from free-range Black Angus cattle, reared on the pastures of the south-west of Ireland, grass-fed in the warmer months and fed cereal and hay in the winter, free from hormones and artificial additives. The beef's delicious flavour is also due to its natural marbling, and steaks are dry-aged on the bone for at least 28 days. Jack's website has a useful guide explaining each type of cut of beef.

Jago Butchers ⬆ ⊘

www.jagobutchersofchelsea.
co.uk
☎ 020 7589 5531
✉ 9 Elystan Street, London
SW3 3NT
🕐 Mon–Fri 8.30am–5pm;
Sat 8.30am–1pm

Jago butcher's shop sits behind London's busy Kings Road among a small enclave of shops on Chelsea Green. Hugely popular with the cosmopolitan locals (this is the little Spain and France of the capital), they know how to prepare meat to both British and continental specifications. The sausages are bestsellers, and include a Cumberland style, wild boar and apple, venison and red wine, pork and leek and some good, plain traditional-style chipolatas. Organic and free-range chickens, English lamb, and plenty of game birds are available in season.

Kent and Sons ⊘

www.kents-butchers.co.uk
☎ 020 7722 2258
✉ 59 St John's Wood High Street, London **NW8 7NL**
🕐 Mon–Sat 8am–5.45pm

This award-winning butcher in north London is the only shop that remains from the retail outlets started by Fred Kent in 1919. Their counters are stocked with free-range, milk-fed English pork, grass-fed and organic beef from Scotland and Wales, lamb reared on West Country pastures, veal from Holland, as well as home-made escalopes, kebabs, satays and other deli items, such as cheeses, pickles, chutneys and cassoulet.

Kingsland Edwardian Butchers ⊘

☎ 020 7727 6067
✉ 140 Portobello Road, London **W11 2DZ**
🕐 Mon–Sat 7.30am–6pm

Kingsland is an old-fashioned, family-run butcher's shop located near the top end of Portobello Road with a bright red awning. Brothers Philip and Hadyn Field dry-cure their own bacon and produce home-made sausages in unusual combinations, such as wild boar and apple, and apricot and garlic. This butcher is also accredited as a Rare Breeds Survival Trust retail outlet, specialising in rare-breed meat such as Gloucester Old Spot and Saddleback pork, salt marsh lamb from Romney Marsh in Kent and Ayrshire grass-fed cattle. Seasonal game can also be purchased, including English partridge, woodcock and teal.

C. Lidgate ⚘ ⊘

www.lidgates.com
☎ 020 7727 8243
✉ 110 Holland Park Avenue, London **W11 4UA**
🕐 Mon–Fri 7am–7pm; Sat 7am–6.30pm

This 150-year-old establishment is run by David Lidgate, the fourth generation of his family to run the butchery. With the help of his son Danny, David chooses organic grass-fed pork, lamb and beef from free-range and organic farms and estates, including Highgrove, home farm of HRH The Prince of Wales, and Gatcombe Park, home farm of HRH The Princess Royal. This popular butcher focuses on quality, with specialities such as home-made sausages, award-winning pies in ceramic dishes (Boeuf Bourguignon, for example), as well as a selection of matured English and French cheeses, plus much, much more. Definitely worth a visit.

Mackens Brothers Ltd

www.mackenbros.co.uk

☎ 020 8994 2646

✉ 44 Turnham Green Terrace,
London **W4 1QP**

🕐 Mon–Fri 7am–6pm;
Sat 7am–5.30pm

Established in 1960, this is a great little butcher in the heart of Chiswick. Expect queues at the weekends, which is only testament to the longevity of the shop. All their meat, sourced from around the UK, is free-range and reared naturally. This butcher can cater to all your needs, whether you want the finest Aberdeen Angus beef or tasty organic sausages.

M. Moen & Sons ✅

www.moen.co.uk

☎ 020 7622 1624

✉ 24 The Pavement, London
SW4 0JA

🕐 Mon–Fri 8.30am–6.30pm;
Sat 8.30am–5pm

This year I have been shopping often at Moen's and am full of admiration. It is a 20-minute drive from where I live but it is always easy to park outside. Overall I am full of praise for the meat, which is exceptionally good value for money. It is also one of those butchers that still offers every cut, every British species of meat, poultry or game that you could wish for, and who makes marinades and ready-to-cook meat dishes that are genuinely appetising. Gary Moen runs a tight-knit, happy ship; the other assistants are delightfully polite. This is also a one-stop shop with huge bowls of olives, cooked meats, fresh seasonal vegetables and fruit, handmade British and other European cheeses, eggs, scrumptious sausage rolls and other pastries including – to the delight of my children – Portuguese custard tarts. Ask for it, and Moen's will probably have it. I tested him, needing caul and farmed rabbit for a photoshoot – and yes, it was no problem. In stock, just like everything else. Any struggling butcher's shop, or ambitious food entrepreneur, should take a look at this business.

Pethers of Kew ✅

☎ 020 8940 0163

✉ 16 Station Parade, Kew
Gardens, London **TW9 3PZ**

🕐 Mon–Fri 7.30am–6.30pm;
Sat 7.30am–5pm

A free-range butchers located next to Kew Gardens Station specialising in top quality meat – grass-fed beef, game, organic sausages, free-range veal, turkeys (around Christmas time) and mutton. Other enticing items to purchase include pickles, chutneys, over 40 varieties of cheese, ham, gammon and their famous award-winning meat pies (steak and kidney, lamb, leek and apricot, and beef bourguignon).

Smithfield Market ⊘

020 7332 3092
Charterhouse Street, London
EC1A 9PQ
Mon–Fri 4am–12pm

You must set your alarm to experience Smithfield market as a hive of activity. Meat has been traded here for over 800 years, making it one of the oldest markets in London. Having undergone a massive refurbishment, this once-ancient market (a livestock market occupied the same site back in the 10th century) has been transformed into a modern temperature-controlled environment within a Grade II-listed Victorian building. Butchers, restaurateurs and caterers flock here to view goods and bargain with one of the 66 stands selling meat, poultry and deli goods. Smithfield is a good place to go if you need a lot of meat for a feast or to buy specialities such as French squabs or game. Be discriminating when shopping in Smithfield, however, and ask each butcher about the origins of what they are selling. These days they are obliged by law to be open about provenance.

Stenton Family Butchers ⊘

020 8748 6121
55 Aldensley Road, London
W6 0DH
Tues, Wed, Fri 8am–6pm;
Thurs 8am–1pm; Sat 8am–5pm

John Stenton has become a favourite butcher, both, in my opinion, to his many customers who live locally and those who travel much further to visit his tiny shop in Brackenbury Village near Hammersmith. He has survived in the capital purely because he has stayed ahead of the game and buys from farms rearing meat naturally, as close as possible to London. He buys chickens from small cooperatives, including Elmwood in Suffolk, he buys Bretby lamb from Staffordshire, beef from Richard Fuller in Yorkshire and organic meat from Childhay Manor in Dorset. He also sells Welsh Black pedigree beef when in season. He is an expert in both British and continental cuts, selling the latter to grateful European expats living in London who love their bavette (trimmed beef skirt) and onglet (feather steaks).

St Marcus Fine Foods ⊙ @ ⊘

www.biltongstmarcus.co.uk
020 8878 1898
1 Rockingham Close,
London **SW15 5RW**
Mon–Sun 9am–6pm

This is a one-stop shop for everything from South Africa, specialising in meat. They produce their own award-winning biltong and gourmet sausages, droewors, stokkies, boerewors, and sosaties on site. The Roehampton shop has been open for over 25 years, providing just about anything you may crave from biscuits and salad dressings to crisps and puddings, however it is still recognised as the first UK company to make biltong and boerewors. Their website is informative and easy to navigate.

H. G. Walter ✪ @ ✪

www.hgwalter.com
☎ 020 7385 6466
✉ 51 Palliser Road, Baron's Court, London **W14 9EB**
🕐 Mon–Fri 8am–7pm; Sat 8am–5pm

A combination of experienced London butcher Peter Heanen, selling meat hung and cut to the highest standards, and a mail order service with a glossy catalogue. Beef is pure-bred Aberdeen Angus, lamb is a cross between Cotswold and Suffolk sheep, and they sell milk-fed English veal and free-range pork from farmer Hugh Norris. Added to this are some beautiful gammons and hams, free-range and organic eggs, ducks, Black Mountain and Cornish Red chickens, guinea fowl and poussins. Game birds are a speciality and include mallard, wood pigeon, partridge and pheasant (in season).

William Rose ✪

www.williamrosebutchers.com
☎ 020 8693 9191
✉ 126 Lordship Lane, East Dulwich, London **SE22 8HD**
🕐 Tues–Sat 8am–5pm

This is a popular butcher's shop on a high street corner in this busy shopping street that boasts more good food shops than most areas of the capital. On Saturday mornings witness a huge queue of customers, anxious to buy the salt marsh lamb from Dulas Bay on Anglesey, Suffolk-cross Texel lamb in spring and summer, and Orkney lamb from September onwards. Venison is sourced from Scotland, pork is from Plantation Pigs in Surrey and beef is from either Scotland or Yorkshire. I wish that more meat in the shop was (like the pork) sourced near the capital, but this place has a loyal following, and the many customers who come here seem unbothered by this.

& Clarke's ⬤ @ ⬤

www.sallyclarke.com

☎ 020 7229 2190

✉ 124 Kensington Church Street, London **W8 4BH**

🕐 Mon–Fri 8am–8pm; Sat 8am–4pm; Sun 10am–4pm

In 1988 Sally Clarke established & Clarke's, a delectable provisions shop next door to her restaurant, selling freshly baked items alongside baskets of seasonal fruit and vegetables and other top quality deli goods. Choose from a variety of classic and flavoured breads such as rosemary, raisin and sea salt, and honey wholewheat. These feature no artificial colourings, preservatives or improvers. Pastries, cakes, muffins, tarts and biscuits are made with French unsalted butter, all baked daily in the restaurant kitchen.

Ambala ⬤ @ ⬤

www.ambalafoods.com

☎ 020 7387 7886

✉ 112 / 114 Drummond Street, London **NW1 2HN**

🕐 Mon–Sun 9am–8.30pm

Mr Mohammed Ali Khan founded Ambala in 1965 with the original shop opening in Drummond Street. Today there are Ambala shops all around the world, famed for their quality Asian confectionery based on ancient recipes using premium ingredients. Their impressive website will tempt any returning customer or novice shopper. Choose from many delicacies including fig halwa (a rich blend of fig, milk, almonds and pistachio, Rasmalai (delicious 'cakes' of curdled milk in a light creamy cardamon sauce) or Special Motichoor Ladoo (a ceremonial sweet made from chopped almonds dusted with pistachio nuts and cooked in a sweet syrup). See website for details of branches.

Bagatelle Boutique ⬤

www.bagatelle-boutique.co.uk

☎ 020 7581 1551

✉ 44 Harrington Road, London **SW7 3NB**

🕐 Mon–Sat 8.30am–7.30pm; Sun 8.30am–6pm

Using the oldest traditions and natural flours supplied by a mill dating back to 1721, Bagatelle bakes over 47 varieties of breads every night. In 1990 the 'boutique' opened in South Kensington providing a typical French boulangerie-patisserie for the area. Bread rolls, fruit loaves, baguettes and sandwich breads are free from preservatives, while their extensive patisserie selection ranges from mini pistachio macaroons and pear and almond tart to crème brûlée and Fontainebleau (layers of almond meringues filled with chocolate mousse).

Baker & Spice ⊙ @ ✿

www.bakerandspice.uk.com
☎ 020 7730 3033
✉ 54–56 Elizabeth Street, London
SW1W 9PB
🕐 Mon–Sat 7am–7pm;
Sun 8am–5pm

Baker & Spice's first shop opened in Chelsea in 1995, where almost everything was made from scratch daily. Famous for its cakes and pastries, they also offer a choice of cooked food and a range of original sourdough breads and breakfast pastries. Seasonal, authentic and organic ingredients are used when possible. Now with three stores in London, a variety of speciality breads are baked daily and are available fresh for collection from 7am and include Pain Campaillou, Pain de Mie (the French version of cholla), Pain de Campagne, and their sourdough-flavoured breads such as potato and rosemary, Russian rye and sultana and fennel.

Blackbird Bakery ✿

☎ 020 7095 8800
✉ 208 Railton Road, London
SE24 0JT
🕐 Mon–Fri 7am–7pm;
Sat 7am–5pm; Sun 9am–4.30pm

What started as a market stall has grown into three Blackbird bakeries. Famous for their excellent bread, all produce is made in their Herne Hill bakery unit using organic flour. Bestsellers include their sourdough, rosemary and olive, farmhouse and granary loaves. They also make a spelt bread for customers with wheat intolerances, and speciality loaves, such as olive and walnut, and onion. Cakes can be made to order and their carrot, banana and date, and chocolate fudge varieties are always popular. They also produce their own granola and jam and sell local honey from Woodside. Phone for details of branches.

The Brew House at Kenwood House

www.companyofcooks.com
☎ 020 8341 5384
✉ The Brew House, Kenwood,
Hampstead Lane, London
NW3 7JR
🕐 Mon–Sun 9am–4pm

Kenwood House is a neo-classical villa set in acres of parkland with incredible views over London. After admiring the Chippendale furniture and beautiful paintings in the main house, head to the servants' quarters that have been transformed into The Brewhouse and The Steward's Room. Head to The Brewhouse where you'll find a large selection of hot dishes and freshly baked cakes, including almond and polenta, and orange and lavender, as well as chocolate and hazelnut brownies and the popular gooseberry and nettle cheesecake. Look out for the original oven in the main room and the wonderfully uneven flagstone floor.

Charbonnel & Walker ⌂ @ ◑

www.charbonnel.co.uk
☎ 020 7491 0939
✉ 1 The Royal Arcade, 28 Old Bond Street, London **W1S 4BT**
🕐 Mon–Sat 10am–6pm

This is an old-fashioned chocolatier dating back 135 years and a place to buy a respected relative something luxurious, such as beautifully made little filled lozenges flavoured with flowers such as violets and roses, or truffles dusted with cocoa powder. There are dark chocolate thins, sugar-coated dragees, peppermint creams and also some high-quality chocolate bars. All is packed in smart boxes with layers of lacy wrapping. High-calorie nostalgia.

The Chocolate Society ⌂ @ ◑

www.chocolate.co.uk
☎ 020 8743 1325
✉ 36 Elizabeth Street, London **SW1W 9NZ**
🕐 Mon–Wed, Fri 9am–7pm; Thurs 9am–8pm; Sat 10am–4pm

With a website designed for any serious chocoholic, The Chocolate Society's small, but perfectly formed, bijou shop and café in Belgravia is even more tempting. As the UK's exclusive retail distributor of Valrhona chocolate, pre-wrapped bars are sold among their selection of truffles, handmade bars to be eaten at certain times of the day, gift boxes of cocoa-dusted almonds, dark chocolate-enrobed ginger, and original Hokey Pokey honeycomb dipped in milk or dark chocolate. Pop in for a cup of their famous, 70 per cent cocoa solid drinking chocolate made from Venezuelan beans. In essence, this is a grown-up's chocolate shop.

Exeter Street Bakery ◑

www.exeterstreetbakery.co.uk
☎ 020 7937 8484
✉ 1b Argyll Road, London **W8 7DB**
🕐 Mon–Sat 8am–7pm; Sun 9am–6pm

The bakery opened in July 2001 and the shop in April 2002. Producing a wide range of fine handmade Italian breads, foccacia, panettone and biscuits, the shop also offers paninis, pizzas and a variety of other Italian delicacies to take away.

Flour Power City £

www.flourpowercity.co.uk
☎ 020 8691 2288
✉ Borough Market, Stoney Street,
London **SE1 1TL**

Matt Jones's natural love of food and years of restaurant experience led him to establish Flour Power City selling various artisan breads, such as 100% rye loaves; baps, rolls and baguettes using Shipton Mill flour and free-range ingredients. Their pastries and cakes are also popular – the famous chocolate brownies (containing 30% Callebaut couverture chocolate and lots of butter and eggs) are a must-try. Find your nearest market stall on their website.

The Flour Station

www.theflourstation.com
☎ 020 8457 2098
✉ Unit 12, Garrick Road Industrial
Estate, Irving Way, London
NW9 6AQ

Set up in 2004, it grew from the original kitchen of Jamie Oliver's Fifteen restaurant in London. Their growing selection of 'craft breads' are hand-made with quality natural ingredients. Dough spends up to 24 hours fermenting and developing, which allows the enzymes to react over time and the natural yeast starter breaks down the gluten to give each loaf individual taste and texture. Inspiration is taken from traditional and international recipes – British loaves, levains and European influenced breads can be found along with Chelsea buns and Eccles cakes. Available from selected fine food stores, delis and markets including Brunswick, Borough, Cabbages and Frocks (Marylebone), Parliament Hill, Queen's Park and Wimbledon. See website for details.

Flourish Craft Bakery £

www.flourishbakery.com
☎ 020 8801 9696
✉ Unit 7 Morrison Yard,
551a High Road, London **N17 6SB**

The business was started by two bakers, Edmund Soliva and Paul O'Connell. With hotel and restaurant experience behind them, they discovered a rundown bagel bakery inside the former Tottenham Brewery in north London and transformed it into their dream premises in 2000. As a self-proclaimed craft bakery, all their breads and pastries are hand-moulded. Classic white bloomers, Irish soda bread, roast onion loaves and long fermentation speciality breads, such as the classic sourdough, can be found at the Pimlico, Notting Hill, Palmers Green and Portobello Farmers' Markets. See website for details.

Gail's ✪

www.gailsbread.co.uk
☎ 020 7794 5700
✉ 64 Hampstead High Street,
London **NW3 1QH**
🕐 Mon–Fri 7am–8pm;
Sat–Sun 8am–8pm

Ran Avidan and Tom Molnar left their city jobs to team up with Gail Stephens, founder of Baker & Spice, to make and sell top quality breads to Londoners. Their first shop opened in Hampstead in 2005 selling quality handmade breads, free from preservatives, flavourings and additives. Their extensive range includes a French wholemeal sourdough, a granary bloomer, a hazelnut and sultana rye, a Paysanne baguette and a three-seed spelt, and treats such as seasonal muffins, biscotti (chocolate, coffee, hazelnut and almond), pain au raisins and florentines to tempt your sweet tooth. Gail's has grown substantially, and now has branches in Northcote Road, Battersea, Chiswick, Queens Park, Noting Hill and St John's Wood.

Hope and Greenwood ⌂ @ ✪

www.hopeandgreenwood.co.uk
☎ 0870 850 9049
✉ 20 Northwood Road, London
SE22 9EU
🕐 Mon–Sat 10am–6pm;
Sun 11am–5pm

Traditional sweets of the flying saucer, humbug, sugar balls, gums and lolly type, sold the old-fashioned way from jars behind the counter in this small shop that has become a temple for children who deserve a treat. Kitty Hope and Mark Greenwood, who trawl Britain looking for the best confectionery, also sell a few chocolates under their own label. I am a fan of their chocolate cappuccino almonds.

Konditor and Cook ✪ @

www.konditorandcook.com
☎ 020 7261 0456
✉ Konditor and Cook,
22 Cornwall Road, London
SE1 8TW
🕐 Mon–Fri 7.30am–6.30pm;
Sat 8.30am–3pm

Underpinning the fine baking at this gorgeous cake shop are the ingredients: free-range eggs and pure butter are used in all Gerhard Jenne's products at this small bakery in Waterloo. The cakes are colourful – imaginative without being pointlessly avant garde – and have an appetising degree of home-made-ness. Jenne has also reinvented the iced mini-cube cake, offering a huge range of colours and witty decorations, plus a bespoke service for every celebration. There is great artisan bread, rolls and excellent croissants. Keep an eye on what this year's Christmas offerings will be. See website for other branches.

Lola's Kitchen

www.lolas-kitchen.co.uk
☎ 020 7483 3394
✉ Unit 2, Primrose Hill Workshops,
Oppidans Road, London **NW3 3AG**
🕐 Mon–Sat 8am–5pm

I do not normally like cupcakes but Lola's are wonderful and she makes brilliant birthday cakes with cupcakes dotted all over the surface; beeswax candles are supplied, too. The ingredients are natural, and children and adults alike will be thrilled with the décor.

Luca's Bakery

www.lucasbakery.com
☎ 020 8613 6161
✉ 145 Lordship Lane, London
SE22 8HX
🕐 Mon–Sat 8.30am–5.30pm;
Sun 9am–5pm

This bakery has been a welcome opening on a busy food shopping street in south London. It sells artisan breads (rye sourdough, robust baguettes), rolls, pastries and tarts, including a lovely and juicy one scattered with onion. It is quite new, so I'd welcome your feedback as it develops.

Macaron 🍴

www.patisserie-macaron.co.uk
☎ 020 7498 2636
✉ 22 The Pavement, London
SW4 0HY
🕐 Mon–Fri 7.30am–7pm;
Sat–Sun 9am–7pm

This wood-panelled patisserie and café just off Clapham Common serves traditional French cakes, as well as savoury items, with a pot of tea on pretty mismatching china. Freshly baked pastries are arranged on the marble countertops; a window into their back kitchen allows you to watch the cooks at work and, of course, the obligatory candy-coloured macaroons are available – flavours include raspberry, bergamot, chocolate, pistachio and coconut.

Melt 🏠 @ 🍴

www.meltchocolates.com
☎ 020 7727 5030
✉ 59 Ledbury Road, London
W11 2AA
🕐 Mon–Sat 9am–6pm;
Sun 11am–4pm

Unlike traditional chocolate shops, Melt is slick, cool and minimalist white. Melted chocolate is poured and spread on to the white marble counters allowing customers to watch the team at work while simultaneously filling the shop with dense chocolate air. Chika Watanabe, head chocolatier, puts together an eclectic mix of flavours – Maldon sea-salted caramels, pinenut and raisin bars, raspberry, mint and white chocolate bonbons, coconut chocolate bars and the Origin hot chocolate blocks (made from four different single origin chocolates), which can be stirred into hot milk to make an instant, deluxe cup of hot chocolate.

Montezuma's Chocolate ✿ @ ✿

www.montezumas.co.uk
☎ 020 3166 1037
✉ 4 Fife Road, Kingston upon
Thames, Surrey **KT1 1SZ**
🕐 Mon–Sat 9.30am–6pm;
Sun 11am–5pm

Montezuma's is now a mini empire, running a small chain of shops that includes this one in Kingston upon Thames, another in east London's Spitalfields, and others in Brighton, Winchester and Chichester. The chocolate, which ranges from snappy bars to truffles, is beautifully made and the raw materials fairly traded. Expect the unusual, with flavours in the chocolate ranging from geranium to chilli to the nice combination of lime and vanilla. I like the 'dainty dollops', small flavoured discs to eat after dinner, and I have had some great festive creations at both Easter and Christmas. This is modern, funky chocolate, the polar opposite of violet creams (mind you, I love violet creams!). See website for branch addresses and the online shop.

Nordic Bakery @ ✿

www.nordicbakery.com
☎ 020 3230 1077
✉ 14 Golden Square, London
W1F 9JG
🕐 Mon–Fri 8am–8pm;
Sat 9am–7pm; Sun 11am–6pm

Tucked behind the bustle of Regent Street is Nordic Bakery, a simple, Scandinavian-style café with tableware and furniture designed by iconic Nordic designers. Their decently priced menu offers products based on genuine Nordic recipes and ingredients: Finnish cinnamon buns, Tosca cake (a Swedish classic of soft sponge cake with crispy layers of almond caramel), coffee cakes with orange and poppy seeds, round rye breads and rye bread sandwiches filled with gravadlax, egg and anchovy, or honey roast ham with Swedish mustard.

The Old Post Office Bakery

www.oldpostofficebakery.co.uk
☎ 020 7326 4408
✉ 76 Landor Road, London
SW9 9PH
🕐 Mon–Sat 7am–5.30pm;
Sun 7am–2pm

The name originates from their original first premises in a disused post office in Clapham. Back in 1982 when the bakery was established, it was one of the first organic bakeries in south London and despite its new location it still aims to produce affordable organic bread. Only Shipton Mill flour from Gloucestershire is used and their bread is certified by the Soil Association. Choose from sourdough, wholewheat, white and speciality loaves, such as date and walnut, sundried tomato and olive. This lovely bread is available from wholefood and independent shops and the Marylebone, Queens Park, Eltham and Oval farmers' markets. See website for stockists.

Ottolenghi ⊘

www.ottolenghi.co.uk
☎ 020 7288 1454
✉ 287 Upper Street, London
N1 2TZ
🕐 Mon–Sat 8am–11pm;
Sun 9am–7pm

Ottolenghi buys only raw ingredients and makes everything from scratch, whether it is their orange and pistachio marshmallows or their pear and cranberry upside-down cake. Yotam Ottolenghi, together with creative partner Sami Tamimi, opened their first premises in Notting Hill in 2002. Now with three other locations around London, the food continues to focus on the Mediterranean with local produce sourced from the UK and Europe, using bold flavours and colours to entice their customers. Classic offerings include the passion fruit and meringue tart, the voluminous chocolate and raspberry meringues and the polenta and pistachio cake. There are also branches in Kensington and Belgravia.

The Parish Bakery

☎ 020 8876 9441
✉ 13 Barnes High Street, London
SW13 9LW
🕐 Mon–Sat 9am–4pm

Barnes is blessed with good high street food shops, and locals love this traditional bakers for its typical white sandwich loaves, bloomers, sausage rolls and croissants. Everything is baked on site, evident by the scent of baking that wafts down the street in the morning.

Paul A. Young ⊘

www.payoung.net
☎ 020 7424 5750
✉ 33 Camden Passage, Islington,
London **N1 8EA**
🕐 Tues–Thurs, Sat 11am–6pm;
Fri 11am–7pm; Sun 12–5pm

Brave chocolate explorers should try the marmite variety. But fear not, there are others – red wine-soaked prunes, sea salted-caramel and hazelnut and almond praline, to name a few. All is handmade daily on the premises. Paul Young's shop is well-regarded in the area, but I'd like to know what you think. See website for details of his other shop in Royal Exchange, City of London.

Peyton and Byrne ♠ @ ✪

www.peytonandbyrne.com

☎ 020 7278 6707

✉ Unit 11, The Undercroft,
St Pancras International, London
NW1 2QP

🕐 Mon–Fri 7.30am–8pm;
Sat–Sun 9am–8pm

Oliver Peyton, the renowned restaurateur, is the founder and chairman of Peyton and Byrne Limited, a very British bakery. With currently four locations in London (see website for details) the bakery prides itself in national classics, such as the Victoria sponge, coffee and walnut cake (with organic buttercream), millionaires shortbread, jammy dodgers and Bakewell tart, to name a few. All items are made fresh every day, using only natural ingredients. The simple packaging in pretty pastel colours makes for good gifts.

Poilâne ♠ @ ✪

www.poilane.fr

☎ 020 7808 4910

✉ 46 Elizabeth Street, London
SW1W 9PA

🕐 Mon–Fri 7.30am–7pm;
Sat 7.30am–6pm

Three thousand loaves of fine sourdough are baked each week at this atmospheric London branch of Appolonia Poilâne's Parisian bakery. For Christmas buy 'festive' bread, apple tarts and boxes of buttery Punitions ('punishment' biscuits). The wood-fired oven is fuelled by scrap wood and each batch of sourdough has a lump pulled off it as a 'starter' for the next batch. It is really wonderful bread and is even worth paying the congestion charge to buy it – making it undoubtedly some of the most expensive bread in the capital. You can buy it via mail order and via other stockists, too. See website for details.

Popina ♠ @ ✪

www.popina.co.uk

☎ 020 3212 0110

✉ Unit 5, Greenlea Park,
Prince George's Road, London
SW19 2JD

In 2000 Isidora Popovic set up Popina with help from The Prince's Trust. Using only quality ingredients sourced from the UK and around the world, Popina has won countless awards over the years for the ever-expanding range of sweet and savoury items that are made daily. Organic chocolate truffle brownies, walnut and vanilla shortbread, hazelnut spelt biscuits, elderflower and gooseberry tart, and spelt apple, carrot and sunflower-seed muffins can be found at quality food shops and key London farmers' markets during the weekend. Buy online and at markets (see website) including Broadway, Clapham, Islington, Marylebone, Pimlico Road, Portobello Road, Queen's Park and Richmond.

Reza Patisserie

020 7603 0924
345 Kensington High Street,
London **W8 6NW**
Mon–Sun 9am–10pm

Reza is amongst a row of small specialist Iranian food shops at the far end of Kensington High Street and specialises in freshly baked Arabic (using nuts and honey) and Iranian pastries (simple and more subtle), sweets, and other cakes and biscuits. Iranian ice cream with rose water and saffron can also be found, and shelves stacked high with nuts, dried fruits, sweetmeats and Iranian sour cherries. Other items, including fruit, vegetables and Iranian caviar are also here.

Rococo Chocolates ⌂ @ ✦

www.rococochocolates.com
020 7935 7780
45 Marylebone High Street,
London **W1U 5HG**
Tues–Sat 10am–6.30pm;
Sun 12–5pm

This veteran shop broke new ground when it opened in the '80s and it still leads the way in the chocolate world. Artistry, wit and good base ingredients make Chantal Coady's chocolates a joy to indulge in. Shop staff are always charming and encourage tasting of the many naturally flavoured chocolate bars. The *trompe l'oeil* range, which includes chocolates shaped and decorated to look like (among a long list) olives, fungi, quails eggs, borlotti beans, cobs of corn and new potatoes, make wonderful presents. Italian nougat, traditional filled chocolates, Christmas, Easter and other festive specialities are gorgeous, too. The King's Road shop was Coady's first, but she now runs other branches (see website) and wholesales widely.

St John Bakery

www.stjohnbreadandwine.com
020 7251 0848
21 St John Street, London
EC1M 4AY
Mon–Fri 9am–11pm;
Sat 10am–11pm;
Sun 10am–10.30pm

Flanking Fergus Henderson's undeniably meat-dominated restaurant is a bakery churning out chewy sourdoughs and Eccles cakes, fat with currants. The intention is to give diners superior bread and wine to take home with them. It does not disappoint.

The Borough Cheese Company

📞 020 7407 1002
✉ Borough Market, Southwark
Street, London **SE1 1TL**
🕐 Thurs 11am–5pm; Fri 12–6pm;
Sat 8am–5pm

Huge effort goes into sourcing a particular artisan brand of French Comté – the only cheese sold on this stall at Borough Market in London. A daring business plan until you taste the cheese, which as the cliché goes is almost without equal. With its flexible texture and rounded flavour of rich cream, walnuts and apples, it has all the special character of a mountain cheese and is something that British cheesemakers cannot yet copy, hence its inclusion in this guide that is for food pirates as well as indigenous cheese enthusiasts.

The Cheeseboard 🄰 @ 🄰

www.cheese-board.co.uk
📞 020 8305 0401
✉ 26 Royal Hill, London **SE10 8RT**
🕐 Mon–Wed, Sat 9am–5pm;
Thurs 9am–1pm; Fri 9am–5.30pm

A friend and Greenwich resident recommended this good shop, which specialises in artisan cheeses made in Britain, but also good quality continental cheeses, too. Expect to find Keen's (my favourite real West Country cheddar), Appleby's Cheshire (a sweet version tinted pale orange), Sparkenhoe Red Leicester, the unusual Katy's White Lavender from Thirsk, pungent Stinking Bishop, fresh Vulscombe goats' cheese and Wigmore (a creamy bloomy rind cheese made from ewes' milk). I am only touching the surface of a 100-strong list...

Gastronomica

www.gastronomica.co.uk
📞 020 7407 4488
✉ Borough Market, Southwark
Street, London **SE1 1TL**
🕐 Thurs 11am–5pm; Fri 12–6pm;
Sat 8am–5pm

Now established as a leading provender of perfectly ripe Italian cheeses and artisan charcuterie, Gastronomica have not lost their loyalty to the London markets where they made their name and where they still sell their amazing cheeses. Specialising in cheeses from Piedmont and Lombardy – they also sell some good pecorini from Tuscany and fresh mozzarella from Campagna in the south. The air-dried hams and sausage are equally impressive. If you can't visit a London market, contact them to see if they supply an outlet near your home.

Hamish Johnston ○ ◐

www.hamishjohnston.com
☎ 020 7738 0741
✉ 48 Northcote Road, London
SW11 1PA
🕑 Mon–Sat 9am–6pm;
Sun 11am–4pm

Cheeses in this Battersea shop are always well-chosen, always in good nick and sold alongside a carefully chosen small range of deli foods, including biscuits and oatcakes, olives (and attractive cheeseboards made from olive wood), juices, virgin olive oil, dried fruit, nuts and fruit pastes. Three glass-covered counters house the cheeses: hard cheese in one, semi-soft and goat in another, and the third selling freshly made and wet cheeses such as ricotta and mozzarella. Mark Newman, who runs the Battersea shop, is passionate about his favourite subject, offering great advice and inside knowledge about which cheeses are 'tasting best' at the time. Unusually for a cheese shop, H. J. will send cheeses via courier anywhere in the UK. Also see page 28.

Jeroboams ○ @ ◐

www.jeroboams.co.uk
☎ 020 7727 9359
✉ 96 Holland Park Avenue,
London **W11 3RB**
🕑 Mon–Fri 8am–8pm;
Sat 8.30am–7pm; Sun 10am–6pm

The Holland Park shop is Jeroboams' flagship food premises selling fine foods and wines and a matured selection of cheeses. The Jeroboams affineur is also located on the avenue, with their own purpose-built maturing rooms. Here the cheeses from around the UK and Europe are individually ripened and matured to reach peak perfection. Cheeses for sale include the Langres (a pungent farmhouse cows' milk cheese from the Champagne-Ardenne region), the Ragstone (a creamy goats' milk log from Hereford) and the Oxford Isis (made by Baron Pouget, its rind is washed in honeyed mead). Find many other fine deli goods in store.
It is pricey, but the quality is paramount.

Jones Dairy ○ ◐ ◔

www.jonesdairy.co.uk
☎ 020 7739 5372
✉ 23 Ezra Street, London **E2 7RH**
🕑 Fri and Sat 8am–1pm;
Sun 9am–2pm

Where the café stands today is where the eight milking cows were fed daily from the haymarkets and exchanged every six months for fresh cows from Wales. This vintage shop is only open three days a week, but expect to find a good selection of pasteurised cheese, such as Somerset Brie, ewes' milk Swaledale, and unpasteurised cheeses such as Caerphilly, Jersey Shield and Double Gloucester.

La Cave à Fromage ○ @ ✿

www.la-cave.co.uk
☎ 0845 1088222
✉ 24–25 Cromwell Place, London
SW7 2LD
🕐 Mon–Thurs 11am–7pm;
Fri–Sat 10am–8pm; Sun 11am–5pm

This is an inviting shop in busy South Kensington, where not only can you buy artisan cheese in top condition, but you can also sit and eat a plate of it with bread for a quick lunch before setting off to the museums on Exhibition Road. Opened in 2007 by Eric Charriaux and Amnon Paldi, the shop predominantly sells mainly British and (some rare) French farmhouse cheeses, some of which they buy when 'young' and use their affineur skills to mature themselves. I love the atmosphere in this shop, which tingles with the scent of ripening unpasteurised cheeses, and enjoy peering at the appetising window displays. If you can't visit their shop, log on to their comprehensive website and buy direct.

La Fromagerie ○ @ ✿

www.lafromagerie.co.uk
☎ 020 7935 0341
✉ 2–6 Moxon Street, Marylebone,
London W1U 4EW
🕐 Mon–Fri 8am–7.30pm;
Sat 9am–7pm; Sun 10am–6pm

This stylish cheese-and-wine specialist stocks a myriad of cheeses: buffalo, cow, sheep and goat; soft, semi-soft, semi-hard, hard, blue; and from over 20 countries. There are around 24 English cheeses, ranging from Cornish Yarg to Appleby's Cheshire – a dazzling selection. The friendly staff will help you make an informed choice – their knowledge of the product enhances the shop and makes it a welcoming place to be. There is a tasting café, serving good quality food, and of course the broad spectrum of wines, each to be matched to particular cheeses. Thought and care have been poured into every corner of this establishment – well worth a visit.

Leadenhall Cheese ○ @ ✿

www.cheeseatleadenhall.co.uk
☎ 020 7929 1697
✉ 4–5 Leadenhall Market, London
EC3V 1LR
🕐 Mon–Tues 9am–5pm;
Wed 9am–6pm; Thurs–Fri 9am–8pm

This is a cheese shop and wine bar located in Leadenhall Market – a historic site where, in 1397, cheesemongers from the countryside were bound by trade law to sell their produce at the market. Discover Leadenhall Cheese's selection, many unpasteurised, from all around Europe. Sue Cloke is the owner and manager and an expert on artisan European cheeses due to her stints working for Paxton & Whitfield (see page 96) and running Harvey

Nichols' cheese department. British varieties on offer include Stilton, Cheddar and many full-bodied goats' cheeses. There are also chutneys, olives, biscuits and knives.

Mootown ○

www.mootown.co.uk
☎ 07974 099035
✉ North Cross Road Market, North Cross Road, East Dulwich, London
SE22 9EV
🕐 Sat 9am–5pm

Tom Hardy is a new cheesemonger selling at London markets (contact for your nearest) who will also discuss the possibilities of home delivery. Fascinated by British artisan cheese, he sells a well-edited number of the best. On my last visit to Mootown, Hardy was selling Teifi (a lovely gouda-style Welsh cheese) and Ardrahan (a pungent, semi-soft cheese from County Cork). He also stocked some fragrant English quince pastes. Mail order is available.

Mr Christian's ⊘

www.mrchristians.co.uk
☎ 020 7229 0501
✉ 11 Elgin Crescent, London
W11 2JA
🕐 Mon–Fri 7am–7pm;
Sat 7am–6.30pm; Sun 8am–5pm

In 1974 Tim Dawson and Glynn Christian founded this ever-popular deli just off Portobello Road. In 2003 it became part of the Jeroboams Group. It is a west London foodie destination serving locals and tourists delicious deli and pantry goods. The fromagerie is stocked with cheeses made by artisan farms and producers, which are then individually matured at their affineur located in Holland Park, so the cheese receives optimal development to attain the ideal maturity and taste for it then to be purchased. Too many temptations here.

Neal's Yard Dairy ○ @ ⊘

www.nealsyarddairy.co.uk
☎ 020 7367 0799
✉ 6 Park Street, London
SE1 9AB
🕐 Mon–Fri 9am–6pm;
Sat 8am–5pm

It is hard to know where to start when describing the extensive list of cheeses on sale at Neal's Yard's shops in Borough and Covent Garden (17 Shorts Gardens). Randolph Hodgson, the owner of Neal's Yard Dairy, has done much to raise the profile of British cheese by helping farmhouse cheese-makers find a market and perfect the cheeses they make. The shop, which must rank as one of the finest in the world, is designed to provide perfect conditions for each cheese whether a cheddar, a blue cheese, soft or fresh. Staff

are immensely knowledgeable and charming. Recommended are Stichelton, Montgomery, Keen's, Mrs Kirkham's Lancashire, St James and some of Neal's Yard Dairy's own creations, which include some beautifully made fresh goats' milk cheeses. Crème fraiche, yoghurt and double cream are also on sale. Londoners hoping to buy locally made cheeses should try Crockhamdale (a firm Wensleydale style), Verulamium and Golden Cross (both goats' milk).

Oddono's Gelati Italiani

www.oddonos.com
☎ 020 7052 0732
✉ 14 Bute Street, South Kensington, London **SW7 3EX**
🕐 Mon–Thurs 11am–11pm; Fri–Sat 11am–12am; Sun 11am–11pm

With a mission to create fresh Italian gelato that could rival his grandmother's, Christian Oddono set up the gelateria in Bute Street and has never looked back. All the gelato is developed and produced daily in their South Kensington premises using closely guarded recipes. They use no additives, colourings or preservatives, just high-quality, individually sourced ingredients. Their range of flavours combines the traditional strawberry and vanilla with the more adventurous vodka lemon and cinnamon, which is fabulous. There are also sorbets and soya-based gelati on offer.

Paxton & Whitfield ⚫ @ ⚫

www.paxtonandwhitfield.co.uk
☎ 020 7930 0259
✉ 93 Jermyn Street, London
SW1Y 6JE
🕐 Mon–Sat 9.30am–6pm

This is the original, old St James' shop that made this cheesemonger a national treasure. There are two other shops in Stratford-upon-Avon and Bath (see website for details). The choice of cheeses from both Britain and the continent is enormous. All are well-cared for and served by knowledgeable staff. Paxton's concentrates on artisan cheese, selling the great West Country cheddars (Montgomery and Keen's), Mrs Kirkham's Lancashire, Colston & Bassett stilton and also modern British cheeses, such as Wigmore. They also run a number of tastings and clubs, and can send selections of cheese by mail order.

Rippon Cheese Stores ⚬ ⦸

www.ripponcheese.com
☎ 020 7931 0628 / 0668
✉ 26 Upper Tachbrook Street,
London **SW1V 1SW**
🕑 Mon–Fri 8.15am–5.15pm;
Sat 8.30am–5pm

A cheese shop with a genuine professional feel, run by experts who take enormous trouble to make sure that every cheese in the shop is in tip-top condition. It may look slightly odd as you walk in – the cheeses sit on open chiller shelves half hidden by blinds – but push the blind aside and there is an easy-to-choose from display with plenty of information written up on 'tasting notes'. At the back of the shop is a second room housing soft and semi-soft cheeses. The range and variety sold by Philip and Karen Rippon is vast. All the continental favourites are here, and great Irish cheeses, but there's a strong British emphasis, too.

The Real Cheese Shop ⦸

☎ 020 8878 6676
✉ 62 Barnes High Street, London
SW13 9LF
🕑 Tues–Thurs 9.30am–5pm;
Fri 9am–5.30pm; Sat 9am–5pm

This neighbourhood shop, established in 1985, sells a variety of new British farmhouse cheeses and specialises in Continental cheeses such as Raclette, Gorgonzola and Brie. Also find olives, nuts, cheese biscuits and chutneys together with free-range eggs and local honey. You can sample the cheese before you buy.

Tray Gourmet Ltd ⦸

www.traygourmet.co.uk
☎ 020 7352 7676
✉ 240 Fulham Road, London
SW10 9NA
🕑 Mon–Sat 8.30am–5.30pm

This corner shop specialises in French groceries, Laguilhon's foie gras, confit and cassoulets, and cheese. The fromagerie has a traditional cheese display counter – usually found only in France – made of wood and marble with sliding cutting tables. Their cheeses are bought directly from Rungis Market, the largest wholesale market in France, and then matured here to guarantee they are at their optimum age. Their website lists a cheese of the month with details on the origin, taste, milk type and strength.

Applebee's Fish ⊘

www.applebeesfish.com
☎ 020 7407 5777
✉ 4 Stoney Street, London
SE1 9AA
🕒 Tues–Fri 9am–6pm;
Sat 9am–4pm

Alongside other fine food establishments in Borough Market, Applebee's Fish offers, among the usual suspects, snapper, halibut, mussels and lobster, plus condiments, crab cakes, skewers and marinades. The fishmongers are friendly and helpful and there is a café and restaurant to enjoy fresh catches of the day or grab one of their shrimp wraps to go.

Atari-Ya

www.atariya.co.uk
☎ 020 8896 1552
✉ 7 Station Parade, Noel Road,
West Acton, London **W3 0DS**
🕒 Tues 11am–6.30pm; Wed–Fri
10am–6.30pm; Sat 9am–7pm;
Sun 10am–7pm

This is the place (or its various branches – see website) to buy the very freshest sashimi fish. I have to admit that on the one hand I feel deep disapproval at the sale of endangered fish for sashimi (Japanese raw fish), but there are species sold here that are utterly heavenly to eat (better than bluefin) and yet sustainably harvested and produced. Step forward Yellow Fin, sometimes called Kingfish, which is a white fish that is so delicious raw, or grilled. The Yellow Fin are farmed in Australia by Cleanseas (www.cleanseas. com.au), fed a sustainable diet (mainly scraps from the fish processing industry), blast frozen and sea freighted to the UK. A rare treat, but one not to miss. Atari-Ya sells all the accoutrements for making and serving sashimi and sushi.

The Barnes Fish Shop ⊘

☎ 020 8876 1297
✉ 18 Barnes High Street, London
SW13 9LW
🕒 Tues–Sat 8.30am–5.30pm

The owner of this fish shop has been serving customers for over 25 years, will advise you on what is in season and can clean and prepare the fish to your requirements. A catering service offers a range of hand-prepared specialities such as cooked Cornish lobsters and seafood kebabs. Other popular items include whole dressed salmon, handmade fishcakes, shellfish platters and bouillabaisse.

Billingsgate Market £

www.cityoflondon.gov.uk/
billingsgate

📞 020 7987 1118

✉ Trafalgar Way, London **E14 5ST**

🕐 Tues–Sat 5am–8.30am

This market has exclusively traded fish since the 16th century. The listed building in which it is housed was opened in 1876 and today it is the UK's largest inland fish market with an average of 25,000 tons of fish being sold each year. There are 98 stands, 30 shops and two cafés to peruse, all covering an area of 13 acres. Fish from the coasts of Aberdeen to Penzance are transported by road overnight to arrive in time for the market's early opening hours. Some stallholders take credit cards, but bring cash to be safe. Look out for Chamberlain & Meadows (Leslie Steadman, tel: 020 7987 2506/2639) for prime wild fish from the British coast and wild salmon, netted in rivers. And also Barton & Hart (Roger Barton, tel: 020 75252341) for a large range of fresh British and imported fish.

The Chelsea Fishmonger @

www.thechelseafishmonger.com

📞 020 7589 9432

✉ 10 Cale Street, Chelsea, London **SW3 3QU**

🕐 Tues–Fri 9am–5.30pm;
Sat 9am–4pm

Rex Goldsmith's shop is ever popular with Chelsea residents despite the presence of a Waitrose supermarket with a fish counter about 200 yards away. All fish is from a sustainable source – line-caught bass and wild Scottish salmon, to name a few. All is always fresh and Goldsmith specialises in selling species popular with Spanish and French expats who live in this area – you will often see octopus, mussels, clams and bream on the counter. He also sells gull eggs in season (April / May) and other delicacies.

Covent Garden Fishmongers ✍

www.coventgardenfishmongers.
co.uk

📞 020 8995 9273

✉ 37 Turnham Green Terrace, London **W4 1RG**

🕐 Tues–Wed, Fri–Sat 8am–5.30pm;
Thurs 8am–5pm

Philip Diamond has been trading fish since 1982, starting in Covent Garden then moving to Chiswick, where together with the help of his son Gary and business partner Eddie Patmore their combined knowledge of fish is bestowed upon local customers. Fish can be prepared to meet all demands – examples include filleted red snapper, salmon steaks and sea bass scaled and gutted. A wide range of shellfish is on offer and their deli is stocked with pre-packed smoked fish, sushi accessories and a condiments corner.

Crustacea Stall at Bibendum ✒

www.bibendum.co.uk
☎ 020 7589 0864
✉ Michelin House, 81 Fulham Road, London **SW3 6RD**
🕐 Tues–Sat 9am–5pm

Located at the busy crossroads of fashionable Brompton Cross is Terence Conran's Michelin House, a local landmark consisting of a French restaurant, oyster bar, café and crustacea stall. Located opposite the café in the forecourt the stall sells crab, hand-picked white crab meat, winkles, shrimp, caviar, clams and smoked fish. Lobsters are available on Saturday mornings from 9am when you can also pick up some home-made mayonnaise to accompany it.

Fin & Flounder ✒

www.finandflounder.com
☎ 0783 8018395
✉ 71 Broadway Market, Hackney, London **E8 4PH**
🕐 Tues–Fri 10am–6.30pm; Sat 9am–5pm; Sun 11am–4pm

I've heard excellent reports about this newish shop. It has knowledgeable staff with a passion for what they sell and a sustainability policy that means they are endorsed by leading bodies such as the Marine Stewardship Council who certify sustainable seafood. The shop also sells a fine selection of cheese and condiments as well as a good range of wines. I'd welcome more feedback on this shop. They will deliver – ring for details.

The Fish Shop at Kensington Place ✒

☎ 020 7243 6626
✉ 201 Kensington Church Street, London **W8 7LX**
🕐 Tues–Fri 9am–7pm; Sat 9am–5pm

Tucked around the corner from Kensington Place restaurant, this wet fish shop supplies the eatery as well as Notting Hill locals. Quality and freshness is guaranteed you will find whole and filleted fish, sustainable langoustines, smoked fish and some of the restaurant's signature dishes for you to take home and cook yourself – fish soup, fish pies and fishcakes.

The Fishmonger Ltd. ✒

www.thefishmongerltd.com
☎ 07880 541 485
✉ 26 Royal Hill, Greenwich, London **SE10 8RT**
🕐 Tues–Fri 8.30am–5pm; Sat 7.30am–4.30pm

With a huge variety of fresh and smoked fish it is reassuring and encouraging that this business still takes traceability and sustainability seriously. They encourage customers to check online or to phone ahead if they are searching for something specific, but there is always a good range available and advice on hand on how to incorporate the daily catch into a tasty meal. To assist in this, there is a wide variety of oils, sauces and condiments, all of which are 'fish friendly' and complement the fresh stock. They also run seafood tastings.

Forman & Field ○ @ ◐

www.formanandfield.com
☎ 020 8525 2352
✉ Stour Road, Fish Island, London
E3 2NT

A derivative of H. Forman & Son, a family business founded in 1905 supplying the finest smoked salmon, caviar and other smoked fresh fish to top hotels and restaurants around the world, Forman & Field is a fine food mail order company specialising in traditional British produce sourced from small independent producers. Among their seven food categories is The Fishmongers, offering fresh fish, such as Dover sole caught on the day of dispatch, prepared fish, such as fishcakes and salmon fillet en croute, smoked salmon, Beluga and Sevruga caviar, a selection of marinated fish and shellfish and Maldon Rock oysters. Their website is attractive to look at and easy to use.

Golborne Fisheries ◐ ◐

☎ 020 8960 3100
✉ 75 Golborne Road, London
W10 5NP
🕐 Mon 10am–4pm; Tues–Sat 8.30am–6pm

Just off Portobello Road lies Golborne Fisheries, a green-fronted corner shop with large display windows. This fishmonger serves local fish-lovers a large range of fresh seafood, including shellfish and exotic fish, all at affordable prices. Friendly staff are always at hand to help.

James Knight of Mayfair ◐

www.james-knight.com
☎ 020 7221 6177
✉ 67 Notting Hill Gate, London
W11 3JS
🕐 Mon–Sat 9am–6pm

The large, open shop front window piled high with wet fish attracts many a customer on this main drag in Notting Hill. A selection of top quality organic fish and crustacea are available from a team who are more than happy to help. They also offer a selection of organic meat and poultry, smoked and marinated fish, dairy products and many other grocery products to complement the fish. They also have a fish counter at Selfridges Food Hall in Oxford Street (see page 68) and the company holds a royal warrant by appointment to Her Majesty Queen Elizabeth II.

Kennards For Food Lovers ●

www.kennardsgoodfoods.com
☎ 020 7404 4030
✉ 57 Lambs Conduit Street, London
WC1N 3NB
🕐 Mon–Fri 8.30am–7pm;
Sat 9.30am–5pm; Sun 11am–5pm

Kennards is a specialist food shop on a lovely street lined with artisan shops in the heart of Bloomsbury. It is a one-stop shop selling the finest British, as well as international, goods such as Doves Farm flour, Prestat chocolates and Seggiano delicacies. The fish counter stocks fresh fish that come straight off a number of small British day-boat fishing fleets. There is limited stock so call beforehand if you require something specific.

La Maree ●

www.poissonneriedelavenue.com
☎ 020 7589 8067
✉ 76 Sloane Avenue, London
SW3 3DZ
🕐 Mon–Sat 9am–5.30pm

La Maree is part of La Poissonnerie restaurant next door, which was started by Peter Rosignoli in 1964, and specialises in fish. La Maree offers a range of fresh quality fish and shellfish. Home-made sauces and fish soups are also available, along with eggs, organic chicken and game when in season.

H. S. Linwood & Son ●

☎ 020 8980 2058
✉ 6–7 Grand Avenue, Leadenhall
Market, London **EC3V 1LR**
🕐 Mon–Fri 6am–3.30pm

Leadenhall's covered Victorian market provides an atmospheric location for this family-owned fishmonger that has been in business for over 100 years. The open-fronted stall displays fresh scallops, snappers, sardines, salmon, sea trout, mackerel and herring. It is also one of the few fishmongers to be open on a Monday, but closed on the weekend.

Moxon's ⊘

www.moxonsfreshfish.com
☎ 020 8675 2468
✉ Westbury Parade, Nightingale
Lane, Clapham South, London
SW4 9DH
🕐 Tues–Fri 9am–8pm; Sat 9am–6pm

An exemplary fishmonger sourcing the best and freshest of
British fish, much of it from the south coast. Robin Moxon
has revolutionised fish shopping in south London and now
has a large and loyal following. Line-caught mackerel from
Cornwall, red mullet, squid and John Dory are regularly on
the counter, but expect a few less familiar types – megrim
soles often turn up, a good-tasting alternative to other flat
fish. The crab is fabulous, too. Some imports are on offer,
including line-caught yellow fin tuna from Sri Lanka and
Icelandic halibut. New branches have opened in South
Kensington's Bute Street, and Lordship Lane, East Dulwich
(see website for details).

Steve Hatt Fishmonger ⊘

☎ 020 7226 3963
✉ 88–90 Essex Road, London
N1 8LU
🕐 Tues–Sat 7am–5pm

This family-owned fishmonger has been trading since 1895
and is somewhat of an institution in Islington. A popular
destination, it offers the freshest of fish from sustainable
sources around the world – wild salmon, oysters, sea bass,
Sevruga and Beluga caviar, samphire when in season, sea
urchins, squid ink and whelks, to name but a few. Game,
such as snipe and woodcock, is also available when in
season. Expect queues.

Walter Purkis & Sons ⊘

www.purkis4fish.com
☎ 020 8883 4355
✉ 52 Muswell Hill Broadway,
London **N10 3RT**
🕐 Tues–Sat 8.30am–5pm

All of the fish found here is wild unless otherwise stated.
They smoke the fish in their own 100-year-old smokehouse
at the rear of the Crouch End shop and sell every type of
wet fish and shellfish. The Purkis family has been supplying
food for over two centuries. Walter founded his business in
1973 and today he runs the Muswell Hill shop while his son
runs the Crouch End shop. Fish is sourced from Billingsgate
Market, Cornwall, Devon, Grimsby, Aberdeen and
Fraserburgh, and more exotic fish and shellfish come
from Europe. See website for details of all the shops.

Abel & Cole ⊙ @ ⊘ ⊙ ⊙

www.abel-cole.co.uk
☎ 08452 626364
✉ 16 Waterside Way, Plough Lane,
London **SW17 0HB**
🕐 Mon–Thurs 8.30am–7.30pm;
Fri 8.30am–6.30pm; Sat 9am–5pm

Keith Abel began his organic empire from his London
home in 1988 selling potatoes door-to-door. Before long
Keith, with Paul Cole's help, was selling novel (at the time)
organic produce, supplied by local farmers, to unsuspecting
customers. From there, Abel & Cole has grown into one of
the UK's leading organic fruit and vegetable suppliers. Their
support for British farmers and beliefs in animal welfare are
paramount. Only seasonal food is sold and packaging is kept
to a minimum. Choose from mixed or non-mixed organic
fruit and vegetable boxes; sizes range from a baby and
toddler box to a family box that will feed five. Visit their
website to view their entire organic range offering
everything from cereal and meat to children's food
and household cleaning products.

Alwand

☎ 020 8742 9009
✉ 140 Uxbridge Road, London
W12 8AA
🕐 Mon–Sun 24 hours

Food writer Simon Hopkinson chose this Shepherd's Bush
shop in a round-up of favourites, so I could not resist a visit
to see its renowned range of fruit and vegetables. He was
right – it is a gem: quinces, great bunches of herbs,
pomegranates, apricots, all manner of citrus, dates and
Hopkinson's adored long, pale-purple, thin-skinned
aubergines.

Andreas Georghiou & Co ⊘

www.andreasveg.co.uk
☎ 020 8995 0140
✉ 35 Turnham Green Terrace,
London **W4 1RG**
🕐 Mon–Fri 7am–6pm;
Sat 7am–5.30pm

Andreas Georghiou's traditional-looking greengrocer
provides acclaimed restaurants and food lovers in west
London with the finest seasonal British fruit and veg, as
well as organic produce sourced from all over Europe, such
as Italian wild mushrooms that are available in the autumn.
Food miles stickers relay the produce's carbon footprint
and minimum packaging is used for their free home
deliveries to local customers.

FarmW5 @ ⊘

www.farmw5.co.uk

☎ 020 8566 1965

✉ On-the-Green, 19 The Green, Ealing, London **W5 5DA**

🕐 Mon–Fri 8am–7.30pm; Sat 9am–7pm; Sun 11am–5pm

FarmW5 is an organic and artisan food shop styled as a market, selling certified organic, seasonally sourced food from over 50 small UK producers and it is the first retailer to be endorsed by the Slow Food Movement. This shop has a coffee shop in the back where fresh coffee beans are ground to order, a fully-stocked deli and dairy area and all the fruit and vegetables are organic, British and biodynamic when available.

Michanicou Bros ⊘ £

☎ 020 7727 5191

✉ 2 Clarendon Road, London **W11 3AA**

🕐 Mon–Fri 9am–6.30pm; Sat 9am–5.30pm

Two Cypriot brothers own this old-fashioned greengrocers located around the corner from Holland Park tube station. The boxes outside piled high with colourful produce are sure to draw you into the slightly chaotic shop where cheeky chappies are keen to serve you, fulfilling any requirement, and if they don't have what you want they will try and source it for you. Produce is from around the world, including exotic fruits and vegetables you would struggle to find in a supermarket. There is free home delivery for locals.

The Natural Kitchen

www.thenaturalkitchen.com

☎ 020 7486 8065

✉ 77 / 78 Marylebone High Street, London **W1U 5JX**

🕐 Mon–Fri 8am–8pm; Sat 9am–7pm; Sun 11am–6pm

Described as a 'food emporium', Natural Kitchen can be found on Marylebone's main shopping street around the corner from the other foodie destinations The Ginger Pig and La Fromagerie (see pages 77 and 95). There is an eat-in café / restaurant and a food-to-go counter. Other produce includes meat, cheese and an abundance of seasonal fruit and vegetables.

The Organic Delivery Company
♻ @ 🌿 ✿

www.organicdelivery.co.uk
☎ 020 7739 8181
✉ A156 Nine Elms Lane, New
Covent Garden Market, London
SW8 5EE
🕐 Mon–Fri 9am–5pm

A small, friendly, family-founded local fruit and vegetable service that is also a worker's cooperative. Certified organic by the Soil Association, you can order a regular vegetable box or have it tailor-made to your own needs. Most vegetables are sourced from farms near London.

Parkside Farm PYO 🅿

www.parksidefarmpyo.co.uk
☎ 020 8367 2035
✉ Hadley Road, Enfield, Middlesex
EN2 8LA
🕐 Tues–Sun 9am–5.30pm

I believe this PYO is the closest to north London than any other, but would love to hear of more. City dwellers need locally grown produce and this really is on the doorstep of London. If you know of any others close to our big city centres, please let me know. There's a good range of soft fruit here, plus vegetables. You can also buy meringues, honey, ice cream and cold drinks for tired pickers.

Pretty Traditional 🌿 💷 ✿

www.prettytraditional.co.uk
☎ 020 8693 7169
✉ 47 North Cross Road, London
SE22 9ET
🕐 Mon–Fri 7am–5.30pm;
Sat 7am–5pm

A traditional London greengrocer selling fruit and vegetables bought at London's wholesale markets, including a quantity of organic produce. New fruit and veg is brought in every day so you can always guarantee it is the freshest available. Owner Chris Burgess has a 'no air-freight' policy on all fruit and vegetables, keeps his prices competitive and tries to source, particularly the organic produce, as locally as possible. When I visited there was a beautiful display of purple sprouting broccoli, white cabbage, sprouts and sprout tops, parsnips, acorn and butternut squash, and organic red-skinned potatoes. It would be hard to argue that this is not the best greengrocers in East Dulwich.

Seeds of Italy ○ @ ◑

www.seedsofitaly.com
☎ 020 8427 5020
✉ A1 Pheonix Industrial Estate,
Rosslyn Crescent, London **HA1 2SP**

Not strictly a fruit and veg shop, Seeds of Italy was established in 1783 and has been passed down through seven generations, making it the world's oldest family-run seed company. The most common and more unusual seeds are available from their easy-to-use website with categories subdivided into sections such as vegetables, fruit, herbs, radicchio and chicory, salad accompaniments, seed collections, even truffle and mushroom spawn. The website also offers store cupboard essentials, such as their own tomato sauce, truffle olive oil and seasonings, as well as their own cookbook *From Seed to Plate*.

▼ HONEY

Chelsea Physic Garden ◑

www.chelseaphysicgarden.co.uk
☎ 020 7352 5646
✉ 66 Royal Hospital Road, Chelsea,
London **SW3 4HS**
🕑 **Apr–Oct** Wed–Fri 12–5pm Sun,
Bank Hols 12–6pm

Situated in the heart of London the honey produced here is probably the rarest in the world. The bees from five hives feast on more than 5000 rare and endangered plant species and each batch is subtly different depending on the time of year. Jars are available in the tea room and, as it is very popular, it is in short supply so you may well be limited to one pot per person – it is worth ringing beforehand to check that it is available. At around £8 a jar it's not cheap either, but aficionados swear by it. The garden was founded in 1673 as the Apothecaries Garden and with the renewed interest in natural medicine is increasingly popular.

Fortnum & Mason ○ @ ◑

www.fortnumandmason.com
☎ 020 7734 8040
✉ 181 Piccadilly, London
W1A 1ER
🕑 Mon–Sat 9.30am–6pm

As expected Fortnum's sell a wide range of honey. Last year they were selling their own, harvested from London hives, some of which were on the roof of the building. This year they have Regent's Park honey, plus lovely, pale 'pooh bear' honey from Brightwell Bees.

Pure London Honey

www.purelondonhoney.com
☎ 07956 367544
✉ Brockwell Park, London
SE24 9BJ

Honey made by beekeeper Orlando Clarke, who says that London is – surprisingly – one of the greener places to produce honey. Clarke has been beekeeping since 1998, when he was introduced to it by a Polish beekeeper, Henry Klobuch, who left him his hives when he died a year later. Clarke uses no chemicals to treat his bees (to protect them from disease) and the honey has multifarious flavours, depending on the time of year and which flowers or blossom the bees are busy with. You can buy his honey from various outlets in London – contact for stockists.

Regent's Park Honey

www.purefood.co.uk
☎ 07973 121800
✉ Pure Food, 58 Witley Court, Coram Street, London **WC1N 1HD**

Honey produced in a limited quantity from bees that work among the gorgeous gardens of Regent's Park and the surrounding area. The variety of blossom determines the flavour of the honey. Through the honey season the honey changes character, gradually becoming stronger and darker. It is manually filtered, but you will sometimes see some cloudiness of left-behind particles of unfiltered pollen. You can buy it in very limited quantities from the Garden Café in Regent's Park and local deli Melrose and Morgan (see page 62).

Urban Bees ⬤ @ ⬤

www.urbanbees.co.uk
☎ 020 7223 4260
✉ 5 Humphrey Court, Battersea, London **SW11 3JA**

Brian McAllum is passionate about bees. He wants to bring them to the inner cities and he has done just that. He has started community apiaries in Latchmere Road and next door to his home on Battersea Square. He currently harvests around 400 lbs of honey a year. The bees predominantly feed on horse chestnut and lime trees and McAllum says, 'It's the best, tastiest honey in the world'. Contact for stockists.

Algerian Coffee Stores

www.algcoffee.co.uk
📞 020 7437 2480
✉ 52 Old Compton Street, London
W1D 4PB
🕐 Mon–Wed 9am–7pm; Thurs–Fri
9am–9pm; Sat 9am–8pm

This famous London shop was established in 1887 and is still selling some of the best coffees available. It is a place that deserves your support. They will send your favourite coffee to you wherever you live (worldwide) as whole beans or ground to the consistency you prefer. There are too many coffees on sale here to list, but you can choose between single estate rare types, organic and Fairtrade or unusual spiced coffees. Alternatively let the guys do the choosing for you and try the 'coffee of the month'. Tea is also available.

Azorie Blue @

www.azorieblue.co.uk
📞 020 7692 5670
✉ 72 New Bond Street, Mayfair,
London **W1S 1RR**

Stocking ethically sourced, top quality Brazilian coffee, Azorie Blue can truly be called a coffee specialist. Available as whole beans or pre-ground, the coffee is blended from Brazilian Arabica and has a uniquely nutty, caramel flavour that is just as good black as with milk. The tins are slick and stylish, matching the coffee itself. This company ensures that its producers are fairly paid and that they cultivate their crops sensitively and sustainably. See the website for stockists or to order online.

Café Direct

www.cafedirect.co.uk
📞 020 7033 6000
✉ Unit F, Zetland House, 5–25
Scrutton Street, London   **EC2A 4HJ**

Café Direct was established just after 1989 when the coffee price collapsed as a way to boost the income of the beleaguered coffee farming community. The company now claims to trade directly with over 40 growing organisations in 14 countries involving over 200,000 people. This company is no minnow, but the coffee now tastes good (to begin with it was a triumph of principles over a decent cappuccino) and companies like Café Direct and Equal Exchange (see page 242) have inspired, most importantly, millions of shoppers. Salut.

Choi Time @

www.choitime.com

☎ 0845 0533 269

✉ 119 The Hub, 300 Kensal Road, London **W10 5BE**

Melissa Choi has drawn on her family's heritage and the Chinese tradition of tea drinking to create a modern and delicious product. The range of artisan teas that Choi Time offers is diverse and glamorous, with each ingredient being ethically sourced in the Hangzou and Fujian regions of China. Easy to prepare, the leaves are of such quality that just a pinch will give three or four full cups of equally deep flavour. In particular, the giant hand-stitched tea bulbs come alive when steeped in hot water. The 'Thousand Year Red', made from the globe amaranth flower, unfurls and blooms in front of your eyes and creates a wonderfully intense infusion. These products are excellent value and make tea-time a special and luxurious experience, one to be prolonged and savoured. See the website for stockists and direct ordering information.

Coffee Plant ♦ ∅

www.coffee.com

☎ 020 7221 8137

✉ 180 Portobello Road, London **W11 2EB**

🕐 Mon–Sat 7.45am–6.30pm; Sun 9:30am–5pm

A shop that began as a small market stall on the Portobello Road: I remember buying the espresso blend for my coffee machine when I ran the café in the bookshop opposite the stall and it was wonderful. The stall became a shop and the roastery, which used to fill the street with heavenly fumes and vapours, is now in Acton. Still the coffees get well-reviewed and the company has moved on to selling largely organic and accredited Fairtrade blends. Bravo.

Drury Tea & Coffee ♦ @ ∅

www.drury.uk.com

☎ 020 7836 1960

✉ 3 New Row, Covent Garden, London **WC2N 4LH**

🕐 Mon–Fri 9am–6pm; Sat 11am–5pm

A central London shop and roastery that has been going for 70 years, specialising in the espresso coffees that the company first started producing in the '50s. There are a total of 16 espresso blends from Reale to Classico, Siena to Gran Riserva, and so on. Buy them either ground or as whole beans, still in the hessian sack (which Drury recommend to cut environmentally unfriendly packaging). You can also buy filter and cafètiere coffee blends, plus teas.

Firefly

www.fireflytonics.com
020 7052 9720
1 Petersham Mews, London
SW7 5NR

Drinks with a growing popularity, made with natural ingredients and to some imaginative recipes. Marcus Whaley Cohen and Harry Briggs are the people behind Firefly, former city workers who decided it was time to curb their habit for sugary drinks and invent something without sugar or chemicals. Research into the medicinal uses of herbs and combining them with natural fruit juices produced Firefly. As someone who prefers to drink either wine or water, I can still say that these give a noticeable 'lift' and are some of the best tasting on the market. See website for stockists.

Fortnum & Mason ○ @ ◐

www.fortnumandmason.com
020 7734 8040
181 Piccadilly, London
W1A 1ER
Mon–Sat 10am–8pm;
Sun 12am–6pm

Experienced tea specialists, stocking a vast range of teas and coffees, this is also a good place to find cordials and juices. There are at least 15 single estate teas, eight or so green teas (including the famous Gunpowder tea), just as many strong black teas to kick start yourself at breakfast and lighter, fragrant black teas to sip in the afternoon. They now sell eight Fairtrade accredited coffees from all over the world including Sumatra, Honduras, Ethiopia and – unusually – Papua New Guinea.

Hampstead Teas and Coffees ○ @ ◐

www.hampsteadtea.com
0207 431 9393
PO Box 52474, London
NW3 9DA

Imaginatively designed boxes containing 25 different Fairtrade organic teas made by this company in north London. They include single origin teas from the Makaibari tea estate in Darjeeling, the first tea garden to be accredited as biodynamic (a more rigorous organic standard linked to traditional farming methods), it is also – unusually – owner-managed hence the good working relationship between the tea company and the estate. The herb teas are also made with biodynamic ingredients. All are available from their online shop.

Jing Tea ⊙ @ ⵁ

www.jingtea.com

☎ 0207 183 2113

✉ Canterbury Court, London
SW9 6DE

Serious south London online tea merchants, selling an astonishing range of grand-sounding teas of every group and type. Among the dried, fresh green teas are Jasmine Pearls (curled scented leaves) and Dragons Well, which is so fresh that they will tell you on which day it was picked and where. White teas include the heavenly Silver Needle tea from China, their own-label Black Ceylon tea is robust and heady, there are herb teas, accredited Fairtrade teas, organic teas and a special section for tea bags for those closet lazies (like yours truly) who cannot be bothered to fill a pot. Sacrilege at the altar of fine tea!

London Tea Co ⊙ @ ⵁ

www.londontea.co.uk

☎ 0203 159 5480

✉ The London Tea Company,
Saunders House, 52–53 The Mall,
London **W5 3TA**

Stylish tea merchants selling a range of herb teas (they are specialists on the health benefits of each one) in fabulously colourful packaging. Some of the infusion recipes are intriguing – like camomile and lavender or strawberry, peppermint and spearmint – but once in the cup they deliciously succeed. See the website for an inspired range and let me know what you think about these infusions.

Make Us A Brew @ ⵁ

www.makeusabrew.com

☎ 0844 8001956

✉ 34 Percy Street, London
W1T 2DG

Whatever next? A tea company called Cuppa Splosh? The latest in a line of tea merchants who want to attract the post-Jamie Oliver tea-drinking generation sells teas called names such as Look Lively! and Big Chill. But they have a nice ethos (there are Fairtrade and organic varieties) and the graphics on the box are a laugh. Great presents for herbal tea-sceptic teenagers.

Miller Harris Tea Room ⊙ @ ✪

www.millerharris.com

☎ 020 7629 7750

✉ 21 Bruton Street, London

W1J 6QD

⏱ Mon–Sat 10am–6pm

Perfumier Lyn Harris probably gets the prize for the very smartest caddies of fragrant tea sold in her tea room or via her website. There are six teas in total, including one Assam flavoured with Brazilian bigarade oil, another with bergamot (like Earl Grey), and one very pretty-tasting tea with added rose petals. All very gorgeous and, yes, you will have to dig deep. Someone will be very appreciative if given this tea as a present.

Monmouth Coffee Company ✪

www.monmouthcoffee.co.uk

☎ 020 7232 3010

✉ 27 Monmouth Street, London

WC2H 9EU

⏱ Mon–Sat 8am–6.30pm

Monmouth Coffee is strategically situated between Covent Garden, Bloomsbury and Soho on the street that lent it its name. It may not be very daring to pick it as London's best coffee shop, but it's pretty near to it. A world-class roasting programme and attention to both espresso-based drinks and filter coffees make it near to top of the pile – the espresso is especially fruity, powerful and dark, and is one of my favourites. The larger Monmouth shop outside Borough Market, with its bread and jam served on a communal table, is a must-stop destination during visits to the great food market.

Postcard Teas ⊙ @ ✪

www.postcardteas.com

☎ 020 7629 3654

✉ 9 Dering Street, London

W1S 1AG

⏱ Mon–Sat 10.30am–6.30pm

Timothy d'Offay is one of the foremost tea experts in the world. He works with some of the world's best small-scale producers and brings his bounty back to central London. Most of these can be tried at the in-store tasting table and all are available in caddies to purchase. There's also a tea school for those unversed in good and bad tea. A must if you live in London or are visiting.

The Rare Tea Company ✪ @

www.rareteacompany.com
☎ 020 7681 0115
✉ 9 Gloucester Court,
33 Gloucester Avenue, London
NW1 7TJ

Tea is a funny thing. Most of what we drink in the UK is industrial and of low quality, but if you search them out there are some very good tea importers and processors – and this one is for real aficionados. The Rare Tea Company's founder Henrietta Lovell has dedicated herself to the serious business of finding the best tea in the world and she has succeeded. As an importer she is also concerned about economic impact and many of the company's teas are Fairtrade. You can buy their teas online.

RDA Organic

www.rdaorganic.com
☎ 020 8871 3917
✉ Target House, 218–220 Garratt
Lane, London **SW18 4EA**

RDA produce organic smoothies and fruit drinks. They are available in Booths and Waitrose and a plethora of good independent stores including Whole Foods, Fresh and Wild and smaller outlets. These are seriously fruity drinks from a small company who deserve to be supported. See website for details of stockists.

Royal Botanic Gardens, Kew – Golden Blend Tea ✪ @ ✿

www.kew.org
☎ 020 8332 3123
✉ RBG Kew Enterprises, Shaft Yard,
Royal Botanic Gardens Kew,
Richmond, Surrey **TW9 3AB**

Kew has collaborated with a plantation in Sri Lanka to produce a bespoke tea for the Botanic Gardens which, with every packet sold, will put a donation towards Kew's global conservation work. The tea is sold in teabags and is certified organic and Fairtrade. It makes a great present and puts a little back, which is nice. You can buy the tea from Kew's online shop via their website.

Tea Palace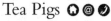

www.teapalace.co.uk

☎ 020 7836 6997

✉ 12 Covent Garden Market,
Covent Garden, London **WC2E 8RF**

🕐 Mon–Sat 10am–7pm;
Sun 11am–6pm

The Tea Palace is just that. An innovative Covent Garden-based tea emporium with more than 100 different teas on offer, from Earl Grey to Oolong, White and Green, camomile and a lot more. These are proper teas, sourced with imagination and verve. They bring a new dimension to something that is very staid and English – tea drinking. Really worth a visit, and if you are not a great tea-drinker there's a great novelty element about it.

Tea Pigs

www.teapigs.co.uk

☎ 020 8568 2900

✉ 1 The Old Pumping Station,
Pump Alley, Brentford, Middlesex
TW8 0AP

Great-looking and great-tasting tea, sold in now characteristic cloth tea bags, which the company call their tea temples. It is all very cool, very hip (with an overly chatty website) and also a rather expensive way to make a cup of tea, but the result is as delicious as claimed. I like the searing green tea – so powerful I began acting like one of those scrooges that uses a tea bag twice. They also make a gently perfumed jasmine pearl tea that is amazing to drink alongside Asian food. Or try the blended herb teas, the black tea – all is an enjoyable luxury. See the website for stockists or order online.

Union Coffee Roasters

www.unionroasted.com

☎ 020 7474 8990

✉ The New Roastery, Unit 2,
7a South Crescent, London
E16 4TL

Jeremy Torz and Stephen Macatonia established their coffee company in 2001, aiming to sell high quality coffee that was ethically sourced. Both travel to coffee producing countries in Africa and South America, discovering distinctive coffees and then building relationships with the communities that produce them. The coffee growers and processors reap greater benefits through dealing direct with Union. Most delicious are the Rwandan coffees, in particular the Maraba Bourbon and the Cup of Excellence. The coffee is roasted on the London premises and is available (as whole beans or ground) online from a very informative website. Alternatively you can contact them to find your nearest stockist.

Midlands

Abbey Parks Farm Shop @ ○

www.abbeyparksasparagus.co.uk
☎ 01205 821610
✉ East Heckington, Lincolnshire
PE20 3QG
🕐 Mon–Sat 9.30am–5pm

The farm shop is set on the family-run farm estate that was established in 1932 and is owned by Ros and Nick Loweth. The delicatessen counter in the shop sells a delightful variety of speciality cheese, meat plates, olives, jams, chutneys, sauces, biscuits and real dairy ice cream. Many of these goods are sourced from local farms around the county. Abbey Parks's speciality, however, is their fruit and veg – they sell mainly home-grown and locally sourced fruit and vegetables, some of which are organic. They are also renowned for their asparagus – the ginjnlim variety. As vegetable suppliers to some of the top London restaurants such as the Ivy, you know you will be buying the best when you visit. Mail order available.

Bells Farm Shop ○

www.bellsfarmshop.co.uk
☎ 01299 251364
✉ Chadwick Bank, Worcester Road,
Hartlebury, Stourport-on-Severn,
Worcestershire **DY13 9RQ**
🕐 Mon–Sun 9am–5pm

A farm shop rated highly with local people with a PYO growing an amazing 200 varieties of fruit and vegetables all year round. Depending on the season you can find peas, purple sprouting broccoli, calabrese, beetroot, asparagus, herbs, strawberries, courgettes and much more.

Berryfields Farm Shop

www.berryfieldsfarm.net
☎ 01676 522 155
✉ Berkswell Road, Coventry, West
Midlands **CV7 7LB**
🕐 Tues–Fri 9am–5.30pm;
Sat 9am–5pm; Sun 10am–2pm

Home-reared fresh pork plus sausages, bacon, pies and ham made on the premises. Other meat is not reared on the farm but brought in from local farms and includes well-hung beef, fresh lamb and free-range poultry. You can also buy other sundry groceries, but don't leave without a pork pie, made to the recipe of the owner's great aunt who in 2010 reached the ripe old age of 102 years old.

Brockhampton Estate

www.nationaltrust.org.uk/
brockhampton
☎ 01885 482077
✉ Greenfields, Bringsty,
Herefordshire **WR6 5TB**
🕐 11am–5pm (seasonal opening
times apply, see website)

The damson and rhubarb jam produced on this National Trust estate are just two of the fabulous home-made products sold on the estate. The company was set up in 2001 and was the idea of Les Rogers, whose aim it was to work with the local tenants to use and add value to their produce. Les and his wife Janet work together using fruit and veg grown at Brockhampton to make a range of jams and chutneys using local, traditional recipes. The damson jam, one of their specialities has been described as 'tart but with a beautiful flavour and great texture'. Award winner of the National Trust's 2010 Fine Farm Produce awards.

Chantry Farm Shop ✿ @ ✔

www.chantryfarm.com
☎ 01332 865698
✉ Kings Newton Road, Melbourne,
Derbyshire **DE73 8DD**
🕐 Mon–Fri 8am–5pm; Sat 8am–
4pm; Sun 10am–2.30pm

The shop sells its own North Country Mule, and the ewes can be seen grazing in the fields around the shop. It also sources grass-fed Longhorn beef from a farm in Staffordshire and pork from Packington, widely admired for its RSPCA-certified high welfare standards. Added to this you can buy free-range poultry and a wide range of other groceries.

Chatsworth Farm Shop

www.chatsworth.org
☎ 01246 583392
✉ Stud Farm, Pilsley, Bakewell,
Derbyshire **DE45 1UF**
🕐 Mon–Sat 9am–5.30pm;
Sun 11am–5pm

There has been a farm shop on the Chatsworth Estate since 1977, set up by the Duke and Duchess of Devonshire to support the local estate farms and sell their produce, as well as other Derbyshire specialities. There is an in-house butchery, bakery, dairy and a vegetable stall outside selling produce from local growers in Melbourne. The various rare-breed meats are outstanding, as are the eggs from a farm in Rowsley. There's milk and cream from the local dairy, smoked fish from the Derbyshire Smokery in Flagg and, of course, game from the estate gamekeepers. Hampers are also available online.

Cook's Farm Shop

www.cooksfarmshop.co.uk
01530 242214
Lane End Farm, Markfield Lane, Newton Linford, Leicestershire **LE6 0AB**
Mon–Fri 9am–6pm; Sat 9am–5pm; Sun 10am–1pm

A nice farm shop loyal to local produce, selling the farm's own Aberdeen Angus beef, free-range pork and free-range poultry. Milk and cream come from Lubcloud Dairy in Loughborough, yoghurt from Manor Farm, Quenby Stilton, honey from Groby and drinks from Belvoir. An interesting range of hen, turkey, duck and bantam eggs is also available.

Doddington Hall Farm Shop

www.doddingtonhall.com
01522 688581
Doddington Hall Doddington, Lincolnshire **LN6 4RU**
Tues–Sat 9am–5pm; Sun 10am–5pm

A farm shop attached to a beautiful Elizabethan house owned by Claire and James Birch. The shop sells vegetables plucked from the recently restored walled kitchen garden, plus meat, poultry and game from local butcher F. C. Phipps of Mareham le Fen, flour from a nearby Lincolnshire watermill, locally baked bread and various cakes and pastries that are made on the premises. It received a number of glowing nominations for BBC Radio 4 Food & Farming Awards 2009. Please let me know what you think, should you get the chance to visit.

Farndon Fields Farm Shop

01858 46488
Farndon Road, Market Harborough, Leicestershire **LE16 9NP**
Mon–Sat 8am–6pm; Sun 10am–4pm

A fabulous-looking farm shop and former winner of FARMA Farm Shop of the Year. Opened in 1983 by the Stokes family, it began selling the farm's own home-grown produce out of the farm garage. Now housed in a larger wooden barn structure, it boasts huge wooden counters stacked with fresh produce and low beams draped with dried hops. There's a PYO (see entry on page 147) and expect to find local milk from Lubcloud Dairy, freshly baked bread, free-range eggs and fresh meat prepared on site at the on-farm butchery. Rated as outstanding and a must-visit place.

Galileo Organic Farm @ ⊘

www.fossewayorganics.co.uk
☎ 07891 522 451
✉ Galileo Farm On The Hill, Fosse
Way, Moreton Morrell, Warwickshire
CV35 9DF

The Peckhams have been farming for the last 10 years, and selling their products to the consumer for the last 5 as a result of the increased demand for high quality, organic produce. Their farm is stocked with animals that complement each other in a free-range environment: chickens, ducks, turkeys, geese, pigs, sheep and cows. Their rare-breed Berkshire and Gloucester Old Spot pigs live in family groups and mature slowly and naturally, allowing them to graze freely and develop the layer of fat that gives the final pork product that wonderful taste. Their chickens are Cornish Game, an old-fashioned breed dating back to the '50s, which are reared naturally and, like the pigs, have a delicate but flavourful meat. You can order online, or call ahead and then pick up an order from the farm direct.

Gonalston Farm Shop ⊙⊘⊙

www.gonalstonfarmshop.co.uk
☎ 0115 966 5666
✉ Southwell Road, Gonalston,
Nottinghamshire **NG14 7DR**
🕐 Tues–Sat 9am–6.30pm;
Sun 10am–4pm

A large shop, specialising in meat from their own farm, locally sourced pork and lamb. It has to be said that there is a certain lack of soul to the place, but the highlight is the Hereford cross beef; fabulous looking rib joints for the weekend were magnificently displayed on a slate counter when I visited. Also, don't miss the authentic Bramley apples that are grown on John Starkey's farm at Norwood Park. Southwell, as any apple nerd will tell you, is home to the first original Bramley tree.

Hillers

www.hillers.co.uk
☎ 01789 773057
✉ Dunnington Heath Farm, Alcester,
Warwickshire **B49 5PD**
🕐 Mon–Fri 9am–5.30pm; Sat–Sun
9am–5pm

For almost 80 years Hillers has been trading in local produce, and they continue to go from strength to strength. Their stock is predominantly sourced on their own farm, or from farms in the Vale of Evesham, in a conscious effort to keep food miles low and quality high. Bread is baked freshly on site throughout the day, filling the shop with a wonderful smell, along with that of their delicious pastries. Their cheese counter is locally renowned and with good reason, as they stock over 100 cheeses and host regular tastings to showcase local specialities. Alongside the cheeses is an array of olives and antipasti, beautifully presented and offering something for every taste and budget. Home-roasted ham, beef and pork, as well as a range of home-made salads, add to a sense of abundance that pervades this establishment. You can call ahead, or look online to check on availability of fresh seasonal produce such as soft fruits, leaf salads and root vegetables. This is a family business that has developed and grown over several generations and puts locality and quality first.

Manor Organic Farm

www.manororganicfarm.co.uk
☎ 01509 646413
✉ 77 Main Street, Long Whatton, Loughborough, Leicestershire **LE12 5DF**
🕐 Wed 10am–5.30pm; Thurs 9am–6pm; Fri 9am–7pm; Sat 9am–4pm

A lovely farm shop run on organic principles by Graeme and Vivienne Matravers, selling home-reared Longhorn / Fresian cross beef and Llleyn breed lamb, plus pork from a local Soil Association-certified farm. The couple also rear turkeys for Christmas and you should get your order in quick. The shop has its own bakery selling beautiful artisan breads. Organic milk and cream is sourced from Lubcloud Dairy, just a few miles away. This is a great place, popular with locals – tell me what you think if you get the chance to drop in.

Marley Farm Shop

☎ 01327 261331
✉ Banbury Road, Byfield, Daventry, Northamptonshire **NN11 6UA**
🕐 Mon–Fri 10am–5.30pm (except Tues); Sat 8.30am–4pm; Sun 9am–1pm; Butchers open Fri 10am–5.30pm

A small farm shop with a lot of promise, selling beef and lamb, fresh produce and some good larder items. My mother-in-law is a regular here and has been delighted with the meat. My family has tried it too, when visiting, and had some superb pork, plus bacon and beef with masses of flavour. Expense has been spared on the appearance of this place, but do not be put off. Locals are delighted to have such a shop in an area where superstores dominate. Please let me know what you think.

Ossams Hill Farm ⊘

www.ossamshillfarm.co.uk
☎ 01538 304587
✉ Grindon, Leek, Staffordshire
ST13 7TS
🕐 Mon–Sun 9am–5pm

A remarkable farm on National Trust property in Staffordshire, specialising in rare breeds of beef and lamb. The shop is open if there is someone there to man it, so do call ahead if making a special journey. Beef breeds include Red Poll, Aberdeen Angus, Beef Shorthorn and South Devon, all of which are suited to the environment here which includes land registered as a Site of Special Scientific Interest (SSSI). Lamb breeds include Derbyshire Gritstone, Swaledale and North Country mules (which are a cross between a Swaledale or other hill sheep and Blue Faced Leicester, or another type with long wool). All cuts are available from the shop.

Syston Farm Shop ⓎⓈ £

☎ 01400 250000
✉ Syston Park, Grantham,
Lincolnshire **NG32 2BZ**
🕐 Tues–Sat 9.30am–4.30pm;
Sun 10am–4pm

A farm shop and café selling fruit and vegetables in season, including asparagus and strawberries, from the farm (with some PYO). There are also locally baked breads, cheese and homemade dishes. This has been highly recommended by locals – please let me know what you think if you go there.

Wayside Farm Shop

www.waysidefarmshop.co.uk
☎ 01386 830546
✉ 50 Pictshers Hill, Wickhamford,
Evesham, Herefordshire **WR11 6RT**
🕐 **Winter** Mon–Sun 9am–5pm;
Summer Mon–Sun 9am–5.30pm

Well, being in the Vale of Evesham you would expect good produce, and this lovely farm shop does not disappoint, selling vegetables sourced from farms no more than 10 miles away. Everything is picked fresh, within the last 24 hours, it is promised – please feed back to me about this. But regulars say you should expect some wonderful asparagus in season, and amazing soft fruit; plus jams and chutneys made with the local produce, cheeses, fresh-baked bread, ice cream, milk, local cider, scrumpy and beer, also local cut flowers.

The Welbeck Farm Shop

www.thewelbeckfarmshop.co.uk
01909 478725
Welbeck, Worksop,
Nottinghamshire **S80 3LW**
Mon–Sat 10am–5pm;
Sun 10am–4pm

There's a friendly feel to this large and airy farm shop, which is gradually expanding to become one of the best in the country. Part of the Welbeck estate, and run by a young entrepreneur, Joe Parente, it has a well-stocked butchery counter featuring beef and lamb from the estate farms, a wide range of game from the estate shoot, and plenty of vegetables, a proportion of them locally grown (I liked the sacks of Doug's Super Spuds). An artisan bakery has recently opened in another of the Welbeck Farm buildings as part of a new school set up by Joe's mother Alison, offering training in artisan food skills (see Welbeck Bakehouse, page 140). The bread is now sold in the shop alongside a wonderful selection of artisan cheeses including blue Stichelton, a raw milk Stilton-style cheese made by cheesemaker supreme Joe Schneider, also at Welbeck. In spite of all the investment, Joe is keeping prices of the meat and vegetables affordable and has also launched a range of ready-cooked foods, so there really is something here for everyone. Next door there is a café, selling simple lunches, coffee and sandwiches.

▼ FOOD MARKETS

24Carrots

www.24carrots.org.uk
Big Peg Car Park, Warstone Lane,
Birmingham **B18 6JE**
Check website for details

The name provides a clue to the location of this market. There are 20–30 stalls organised by the local residents of the Jewellery Quarter in the heart of Birmingham City Centre, home to over 400 jewellery businesses. The goal of the market is to become a fully self-funding social event benefiting the community. There is fresh local produce grown by farmers, local schools and neighbourhood allotments, as well as the usual baked goods, dairy products and meats typically found at farmers' markets. See website for varied opening dates.

Atherstone Farmers' Market 💷

01827 715341
Market Square, Atherstone,
Warwickshire **CV9 1BB**
Monthly, 3rd Sat 9am–2pm

Locals are urged to use the farmers' market or lose the farmers' market. It would be a great pity if it was lost through lack of use. Generally reports have been good: there are lots of local veg, good cooked foods and nice supplies of local meat and game in season. I'd like to hear a bit more about this market so all feedback welcome.

Brigg Farmers' Market 💷

01724 297356
Brigg Marketplace, Brigg,
North Lincolnshire **DN20 8LD**
Monthly, 4th Sat 9am–3pm

Brigg is a historic market town that hosts this farmers' market every fourth Saturday. Local butchers, grocers and speciality shops alongside the market create a lively atmosphere – no wonder it was awarded Rural Farmers' Market of the Year in 2008. With some of the country's best farmland in the area expect to find fantastic fruit, vegetables, dairy products and meat.

Kings Norton Farmers' Market 💷

**www.kingsnortonfarmersmarket.
org.uk**
07966 434177
The Green, Kings Norton,
Birmingham **B38 8RU**
Monthly, 2nd Sat 9am–2pm

This market's original patent was established in 1616 and later re-established in 2005. The National Farmers' Retail and Markets Association voted this market the West Midland's Farmers' Market of the Year in 2008. Over 25 producers sell meat, fish, plants, fruit, vegetables, organic and non-organic produce as well as Fairtrade items.

Leicester Farmers' Market 💷

**www.leicestershirefoodlinks.
org.uk**
01509 881 386
Humberstone Gate, Leicester
LE1 3PJ
Monthly, 1st Thurs 10am–4pm

Leicester has a Food Links programme that encourages residents to buy local food from farmers. Organisations like this can make a big difference. Due to their lobbying last November the market moved to Humberstone Gate, where it has been a big hit. Apart from selling daft ostrich burgers there are more than 25 stalls selling game, poultry, fish, cheese and fresh apple juice. You can even get a cup of home-made soup and a handmade dog biscuit!

Lincoln Farmers' Market ⓕ

www.lincolnshire.gov.uk
☎ 01522 545711
✉ City Square, Lincoln **LN2 2AA** or
High Street, Lincoln **LN5 7AL** or
Castle Hill, Lincoln **LN1 3AA**
🕐 1st Fri (**City Square**); 3rd Sat
(**Bailgate**) 9am–4pm

Lincoln's farmers' market is held somewhat confusingly three times a month at three different locations. You should find a lot of good produce: not only are there some quality traditional meat suppliers in the area, it is potato and broccoli country, so expect fresh vegetables. I have seen some amazingly lush purple sprouting broccoli here in winter, not a woody stem in sight. There are several other farmers' markets in the county, see www.visitlincolnshire.com/food-and-drink/farmers-markets for dates and venues. The city also has a good covered market with some decent butchers and greengrocers selling locally grown produce. Cornhill covered market is open Monday to Saturday.

Louth Farmers' Market ⓕ

☎ 01507 329568
✉ Corn Market, Louth, Lincolnshire
LN11 9DP
🕐 **Twice monthly** 4th Wed,
2nd Fri 9am–4pm

Lincolnshire Poacher cheese, locally reared lamb, beef, venison, gourmet fishcakes and smoked trout products, plus much more can be found in this thriving market. Louth is an old-fashioned town, not only with a great street market, but a high street packed with good food shops. The superstores long to move into Louth – application for one enormous store was turned down in 2009. Hopefully the local council planners will continue to work to preserve the character of this special place for food.

Moseley Farmers' Market ⓕ

www.moseleyfarmersmarket.
org.uk
☎ 0121 449 3156
✉ Village Green, Moseley,
Birmingham **B13 8HW**
🕐 **Monthly**, 4th Sat 9am–3pm

Moseley has become a very impressive market. There are over 50 stalls offering a variety of tempting produce. Local farms and other specialist producers can be found here, including Lyon Farm mutton and lamb, Hilltop Farm sausages, steamed puddings and tarts from The Pudding Shop, fresh eggs, Hopesay Glebe Farm's organic vegetables and Shropshire and Herefordshire honey.

Oakham Farmers' Market

☎ 01780 722009
✉ Gaol Street, Oakham, Rutland
LE15 6DT
🕐 **Monthly**, 3rd Sat 8am–1pm

Rutland has quite a reputation for food. Around 30 producers attend this market, which has proven popular with locals. A wide variety of produce is available ranging from meat, eggs and cheeses to the more mundane cakes. You can also buy hot food at the market, ready to eat.

DELIS AND SPECIALISTS ▼

Ceci Paolo ⭕ @ ⦿

www.cecipaolo.com
☎ 01531 632976
✉ 21 High Street, Ledbury,
Herefordshire **HR8 1DS**
🕐 Mon–Sat 9.30am–5pm

Expensive it may be, but this famed Ledbury deli sells nothing but high quality produce. Admittedly, much is imported from Europe, but if you live in Herefordshire and want to indulge in a love for Italian ingredients, Ceci Paolo is a port in a storm. The range is vast – you might find Roscoff onions and garlic from Brittany, or Italian tomatoes, Muscat grapes and red peppers. Charcuterie, oils, chocolates (including the amazing Zotter) and artisan cheeses are always in stock. This, by the way, is not just a food shop – lighting, clothes and furniture are also on sale.

Comestibles Delicatessens ⭕ @ ⦿

☎ 01522 520010
✉ 82 Bailgate, Lincoln
LN1 3AR
🕐 Mon–Sat 9am–5pm

Julie Morris's deli is a good place to buy the much-admired, subtle but strong-flavoured, local cheddar-style cheese, Lincolnshire Poacher, and another called Cote Hill Blue, a very rustic-looking blue-veined cheese made locally by Michael and Mary Davenport with milk from their own herd. I also found Bowland cheese here, a sweet concoction of Lancashire cheese, apple and raisins coated in cinnamon (it shouldn't be nice, but it is). The range of deli foods also includes salads, home-made cheese tarts and olives.

A.W. Curtis & Sons ✪ @ ❂ ✦

www.curtisoflincoln.com
☎ 01522 527212
✉ Long Leys Road, Lincoln
LN1 1DX
🕐 Mon–Sat 8.30am–5pm

A truly traditional grocer that has 21 shops in Lincoln itself and more in the region. Combining a bakery, butchery and general stores, Curtis & Sons do sticky buns and custard tarts alongside Linconshire sausages and bacon chops (made with local pork) and good, honest root vegetables from the city. Visit their shops for the plum bread, ham and pork pies. You cannot help but celebrate their survival in superstore-dominated Britain, and also admire their loyalty to local fresh foods. See website for details of their other branches and their mobile shops.

Delilah Fine Foods ✪ @ ❂

www.delilahfinefoods.co.uk
☎ 0115 948 4461
✉ 15 Middle Pavement, Nottingham
NG1 7DX
🕐 Mon–Fri 8am–7pm; Sat
9am–7pm; Sun 11am–5pm

Nottingham's acknowledged favourite café-deli is run by Sangita Tryner. The shop has a small kitchen at the back where Tryner and her team prepare tapas and frittatas for customers to take away or eat at the bar in the shop. Added to this is a good range of deli foods, including over 200 cheeses, 50 different types of charcuterie and some useful store cupboard items. Loose olives from Olives et Al (see page 325), Alderton ham (which is excellent), Stichelton cheese made nearby at Welbeck (see page 145) and Dolly Smith's Indian pickles (which, again, I can highly recommend) are among her bestsellers.

Fresh Basil

www.freshbasil.co.uk
☎ 01773 828882
✉ 23 Strutt Street, Belper,
Derbyshire **DE56 1UN**
🕐 Mon–Sat 6.30am–4pm

Housed in a converted former fire station, they have a range of over 60 cheeses and there are continental meats, home-made salads and marinated olives and pâtés. There is a real focus on locally sourced foods and they try as far as possible to purchase from small independent farmers and growers in the vicinity. They also have a small café serving light meals, snacks, tea and coffee.

Gringley Gringo ⬤ @

www.gringleygringo.com
☎ 01909 808515
✉ Mayflower Cottage, Clumber
Park National Park, Near Worksop,
Nottinghamshire **S80 3BQ**

Lovely chilli sauces made with home-grown produce at
Mayflower Cottage, inside the boundary of the National
Trust's Clumber Park. Into the pot go the freshest chilli
peppers, tomatoes and onions, to make a sauce that is a
worthy winner of one of the National Trust's 2010 Fine Farm
Produce awards. Gringly Gringo is run by Debbie Porter and
Sarah Priestly who keep the carbon footprint low, sourcing
all other ingredients locally where possible. Contact for
stockists, or buy from National Trust shops at
www.nationaltrust.org.uk. Home delivery available.

The Handmade Scotch Egg Company ⬤ @

www.handmadescotcheggs.co.uk
☎ 01885 490520
✉ The Old Cookhouse,
5 The Hop Pocket, Bishop's Frome,
Herefordshire **WR6 5BT**

This company has become a favourite with regulars at
farmers' markets and now supplies a growing list of
speciality outlets. 'Reassuringly old-fashioned' is the
company's motto and that is exactly what they are. Using
only free-range pork and eggs, there are around 30 varieties
and these are also available online. See website for details.

Leverton & Halls Deli ⬤

☎ 0121 451 1246
✉ 218 Maryvale Road,
Bournville, Birmingham **B30 1PJ**
🕐 Tues–Fri 8.30am–5.30pm;
Sat 8am–4pm

Dee Leverton was born in the city and is devoted to her
stylish organic shop and Fairtrade café serving terrific,
eco-friendly bacon and eggs and tasty home-made food.
You can buy fresh local and organic vegetables, heavenly
breads from nearby Cotteridge Bakery and general organic
groceries. In spring 2010 the shop underwent a
refurbishment with funding from Birmingham City Council.

Louth Wholefood Co-Op Ltd ●

www.louthwholefoodcoop.co.uk
☎ 01507 602411
✉ 7–9 Eastgate, Louth, Lincolnshire **LN11 9NB**
🕐 Mon–Fri 9am–5.30pm;
Sat 9am–5pm

An earnest shop started by friends who wanted to feed their children better food. It is also a workers' cooperative, the first of its type to be started in the UK. The range on sale is large, with plenty of organic and Fairtrade foods – honeys, dried fruit and nuts, wholegrain breads, chocolate and much, much more.

Nima Delicatessen

☎ 0121 442 4205
✉ 103 Alcester Road, Birmingham **B13 8DD**
🕐 Mon–Fri 9am–7pm;
Sat 9am–6pm; Sun 10am–6pm

Salvation for food lovers in this area with few food shops is at hand in Ziba and Hamid Asl's deli, selling everything from dried morels to quince paste, nibbed pistachios to fresh yeast. Seventeen varieties of coffee perch above Mr Asl's head as he sits serenely reading at the counter. His shop typifies global Birmingham.

The Pickled Village ⌂ @ ●

www.thepickledvillage.co.uk
☎ 01780 450774
✉ 15 Main Street, Bulwick, Northamptonshire **NN17 3DY**
🕐 Tues–Fri 9am–5pm;
Sat 9.30am–4.30pm

Here you can buy tangy, perfectly made marmalades in half a dozen different citrus fruit combinations, made by Camille Ortega McLean in small batches. All are sold in her quirky Northamptonshire shop as well as via mail order. I liked the 'Undecided Breakfast' marmalade, made with three different fruits and a dash of booze, but also the 'Refreshing Breakfast' marmalade with its liquid texture and thin-cut peel. The shop also sells home-made cakes and sausage rolls. A fun place to visit – tell me what you think.

Rizos Greek Speciality Shop ⌂ @ ●

www.rizosonline.co.uk
☎ 01562 863204
✉ 84 New Road, Kidderminster, Worcestershire **DY10 1NT**

This online shop is the place to buy the best Cretan oregano, olive oil and olives, wonderful Cretan 'Minoan' honey, Zanae tomato paste, dried white gigantes beans (which are indeed very large), plus other spices, sea salt and the most fragrant dried thyme and lavender in little sacks, which is used to flavour roasted lamb. You can even buy a can of horta (highly nutritious, cooked wild greens).

Royston's Deli

`www.roystonsdeli.co.uk
☎ 01507 604143
✉ 75 Eastgate, Louth, Lincolnshire
LN11 9PL
🕐 Tues–Fri 9am–5pm; Sat 9am–4pm

When visiting this deli you will be hit by a waft of home cooking. In the kitchens at the back of the shop the team is working hard to produce a great selection of home-made ready meals, pastries and breads. Their baking contains free-range eggs, the flour is organic and the rich butter is from Longly farm. They endeavour to use local products wherever possible. The meat in the deli is from the local butcher Meridian Meats, and the fruit and veg are grown locally by owner Chris's girlfriend's grandmother, and so are very seasonal. As well as the wide selection of local products they also sell a variety of fine delicatessen foods from around the world, such as Spanish olive oils and vinegars.

Sealwood

www.sealwood.com
☎ 01283 760841
✉ Sealwood Lane, Linton,
Derbyshire **DE126PA**

Caroline Royston and Andrew Gray grow vegetables and salad leaves for a popular local delivery scheme for which they also source a number of foods from local producers . Meat is from Woodhouse Farm or Manor Organic Farm; eggs are from Mulberry Farm; milk is from Lubcloud organic dairy; there are honeys from beekeeper Harry Cook or from the First Honey Cooperative; cheese from Innes; and bread from Smithards bakery in Ashby de la Zouch.

Tree Harvest ⊙⊚⊘

www.tree-harvest.com
☎ 01531 650764
✉ The Granary, Lintridge Farm,
Bromsberrow Heath, Ledbury,
Herefordshire **HR8 1PB**
🕐 Mon–Fri 9am–5pm;
Sat 9am–1pm

An online delivery service that began as a tree nursery and has now extended into selling a plethora of ethically sourced, plant-related items including an astonishing variety of culinary herbs, dried fruit, nuts, bee pollen, floral waters and dried flowers. Note that not all the items in the catalogue are for culinary use.

Coopers Family Butchers Ltd

www.coopersfamilybutchers.
co.uk
🕿 0121 526 2181
✉ 195 Walsall Road, Darlaston,
Wednesbury **WS10 9SW**
🕒 Tues–Thurs 7am–4.30pm;
Wed 7am–3.30pm;
Fri-Sat 6am–4.30pm

Here's a wonderful place, the kind of butcher our grandparents and great-grandparents would have known, and that makes imaginative use of cheap cuts, selling polony (red-coloured, hot-smoked sausage), faggots, black pudding, brawn and even chittlerlings (pork casings). It is the oldest butcher in Darlaston and remains devoted to the great meat dishes of the Black Country, including cooked meats, lovely chicken and ham or game pies, and traditional and flavoured pork sausages.

The Country Victualler Alderton Hams

www.alderton.co.uk
🕿 01636 636465
✉ Winkburn Hall, Newark,
Nottinghamshire **NG22 8PQ**

Richard Craven Smith Milnes has developed a wonderful ham with a juicy, delicately flavoured centre and marmalade smeared on the outside. The hams are salted then partially steamed before being roasted in bread ovens. Andrew Cook is in charge of the whole operation, producing some very accomplished results. Game terrines and chicken liver pâté are also available. All available via online mail order.

A. Dales & Sons

🕿 01507 602698
✉ 120 Eastgate, Louth,
Lincolnshire **LN11 9AA**
🕒 Tues–Wed 8am–4pm;
Thurs, Sat 8am–1pm; Fri 8am–5pm

It is unusual to see a poulterer in any town, but Louth, with its astonishing number of independent butcher's shops, is a likely place to find one. A. Dales & Sons was opened in 1896 by the present owner Peter Dales's great grandfather. All chickens are sourced locally, there are game birds on offer, when in season, and always a selection of fresh-looking muddy vegetables.

Dukeshill Ham Company ✿ @ ✪

www.dukeshillham.co.uk
☎ 0845 3700129
✉ Lodge Park, Hortonwood 30,
Telford **TF1 7ET**

A good forward-looking company that came to my attention when I sampled one of their potted ham hocks, an inexpensive terrine of perfectly cured, delicate-tasting ham set in jelly. Since then I have tried curer Neale Hollingsworth's hams, which are made using naturally reared pork, plus the bacon chops and streaky bacon chops. What I like about this online company is how they have spotted the need to offer cheaper cuts, but also the necessity of sticking to their principles. Faggots, roasted hocks and Cumberland sausages are also available along with artisan cheeses and other deli items.

Elite Meats ✿ @ ✪

www.elitemeats.co.uk
☎ 01522 523500
✉ 89 Bailgate, Lincoln
LN1 3AR
🕐 Mon–Sat 8am–5.30pm

Elite Meats sells Lincolnshire dry-cured bacon, magnificent ribs of well-hung Red beef, handmade sausages, game birds, tripe and onions and a variety of eggs including hen, quail, duck and goose. Other must-try items include haslet (a loaf made with chunky sausage meat, chopped liver and onion) and the pies made in Ruskington. Dripping and lard are rendered on the premises and there's a rotisserie, making it possible to take home a ready-roasted chicken. Lincolnshire plum bread, made in Navenby, is also on sale.

Goodman's Geese ✿ @ ✪

www.goodmansgeese.co.uk
☎ 01299 896272
✉ Walsgrove Farm, Great Witley,
Worcestershire **WR6 6JJ**
🕐 End Sept–Dec, Fri 9.30am–5.30pm

Running as a seasonal business since the early 1960's, it caters more or less for the Christmas market. Judy Goodman's birds are revered by chefs, critics and the farm's many private customers. They testify that Goodman's free-range system, additive-free diet and, above all, passion for her farm is evident in the flavour of the meat. Her geese are also available at London butchers M. Moen & Sons and Mackens Brothers Ltd (see page 80), Harvey Nichols' food halls and elsewhere – see website for stockists. Nothing, however, beats a personal visit.

A. H. Griffiths Butchers

01548 872141

11 Bullring, Ludlow, Shropshire
SY7 0LB

Mon–Fri 7.30am–5pm;
Sat 7.30am–4pm

One of several butchers in Ludlow, a town that, in spite of having a large supermarket, has retained its high-street food shops and holds a huge and well attended food festival every September. Griffiths sell, as you might expect, the best meat from the Marches (Welsh border counties) – exceptional native beef and lamb, naturally reared pork and chicken. A very traditional butchers in every way, their bacon and pies are beloved of locals and the black pudding is exceptional. There is another branch in Leintwardine.

Huntsham Farm ⊙ @ ⊘

www.huntsham.com

01600 890296

Ross-on-Wye, Herefordshire
HR9 6JN

Richard Vaughan's beef, especially his Middle White pork, is well known to many of the best UK chefs. Reared in a specialist programme, the reputation of his Middle White has elevated pork from being a dull meat to find on a menu, to something ranking alongside the best sirloin (which he also sells). Happily, he supplies private customers by mail order. It is not cheap, but he will send you a lot of cuts in a box, plus offal, maybe with sausages. Get the freezer ready.

Jacksons Butchers Ltd

01507 602797

118 Eastgate, Louth,
Lincolnshire **LN11 9QE**

Mon–Fri 8am–5pm;
Sat 8am–1pm

This is the land of some unusual, almost forgotten, English meat specialities and there are few better places to buy Lincolnshire chine (cured pork shoulder, boned and stuffed with parsley) or haslet (a well -seasoned meatloaf made from sausage meat, liver and onion which can be utterly good or rather revolting). Jackson's version is a marvel and a must-buy, however, backed up by the fact that he has been Lincolnshire Butcher of the Year on five separate occasions since 1990. Handmade sausages, stuffings and pork pies with beautiful crisp pastry are also made on the premises. The bacon, smoked over hickory chips, is also excellent.

Long Horn Beef Company ⊙ @ ⦿

www.thelonghornbeefcompany.
co.uk
⊙ 01949 850 993
✉ Whatton Manor Farm, Whatton
in the Vale, Nottinghamshire
NG13 9EX

Whatton Manor is a thoroughbred stud farm (they bred Eagle Mountain, the second placed horse in the English Derby a few years back). They also breed Long Horn cattle and have recently started selling locally. The cows feast on the same pasture as the racehorses. Between 24–30 months' old the cattle are slaughtered just 2 miles away and hung for a minimum of 24 days. You can buy 12 kg boxes for £100 and the venture has been such a success that owner, Ed Player, has upped the stock from 12 to 25 beasts in his first year of operation. They will deliver, but ring first to see what is available.

Meridian Meats ⊙ @ ⦿

www.meridianmeatsshop.co.uk
⊙ 01507 603357
✉ 108 Eastgate, Louth,
Lincolnshire **LN11 9AA**
🕐 Mon–Wed, Fri 8am–5pm;
Thurs 8am–1pm; Sat 8am–3pm

Meridian Meats sells some superb extra-mature beef. The Longhorn and Dexter is raised on their own farm in nearby Tetford and then transported to a local abattoir. It is then hung for a minimum of 21 days. This shop has a very good reputation and the Longhorn beef was recently voted the best in the UK by *Country Life* magazine. All the meat is fully traceable. If you require a specific breed, ring first or email from the website.

J. W. Mettrick & Son ⊙ @ ⦿

www.mettricksbutchers.co.uk
⊙ 01457 852239
✉ 20 High Street, Glossop, High
Peak, Derbyshire **SK13 8BH**
🕐 Mon–Fri 8am–5pm;
Sat 8am–4.30pm

A previous winner of the BBC Radio 4 Food & Farming Award for Best Retailer, John Mettrick is not only a fantastic traditional butcher selling the best locally reared meat, but (unusually) the owner of an abattoir. His is one of the last remaining small-scale butchers in Britain buying local livestock from nearby farms and carrying out all processing himself. This total control of his stock ensures that he is selling meat of the highest standard that is 100 per cent traceable. Beef is Aberdeen Angus cross from farms in the Peak District and Cheshire that have supplied Mettrick's for 20 years. There is High Peak lamb from a local producer group, pork is from Derbyshire farms and the chicken is barn-reared and excellent value. There is also an efficient online shop.

Muckleton Meats

www.muckletonmeats.com
☎ 01939 251128
✉ Bank Farm, Muckleton, Telford,
Shropshire **TF6 6RQ**
🕐 Mon–Fri 8am–5pm;
Sat 8am–4.30pm

Since 1994 Bank Farm has been breeding Gloucester Old
Spot pigs. Reared as naturally as possible in arks, these pigs
are free of additives, antibiotics and growth promoters. As a
result, the characteristically delicate taste of the Old Spot is
preserved in the end product. Their online shop offers every
possible cut, but the pork belly is particularly good as the
thick layer of fat makes for succulent meat and wonderfully
crunchy crackling.

Northfield Farm

www.northfieldfarm.com
☎ 01664 474271
✉ Whissendine Lane, Cold Overton,
Oakham, Rutland **LE15 7QF**
🕐 Mon 9am–4pm;
Tues–Fri 8am–5pm; Sun 10am–3pm

Following redundancy, former City banker Jan McCourt
started Northfield Farm in 1997. Specialising in Dexter and
Longorn Ccattle, as well as local cheeses (he's in the heart of
Stilton country), the business has thrived and people rave
about the beef in particular. It's also available at Borough
Market in London (see page 42).

Packington Poultry

www.packingtonpoultry.co.uk
☎ 01283 711547
✉ Blakenhall Park, Bar Lane,
Barton-under-Needwood,
Burton upon Trent, Staffordshire
DE13 8AJ

They specialise in slow-reared chickens, fed
a natural diet, which are free to roam and peck around the
field of this Staffordshire Farm. The chickens are a squat-
shaped breed, with plenty of breast meat, now with a loyal
following that rank their flavour and texture to be among
the best. These chickens are widely available in London.
Call to find your nearest stockist.

The Parson's Nose

www.parsonsnose.co.uk
☎ 01886 880617
✉ Grove Court, Green Hill,
Nr Suckley, Worcestershire
WR6 5EJ
🕐 Tues–Fri 10am–4pm

Andrew Dobson is passionate about animal welfare and his
farm shop has a very good reputation with locals, who are
devotees. The pork and black pudding, sausages and superb
well-hung beef are bestsellers. He visits farmers' markets in
the area, as well as travelling further afield to the farmers'
markets in London.

Pink Pig Organics 🔆 @ 🍃

www.pinkpigfarm.co.uk
☎ 01724 844466
✉ Holme Hall, Holme, Scunthorpe,
Lincolnshire **DN16 3RE**
🕐 Mon–Fri 9.30am–5pm;
Sat 9.30am–5.30pm;
Sun 10am–4pm

An organic pig farm with a shop attached, run by a cheerful team who are very proud of their products. Specialities include (of course) fresh pork and especially the sausages, home-cured bacon and ham. There are other good things in the shop, bought from local producers, including free-range chickens and a wide range of seasonal organic vegetables.

Robert Foster & Son Ltd 🔆 🍃

☎ 01522 523369
✉ 111 Monks Road, Lincoln
LN2 5HT
🕐 Mon–Tues, Thurs–Fri 7.30am–
5pm; Wed 7.30am–12pm;
Sat 7.30am–1pm

This is the place to come for the famous Lincolnshire Red beef, a local breed that is matured on the bone for at least 15 days. This is a good traditional butcher's shop with a great range of fresh pork, lamb and poultry, mostly locally sourced. The over-the-counter service is helpful – you can always ask how long a joint needs cooking in the oven or what you can do with one of the cheaper cuts.

Rossiters Organic Butchers 🍃

☎ 0121 458 1598
✉ 247 Mary Vale Road, Bournville,
Birmingham **B30 1PN**
🕐 Tues, Thurs–Fri 8am–5.30pm;
Wed 8am–1pm; Sat 8am–4pm

This mainly organic butcher's shop forms part of a small foody enclave in picture-perfect Bournville, the old Cadbury workers' village on the outskirts of Birmingham. All meat is sourced from farms in Warwickshire. The majority is certified organic, but slightly cheaper, free-range non-organic sausages are also on sale. I was especially impressed by Steve Rossiter's dry-cured bacon.

Seldom Seen Farm 🔆 🍃 🐓 🍂

www.seldomseenfarm.co.uk
☎ 0116 259 6626
✉ Billesdon, Leicestershire
LE17 9FA
🕐 Mon–Sat 9.30am–5pm
(Dec only)

This farm has been going for 30 years, rearing free-range geese and turkeys just for the festive season. All their efforts go into the month of December: over 4000 geese and 700 turkeys are all reared to mature at Christmas. They do a highly regarded and extremely succulent three-bird roast (a boned pheasant inside a boned chicken inside a boned goose) and there are other seasonal things, too. In summer and autumn you can visit and pick your own raspberries and blackberries. Added to the poultry production, they make mince pies and even sell holly wreaths. The service is very personal and the Symington's, who own the farm, insist on speaking to each and every customer directly to get precise requirements regarding mouths to feed and weight of bird. That really is service.

Standley's Barn Farm

www.standleysbarn.com
www.nationaltrust.org.uk
☎ 01332 862762
✉ Calke Abbey Estate Shop, Ticknall, Derby **DE73 1LE**
🕐 Mon–Sun 10.30am–5pm

Beef from traditional breeds, reared by Joe and Will Hallifield at their farm within the lovely Calke Abbey Estate (which is National Trust owned). The Hallifields' cross their Sussex and Red Lincoln cows with a 'stabiliser' bull to keep the cattle small so they do not overgraze, producing meat that has a very traditional, small grain. A 2009 winner of the National Trust's Fine Farm Produce award, the meat is sold in the abbey's shop but also from the farm on Fridays and Saturdays – call ahead.

D. W. Wall & Son Butchers 🌣 🖉

www.wallsbutchers.co.uk
☎ 01588 672308
✉ Wilton House, Corvedale Road, Craven Arms, Shropshire **SY7 9NL**
🕐 Mon–Tues, Thurs–Fri 7.15am–5pm; Wed, Sat 7.15am–1pm

Walls is Shropshire's only accredited rare-breeds butcher and one with a great reputation. Family-owned and run, they source beef, pork and lamb from farmers who specialise in traditional species. Expect to find Red Poll, Irish Moiled and White Park beef; Kerry, Soay and Castlemilk Morit lamb or mutton; and British Lop and Large Black pork. This is a place that believes strongly in farm diversity. Ring if you are after a particular breed, but it's worth visiting on the off chance.

Baines Bakery and Tea Shop ○●

☎ 01572 823317
✉ 3 High Street West, Uppingham,
Rutland **LE15 9QB**
🕐 Tues–Fri 10am–6.30pm;
Sat 9am–5pm; Sun 11am–4pm

The Baines family have been running the shop since 1867 so they must be doing something right. They use strong, untreated flour for the bread and pork from their own home-reared pigs for the sausage rolls. Of particular note is their home-made almond paste, which has a very good local reputation. They also sell a selection of teas and chutneys. Contact for delivery.

Hambleton Bakery ○

www.hambletonbakery.co.uk
☎ 01572 768936/01572 812995
(home delivery)
✉ Cottesmore road, Exton,
Oakham, Rutland **LE15 8AN**

Julian Carter is a master baker, the latest in a family of bakers from Bath and Liverpool that go back generations. He describes his bread as artisan – made by hand – and is especially proud of his Hambleton sourdough and 'local' bread made using a fermentation process that takes 24 hours, and baked in a wood-fired oven. Other specialities include griddle-cooked English muffins (the yeast type – not the cupcake version), wholemeal, walnut and fruit loaves. The bakery comes highly recommended by a very discerning local cook, Julia Moore, who lives in Rutland and is one of this guide's most trusted contributors. Home delivery available.

I Should Cocoa ●●

www.i-shouldcocoa.co.uk
☎ 01773 880181
✉ 2 Strutt Street, Belper,
Derbyshire **DE56 1UN**
🕐 Mon–Sat 9am–5pm

The handmade chocolates in this Derbyshire shop manage to cross the spectrum from very traditional (rose creams, praline creams, strawberry ganache) to modern, where you will find some more extreme mixology going on. Customers rate the peanut butter and jam-filled milk chocolates, and the jasmine-tea centres dipped in dark chocolate – and the novelty-shaped chocolates make great presents. You can also drink spice-infused hot chocolate in the café or eat a non-chocolatey light lunch.

Pocklington's Bakery ⊕ £

www.pocklingtons-bakery.co.uk
☎ 01507 600180
✉ 2 Market Place, Louth,
Lincolnshire **LN11 9NR**
🕐 Mon–Sat 8am–4pm

A good, traditional bakers' shop, run by Christopher and Tina Pocklington, in a town packed with high street shops (recently threatened by the spectre of Louth's first – and very controversial – superstore). There are three other branches, in Ashby, Grimsby and Scunthorpe. Pocklington's Lincolnshire Plum bread is famous and is also available from many local shops. This is the kind of bakery where you can buy a beautifully made bloomer or good, crusty farmhouse white baked that morning. Added to all this temptation is the fact that the Pocklington family bake using flour milled from wheat grown in the Lincolnshire Wolds.

True Loaf Bakery ⊕ @ ✿

www.trueloafbakery.co.uk
☎ 01652 640177
✉ Mount Pleasant Windmill, North Cliff Road, Kirton-in-Lindsay,
Lincolnshire **DN21 4NH**
🕐 Tues–Sun 10am–5pm

Mervyn and Marie-Christine Austin are both millers, running the Mount Pleasant Windmill where they grind grain between stones, and also bakers. The flour is organic and the 30 or so different breads, which are baked in a wood-fired oven, are wonderful. The numerous cakes (also served in an adjoining tea room) come highly recommended. You can also buy wholefoods in the shop. Look out for the sourdough pain levain, the seeded breads (choose between flax and walnut, dactylla-sesame and poppy seed) and the herb fougasse. Mail order available.

Welbeck Bakehouse

www.welbeckbakehouse.com
☎ 01909 500129
✉ Lower Motor Yard, Welbeck, Worksop, Nottinghamshire
S80 3LR
🕐 Mon–Sat 10am–5pm;
Sun 10am–4pm

Bread handmade to a very high standard in a newly created bakehouse where there are two wood-fired ovens. Sold in the Welbeck Farm Shop (see page 124), the bread is made just a few hundred yards away in a beautiful old building within the confines of Britain's only School of Artisan Food. Founded by Alison Parente, a keen baker who is passionate about bread, you can expect to find perfectly made rye and white sourdoughs, fruit breads, 'Welbeck' brown made with malthouse flour, ciabatta and seeded pagnotta. There are great expectations for this new bakery.

Ansteys of Worcester ○ @ ◐

www.ansteys.com
☎ 01905 820232
✉ Broomhall Farm, Worcester
WR5 2NT

Colin Anstey's team make a number of cheeses, which you can buy online. Anstey began making cheese 24 years ago, but the main cheesemaker is Debbie Hopkins, responsible for the popular Worcester White, a cheddar-type, and Double Worcester, a variation on Double Gloucester. These cheeses are made with pasteurised milk, but the dairy also makes a good, raw-milk, hard-textured goats' cheese. You can also buy biscuits and pickles and add them to your hamper. See the comprehensive website.

Appleby's Cheese

www.applebyscheese.co.uk
☎ 01948 840387
✉ Monnkhouse, Broadoak,
Shrewsbury, Shropshire **SY4 3HP**

The late Lucy Appleby was one of the most accomplished cheesemakers of her generation who took a bold and ultimately successful stand against attempts to have unpasteurised cheesemaking banned in the UK. She fought a battle against the standardisation of artisan cheese and, in particular, her own Appleby's Cheshire. Now Appleby's unpasteurised Cheshire and Double Gloucester is sold throughout the UK. This is my daughter's favourite cheese and although it is available in M&S and Waitrose, don't let that put you off. The cheese, which has a firm, slightly crumbly texture and rich hazelnut tint to the flavour, is a marvel and both stores should be applauded for stocking it.

Bluebell Dairy

www.bluebelldairy.co.uk
☎ 01332 673924
✉ Brunswood Farm, Locko Road,
Derby **DE21 7BV**
🕐 Mon, Wed–Sun 10.30am–
5.30pm

The Brown family has been farming on the outskirts of Derby for more than 60 years. Three years ago they started making ice cream and latterly opened a farm shop where they attempt to source everything within a 30-mile radius. Local cheeses, eggs and some farm-grown beef is all on offer. It has proved to be a real winner with locals and this year the Browns were finalists in the Farmer of the Year category in the BBC Radio 4 Food & Farming Awards – a real accolade. Visit if you can.

The Cheese Shop, Louth ⊙ @ ⊘

www.thecheeseshoplouth.co.uk
☎ 01507 600407
✉ 110 Eastgate, Louth, Lincolnshire
LN11 9AA
🕐 Mon–Sat 9am–5pm

Paul Adams's shop has a very good reputation, both locally and nationally, selling a range of nicely matured artisan cheeses from all over Europe. A few more British cheeses on offer would make this an excellent shop; it would also be nice to find some unusual continental cheeses as those they do sell can be a bit run-of-the-mill. Having said that, this is still a very good shop and Adams really knows what he is doing when it comes to selling a cheese in good condition. Do support him.

The Cheese Society ⊙ @ ⊘

www.thecheesesociety.co.uk
☎ 01522 511003
✉ 1 St Martin's Lane, Lincoln
LN2 1HY
🕐 Mon–Sat 10am–4.30pm

A café-restaurant and shop with a smallish counter packed with an astonishing number of cheeses. Many are locally made, but there is also a wide range of British and continental artisan cheeses. Look out, of course, for the delicious Lincolnshire Poacher (see page 144), a cheddar with a more authentic flavour than most cheddar made the world over. Kate O'Meara brings cheese fans together here either to buy cheese or sit and eat a dish with cheese – I loved the Lincolnshire cauliflower and cheddar soup and the blue cheese risotto. Other good local cheeses include Cotehill Blue (a new cheese with much promise) and Billy's Best (an organic goats' cheese made by Patty Phillips).

Colston Bassett Store @ ⊘

www.colstonbassettstore.com
☎ 01949 823717
✉ Church Gate, Colston Bassett,
Nottinghamshire **NG12 3FE**
🕐 Tues–Fri 10am–5pm;
Sat 10am–4.30pm;
Sun 10.30am–4pm

This is a village shop that has undergone a revamp in the village where the best Stilton cheese is still made, Colston Bassett. Here you can also buy traditional bacon, sliced in front of you on the shop's original bacon slicing machine. The Colston Bassett cheese is on sale along with some others and there's bread from Turners, which is also in the village. Pies are made by Mrs Elizabeth King, a famous pork pie-maker in nearby Cropwell Butler. Vegetables from local farms are also on sale and there's a restaurant and café next door.

Cropwell Bishop Creamery

www.cropwellbishopstilton.com

☎ 0115 989 2350

✉ Cropwell Bishop, Nottingham,
Nottinghamshire **NG12 3BQ**

🕑 Mon–Fri 9am–5pm

The Skailes family are third-generation Stilton cheesemakers.
They employ local people and have a knack of hanging on
to the people they employ, some having been with them for
more than 25 years, a sign of a good company. Cropwell is a
good robust Stilton that has many fans. The creamery
welcomes personal callers.

The Dairy House

www.thedairyhouse.co.uk

☎ 01544 318815

✉ Whitehill Park, Weobley,
Herefordshire **HR4 8Q**

Four organic farms in Herefordshire have collaborated to
produce the highest quality milk from a combination of
Friesian and Jersey dairy cattle. They produce milk, but
perhaps more significant is the skill they use to make some
of the most sublime cream cheeses, yoghurt and cream I
have tasted – proof that the more care you take with the
welfare of your cattle, the better the milk and cream will
taste. Their products are now widely available, contact them
(or see their website) and they will locate your nearest
supplier or recommend a mail order service.

Dennetts Ice Cream

www.dennetts.co.uk

☎ 01522 511447

✉ 3 Bailgate, Lincoln **LN1 3AE**

🕑 **Easter–Dec** Mon–Sun 10am–
sunset; **Jan–Easter** Fri–Mon
11am–5.30pm

Robin Dennett's grandfather began making ice cream over
75 years ago using cream from his own herd of Friesian
cattle, and the family still run the old ice cream parlour in
Lincoln's city centre, proudly scooping from a choice of over
36 flavours into cones for delighted visitors. The ice cream is
made with real dairy cream and natural flavours, but sadly –
as with so many dairy ice creams – there are the usual
emulsifiers binding it. You can't taste them, and the ice
cream tastes good per se, but I wish they were not there all
the same. On a lighter note, these ice creams are freshly
made and tempting – including cherry, pistachio, orange
and liquorice and, of course, a sumptuous chocolate.

Leicestershire Handmade Cheese Company

www.leicestershirecheese.co.uk
☎ 01455 213863
✉ Sparkenhoe Farm, Main Road
Upton, Nuneaton, Warwickshire
CV13 6JX
🕐 Fri 8am–12pm

David and Jo Clarke started making Sparkenhoe, a traditional Red Leicester cheese in November 2005. They use the milk produced from their own herd of naturally reared cows, which is pumped straight from the parlour directly into the vats in the creamery, ready to make the cheese. The cheese is made authentically using unpasteurised milk and annatto, a natural plant dye obtained from a South American bush. This gives the cheese its wonderful red colour, but does not alter the taste in any way. Matured for four months, the end product is tangy and creamy with a versatile texture, excellent on its own or used in recipes.

Lightwood Cheese ❶ ❷ ❸

www.lightwoodcheese.co.uk
☎ 01905 333468
✉ Heath Grange Farm, Lower
Broadheath, Worcester **WR2 6RW**

Handmade and using unpasteurised milk, Lightwood cheeses have a good reputation but I'd like more feedback. The company also has the admirable policy of not doing business with supermarkets so they rely on selling at farmers' markets, farm shops and delis (see website for a list of stockists). For that reason they are worth supporting. They encourage farm visits, where you can taste the cheese before buying, but do ring first.

Lincolnshire Poacher ❶ @ ❷

www.lincolnshirepoacher
cheese.com
☎ 01507 466987
✉ F. W. Read & Sons Ltd, Ulceby
Grange, Alford, Lincolnshire
LN13 0HE
🕐 Mon, Wed, Sat, 7am–1pm;
Tues, Thurs–Fri 7am–4.30pm

One of the best cheddars in the UK, but not made in the south-west. Lincolnshire Poacher ranks among my group of pet 'orphans' – foods that are outside producer group families (in this case the West Country Farmhouse Cheeses), but are just as good, if not better. Anyway, this is a great cheese, mellow and only gently acidic, yet powerfully fruit-hued, smooth-textured and fragrant. It wins endless prizes – quite rightly – and is made by Simon and Tim Jones.

Mousetrap Cheese ❶ @ ✪

www.mousetrapcheese.
streamlinenettrial.co.uk

☎ 01568 720307
✉ The Pleck, Monkland, Hereford
HR6 9DB
🕐 Mon–Sun 10.30am–5.30pm

Mousetrap is an interesting outfit. They make their own Herefordhire cheese by hand at the creamery where you can watch it being made and make purchases (see website for details). They also have three shops in the area selling a wide range of cheeses, as well as their own. Creamy and very crumbly, all their cheese is made using unpasteurised milk. A great business and well worth a visit.

September Organics ❶ @ ✪

www.september-organic.co.uk
☎ 01544 312910
✉ Unit 5, Whitehill Park, Weobley,
Herefordshire HR4 8QE

This is a very unusual artisan ice cream company that can deliver its special organic ice cream from the dairy in Herefordshire to your door (minimum order is six 500 ml cartons). Double cream, eggs and much of the fruit is sourced locally. Flavours include brown bread, apple and cinnamon, honey and ginger, elderflower, strawberry and butterscotch. Having tasted many of these, I can recommend them highly. Contact them for stockists.

Stichelton Dairy ❶ @

www.stichelton.co.uk
☎ 01623 844883
✉ Collingthwaite Farm, Cuckney,
Mansfield, Nottinghamshire
NG20 9NP

Joe Schneider is a native New Yorker with a passion for making cheese. He and Randolph Hodgson of Neal's Yard Dairy got together to produce Stichelton, a cheese that is a Stilton in everything but name – and far superior in the minds of many. This is a wonder: creamy, delicately veined and packed with bittersweet tones. As it ripens, the fruit in the flavour increases, sometimes developing a rich apricot-coloured juice on the rind. Joe is a true artisan and his cheese a wonder. I cannot recommend this cheese highly enough. Buy online or see website for stockists.

▼ FISH AND SEAFOOD

Igloo Seafoods ●

☎ 01507 603933
✉ 15 New Street, Louth,
Lincolnshire **LN11 9PT**
🕐 Mon–Sat 9am–5pm

Lesley Tyler's father was a fish merchant working from Grimsby beach and all the fish (which is superbly fresh) is bought from the nearby port. The haddock is smoked with turmeric by Lesley's brothers and on the day of my visit there was a good variety on display including grey mullet, mackerel, mussels, plaice, sprats and crabs from Whitby. Fish pies, fishcakes and baked soused herring are all prepared on the premises.

The Little Fish Shop

www.littlefishshop.plus.com
☎ 07951 449658
✉ 20 Market Street, Tenbury Wells,
Worcestershire **WR15 8BQ**
🕐 Tues, Fri 8am–5.30pm;
Wed–Thurs 8am–5pm; Sat 8am–1pm

The fish in Mr James's shop is known for its freshness and if you ask, he should be able to tell you exactly where everything is sourced. This site had been a fish shop since the 19th century. It briefly became a wholefoods shop until James, who loved fish yet had no background in the fish business, decided to train to become a fishmonger and opened up there in 2008. What I love about this shop is the variety and especially the less familiar species he sells, including witch, dab, brill, ling, pollock, John Dory, gurnard and squid.

▼ VEGETABLES AND FRUIT

Court Farm ●

www.courtfarmleisure.co.uk
☎ 01432 760271
✉ Tillington, Hereford,
Herefordshire **HR4 8LG**
🕐 **May–Dec** Mon–Sun
9.30am–6pm

A great-looking shop, packed (depending on the season) with the huge amount of produce that is grown on the farm. Alternatively head out to the fields yourself (for better value) and pick your own asparagus, beans, strawberries etc. The farm also grows cobnuts – look out for them from August – and sells free-range meat, dairy and eggs. Opening times are approximate so do check and call ahead for opening hours in January to April.

Farndon Fields Farm Shop 🐄

01858 464838
Farndon Road, Market Harborough, Leicestershire **LE16 9NP**
Mon–Sat 8am–6pm; Sun 10am–4pm

A fabulous-looking farm shop and winner of FARMA Farm Shop of the Year in 2008. Opened in 1983 by the Stokes family, it began selling the farm's home-grown produce out of the farm garage. Now housed in a larger wooden barn , it boasts huge wooden counters literally stacked with fresh produce and low beams draped with dried hops. There's a pick-your-own (check for seasonal opening hours) and expect to also find local milk from Lubcloud Dairy, freshly baked bread, free-range eggs and fresh meat prepared on site at the on-farm butchery. See also page 120. Rated as outstanding and a must-visit place.

Fern Verrow Vegetables

01981 510288
St Margaret's, Nr Hereford, Herefordshire **HR2 0QFP**

Fern Verrow is a biodynamic 30-acre smallholding in the foothills of the Black Mountains. They have a continual supply of seasonal vegetables that are sold at Borough Market on Saturdays only (9am–4pm). One week there will be a new crop of golden beetroot on sale; another week there might be some globe artichokes, orchard fruit, some of the farm's robust roasting hens or cuts of well-hung Dexter beef. Salad leaves are almost always available, along with herbs. Nigel Slater is a huge fan of Fern Verrow and raves about the quality, taste and texture of the produce he buys there. His endorsement is good enough for me, but it remains a pity that this grower, with all the green credentials it possesses on the farm, has no farm gate sales or box schemes for locals.

Fresh From The Fields £

07939 550336
228 Rookery Lane, Lincoln, Lincolnshire **LN6 7PH**
Mon–Fri 9am–4pm; Sat 9am–3pm

A good Lincolnshire produce shop, accessible through Curtis and Sons. On the day I called in, there was an impressive show of locally grown bunched carrots, romanesco, muddy spuds, curly kale, Brussels sprouts and cauliflowers. Being in a county where there is a substantial quantity of vegetable farming, you would expect all shops to stock local veg, but this shop is sadly the exception and not the norm. You will find a good quantity of locally grown veg in Lincoln's market, however, which is open daily.

Gwilliams Farm Shop 🅿🅾

☎ 01905 756490
✉ Ombersley Road, Claines,
Nr Worcester, Worcestershire
WR3 7RH
🕐 Mon–Sat 9am–5pm

Strawberries and raspberries are the main soft fruit crop growing on this PYO farm. You will not always have to do the hard work, however, as there is a farm shop, too, which also sells some produce that is sourced locally.

Packington Moor Farm 🅿🅾

www.packingtonmoor-events.co.uk
☎ 01902 735724
✉ Bognop Road, Essington,
Wolverhampton, Staffordshire
WV11 2BA
🕐 **Jun–early Aug** Mon–Sun
9am–8pm **Late Aug–May** Tues–Sat
9am–5pm; Sun 10am–pm

A produce farm where you can pick your own soft fruits and vegetables or buy orchard fruit, but which is also a butchery and farm shop (see page 136). The fruit farm is part of the LEAF scheme, which aims to boost the wildlife population on the farm, while not being organic. Thirty crops are grown: all the red fruits (including tayberries and marion berries), damsons, plums, French beans, broad beans, pumpkins, squash, spinach, peas, shallots and more.

Robinsons of Louth 🥬 🐄

☎ 01507 602499
✉ 125 Eastgate, Louth, Lincolnshire
LN11 9QE
🕐 Mon–Sat 8am–5pm

Chris Robinson is a fifth-generation greengrocer whose shop sells an abundance of locally grown Lincolnshire produce. He buys soft fruits from a farm four miles away, potatoes from Alford, apples directly from orchards close by and most of the green vegetables he sells are from Wainfleet.

Sid's Greengrocers

☎ 07738 856 273
✉ 14 Queen Street, Bottisford,
Leicestershire **NG13 0AH**
🕐 Mon 8am–5pm; Tues 8am–2pm;
Thurs and Fri 8am–5pm;
Sat 8am–2pm

A traditional village greengrocers with a loyal following, selling fresh vegetables and fruits, local whenever possible. This is a much-loved shop dong a great service – greengrocers remain the most vulnerable of high-street food shops. Bottisford also boasts a butcher (A. E. Taylor & Sons,) the Malt House Deli and a bakery (Jeans) – bliss for traditional shoppers.

Woodlands Farm Organic Box Scheme @ ◐ ◉

www.woodlandsfarm.co.uk
☎ 01205 724778
✉ Kirton House, Kirton, Nr Boston, Lincolnshire **PE20 1JD**

An organic box scheme, and winner of the 2008 Organic Food Award, offering a good choice of differently sized vegetable, fruit or mixed boxes. A large box could contain cauliflower, tomatoes, potatoes, onions, celeriac, turnips, spinach, savoy cabbage, leeks, broccoli, green kale, carrots and lettuce. The farm is currently setting up a 300-acre biodynamic farming pilot using very traditional, integrated and sustainable farming techniques to produce cereals, vegetables, pork and poultry. You can sign up for their e-newsletter and you'll also find their produce at local farmers' markets – see website for details. Keep an eye out for this produce and let me know what you think.

HONEY ▼

Honey at Bailgate Books ◉

www.bailgatebooks.com
☎ 01522 579222
✉ Malt Kiln House, Everton Road, Mattersley, Nottinghamshire **DN10 5DS**

Nicholas Wollaston is an antiquarian book dealer and an avid beekeeper. He has 20 hives in total, reaping around 100 lbs of honey a year, sometimes more. His bees feed on mixed woodland, village flowers and trees. He also has hives at a nearby lavender farm but reports that they 'don't seem to like lavender'. Available from Malt Kiln House or at the Post Office in Mattersley (open Mon–Fri 9am–5pm). See website for details.

Lyveden New Bield

www.nationaltrust.org.uk/
lyveden
☎ 01832 205385
✉ Near Oundle, Northamptonshire **PE8 5AT**
🕐 Mon–Sun 10.30am–5pm (seasonal opening times apply, see website)

Beehives were brought to this estate four years ago when the National Trust began working to make a wildlife habitat here. The wildflower meadows, traditional hedgerows and orchards provide the Lyveden New Bield bees with a pollen and nectar source from a number of different blossoms, from March through to October. The late honey the bees produce at Lyveden is described as 'rich and inviting with a smooth and subtle sweetness', and was a winner of one of the National Trust's 2010 Fine Farm Produce awards.

▼ DRINKS

Belvoir Fruit Farms ⊙ @

www.belvoirfruitfarms.co.uk
☎ 01476 870286
✉ Belvoir, Grantham, Lincolnshire
NG32 1PB

Belvoir make lovely, old-fashioned cordials and pressés. Run by the delightful Pev Manners whose parents first started making elderflower pressé and fruit cordials using elder blossom picked from the hedgerows near the family home at Belvoir, it's now a more serious business than a kitchen table-top one. I stock up on these products religiously, particularly in the summer months. They have a fantastic flavour and the company has a nice ethos and cares for its employees. See website for details of stockists.

Broomfields Apples ⊙ @ ✿ ⊙

www.broomfieldsfarmshop.co.uk
☎ 01905 620233
✉ School Plantation, Holt Heath,
Worcester **WR6 6NF**
🕐 Mon–Fri 8.30am–5pm; Sat 9am–5pm; Sun 10am–5pm

The Broomfield family has been growing apples since the '30s. They started a farm shop in the '60s, which must have been one of the first in the country, and now grow a huge range of apples and pears, including unfamiliar varieties such as Jupiter, Crispins and Lord Lambourne. As well as sending apples by mail order, they press their own apple and pear juice on the farm and sell it in their farm shop.

Copella

www.copellafruitjuices.co.uk
☎ 0800 8766 946
✉ Tropicana Ltd, PO Box 6642,
Leicester **LE4 8WZ**

Copella has been pressing apples since 1969 at Boxford Farm in Suffolk. Although they are big, they are good; no colourings or preservatives are added. This may not be the best apple juice, but it is widely available and I like it.

Goodness Direct ⊙ @ ✿

www.goodnessdirect.co.uk
☎ 0871 8716611
✉ South March, Daventry,
Northamptonshire **NN11 4PH**

A highly efficient mail order service whose policy is to sell only natural or organic foods. They are also strong on ethical sourcing, which makes them a good one-stop shop for drinks, whether you are buying bottled water, fruit juice or cordials, herb infusions (which they sell an awful lot of), plus tea and coffee from a sustainable, Fairtrade source.

Imperial Teas of Lincoln ⊙ ⓐ ⬤

www.imperialteas.co.uk
☎ 01522 560008
✉ 47 Steep Hill, Lincoln **LN2 1LU**
🕐 Mon–Sat 10am–5pm;
Sun 11am–4pm

The last time I visited this shop it was in a premises across the road, but it has now moved and is in the larger 'Norman House', doubtless a good thing as there will be even more tea and coffee to buy. You could spend days here, utterly fascinated, listening to these experts take you through all the range and telling you stories of the origins of the teas. I especially love the flowering teas, handmade bouquets (pricey, I am afraid to say) that unravel into beautiful displays in boiling water (you will need a glass tea pot to see this). Also great are the many coffees – look out for the Sumatran Kopi Luwak – which have actually passed through the digestive system of a wild Sumatran cat. A hot drink will not get more far out than that!

Jus Apples ⊙ ⓐ ⬤ ⬤

www.jusapples.co.uk
☎ 01531 670749
✉ Birchley, Aylton, Ledbury,
Herefordshire **HR8 2QH**

The Skittery's have a small business making apple juice and also supply other small businesses in their area. The juice is very well thought of locally and each type sold is a single variety juice – there are no blends. Look out for Cox's Orange Pippin, Bramleys, Lord Lambourn and Discovery. They process and pasteurise around 30,000 bottles annually. It's available at local farm shops, B&B's, restaurants and delis (contact for stockists). You can collect from the Skittery's, but do ring beforehand because there is no shop.

Northern Tea Merchants ⊙ ⓐ ⬤

www.northen-tea.com
☎ 01246 232600
✉ 193 Chatsworth Road,
Chesterfield, Derbyshire **S402BA**
🕐 Mon–Sat 9am–4.30pm

I love this proper tea and coffee shop, which has a studious approach to selling the national favourite pick-me-up. Its walls are literally lined in packages of every sort from all over the world. White teas picked early, fresh green teas from China, and African and South American coffees. There is much here to fascinate, plus Fairtrade blends, too.

Pixley Berries

www.pixleyberries.co.uk
01531 670228
Pixley Court, Pixley, Ledbury,
Herefordshire **HR8 2QA**

Pixley blackcurrant cordial is delicious and while the mixtures are not so successful (blackcurrant and ginger for instance lacks ginger flavours), the drinks are superb diluted with water. The fruit is grown at Pixley Court, a farm in rural Herefordshire where a recently installed pressing station means the company retains control of the drinks from start to finish. Full traceability, in other words. The drinks are available in Waitrose, Morrisons, farm shops and small retail outlets throughout the West Midlands. See website for details of stockists.

The Teahouse ❶ @

www.theteahouse.co.uk
07880 550751
The Teahouse, Mayswood Road,
Warwickshire **B95 6AX**

Check out the huge range of teas available online. It joins a growing band of tea enthusiasts who want to up the ante and get us all drinking high quality teas that are ethically sourced and interesting. Tea is now where coffee was 10 years ago. We are becoming more aware of the good, the bad and the indifferent and The Teahouse, tucked away in the backwaters of Warwickshire, is showing the way. They are very keen on whole leaf tea and have an interesting and varied selection. Very interesting and worth supporting.

Trumpers ❶ @ ✿

www.trumperstea.co.uk
01432 379122
1 St James Terrace, Green Street,
Hereford **HR1 2QJ**

Fairtrade teas sold in cheerful tin tea caddies with brightly splashed graphics. Inside is the important bit, however, and Trumpers sell some awesome varieties. Impressive is their green tea, sourced from China's Fujian Province. The tea, which is called Pi Lo Chun, is hand-rolled into distinctive small spirals and is deliciously robust, enough to make a second pot with the same leaves. They also sell three of my favourite herbals: fennel, lemon verbena and peppermint. Highly recommended.

North East and Yorkshire

Ainsty Farm Shop ❂

www.ainstyfarmshop.co.uk
☎ 01423 331897
✉ York Road, Green Hammerton,
York, North Yorkshire **YO26 8EQ**
🕐 Tues–Thurs, Sat 9am–5.30pm;
Fri 9am–6.30pm; Sun 10am–4pm

Stuart and Lily Beaton's shop off the A59 has an in-house butchery cutting beef, pork and lamb from local farms. Such shops are a lifeline for local farmers and very deserving of support. Stuart Beaton started with his own flock of sheep when he was just five years old! The standard of welfare is high, no GM feed and an on-farm cold room and butchery mean that meat can be cut to individual requirements. Local game is available in season, including rabbit, venison and pheasant. This is also the place to go for genuine Yorkshire curd tart.

The Balloon Tree Farm Shop ❂ ❂

www.theballoontree.co.uk
☎ 01759 373023
✉ Stamford Bridge Road,
Gate Helmsley, York **YO41 1NB**
🕐 Mon–Sat 9am–6pm;
Sun 10am–5pm

The Machin family are adventurous growers, producing just about everything from asparagus to peppers. They also sell rare-breed meat and use it in their ready-made foods. This is an exemplary place to shop. The Longhorn cattle is matured for a minimum of three weeks. Otherwise they source mainly from local farmers in Yorkshire. Fruit and vegetables are harvested daily and chosen for flavour, not shelf-life. Cakes are also produced in-house and the staff (family and locals) are helpful and knowledgeable. (See also page 182).

Blacker Hall Farm Shop

www.blackerhall.com
☎ 01924 267202
✉ Branch Road, Calder Grove,
Wakefield, West Yorkshire
WF4 3DN
🕐 Tues–Fri 9.30am–6pm;
Sat 9am–4.30pm; Sun 10am–4pm

An award-winning farm shop, with its own butchery and bakery, run by John and Anne Garthwaite, and their son John and his wife Mary, housed in a beautiful old stone barn. The astonishing claim is that 90 per cent of the food sold in the shop is produced on the premises, so this is well worth a look. The beef, pork and lamb is almost all home-produced, and the beef is hung for a minimum of 21 days. The bakery is run by Anne, who bakes in small batches using ingredients from the farm or local producers. The smell of her pies, buns and cakes is a huge draw for customers.

The Blagdon Farm Shop @ 🍴 🕐

www.theblagdonfarmshop.co.uk
📞 01670 789924
✉ The Milkhope Centre, Blagdon,
Newcastle upon Tyne **NE13 6DA**
🕐 Tues–Sat 10am–5pm;
Sun 11am–4pm

This is quite a smart and shiny farm shop, but with a good heart and some excellent quality meat, vegetables and dairy foods. The beef is stunning (Belted Galloway, hung for a good long time on the bone) and the Saddleback pork delicious. There is a nice range of Northumberland artisan cheeses. Vegetables include potatoes from Tritlington Hall, plus more from the walled garden at Blagdon.

Keelham Hall Farm Shop

www.keelhamhallfarmshop.co.uk
📞 01274 833 472
✉ Brighouse and Denholme Road,
Thornton, Bradford **BD13 3SS**
🕐 Mon–Fri 8am–8pm;
Sat 8am–7pm; Sun 9am–5pm

A finalist in the National Farmers' Retail & Markets Association (FARMA) awards, 2010. Run by brother and sister James and Victoria Robertshaw, this is a hard-working farm shop that opens admirably long hours and is a great asset to the area, selling affordable locally sourced food. The lamb is home reared, and other fresh meat is from nearby farms; all is butchered on the premises. The butcher also makes sausages and other good things using locally reared meat, and has won numerous awards – including one for sausages made with the outrageous combination of rhubarb and mango. Fruit and vegetables are sourced in the region, too, though only when available. A great place – well worth a visit.

Lowfields Farm Shop

www.lowfieldsfarmshop.co.uk
📞 01388 746900
✉ Willington, Crook, Durham
DL15 0TP
🕐 Tues–Sat 10am–5pm;
Sun 10am–4pm

Stocking cuts of beef, lamb and pork from the Lowfields Farm itself, the butchery counter in this thoughtfully arranged and homely shop is a delight. Home-cured bacon sits alongside chubby, hearty-looking sausages and chops. A real variety of dried and store goods is also available, and it is clear that the Moralee family has thought carefully about the expectations and needs of local, regular customers, as well as those from further afield. They succeed in promoting the benefits of local food as well as showcasing its quality by providing as much of it as possible in its raw, natural state. Their online shop is currently under construction

Moorhouse Farm ✆

www.moorhousefarmshop.co.uk
☎ 01670 789016
✉ 21 Station Road, Stannington,
Morpeth, Northumberland
NE61 6DX
🕐 Tues–Sat 9.30am–4.30pm;
Sun 10am–3.30pm

Ian and Victoria Byatt's admirable shop now has a huge following, thanks to their offering locally sourced meat and poultry, dairy foods, vegetables and bread at affordable prices. Close to Newcastle upon Tyne, they have been delighted to see shoppers coming out from the city to buy from them, bypassing the out-of-town superstores. The meat on the butchery counter is reared on their own family farm and slaughtered locally; beef is hung for at least 15 days for extra flavour and tenderness.

Newby Hall Farm Shop

www.newbyhall.com
☎ 01423 326452
✉ Leeming Lane, Langthorpe,
Boroughbridge, North Yorkshire
YO51 9DE
🕐 Mon–Sat 9am–6pm;
Sun 10am–5pm

A shop making a big effort to source locally, claiming over 90 per cent of the content to come from within 40 miles. This includes locally grown vegetables, milk, cream, cheese and eggs. The naturally reared fresh meat sold in the shop comes from the estate's own farms, and there is a wide range of game through the winter months.

North Acomb Farm Shop ✆

www.northacombfarmshop.co.uk
☎ 01661 843181
✉ North Acomb Farm, Stocksfield,
Northumberland **NE43 7UF**
🕐 Tues–Thurs, Sat 9.30am–5pm;
Fri 9.30am–5.30pm;
Sun 9.30am–1pm

Robin and Caroline Baty are farm-shop pioneers, having opened their shop in beautiful Stocksfield 25 years ago. There is no complacency here. The produce, especially the pork from Welsh pigs who are reared in a barn beside the shop, is top grade. On arrival, expect a flurried greeting from Jemima, the couple's old English Buff goose. Must-buys include lovely blood pudding (the real thing, never made with dried blood), sausages, beef and lamb. It is not a big shop, but there is hardly an item you wouldn't want to buy – the home-churned butter, meat pies, locally milled Northumberland flour from Gilchesters (see page 171), Carroll's 'heritage' potatoes and delicious heather honey with comb collected by Alan Swan at Swalwell. A well-edited shop and great value.

The Organic Pantry ⊙

www.theorganicpantry.co.uk
☎ 01937 531693
✉ St Helens Farm, Newton Kyne,
Tadcaster, North Yorkshire
LS24 9LY
🕐 Mon–Sat 9am–5pm;
Sat 9.30am–12.30pm

Organic fruit and vegetables, grown on the farm, available in a box scheme or from the shop, where you can also buy fresh, naturally reared organic meat, milk, cheese, eggs and general grocery items. Not all the vegetables in the boxes are home-grown, but you can check the website to see where they come from and for the latest crop list, updated each year. The shop will note your likes and dislikes, and tailor a box to your preferences. The farm has planted an apple, pear and plum orchard and has plans for a duck pond and herb garden. A nice business that is going places – please keep me updated.

Redcliffe Farm Shop

www.redcliffefarmshop.co.uk
☎ 01723 583194
✉ Redcliffe Lane, Lebberston,
Scarborough, North Yorkshire
YO11 3NT
🕐 Mon–Sat 9am–5pm;
Sun 11am–5pm

A shop run by farmer's son Martin Brown that is loyal to the farmers of the region, sourcing fresh meat from a group of local farmers, and also selling the Brown family's own excellent grass-reared beef and free-range eggs. He buys fresh produce from Stuarts, a regional wholesaler who specialises in buying Yorkshire produce when possible.

Whirlow Farm Shop

www.whirlowhallfarm.co.uk
☎ 0114 262 0986
✉ Whirlow Lane, Sheffield
S11 9QF
🕐 Mon–Sun 10am–6pm

All fresh produce sold in this great farm shop is grown at Whirlow Hall Farm, and includes fresh pork, sausages, bacon and gammons (raw ham), as well as lamb from sheep that can be seen in the field outside the shop window, and eggs from free-range hens. The beef is hung for a generous 28 days – it is advised that you pre-order as it is only produced in limited quantities. Local preserves, cakes and dairy food are also available.

Alnwick Farmers' Market 💷

www.alnwickmarkets.co.uk
☎ 07894 402766
✉ Market Place, Alnwick
NE66 1HS
🕐 **Monthly**, last Fri 9am–2pm

Seasonal specialities such as hill lamb (from August to March) are available at this market located near Alnwick's medieval market cross. You'll also find vegetables, soft fruits, cheese, home-baked cakes and pies, fish, pork, beef, jams, pickles and mussels (from September to April). Local crafts are also available.

Durham Farmers' Market 💷

www.durhammarkets.co.uk
☎ 0191 384 6153
✉ Market Place, Durham **H1 3NJ**
🕐 **Monthly**, 3rd Thurs
8.30am–3.30pm

The north-east of England is rich in producer heritage and it is a bit of a surprise that the Durham Farmers' Market took so long to get going. It has more or less established itself now, right in the centre of town. Stalls sell bread and also locally grown grains, such as pearl barley and oats. There are also seasonal vegetables, game in season from the big northern estates, and hill lamb from local farms.

Holmfirth Farmers' Market 💷

☎ 01484 223730
✉ Holmfirth Market,
38 Huddersfield Road, Holmfirth,
West Yorkshire **HD9 3JH**
🕐 **Monthly**, 3rd Sun 8am–2pm

Holmfirth is the town that was made famous as the home of the BBC TV cult series, *Last of the Summer Wine*. It is a smallish market town just north of the Peak District. It holds a farmers' market every third Sunday, which is very popular with locals and visitors. All the free-range eggs, naturally reared beef, pork and lamb, plus artisan cheeses and breads are sourced within a nearby radius. Held in the town's market hall, the farmers' market has an authentic feel – and, not least, shelter from the rain and cold!

Leeds Farmers' Market €

www.leeds.gov.uk
☎ 0113 2145162
✉ Leeds Kirkgate Market, George
Street, Leeds, West Yorkshire
LS2 7HY
🕐 **Twice monthly**, 1st and 3rd
Sun 9am–2pm

This twice monthly market can house up to 70 stalls,
and locals report a fantastic presence of good vegetable
suppliers, including organics. In winter you can buy the
beautiful, pink forced rhubarb from near Wakefield; there
are stallholders selling artisan cheese, free-range eggs,
naturally reared meat, preserves and ready-cooked food for
you to take home and reheat. More eclectic sellers offer
Caribbean pickles and locally grown chillies.

Newcastle Farmers' Market €

www.newcastlecityfarmersmarket
.com
☎ 0191 211 5533
✉ Grainger Street, Newcastle upon
Tyne **NE1 5QQ**
🕐 **Monthly**, 1st Fri 9.30am–2.30pm

The produce from Newcastle's surrounding area is superb
and all reports about the Grainger Street farmers' market
have been good. There are some lovely local cheeses, fresh
seasonal veg and fruit, free-range poultry and you should be
able to find some excellent beef. There are usually around
25 stalls – a good number guaranteeing plenty of variety.

North Allerton Farmers' Market €

www.ndfm.co.uk
☎ 01748 884414
✉ Town Hall, North Allerton,
North Yorkshire **DL7 8LW**
🕐 **Monthly**, 4th Wed 8.30am–3pm

North Allerton is part of the North Dales Farmers' Markets,
a group of like-minded farmers selling a plethora of different
produce around the area. Yorkshire Dales Meat sells beef;
and M. & T. Betney sells dry-cured bacon, gammons, hams
and sausages. There's a stall selling a wonderful array of
poultry including Kelly Bronze turkeys, chicken and guinea
fowl. Not all of the producers go to the same market, so it is
worth checking if a particular one is going to be at North
Allerton. See website for details.

Otley Farmers' Market €

www.otley-online.co.uk
☎ 01943 851204
✉ Market Square, Otley,
West Yorkshire **LS21 1HD**
🕐 **Monthly**, last Sun 9am–1pm

The majority of this town centre is 18th century or older and has
a Conservation Area status. As well as the monthly farmers'
market selling the best of local produce, there are bakeries and
butchers around the market square that are also worth a visit.

Richmond Farmers' Market 💷

www.ndfm.co.uk
☎ 01748 884414
✉ Market Square, Richmond,
North Yorkshire **DL10 4QN**
🕐 **Monthly**, 3rd Sat 8.30am–2pm

Richmond is one of the prettiest towns in the Dales area of Yorkshire. The farmers' market, held on the third Saturday of every month, is well attended. Of note is Yockenthwaite lamb, reared on the hills; lovely, fresh seasonal fruit and vegetables from Bluebell Organics' walled garden; a stall selling delicious burgers made from well-hung buffalo beef; and good pork sausages made by Langthornes.

▼ DELIS AND SPECIALISTS

Appletons Pie Shop 🌱 💷

☎ 01765 603198
✉ 6 Market Place, Ripon,
North Yorkshire **HG4 1BP**
🕐 Mon–Sat 7am–5pm

Wonderful hot pork pies are handmade in the tiny kitchen at the back of the shop. Fantastic sausages, hazlet, black puddings and bacon, too. This really is a shop not to be missed and is well worth a detour. Long-time owner Roger Gaunt sold the shop in 2010. New owners Anthony Sterne and Leigh Hughen are continuing the tradition.

Belsay Shop 🍏

☎ 01661 881207
✉ 12 The Arcade, Belsay,
Northumberland **NE20 0DY**
🕐 Mon–Fri 7.15am–7pm;
Sat–Sun 8am–6pm

An elegant village shop and post office in North Tyne, run by Stephanie Farron, selling good bread from nearby Castle Bakery, made with flour from a local farm and mill Gilchesters (see page 171), and vegetables from Little Harle Farm. There is beef from the same farm, when available, bacon from Moorhouse Farm, also close by, and you can place an order for very fresh fish supplied by excellent local fishmongers Ridley's, near Hexham (see page 176).

Bleiker's ⊙ ⊚ ⊘

www.bleikers.co.uk
☎ 01423 711411
✉ Bleiker's Smokehouse,
Glasshouses Mill, Glasshouses,
North Yorkshire **HG3 5QH**
🕐 Mon–Fri 10am–4pm

I know Jörg and Jane Bleiker's smokehouse well and can say that it is one of my favourites in Britain. Amazing trout cured with gin; organic smoked bacon; and beetroot-cured salmon. The conventional salmon comes hot-smoked, cold-smoked and supplied from an accredited Freedom Foods farm in Scotland. Free from additives, too. The mail order service is exceptionally good.

Café Royal ⊘

www.sjf.co.uk
☎ 0191 231 3000
✉ 8 Nelson Street,
Newcastle upon Tyne **NE1 5AW**
🕐 Mon–Sat 8am–6pm;
Sun 10am–4pm

This is an elegant tea room with a food store attached, popular with shoppers in the city centre who want to rest their legs, but not necessarily their credit cards. A big, bustling place, run with a lot of vision and energy and putting paid to any idea that food shops 'up north' fall behind their swish London counterparts. Aside from some scrumptious patisserie (a raspberry and ricotta muffin will never be forgotten), there are wholesome artisan breads made with Gilchesters flour (wheat grown and milled about 15 miles away – see page 171) locally made jams (Rosebud in Yorkshire) are also available.

Deli at Darras ⊙

www.deli-at.co.uk
☎ 01661 860206
✉ 13 Broadway, Darras Hall,
Ponteland, Northumberland
NE20 9PW
🕐 Mon–Sat 8.30am–5.30pm;
Sun 10am–4pm

Deli owner David Urwin tells me he has changed a few things since my last visit to Northumberland when I went to his second shop, which is now closed. His Darras Hall shop sells vegetable boxes from North East Organic Growers, fresh locally sourced beef, pork and lamb from Northumbrian Quality Meats, plus Richard Woodhall's famous Cumberland sausage and dry-cured bacon. It also sells a wide range of charcuterie, olives and olive oils, plus locally made pies and toffee pudding from Lancashire. Urwin has also added a café. The word is that locals love it, but your comments on the changes would be very welcome.

Donaldson's

07900 961655
73 Front Street, Stanhope,
Weardale, County Durham
DL13 2TZ
Mon–Sat 9am–5pm;
Sun 10am–1pm

This proper grocers run by Richard and Denise Salkeld was a finalist in the 2009 BBC Radio 4 Food & Farming Awards. The shop is only small, but its shelves and central aisle are stacked with a large, well-chosen range of ingredients – some fresh, some to put in the store cupboard. There is no large supermarket in this area of the Dales, so locals are grateful to have this shop where you can buy, for instance, all you would need to make a good curry, from spices to coconut milk, or all the raw materials required to make a good loaf of organic bread. They stock a wide range of Suma foods, including cans of organic beans and pulses, and a huge range of aromatics. It is nice to see that they sell local products including eggs and lamb from a farm half a mile away, milk (including organic) bottled at a nearby dairy, and honey and honey products from Rowse. Vegetables are on shelves behind the counter and are weighed out for you – lovely and old-fashioned.

Fenwick ⬤ ⬤

www.fenwick.co.uk
0191 232 5100
39 Northumberland Street,
Newcastle upon Tyne
NE99 1AR
Mon–Wed, Fri–Sat 9am–6pm;
Thurs 9am–8pm; Sun 10am–4pm

A traditional, department-store food hall in modern surroundings, housing a good wet fish counter and a butchery selling organic Northumbrian Heritage Meats (including Blackface lamb from the hill country near the city). There's milk from Embleton Hall, County Durham, fresh seasonal vegetables, some grown locally, and a well-stocked larder of store cupboard foods. They will do mail order for delivery within 50 miles.

First Season

www.firstseason.co.uk
01947 601608
1 St Ann's Lane, Whitby, North
Yorkshire **YO21 3PF**
Mon–Sat 9am–5pm

An innovative wholefoods shop selling fresh, local seasonal vegetables, eggs from Pasture Cottage and potatoes from Mickleby. Locally sourced organic and speciality breads are delivered daily by a local supplier. They also do wheat- and gluten-free foods.

Gibside Larder and Community Farmers Market

www.nationaltrust.org.uk (then link to Gibside Larder using the search function)
☎ 01207 541 829
✉ Near Rowlands Hill, Gateshead, Northumberland **NE16 6BG**
🕐 Mon–Sun 11am–5pm, Mar–Oct; 11am–4pm, Nov–Feb; farmers' market: **monthly**, 3rd Sat

Gibside Estate is a National Trust property and the trust is now working hard to bring local food to visitors of the house. The Gibside Larder is part of the gift shop, and sells fresh produce including beef and lamb from the nearby Wallington Estate, local game, dry-cured bacon, Northumbrian virgin rapeseed oil and a wide range of cakes and preserves. The monthly farmers' market offers the same produce, and more.

Henshelwood's Deli

www.deliyork.co.uk
☎ 01904 673877
✉ 10 Newgate, York **YO1 7LA**
🕐 Mon–Sat 9am–5pm; Sun 11am–4pm

Kirk and Ali Vincent are relative newcomers to the city, using local produce bought from the market on their doorstep in their ready-made foods, which include ham hock and parsley terrine, and white crab pâté. Over 25 British artisan cheeses, 10 of them made in Yorkshire, are stocked. They also have an outside catering business. Henshelwood's has a good reputation.

Honey Tree

www.webreform.co.uk/ht/
☎ 0191 240 2589
✉ 68 Heaton Road, Newcastle upon Tyne **NE6 5HL**
🕐 Mon–Wed 10am–5pm; Thurs–Fri 10am–6pm; Sat 10am–4pm

A wholefoods shop and general stores with a good atmosphere – it describes itself as a 'social enterprise' – selling organic eggs, locally milled organic flour, some nice, gooey polenta cakes, game from nearby shooting estates, organic free-range meat, poultry and organic chocolates.

Hunters of Helmsley @

www.huntersofhelmsley.com
☎ 1439 771307 13
✉ Market Place, Helmsley, North Yorkshire **YO62 5BL**
🕐 Mon–Sun 8am–5pm

Chris and Christine Garnett have owned Hunters since 2008. As both of them come from farming families, with personal backgrounds in catering and retail, the pair are passionate about how and where food is produced. Their deli counter features Yorkshire hams as well as local beef and pork cooked on the premises. Their generous sandwiches are a meal in themselves, and can be filled with anything from the counter – bacon, black pudding, sausage or salami – or you can indulge in a top-notch pork pie or quiche. Two rooms filled with fine, hand-chosen, imported goods provide everything for the store cupboard or a special treat, and are rightly called the 'Aladdin's Cave'. Of particular note is the range of locally made fruit wines, sloe gin and cider. The range at Hunters is constantly evolving, but the essence of a traditional store is maintained with care.

Il Piccolo 🖊

www.ilpiccolo.co.uk
☎ 01434 634554
✉ St Helen's Street, Corbridge, Northumberland **NE45 5BE**
🕐 Mon–Sat 9am–5pm

A fun shop and café in vibrant Corbridge, run by the enthusiastic Manni Corto. It is impossible not to stay and drink proper Italian coffee after having stocked up from Corto's well-stocked larder of typical Italian specialities. These may include breads, pasta, risotto rice, cheeses or prosciutto (including a nice one made from wild boar), but there is also a choice of a few Northumberland specials, including honey and flour from a nearby mill.

Le Langhe 🏠 @

www.lelanghe.co.uk
☎ 01904 622584
✉ The Old Coach House, Peasholme Green, York **YO1 7PW**
🕐 Mon–Thurs 11am–5.30pm, Fri 10am–5.30pm; Sat 9.30am–5.30pm

While the content of this shop is clearly of Italian, not Yorkshire, origin, independent deli-owner Otto Bocca deserves mention for his exceptional Piedmont charcuteria and cheeses, including an extraordinary cheese matured in the must from the wine harvest. Its aromas had an interesting effect on my fellow train passengers as I travelled home from my last visit. This is also the place to go to for unusual Italian wines, including the great Barolo. Since my visit, Otto has moved the shop to a bigger location, adding a larger restaurant and café. I look forward to seeing the new place and would love to hear your views. There's also a comprehensive online shop.

Lewis & Cooper ❶@

www.lewisandcooper.co.uk
☎ 01609 772880
✉ 92 High Street, Northallerton,
North Yorkshire **DL7 8PT**
🕐 Mon–Fri 8.30am–5.30pm; Sat
8am–5.30pm; Sun 11am–4pm

This is a food emporium that has been running in some shape or form for over a century. Today it specialises in wine and fine foods, ranging from Russian caviar and Chatka crab, to York ham and handmade plum pudding. Their dry-cured bacon is truly delicious, as is the beef Cumberland sausage (which is reassuringly low in fat). The variety of food available is terrific, even though each item has been hand-chosen and taste-tested to ensure that it is of the highest quality. This is not only a traditional food hall, but it is also a piece of local history. The range is constantly changing and Lewis & Cooper will, with pleasure, always endeavour to source a rare relish or elusive cheese for individuals. Everyone here clearly enjoys their work and takes great pride in placing Yorkshire produce next to some of the finest products in the world – a place that it deserves.

Rafi's Spice Box ❶ @

www.spicebox.co.uk
☎ 01904 638119
✉ 17 Goodramgate, York
YO1 7LW
🕐 Mon–Sat 10am–5.30pm

Rafi's Spice Box is something of an institution. The shop and mail order business prepares more than 25 'curry packs' for people to cook at home. Each mix is prepared by hand using Indian spices to make a bespoke curry. Customers can call and discuss curry ideas with Rafi.

Shepherd's Purse

www.theshepherdspurse.com
☎ 01947 820228
✉ 95 Church Street, Whitby, North
Yorkshire **YO22 4BH**
🕐 Mon–Sun 9.30am–5.30pm

This nice general shop on hilly Church Street is not exactly packed with food (there's a range of clothes and candles laid on to please Whitby's visiting 'goth' pilgrims), but it does have a decent selection of local cheeses, including Blackstick Blue, Mrs Bells' Blue, Swaledale, Yorkshire 'Feta', Wensleydale, Sage Derby and Cotherstone. Also available are Lindisfarne mead (a honey liqueur), locally baked bread and flour milled by Spaunton in Yorkshire. Coffees, tea and spices are also available.

Steenbergs Organic ❁ @ ✿

www.steenbergs.co.uk
☎ 01765 640088
✉ 6 Hallikeld Close, Barker Business
Park, Melmerby, Ripon, Yorkshire
HG4 5GZ
🕐 Mon–Fri 9am–5pm

Axel and Sophie Steenberg's spices and teas are of the
highest standard. The company was established in 2003 and
due to demand for its products has had to move three
times. Now in an eco-friendly factory, they sell Fairtrade
spices by mail order and to other retail outlets, as well as
from the factory gate. Beautiful packaging; lovely business.
(See also page 180).

Stewart & Co Fine Food and Butchery ✿

www.stewartandcofinefood.co.uk
☎ 0191 281 4838
✉ 36–38 Brentwood Avenue,
West Jesmond, Newcastle upon Tyne
NE2 3DH
🕐 Mon–Fri 8.30am–7pm;
Sat 8.30am–6pm; Sun 10.30am–5pm

A very stylish deli-café in a popular residential area where
you can sit down to tea or coffee after browsing a well-
edited range of speciality foods, many of them sourced
in the north of England. The focus is more on local than
organic. There is bread from Castle Bakery, free-range eggs
from Sunny Hill Farm in Northumberland, fresh lamb from
a farm in Ingram Valley, Rington's teas (from Newcastle),
coffee from Pumphrey's of Blaydon (see page 180),
Gilchesters flour (see page 171), organic vegetables from
nearby Tritlington Hall, plus milk and cream from organic
Acorn Dairy. This is a shop that has that extra notch of
appeal, thanks to its great location on a quiet street, a well-
chosen larder and good ideas and skills in the kitchen.

Weeton's

www.weetons.com
✉ 23/24 West Park, Harrogate
HG1 1BJ
🕐 Mon–Sat 9am–7pm;
Sun 10am–6pm

Supporting over 50 local farmers, Weeton's was established
in 2005 and set out to stock their elegant premises with the
very best meat, groceries, deli and bakery goods that the
Harrogate area can offer. They have achieved an upmarket,
luxury range of goods while maintaining a down-to-earth
feel to the shop itself, with a stunning array of clearly
marked British and imported cheeses; top quality beef,
lamb, pork, poultry and game; delicious home-made pies
and pasties; and a range of store goods to tantalise the
most discerning palate. Weeton's spoils the customer with

locally sourced produce. Each area of the shop is carefully stocked and managed by clued-up staff, be it in baking or butchery. Promoting the 'eat local' message, Weeton's is the best of Yorkshire through and through.

BUTCHERS ▼

Barnards Butchers

01947 880322
Main Street, Fylingthorpe,
Robin Hood's Bay, North Yorkshire
YO22 4AU
Mon 8am–1pm; Tues–Fri
8am–5pm; Sat 8am–12pm

All beef, pork and lamb are sourced from within a 30-mile radius in this tiny shop close to the coast. Specialities include beef, pork and lamb sourced from local farms. Free-range eggs and poultry are always available, and the enterprising owners Paul and John McQue also bake bread and cakes, and even deliver home-made pizza locally on Wednesdays, Thursdays and Fridays.

H. Coates and Son

www.coatesbutchers.co.uk
0191 386 2474
26 Front Street, Framwellgate
Moor, Durham, Co Durham
DH1 5EJ
Mon–Fri 8am–4.30pm;
Sat 8am–4.30pm

A butcher's shop that has been open for over 50 years selling a combination of Scottish and locally sourced meat. Beef and lamb are predominantly from Scotland, free-range poultry comes from the Blagdon Estate in Northumberland and there are barn-reared chickens from Cumbria. You can buy good value meat hampers for the freezer and the shop also makes its own shepherd's pie, pasties, beef mince pie, bacon and egg pie and a variety of braises and stews. Deli items such as olives, cheeses and charcuterie are also available.

Cranstons Butchers

www.cranstons.net
01434 602271
7 Cattle Market, Hexham,
Northumberland **NE46 1NJ**
Mon–Fri 6am–5pm

A butcher famed for its bacon (the dry-cured streaky and back has won multiple prizes), but who also makes an unusual and delicious Cumberland sausage with added black pudding – another award-winner. This is a branch of a butcher based in Penrith, Cumbria, selling meat sourced in the north of England, not only in Cumbria, but also Northumberland and Yorkshire. Also excellent is the fresh Tamworth pork reared nearby by part-time farmer Liz Nixon, who works in the shop. There are four other branches – see website for details.

George Payne ○ @ ◐

www.georgepaynebutchers.co.uk
☎ 0191 236 2992
✉ 27 Princes Road, Brunton Park, Gosforth, Newcastle upon Tyne **NE3 5TT**
🕐 Mon–Wed 8am–5pm; Thurs 7.30am–5.30pm; Fri 7.30am–6pm; Sat 7.30am–2pm

George Payne sources his pork and beef from two farms in Northumberland and likes to keep his produce local. His city shop has been likened to an old-fashioned French butcher's and he is the recipient of a Rick Stein Food Hero award. The free-range chickens are reported as being 'superb' and Payne also sells meat from a local herd of Belted Galloways.

B. W. & D. J. Glaves & Sons Ltd ◐

www.glavesbutchers.co.uk
☎ 01723 859523
✉ 37 Cayley Lane, Brompton-by-Sawdon, Scarborough **YO13 9DL**
🕐 Mon–Fri 7am–5.30pm; Sat 7am–12.30pm

Established in 1973, Glaves is a family-run business. All the meat sold in the shop comes direct from the family farm and is processed under one roof. Sausages, cured hams, pies, sandwiches and burgers are also all made on site using the produce from the farm, keeping food miles to an absolute minimum and ensuring the quality of the ingredients. As the animals are all butchered on site by experts, the quality of the butchery is consistent and particular cuts can be requested without issue. The produce here is as local as it gets, and delicious as well.

A. P. Jackson ◐

☎ 01947 820085
✉ 10 High Street, Ruswarp, Whitby, North Yorkshire **YO21 1NH**
🕐 Mon 8am–1pm; Tue 8am–5pm; Wed–Sat 8am–8.30pm

Alastair Jackson not only sells great, locally sourced fresh meat (the source of the beef is highlighted on a wall poster), but some truly extraordinary pork pies. The locals know this, too, so prepare for a bit of a queue. Pastry is perfect (flaky, thinly rolled then baked to a good, deep-golden brown) and the filling seasoning is spot on. Alternatives to plain pork include a fruity, pleasantly sweet pork and apple, and a well-judged Stilton and pork.

Radford Butchers 🏠 🖊 £

01947 810229

81 Coach Road, Sleights, Whitby, North Yorkshire **YO22 5EH**

Mon–Fri 8.30am–5.30pm; Sat 8.30am–5pm

Dry-cured hams hang from the ceiling in fifth-generation butcher Andrew Radford's shop, some prepared in a Guinness and molasses cure, others simply dry-cured. Fresh meat from local farms is also top quality (Ryedale lamb and pork from Liverton) and there are pâtés, pies and cooked meats, plus comforting bread and butter pudding and deli items on offer.

A. A. Swarbrick

01765 602 776

25 Westgate, Ripon, North Yorkshire **HG4 2BQ**

Mon–Sat 8am–5pm; Wed 8am–1pm

Great traditional Yorkshire butchery, selling beef, pork and lamb sourced locally and exceptional home-cured bacon and ham. Established 30 years ago, a great high street survivor and well worth seeking out.

Yorkshire Game Ltd 🏠 @ 🖊

www.yorkshiregame.co.uk

01748 810212

Station Road Industrial Park, Brompton on Swale, Richmond, North Yorkshire **DL10 7SN**

Mon–Thurs 8am–4.30pm; Fri 8am–2.30pm

Richard Townsend and Ben and Percy Wheatherall supply fresh, oven-ready game sourced from shoots and estates in the north of England and Scotland, then processed at a modern plant in North Yorkshire. The emphasis here is on quality – you will not be sent birds peppered with shot or that have been improperly stored or hung. Choose from a comprehensive range including venison (mainly red deer and roe), grouse, pheasant, partridge, wildfowl (mallard, but also teal when available), woodpigeon, hare and rabbit.

Allendale Bakery ⊘

www.allendalebakery.com
☎ 01434 618879
✉ Unit 2, Allendale, Hexham,
Northumberland **NE47 9EQ**
🕐 Mon, Wed–Sun 10am–4.30pm

Situated in the revitalised Allen Mill near Hexham, the Allendale Bakery is an organic breadmaker with tea (and coffee) rooms attached. The bakery has a good reputation and bakes a wide variety of breads – perhaps rather too many (sometimes it is nicer to visit a baker that makes five great loaves). But the Allendale Bakery is committed to baking real additive-free bread and should be commended. At the end of 2009 it started running bread-making courses catering for beginners to advanced. The revitalisation of Allen Mill is a worthy cause and the bakery a great addition.

Bondgate Bakery ⊙⊘

☎ 01943 467516
✉ 30 Bondgate, Otley, West
Yorkshire **LS21 1AD**
🕐 Mon–Fri 7.30am–5pm;
Sat 7am–5pm

Baker Stephen Taylor bakes slow-made bread and cakes using only natural ingredients (free-range eggs in the cakes, for example). From sunflower seed and honey bread to nicely chewy baguettes and rolls dusted with flour; also muesli bread. There is something here for all tastes – even a slimmer's cake that is egg-, sugar- and fat-free. Among the confectionery there's flapjacks, fruit bun loaves, frangipans and raspberry coconut slices. This is as good as traditional British baking gets – and bakers Stephen Taylor and Chris Hartley are the pride of it.

Botham's of Whitby ⊙@

www.botham.co.uk
☎ 01947 602823
✉ 35 / 39 Skinner Street, Whitby,
North Yorkshire **YO21 3AH**
🕐 Mon, Wed 8.30am–4.45pm;
Tues, Thurs–Sat 8.30am–5.15pm

A traditional bakery making and selling local specialities that reflect Whitby's seaport heritage, such as Whitby Gingerbread and hand-baked spiced Shah biscuits. It is also the place to go for excellent sausage rolls and Yorkshire Brack (a fruity tea bread). As far as food goes, Whitby is a renaissance town and this shop is well worth a visit.

Gilchesters Organics

www.gilchesters.com

☎ 01661 886119

✉ Gilchesters Organic Farm,
Hawkwell, Northumberland
NE18 0QL

An unusual farm growing traditional wheat breeds, including spelt and rye, in an organic system alongside an admirable programme to restore wildlife. Farmer Andrew Wilkinson also runs a centre for organic cereal research, conducting trials for Newcastle University into the health benefits of pre-war breeds of wheat. He mills the grain on the farm making a variety of beautiful flours, including some unusual types such as semolina, which makes a delicious if rather oddly grey-coloured pasta. His wife Sybille is a great baker and has recently developed a range of spelt biscuits for cheese and other snacks. Gilchesters flour is sold by many good independent outlets – see website or contact for details of stockists.

The Handmade Bakery

www.thehandmadebakery.coop

☎ 07894 036742

✉ 14 Carr Lane, Slaithwaite, West
Yorkshire **HD7 5AN**

🕐 Tues–Fri 9am–5pm;
Sat 9am–3.30pm

What began as a community, not-for-profit baking project to encourage local people to take up making real bread has developed into a wonderful bakery that is expanding excitingly. All bread is slowly made – the leavening process takes between 16 and 24 hours. Breads available include traditional British favourites, Scandinavian rye and other continental specialities. The Yorkshire Leaven, Sisu 100 per cent Rye and Pain de Campagne are extra special. If you are a local, or passing through – do seek this place out.

Thompson's Bakery ⊘

www.geordiebakers.co.uk

☎ 0191 286 9375

✉ 385 Stamfordham Road,
Westerhope Village, Newcastle upon
Tyne **NE5 5HA**

🕐 Mon–Fri 8.30am–4pm;
Sat 8.30am–3pm

Recommended to me by local millers who are part of the Real Bread Campaign, this is a traditional bakery selling sandwich tins, good granary loaves, a wide range of pastries, traditional sticky or filled sweet buns and celebration cakes. I am assured all bread is baked from scratch and the quality is good enough for their bread to be sold in local farm shops and grocers. The next plan for the Geordie bakers (as they dub themselves) is to sell a local loaf made with flour stone-milled from Northumberland wheat. Sounds good – look out for it.

Brymor Ice Cream

www.abmoore.co.uk

☎ 01677 460337

✉ Higher Jervaulx Farm, Masham, Yorkshire **HG4 4PG**

🕐 Mon–Sun 10am–6pm

Produced from the milk of a small herd of Jersey cows, the ice cream is made on the farm by the Moore family and they have an in-situ ice cream parlour, too. It's a pretty genuine set-up and definitely worth a visit. The ice cream is also available in a limited amount of retail outlets, including some supermarkets. See website for details of stockists.

The Cheese Board ⬆ @ ❂

www.thecheeseboard.net

☎ 01423 508837

✉ 1 Commercial Street, Harrogate, North Yorkshire **HG1 1UB**

🕐 Mon–Fri 9am–5.30pm; Sat 9am–5pm

Gemma Ackroyd's shop was established 25 years ago, and still specialises in selling artisan cheese, kept in perfect conditions displayed on shelves made either from marble or wood. She sells a variety of cheeses made in artisan dairies in the north of England, including Coverdale and Bedale (two modern Yorkshire cheeses) and the almost unbeatable King Richard III Wensleydale. Other natives include Fountain's Gold, Cotherstone from Co Durham, Coquetdale from Northumberland, Swaledale from Cumbria and Mrs Appleby's from Cheshire. Continental cheeses are also available.

Doddington Dairy ⬆ @ ❂

www.doddingtondairy.co.uk

☎ 01668 283010

✉ North Doddington Farm, Wooler, Northumberland **NE71 6AN**

Margaret Ann (Maggie) Maxwell makes the raw-milk cheese on this delightful dairy farm at the foot of the Cheviots. All milk, which is used untreated, is from the farm's own herd. Maggie, a new cheesemaker who is already winning prizes, makes a range including Baltic and Admiral Collingwood, both washed in locally brewed ale (including Newcastle Brown). The cheeses can be bought online. The second string to the dairy is their range of ice creams, basics made with natural egg and fresh ingredients, flavoured with real chocolate, vanilla etc, and a new, pretty range of flower- and spice-scented ice creams that include rose, or saffron and cardamom. The ice creams and cheese are available in many local stores; phone or see website for stockists.

The Northumberland Cheese Company ⊕ @ ✦

www.northumberlandcheese.
co.uk
☎ 01670 789798
✉ The Cheese Farm, Green Lane,
Blagdon, Northumberland **NE13 6BZ**
🕐 Mon–Sun 10am–5pm

A popular dairy, much admired by locals and whose many (and believe me there are a lot) cheeses are sold in local shops. Contact for stockists or buy online. The company was started by Mark Robertson whose first cheese, Redesdale, made with ewes' milk, was launched in 1984. Various others (using goat, ewe and cows' milk) have followed, including Coquetdale, Reiver, Elsdon, Chevington and Nettle. All are honest, good quality cheeses; nothing too controversially strong or pungent, handmade and welcome on any table.

Shepherds Purse Cheese ⊕ @ ✦

www.shepherdspurse.co.uk
☎ 01845 587220
✉ Leachfield Grange, Newsham,
Thirsk, North Yorkshire **YO7 4DJ**

Shepherds Purse started making cheese in 1989 and now makes a range of 14 cheeses, including cows' and ewes' milk cheeses, at its creamery in Thirsk. It is a family-run concern that has scooped several awards. In the '90s they started making the first blue cheese in Yorkshire – and the company goes from strength to strength. I love the Yorkshire Blue, a creamy, delicately veined blue that has a light yeasty rind, and the Byland Blue, a more Stilton-esque cheese with a firmer texture.

Swaledale Cheese Company ⊕ @ ✦

www.swaledalecheese.co.uk
☎ 01748 824932
✉ Mercury Road, Gallowfields,
Richmond, North Yorkshire
DL10 4TQ
🕐 Mon–Fri 7.30am–3pm

Swaledale cheesemaking was virtually extinct when Mandy Reed and her late husband David decided to start production. At the time there was just one cheesemaker, a Mrs Longstaff. In 1986, the Reeds acquired the recipe for Swaledale cheese from Longstaff and re-established authentic Swaledale, a hard ewes' milk cheese with plenty of rich character. It has been a great success and Mandy Reed now produces nearly two tons of award-winning Swaledale each week.

Wensleydale Cheese Shop ⏏ @ ✦

www.wensleydale.co.uk
☎ 01969 667664
✉ Wensleydale Creamery, Gales
Lane, Hawes, North Yorkshire
DL8 3RN
🕐 Mon–Sat 9.30am–5pm;
Sun 10am–4.30pm

Less a shop than a Wensleydale theme park, a place where you can watch the cheese being made and have the whole Wensleydale cheese experience. But get past the tourist tat and the Wallace and Gromit cheesy merchandise and you will find real cloth-wrapped traditional cheeses, the insides typically lemony and crumbly textured. These are also available online and are excellent value for money. Great everyday cheese for sandwiches or eating with salad, York ham and pickles.

▼ FISH AND SEAFOOD

Cross of York ✦

☎ 01904 627590
✉ 3–4 Newgate Market, York
YO1 7LA
🕐 Tues–Sat 8am–5pm

This is a good wet fish shop on the market place in York, run by Andrew and John Kenny, selling mainly British-caught fish (most from Scotland, but also landed at Scarborough, Whitby, ports in Devon and Newquay). Organically farmed salmon, line-caught wild sea bass and bream are bestsellers. Look out, also, for the excellent brown crab from Whitby.

Fortunes £

www.fortuneskippers.co.uk
☎ 01947 601659
✉ 22 Henrietta Street, Whitby,
North Yorkshire **YO22 4DW**
🕐 Mon–Sat 9am–3pm;
Sun 10am–12pm, 1.30–2.30pm

One of Britain's most charming smokehouses, evocative of another age, Fortunes is perched high on the hill above the bay and fishing port at Whitby, where they have been smoking kippers for ever. Decades of smoking over oak shavings has blackened the shed – you are left in no doubt these are the real thing. The kippers are sold in pairs and wrapped in newspaper. To go to Whitby and not visit Fortunes is almost criminal – note the opening times are fairly brief.

Latimer Fish Deli

www.latimers.com

☎ 0191 5292200

✉ Shell Hill, Bents Road, Whitburn, Tyne & Wear **SR6 7NT**

🕐 Mon 8am–5pm (August only); Tues–Sat 8am–5pm; Sun 9am–4pm

An unsusual deli specialising in fish, making up seafood platters using locally caught fish and also producing fish soups, fish pies and fishcakes. The shop is housed in a large, bright room, and blackboards on the wall advertise the daily specials. The pies and fishcakes will be made using whatever white fish is available, depending on season and availability. Either buy to take home, or eat the same in the café where there is also a range of other dishes including salads and cakes.

Lindisfarne Oysters ♠ @ ⚡

www.lindisfarneoysters.co.uk

☎ 01668 213870

✉ West House, Ross Farm, Belford, Northumberland **NE70 7EN**

Christopher and Helen Sutherland farm rock (Gigas) oysters in the exceptionally clean waters within the Lindisfarne Nature Reserve. These oyster grounds are thought to have been established in the 14th century and once supplied the monks at the Lindisfarne Priory. The grounds changed hands and fell into total decline until the Sutherland family began farming oysters in 1989, noticing oyster shells at low tide and rediscovering the beds. Telephone and they will send the oysters (which are excellent value, by the way) direct to your door.

H. G. Lovitt

☎ 01723 513211

✉ 7 Mitford Street, Filey, North Yorkshire **YO14 9DX**

My friend Chris Hirst, the food writer, is a local and lists this fishmonger as one of the best in Yorkshire. A great source of locally caught fish typical of the area, expect to find ling, pollock, halibut, and cooked and live crab. There is also fresh salmon and sea trout (in season) and good smoked haddock and cod. Since you are in Filey, it is also worth popping along to Mrs Jenkinson's shellfish stall on Coble Landing, where you will also be able to buy excellent crab and lobster. 'Just the sort of place you hope to find at the seaside,' Chris says. Call for opening hours.

Ocean Pantry

01723 350400

West Pier, The Harbour, Scarborough **YO11 1PD**

Mon–Sat 9.30am–4pm

The fish sold at this shop, which comes highly recommended by locals, is mostly landed at Scarborough and by all accounts is as fresh as can be. Expect to find the usual local types: haddock, John Dory, halibut, cod and some good smoked fish including kippers, smoked salmon and haddock.

Ridley's Fish & Game ○ ◉ ◗

www.ridleysfishandgame.co.uk

01434 609246

Unit No 15, Acomb Industrial Estate, Acomb, Nr Hexham, Northumberland **NE46 4SA**

Mon–Sat 7am–6pm

Carolyn and David Ridley's remarkable shop has plenty of the freshest fish, sourced from day boats in Sunderland and prepared for you at the counter by the skilled, informative and helpful staff. Craster kippers, wild mussels from Holy Island (when available), hand-dived scallops, crab and lobsters. You can also buy rabbits, venison and woodpigeon all year round and frozen pheasant – all 100 per cent traceable. Do not miss.

Thundercliffe's Fruits From The Sea

01723 500552

38 Ramshill Road, Scarborough, North Yorkshire **YO11 2QG**

Tues–Sat 9am–5pm

Everyone who knows the area recommends this shop. Peter Thundercliffe was a fisherman, but he's been a fishmonger for about 16 years now. Freshness is key and Thundercliffe buys from local boats where possible, so you can expect to find halibut, haddock, ling and other species typical of the area. There is also a deli section, selling home-made fish pies and fishcakes.

The Whitby Catch ○ ◉ ◗

www.thewhitbycatch.co.uk

01947 601313

1 Pier Road, Whitby, North Yorkshire **YO21 3PT**

Mon–Sun 9am–5.30pm

Since the Whitby Fishing Fleet was reduced by over half during the last decade due to EU conservation measures, the remaining few (under 10) local boats have taken steps to save what remains of the Yorkshire town's fishing business. A shop dedicated to Whitby fish is now open on the harbour, the brainchild of Bill Rae, selling the highest quality sustainably caught fish straight from the boats (via the auction market). This a great-looking shop with a glass panel at the back through which you can watch the fish being prepared by the fishmongers. There's a good variety of wet fish to buy – with a clear conscience – but also smoked fish prepared at Nobles Smokehouse, also in town.

VEGETABLES AND FRUIT ▼

The Balloon Tree Farm Shop

www.theballoontree.co.uk
☎ 01759 373023
✉ Stamford Bridge Road,
Gate Helmsley, York, East Yorkshire
YO41 1NB
🕐 Mon–Sat 9am–6pm;
Sun 10am–5pm

A soft fruit farm that was established 20 years ago, whose red fruits are chosen for flavour and – they say with pride – not for shelf life. You can also pick peas, broad beans and runner beans and there's a nicely thought out PYO trail. Other vegetables grown on the farm are available in the shop all year round. The farm shop (see page 154) also sells beef, cakes and puddings (made by the shop's in-house baker Phyllis Thompson), local cheeses and deli foods.

Brocksbushes Farm

www.brocksbushes.co.uk
☎ 01434 633100
✉ Corbridge, Northumberland
NE43 7UB
🕐 **Winter** Mon–Sun 9.30am–6pm;
Summer Mon–Sun 9.30am–7pm

In summer this is the place for soft fruits; asparagus will be ready in May. The strawberries and gooseberries begin in June; raspberries, red currants and tayberries in July. The fruit is wonderful and, being just picked, it keeps better than any you buy that has sat in a supermarket chiller. It's good value, too, so make jams and chutney from your pickings. The shop also sells home-cooked hams made from local pork, cheeses, breads and ready meals.

Green Valley Grocer

www.slaithwaite.coop
☎ 01484 598050
✉ 14 Carr Lane, Slaithwaite,
West Yorkshire **HD7 5AN**
🕐 Mon, Wed, Fri 9am–5.30pm;
Tues 9am–5.30pm; Thurs 9am–7.30pm;
Sat 9am–3.30pm

This was a long-standing greengrocers shop that had been trading for more than 100 years and was about to shut. The local residents, fearing a lack of choice, stepped in and it is now a community-owned shop with 100 shareholders. They've had huge support from the wider community; they promote local and organic food and are slowly building up a network of local producers. They also sell wholefoods, fish, jam and honey – and it is exceeding all expectations.

Justin S. Smart 🌐

01434 609497
15 Causey Park, Hexham, Northumberland **NE46 2BJ**
Mon–Fri 8.30am–5pm; Sat 8.30am–1pm

Here you will find an astonishing array of locally grown fruit and veg in a region where you would least expect it. Smart's range includes plenty of fresh root vegetables, all supplied from a farm near Dalston, plus some beautiful produce grown by Northumbria Daybreak, a college initiative for adults with learning difficulties. Local kitchen gardeners can also bring their surplus harvest here, so you never know what you might find – there were plums, apples, pears, carrots, parsnips, gooseberries and raspberries on my visit.

The Market Garden 🌐

www.themarketgarden-
sandslane.co.uk
07710 218123
Sands Lane Nursery, Sands Lane, North Cave, East Yorkshire **HU15 2JQ**
Mon–Sun 9am–5pm

This dynamic farm shop sells the farm's own range of vegetables and fruit. You can also pick your own. Expect to find all the red soft fruits, including strawberries, right up until November handily planted in waist-high troughs.

Pasture Cottage Organics 🌐🌐🌐

01947 840075
Pasture Cottage, Bog House Farm, Mickleby, Saltburn-by-the-Sea, Cleveland, North Yorkshire **TS13 5NA**
Mon–Sun 9am–6pm

Jenny and William Summerson farm 87 acres of land with 12 acres certified as organic. They sell an impressive range in their little shop including potatoes, carrots, parsnips, onions, beans, tomatoes and beetroot. Look out also for the farm's own eggs. They will also make up boxes.

HONEY ▼

Chain Bridge Honey Farm ○ @ ◉

www.chainbridgehoney.co.uk

📞 01289 386362

✉ Horncliffe, Berwick-upon-Tweed, Northumberland **TD15 2XT**

Lovely, waxy set honey made on the border of England and Scotland by the Robson family on their farm in Horncliffe. The farm was established in 1948 by William Robson (senior) and is now run by his son Willie and daughter-in-law Daphne. It has gradually expanded and now has over 2000 hives distributed within a 40-mile radius of Berwick. You can order their products online or check the website for details of stockists.

DRINKS ▼

Elizabeth Botham & Son ○ @ ◉

www.botham.co.uk

📞 01947 602823

✉ 35 / 39 Skinner Street, Whitby, North Yorkshire **YO21 3AH**

🕐 Tues, Thurs–Sat 8.30am–5.15pm; Mon, Wed 8.30am–4.45pm

I trust these Yorkshire bakers to know their tea – and their Resolution blend, named after the vessel built in Whitby for Captain Cook's voyages, is a firm, muscular blend of Assam, Ceylon and East African leaves. Fans of this tea, which is also served in the tea rooms of Botham's various traditional shops (see website) can now buy it – and the shop's own blends of coffee – via mail order.

Fentimans ○ @ ◉

www.fentimans.com

📞 01434 609847

✉ 6 Rear Battle Hill, Hexham, Northumberland **NE46 1BB**

Fentiman makes grown-up fizzy drinks (I only say this because my teenage child will not touch them), among which is an outstanding ginger beer made to a recipe obtained by Thomas Fentiman in 1905. Made using the 'botanical brewing' method, combining ginger root with water, herbs, sugar and yeast, the ginger beer is still made much the same way as it always was, though it is now pasteurised and carbonated to replace bubbles lost in the treatment. Lemonade and other good sparkling drinks are available. See website for stockists or order online.

Pumphrey's Coffee ❶ @ ✿

www.pumphreys-coffee.co.uk
☎ 0191 4144510
✉ Bridge Street, Blaydon,
Tyne & Wear **NE21 4JH**
🕐 Mon–Sat 9am–5pm

An old-fashioned coffee company (established 1750) run
by Stuart and Malcolm Archer. The company is a member
of the Newcastle Fairtrade Partnership, sourcing beans from
producer groups who receive a proper wage. They roast
the beans themselves in the traditional way over flames in
100-year-old roasting drums. They sells dozens and dozens
of coffees, both single origin and blends, both in the shop
and online.

Steenbergs Organic ❶ @ ✿

www.steenbergs.co.uk
☎ 01765 640088
✉ 6 Hallikeld Close, Barker Business
Park, Melmerby, Ripon **HG4 5GZ**

I have always liked Axel and Sophie Steenberg's principled
company, which specialises in high quality organic and / or
Fairtrade spices (see also page 166), but it would not be fair
to leave out their beautiful teas from this chapter of the
guide. They sell a huge range, most accredited by the
Fairtrade Foundation, and many in funky-looking tins
(great presents) that keep the tea nice and fresh. Choose
from some impressive grassy green teas, delicate
unfermented, dried white teas and full-on matured black
tea. Herb teas are also available. Order online.

Taylors of Harrogate ❶ @ ✿

www.taylorsofharrogate.co.uk
☎ 01423 814000
✉ Taylors of Harrogate Ltd, Pagoda
House, Plumpton Park, Harrogate,
North Yorkshire **HG2 7LD**

A tea and coffee company that has undergone a major
transformation from selling standard blends in twee
gift caddies to the kind of teas and coffees that suit
contemporary ethics, packed in colourful bags covered in
feel-good graphics and images. Awarded the Queens Award
for Sustainable Development in 2007, Taylor's now sell 11
Fairtrade coffees and (yet still only) one Fairtrade tea (their
breakfast blend). It is very good work from a traditionalist.
I have often bought their organic Fairtrade coffee from
Nicaragua, which is great value as well as very drinkable
cafetière coffee.

Thorncroft 🏠 @

www.thorncroftdrinks.com
☎ 01642 791792
✉ 4 Selby Way, Durham Lane
Industrial Park, Stockton-on-Tees
TS16 0RB

Thorncroft Traditional Cordials are plant-based drinks, not fruit cordials, with a hedgerow theme and an emphasis on natural flavour. They are all also associated with health benefits – hardly surprising as most of them have their roots in ancient herbal medicine. Choose from elderflower, pink ginger, rosehip, cranberry and hibiscus. The website is worth a look also, even for the whacky philosophy alone!

Traidcraft 🏠 @ 🌿

www.traidcraftshop.co.uk
☎ 0845 330 8900
✉ Kingsway, Gateshead, Tyne and
Wear **NE11 0NE**

Traidcraft sell a huge range of Fairtrade products both edible and not, but I want to feature them at least for selling a good Fairtrade cocoa for making hot chocolate, and also because they sell decent, affordable fairly traded tea and coffee. This is the place to come and buy big tubs of instant coffee for the office and large bags of excellent Indian tea-bagged tea, which are great value (I calculated just over 2p each at time of going to print).

North West

Bashall Barn

www.bashallbarn.co.uk
☎ 01200 428964
✉ Bashall Town, Clitheroe,
Lancashire **BB7 3LQ**
🕐 Mon–Fri 9am–5.30pm;
Sat–Sun 10am–5.30pm

There is a hint of glamour to this smart farm shop, housed in an old barn high on a hill in a fairly remote area of the Ribble Valley. But there is a lot to recommend it, including a strong line of locally sourced food and specialities, including the great Lancashire cheeses, home-baked Eccles cakes, jam tarts and lovely, appetising potato-topped meat pies sold in ceramic oven-proof dishes that you can return to the shop after use. Upstairs there is a café and next door the Bowland Brewery, making award-winning beer and stout from local malted grains and real hops. Try the Cromwell Stout – a great alternative to Guinness.

Church Farm 🔵

www.churchfarm.org.uk
☎ 0151 648 7838
✉ Church Lane, Thurstaston,
Wirral, Merseyside **CH61 0HW**
🕐 Wed–Sun 10am–5pm

A 60-acre smallholding on the Wirral selling home-bred Saddleback pork, home-grown soft fruit and asparagus in season, and greenhouse-grown salads such as mizuna, mustard, rocket and chard. Bestsellers are local jams, honeys, cakes and bread. They also have a café serving light lunches. They encourage school visits and have a thriving PYO.

Davenport Farm Shop 🔵

www.davenportsflorists.co.uk
☎ 01606 853241
✉ Bridge Farm, Warrington Road,
Bartington, Northwich, Cheshire
CW8 4QU
🕐 Sun–Mon 10am–4pm;
Tues–Fri 10am–6pm;
Sat 9am–5pm

A multi-award-winning shop Davenport's boasts Northwest Regional Finalist – Best Food Category, Countryside Alliance 2008 and Vale Royal Family Business of the Year 2008, to name but a few. Visiting the farm shop has often been likened to visiting an Ironbridge period shop as it has been fitted out using antique and old furniture. It has one of the largest ranges of locally made food and drink from small suppliers working within a 25-mile radius, including locally brewed beer. They specialise in home-grown tomatoes, which are grown without pesticides and are delicious, tasting just like they should do. They also offer a wide range of the best food and drink from around the UK, some of which is organic, and try to ensure that there is something for everyone by selling food for special diets such as gluten-free, wheat-free and diabetic. Their popular bakery foods include a juicy lemon drizzle cake, coffee and walnut sponge, and freshly baked bread.

Fairfield Farm Shop and Country Café ○⊘

www.fairfieldfarm.co.uk
☎ 01254 813812
✉ Fairfield Farm, Longsight Road,
Clayton Le Dale, Blackburn,
Lancashire **BB2 7JA**
🕐 Mon–Fri 7am–4.30pm;
Sat 8am–5pm; Sun 10am–4pm

Louise and Philip Edge make farm shopping affordable to all, selling their own home-reared pork and highly regarded lamb and beef from a farm nearby in Bolton-by-Bowland. The pork is indoor-reared, but unlike buying non-free-range pork from a supermarket, you can discuss the welfare of the pigs with the couple and be reassured that the pork is local. There is an admirable choice of cheap cuts on offer.

Holker Food Hall ○

www.holkerfoodhall.co.uk
☎ 01539 559084
✉ Cark, Grange-over-Sands,
Cumbria **LA11 7PL**
🕐 Mon–Sun 10.30am–4pm

A grand food hall that is a notch up from a typical farm shop yet still accessible, opened by the owners of the Holker estate seven years ago as an outlet for food produced by their tenant farmers. The shop is best known for the lamb grazed on the wild grasses growing on the marshes of Morecambe Bay, available from July to the end of the year. Good quality bread, game birds and venison from the estate, plus ale, damson gin and artisan cheeses made in Cumbria and neighbouring Lancashire are also available. They also hold monthly food fairs where local producers sell their food. There is a range of Italian specialist foods, which is handy if you live in the sticks and want excellent olive oil or pannetone.

Howbarrow Organic ● ● @

www.howbarroworganic.co.uk
☎ 01539 536330
✉ Cartmel, Grange-over-Sands,
Cumbria **LA11 7SS**
🕐 Tues–Fri 8am–5pm

Hidden up a track behind Cartmel racecourse is a
smallholding with a gem of a farm shop, run by the
appropriately named brothers Tom and Richard Cropper.
The Croppers grow an astonishing range and quantity of
fruit and vegetables organically in polytunnels – cover
that is very necessary in an area not known for its hot
summers. They operate a box scheme, delivering to over
600 customers in the region, and also buy from local
growers throughout the year. Locally reared meat,
poultry and bread is also on sale.

Low Sizergh Barn

www.lowsizerghbarn.co.uk
☎ 01539 560426
✉ Low Sizergh Farm, Sizergh,
Kendal, Cumbria **LA8 8AE**
🕐 Mon–Sun 9am–5.30pm

An organic farm producing milk, cream and vegetables, sold
in a 17th century barn along with a huge range of British
artisan cheeses, locally sourced meat, poultry and game,
plus jams and chutneys made with Cumbrian produce. You
can also drink tea in the shop and watch the daily milking
on the farm.

Plumgarths Farm Shop ● @

www.plumgarths.co.uk
☎ 01539 736300
✉ Lakelands Food Park, Kendal,
Cumbria **LA8 8LX**
🕐 Mon–Sat 9am–5pm

John Geldard sells Lakeland beef, lamb from the nearby salt
marshes and many other local foods, including damson gin
from Strawberry Bank Liqueurs. Established for many years
this is a popular one-stop place to pick up a good range of
groceries, most sourced locally. But it is their meat that
Plumgarths are known for. Sourced from local farmers there
is a good mail order and online service; and BBC Radio 4
Food Programme's Sheila Dillon gives it top marks.

Westmorland Services

www.westmorland.com
01539 624511
Orton, Penrith, Cumbria
CA10 3SB
Tues–Thurs 9am–6pm;
Fri–Mon 9am–7pm

An unusual and famous motorway service station housing a farm shop selling meat from the landowner's own farm, plus lots of other local produce. It is a place that is very loyal to the region. Opened originally by farmer John Dunning who, when the M6 was built, opted to open his own place rather than have one of the chains selling low grade food. It is now run by his equally dedicated daughter, Sarah, who has installed a new and stylish butchery alongside a new café. Dave Morland is the expert at work here, hanging beef sides to perfection, curing bacon and offering every cut from cheap and cheerful offal to sirloin. In the shop you will find Cumbrian favourites – cured bacon and ham from Sillfield Farm (see page 196), Swaledale cheese, Morecambe Bay potted shrimps and much more. Eat in the café or take away a burger from the van – again, all is local meat.

Willington Fruit Farm Shop

www.willingtonfruitfarm.co.uk
01829 751216
Hillside Farm, Chapel Lane,
Willington, Tarporley, Cheshire
CW6 0PH
Mon–Sun 9.30am–5pm

A shop that is Cheshire to its core – just about everything is from within the county boundary: honey, home-pressed apple juice, free-range eggs and cheese (the delicious, creamy, crumbly Cheshire cheese, of course). There are 15 varieties of apples; a range of soft fruit (strawberries, raspberries, blackcurrants, gooseberries – you can pick your own when in season), plus fresh herbs from the farm's own herb garden.

Ashton Farmers' and Producers' Market £

0161 342 3268

Wellington Road, Ashton-under-Lyne, Lancashire **OL6 6DL**

Monthly, last Sun 9am–2pm

Readers of the *Observer Food Magazine* voted this farmers' market the best in the north west. Located in the heart of Tameside, with over 70 stalls, it is the largest in the region. Find salad, vegetables, cheeses, honey, lamb, chutneys, ostrich, fudge, venison, smoked fish, home-baked goods, plus food-to-go, including a hot hog-roast carvery.

Brough Farmers' Market £

www.broughfarmersmarket. org.uk

01768 342135

Memorial Hall, Brough, Cumbria **CA17 4AX**

Monthly, 3rd Sat 9.30am–1pm

Held indoors at the Memorial Hall. the market is supported by the Cumbria Community Foundation, has an active website and is very well organised by a good body of committed local people. Because Cumbria is predominantly a livestock county there are no less than four stalls selling meat – from venison, to Herdwick mutton and Dexter beef. There are vegetables brought in from Lancashire because very few are grown in Cumbria. There's also a traditional baker, plus a stall serving various artisan cheeses and one selling trout.

Chester Produce Market £

www.farmers-markets.co.uk

0845 1668022

Chester Town Hall, Town Hall Square, Northgate Street, Chester **CH1 2HF**

Monthly, 1st Wed 9am–4pm

Good seasonal produce from all over the north west – home-baked breads, naturally reared and organic meat, welfare-friendly poultry, fresh organic vegetables, cheeses and other dairy foods. Look out for the rare-breeds meat stall selling Dexter beef, plus unusual breeds of pig, game from local shoots and, of course, the great wet and fresh textured artisan Cheshire cheeses.

Cranstons Cumbrian Food Hall

www.cranstons.net
☎ 01768 868680
✉ Ullswater Road, Penrith, Cumbria
CA11 7EH
🕐 Mon–Sat 8am–6pm;
Sun 10am–4pm

The main branch of a chain of Cumbrian butchers that also incorporates a larger food hall with a wet fish counter, a wide range of vegetables and fruits – many of which are locally grown – a deli and pies counter. Locals describe Cranston as a lifesaver, a 'supermarket' selling exclusively local meat – which means much to this livestock-farming area. The meat is not all naturally reared – pork and chicken are indoor-grown unless specified free-range – but the beef and lamb are great, and likely to be grass-fed, given that this is a hill farm region. Run by an enterprising family, there's a huge butchery behind the shop that supplies Cranstons' other butcher shops in the area. I was glad to see so many farmers shopping in this shop when I visited – it offers good value for money and yet reassurance that the meat is not brought in from miles away. In 2010 the shop was a finalist as best local retailer in the BBC Radio 4 Food & Farming Awards, of which I was a judge.

Liverpool Wholesale, Fruit, Vegetable and Flower Market 🍋

☎ 0151 233 2165
✉ Edge Lane, Old Swan, Liverpool
L13 2EP
🕐 Mon–Fri 4am–1pm;
Sat 4am–9am

Liverpool has had a fruit and vegetable market since 1859. The building housing the market was destroyed in the war and reopened in 1969 as a new larger construction that sits on 20 acres. This wholesale market, which also welcomes locals, sells a huge variety of affordable fresh fruit and vegetables, as well as hundreds of beautiful flowers from around the world. Mondays and Thursday are the best days for flower trading.

Orton Farmers' Market 🍋

www.ortonfarmers.co.uk
☎ 01524 781003
✉ The Green, Orton, Cumbria
CA10 3RG
🕐 **Monthly**, 2nd Sat 9.30am–2.30pm

Despite this village's remote location and despite it having only 261 residents, their farmers' market boasts over 40 local farmers, growers and producers selling a huge variety of quality produce. Game is readily available when in season, as is Allendale Brewery's local ales, Bluebell Organics fresh vegetables, Deer 'n' Dexter farmed venison and rare breed beef, Pickled Pink chutneys and Country Fare's jams and gingerbreads, to mention just a few items on offer.

Wirral Farmers' Market 🏵

www.wirralfarmersmarket.co.uk
☎ 0151 643 1393
✉ Village Hall, Grove Street,
New Ferry, Merseyside **CH62 5AX**
🕐 Monthly, 2nd Sat 9am–1pm

More than 30 stalls sell some of the north-west's best produce at this indoor market. Expect to find a huge variety to tempt your taste buds, including Lomber Hey Farm's handmade speciality sausages, Born and Bread's fantastic loaves, Capra's artisan goats' cheese, Ian Lloyds hen, duck and goose eggs, Derimon's smoked fish, The Pudding Compartment's handmade puddings, plus lots more.

▼ DELIS AND SPECIALISTS

Barbakan Delicatessen

www.barbakan-deli.co.uk
☎ 0161 881 7053
✉ 67–71 Manchester Road,
Chorlton-cum-Hardy, Manchester
M21 9PW
🕐 Mon–Fri 8.30am–5.30pm;
Sat 8.30am–5pm

Manchester's best bread is baked on the premises – 40,000 loaves a week, no less. Look out for their French campaillou, light rye sourdough and fresh soda breads. They stock plenty of locally made goods including organic Clever Cow Dairy milk, Clippy's apple pickles, honey from Rosebay apiaries and Osa African sauce. Local meats and around 50 pasta shapes mean queues round the block. A big reputation.

Cartmel Village Shop 🏵 @ 🏵

www.cartmelvillageshop.co.uk
☎ 015395 36280
✉ Parkgate House, The Square,
Cartmel, Cumbria **LA11 6QB**
🕐 Mon–Sat 9am–5pm;
Sun 10.30am–4.30pm

The village shop where the now nationally available Cartmel Sticky Toffee Pudding was invented also sells locally produced foods including eggs, cream and butter, freshly baked bread, preserves, ales and cheeses. The puddings themselves are now made on an industrial estate near Morecambe Bay, but still with good ingredients, including free-range eggs, real butter and cream.

Food by Breda Murphy ✆

www.foodbybredamurphy.com
☎ 01254 823446
✉ Abbots Court, 41 Station Road, Whalley, Near Clitheroe, Lancashire **BB7 9RH**
🕐 Tues–Sat 10am–6pm

Breda trained at Ballymaloe in County Cork, Ireland, a place that rarely fails to unleash some stylish and skilled graduates. Food here reflects that special, relaxed style that pays great attention to seasonality. The shop sells Breda's own jams and chutneys, fish pies and other ready-made foods, with all the fresh ingredients sourced locally.

J. & J. Graham of Penrith ⊙ ⊚ ✆

www.jjgraham.co.uk
☎ 01768 862281
✉ 6–7 Market Place, Penrith, Cumbria **CA11 7BS**
🕐 Mon–Sat 9am–5pm

This is Penrith's oldest, smartest deli, housed in a shop with a fascinating history. The company was established in 1793 as an agricultural supplier selling seed, fertiliser, candles and groceries to farms in the area. Now it sells good hams and bacon made in Waberthwaite, pies and pâtés from the Eden valley and some local cheeses. You can order online, but irritatingly only limited produce.

Hang Won Hong

☎ 0161 228 6182
✉ 58–60 George Street, Manchester **M1 4HF**
🕐 Mon–Sun 10am–7.30pm

After stopping (without fail) at the restaurant Yang Sing at 34 Princess Street for some of their handmade-that-morning, steamed prawn dumplings and cuttlefish bumblebee dim sum, nip round the corner to buy fresh Chinese cabbage and everything you need to make your own from this well-stocked supermarket.

Huntley's Food Hall

www.huntleys.co.uk
☎ 01772 872814
✉ Huntley Gate Farm, Whalley Road, Samlesbury, Preston, Lancashire **PR5 OUN**
🕐 Mon–Sat 8.30am–7pm

Huntley's Food Hall prides itself on selling 'local and quality food'. Aiming also to produce as much as possible in-house, it has its own artisan baker whose selection of pies are sure to keep you coming back. The bakery also produces a number of sweet treats and freshly baked bread. The in-house butcher stocks a number of meats from the farm. Fruit and veg available are all locally grown when in season, and in the summer months there is also a PYO option. The deli counter has a range of 100 cheeses, from local Lancashire cheeses to the much sought after Blue Vinny. There is also a wonderful selection of handcrafted chocolates from local chocolatier Choc Lorie and a spectacular array of 80 flavours of ice cream to choose from. For food lovers this is the perfect place to get lost among the exciting variety of goods.

The Old Smokehouse ○ @ ∅

www.the-old-smokehouse.co.uk
☎ 01768 890270
✉ Brougham Hall Foods,
71 Clifford Road, Penrith, Cumbria
CA11 8PU

Richard Muirhead runs this small smokehouse at Brougham Hall and sells excellent smoked wild salmon caught in Cumbria, plus kippers (herring), trout and a number of meaty smoked foods, including Cumberland sausage, ham, beef and bacon. Not even vegetables escape 'lighting up'. They also stock a wide variety of smoking equipment so you can prepare your own smoked food at home.

Taste! Food Hall

www.rheged.com
☎ 01768 868000
✉ Rheged Centre, Redhills, Penrith,
Cumbria CA11 0DQ
🕐 Mon–Sun 10am–5pm

If J. & J. Graham (above) is the oldest and smartest deli in Penrith, this food hall is the newest and slickest. It forms part of the Rheged centre, a sort of visitors' centre run by the wonderful family who started the Westmorland Services food shopping and cafés at Teebay Services. It is a comprehensively stocked food shop full of great, locally made foods including meat from the family's own farm at Orton, Sillfield bacon and ham, damson gin from the Lake District and, of course, Cumberland sausages. The café in the same building makes delicious warming soups and other good things to knock the edge off the cold and wet outside.

Wild at Heart

☎ 0161 881 2389
✉ 1 Railway Terrace, Chorlton,
Manchester M21 0RQ
🕐 Mon–Fri 8.30am–6pm;
Sat 9am–6pm; Sun 10am–5pm

Veena Josh and Rob Goater's (almost all) organic fine food shop and café sells organic poultry, lamb and beef from Mansergh Hall, eggs from Knutsford, and apple juice from Cheshire. Organic baby food from So Baby is also available. The unfiltered borage honey from Littleover Apiary is a speciality.

This shop, which has a policy of employing local people and fighting back against the multiples, deserves your support.

BUTCHERS ▼

Chestnut Meats

www.chestnutmeats.co.uk
☎ 01829 260437
✉ Rudmore Green Farm, Rudmore Green, Spurstow, Tarporley, Cheshire **CW6 9RL**
🕐 Fri only, ring first.

This is a really innovative award-winning enterprise. Tim and Marnie Dobson milk over 100 cows and the milk is sold to a local cheesemaker, Joseph Heler. They sell home-reared free-range pork and Hereford beef and, unusually, goat meat, which is gradually catching on as more restaurants put it on the menu and it attracts media attention. The family also run day farming courses, where small groups of individuals become farmers for the day. A good variety of lamb, pork, beef and goat is available, and home delivery can be arranged. The awards are more than justified.

Cowmans Famous Sausage Shop

www.cowmans.co.uk
☎ 01200 423842
✉ 13 Castle Street, Clitheroe, Lancashire **BB7 2BT**
🕐 Mon–Tues, Thurs–Fri 7.30am–5.30pm; Wed 8am–12.30pm; Sat 7am–4.30pm

Sometimes the heart sinks when you come across a 'sausage specialist', especially one that boasts 78 varieties. It can be sausage-making for the sake of it with not one intelligently devised combination stuffed into a single casing. And, as for the ethics . . . But Cowmans promised to be different – and it was. Butcher Cliff Cowman is passionate about the meat content in his sausages, insisting on using at least 75 per cent pure meat and belly fat with no nasty ground-up connective tissue, common in 'cheat' sausages. Among the good flavours I tried were pork and garlic, pork and chestnut, and pork and plum. Old-fashioned spicy beef and Moroccan Merguez were good and there is a nice honey and pork sausage for children. This is a terrific shop that is fun to visit, run by an enthusiast who deserves his success.

E. W. Edge & Sons Butcher ●

☎ 01244 675156
✉ 54–56 Handbridge, Chester,
Cheshire **CH4 7JF**
🕐 Mon, Thurs 8am–1.30pm;
Tues–Wed 8am–5.30pm;
Fri 8am–5pm; Sat 8am–4pm

Bruce Edge butchers and sells beef reared on his own family's smallholding in Cheshire. He also sells a decent range of fresh meat, all of it from British farms. Free-range chickens and eggs are also on sale.

T. M. Ewbank ● ●

☎ 01768 351462
✉ 12 Boroughgate, Appleby-in-
Westmorland, Cumbria **CA16 6XB**
🕐 Mon, Thurs 7.30am–12.30pm;
Tues–Wed, Fri-Sat 7.30am–5pm

This is a very traditional butcher's shop, selling meat reared and slaughtered by the Ewbank family. All is cut and laid out on marble counters with no price tickets. Just point to the piece you fancy and it will be weighed out and priced in front of you. The sausages are just about perfect – the right balance of meat, fat and bread with a touch of subtle seasoning.

W. H. Frost (Butchers) Ltd ●

☎ 0161 881 8172
✉ 12–14 Chorlton Place, Chorlton-
cum-Hardy, Manchester **M21 9AQ**
🕐 Mon–Sat 7am–5pm

Never accuse a northern city of being the Gobi Desert of food – Chorlton in Manchester has a proud list of good food shops, including this butcher, Jack Frost, selling Middle White (a traditional breed famous for flavour) bacon, locally sourced beef and lamb, and free-range poultry from Cheshire.

Grange Farm Red Poll Beef ● ●

🌐 www.redpollbeef.eu
☎ 01244 300655
✉ Warrington Road,
Mickle Trafford, Chester **CH2 4EB**
🕐 Sat 10am–1pm
other times by appointment

Eight years ago, farmer Huw Rolands chose to farm the Suffolk breed Red Poll for beef and give up unprofitable dairy farming. The Red Poll are the most suitable breed for the soggy pasture on his farm, but the best thing about Rolands's enterprise is the way that he rears the animals to a minimum three years' old. This is almost twice the age of a conventional beef breed and produces meat with an astonishing depth of flavour and a fine small grain. Phone to place an order and they will send your meat to you.

The Great Tasting Meat Company

www.greattastingmeat.co.uk
01270 625781
Gate Farm, Poole, Nantwich, Cheshire **CW5 6AL**
Tues–Sat 9am–6pm

A farm shop housed in an old dairy barn, this place specialises in rare and native British breeds including pure-bred Hereford and Aberdeen Angus beef, Gloucestershire Old Spot, Saddleback and Large Black pork, plus Suffolk lamb. All livestock are slow-grown on a natural diet, a system that farmer / owner Andrew Jackson credits for the great flavour of their meat. The golden tint in the fat on the beef comes as a result of grazing on ancient pasture, he tells me, and he may have a point. Local free-range eggs, laid on a farm only two miles away, are also on sale.

Heritage Meats

www.heritagemeats.co.uk
01539 441433
Yew Tree Farm, Coniston, Cumbria **LA21 8DP**
Farm gate sales are available, but ring first

Caroline and Jon Watson's beautiful farm in the Lake District was once owned by the children's author Beatrix Potter. Supported by landlord the National Trust, the farm is now home to some lovely rare-breed cattle and sheep, and a thriving mail order meat business. Beef cattle are the cuddly-looking 'belties', the gentle Belted Galloway breed with their black fore and hind quarters divided by a white 'belt' around the belly. The lamb is Herdwick, a local hefting, or territorial, breed that lives on the surrounding fell country in all weathers grazing wild pasture. Killed as hoggets, a minimum of one year old, the meat from these slow-growing, naturally fed sheep has an exceptional flavour. Both animals play a vital part in maintaining the condition and appearance of the Lakeland fell country, so this is a business well worth supporting.

Marsden Bros

01539 720033
6 New Shambles, Kendal, Cumbria **LA9 4TS**
Mon–Thurs 9am–5pm; Fri 8.30am–5pm; Sat 8am–3pm

If it is a Cumberland sausage you are after, many Kendal people will send you here. Marsden's sausage is coiled in the traditional way, not linked, and filled with chopped pork shoulder and belly, then seasoned with pepper, marjoram, mace and sage. You can phone orders through and then collect in the shop.

Paul Butchers ●

☎ 01539 559292
✉ 13 Market Street, Flookburgh,
Grange-over-Sands, Cumbria
LA11 7JU
🕐 Mon, Sat 9am–4pm;
Tues–Fri 9am–5pm

Paul Skyrme's shop in Flookburgh is highly recommended by locals, who are full of praise for his home-made sausage rolls and fresh meat, which is sourced from farms in the north west of England. I was a little underwhelmed by the appearance of the shop, but to be as busy as he was on the day of my visit speaks for itself.

Roy Porter Butchers ♠ ●

www.ribblevalleyfoodtrail.com/
roy-porter-butchers.htm
☎ 01200 441392
✉ 9 Bridge Road, Chatburn,
Clitheroe, Lancashire **BB7 4AW**
🕐 Mon, Wed, Sat 7.30am–
12.30pm; Tues, Thurs–Fri
7.30am–5.30pm

This is one of those shops where if you talk to fellow customers in the queue they will tell you they have driven 40 miles to buy the meat. The main point of interest here is in native breeds sourced locally or from longstanding suppliers. Dexter, Hereford, Aberdeen Angus, White Park and Highland beef (all hung for at least 21 days), Grindleton and Herdwick lamb (and mutton), plus Gloucester Old Spot, Tamworth and Saddleback pork (hung for 10 days so it produces the crispest crackling). Game is always available in season and there is a constant supply of rabbit from Settle. Among the deli foods you will find home-made pies and some good locally made artisan cheeses, including Garstang Blue.

Sillfield Farm ♠ ● @

www.sillfield.co.uk
☎ 01539 567609
✉ Endmoor, Kendal, Cumbria
LA8 0HZ
🕐 Fri–Sat 10am–5pm;
Sun 10am–4pm

Peter Gott has earned a nationwide reputation for his sausages, hams and bacon made from meat from his own naturally reared rare-breed pigs and wild boar. You will often see his stall in markets (including Borough Market in London) and at county fairs and food shows. Recently, however, he has opened his own farm shop where you can buy his and other locally sourced products. He makes subtly delicious chipolatas (favourites with fussy children), plus superb dry-cured bacon and pancetta. Fresh cuts of pork, hill lamb and mutton are also available. Gott, who is the most generous-spirited of farmers and always there to support others attempting to start a small food business, has a huge interest in European curing methods and now makes a mean Parma-style ham.

More? The Artisan Bakery ⊙ @ ⊘

www.moreartisan.co.uk
☎ 01539822297
✉ The Artisan Bakery, Mill Yard, Staveley, Nr Kendal **LA8 9LR**
🕒 Mon–Sun 7.30am–4.30pm

More? has been up and running since 2006, producing fresh bread every single day for the local community. The emphasis here is on quality ingredients, careful processes and imaginative recipes – the result is inspirational and delicious, ranging from sourdough to rye breads. Their Muddees – a rich brownie mix that is as soft and unctuous in the middle as it is crisp and delicate on the outside – are outstanding and hold their own against the more ornate, though equally delicious, puddings on offer. More? also runs an online ordering service, though visiting and inhaling the wonderful smell of continuous baking is not to be missed.

Staff of Life ⊙ ⊕

www.artisanbreadmakers.co.uk
☎ 01539 738606
✉ 2 Berrys Yard, off Finkle Street, Kendal **LA9 4AB**
🕒 Mon–Fri 8.30am–5pm; Sat 8.30am–4pm

Baker Simon Thomas likes to call himself 'experimental' so you get bread using flours from a local restored watermill, including a damson sourdough using the fermented yeast of the fruit sourced from the Lyth Valley. He also sells his bread through Booths supermarkets. Visit the bakery from 8.30am, but bear in mind that the opening hours are approximate. Eccentrically, the shop is open until the bread sells out – and we guess that is anytime between noon and 5pm.

The Toffee Shop ⊙ @ ⊘

www.thetoffeeshop.co.uk
☎ 01768 862008
✉ 7 Brunswick Road, Penrith, Cumbria **CA11 7LU**
🕒 Mon–Sat 9am–5pm

Pat and Neil Boustad's shop is famous. It sells the best butter toffee on the market, plus a good 'tablet' type fudge with a lot of 'snap'. Pure butter is used in a recipe that has remained unchanged for 90 years. All products come smartly packed in card boxes lined with wax paper.

Village Bakery

www.village-bakery.com

☎ 01768 881811

✉ Melmerby, Penrith, Cumbria

CA10 1HE

🕐 Mon–Sat 9am–4pm;
Sun 9.30am–4.30pm

Started by Andrew Whitley, the Village Bakery was one of the first rural bakeries to install traditional wood-fired ovens and bake loaves using organic flour. The bakery grew from a tiny seed to something much bigger. Whitley is no longer the owner, preferring to run bread courses and teach artisan baking skills, but the bakery still has a small shop on the original site at Melmerby and is still the best place to buy the brand's bread. Loaves are rustic-European in character, with domed French Campagne-style bread, Rossisky Rye and Pane Toscano being bestsellers.

The Watermill

www.organicmill.co.uk

☎ 01768 881523

✉ Little Salkeld, Penrith, Cumbria

CA10 1NN

🕐 Mon–Sun 10.30am–5pm

Ana and Nick Jones mill flour from organic wheat in a watermill they restored themselves back in 1975. All the grain is British and you can also buy bread, oats, cakes, organic bakers' yeast and preserves. If you are really bitten by the baking bug, you can also take a course here in either breadmaking or milling.

▼ DAIRY

Abbot Lodge Jersey Ice Cream

www.abbottlodgejersey
icecream.co.uk

☎ 01931 712720

✉ Abbott Lodge Jersey Ice Cream, Clifton, Nr Penrith, Cumbria

CA10 2HD

🕐 Mon–Sun 11am–5pm

Steven and Claire Bland produce over 30 different ice creams on their farm, which is part of the Lowther estate in Cumbria, using milk from their pedigree Jersey herd. They sell it at the farm gate and serve sundaes and ices in their café. This is a dairy story like many others, of a farming family sick of making little money from milk sales to the larger dairies and how they have successfully diversified. Tragedy struck, however, in 2001 when they lost their herd to foot and mouth disease, but they have picked up, restocked and started again. They deserve your support.

H. S. Bourne ○ ◎ ✅

www.hsbourne.co.uk

☎ 01948 770214

✉ The Bank, Maples, Cheshire
SY14 7AL

🕐 Telephone first for farm gate sales

Cheshire cheese is one of England's oldest cheeses. Invented before cheddar it has a loose, almost wet character and a unique freshness. Unfortunately, like many British cheeses, its reputation has been diluted by the generic block version that is widely available. I don't want to dent the appetite for commercial cheese with snobbery because it is more or less an honest food, but come across the real thing and it is obvious you are enjoying something totally different. Bourne's cheese is made in traditional round moulds and matured for up to one year. The family has been making cheese since 1930 and aims to make something close to the historic version. Contact for stockists, buy from Borough Market (see page 42) or buy online and at the farm gate.

The Cheese Shop ○ ◎ ✅ £

www.chestercheeseshop.co.uk

☎ 01244 346240

✉ The Cheese Shop, 116 Northgate Street, Chester, Cheshire CH1 2HT

🕐 Mon–Sat 8.30am–5.30pm;
Sun 10.30am–4.30pm

A source of speciality cheeses in Chester for more than 25 years, Carol Faulkner stocks over 200 different cow, goat and ewe artisan cheeses (pasteurised, unpasteurised and vegetarian) in her shop near the cathedral in Chester. She specialises in Lancashire and Cheshire cheese, the loose-crumbed 'wet' varieties that have their origins in Roman Britain. Part of her success as an affineur lies in the old cellar under her shop that provides perfect conditions in which to mature her produce.

Cheesie Tchaikovsky ✅

☎ 01200 428366

✉ 38 York Street, Clitheroe,
Lancashire BB7 2DL

🕐 Mon 8.30am–2pm;
Tues–Fri 8.30am–4.30pm;
Sat 8.30am–3pm

This is a 'must-visit' place on the Ribble Valley Food trail, selling locally made cheeses on Clitheroe's main street, plus other artisan-made examples from further afield in the UK and Europe. There are also home-baked breads on sale, made with flour from a mill called the Little Salkeld.

Martin Gott ⊙ @ ⊘

www.holkerfoodhall.co.uk
📞 015395 59084
✉ Holker Food Hall, Cark, Grange-over-Sands, Cumbria **LA11 7PL**
🕐 Sun–Fri 10.30am–5.30pm

Martin Gott is a talented young cheesemaker and the son of artisan food campaigner Peter Gott (see Sillfield Farm page 196). Gott now makes cheese from raw ewes' milk at the creamery on the Holker Estate. He produces St James (a washed-rind cheese named after the late, great cheesemaker James Aldridge) using raw milk from his flock of Lacaune sheep, the same sheep whose milk is used by the French to make Roquefort. The cheese takes two years to develop – it can be crumbly when less ripe, but still good, or smooth and creamy. Its flavour has lovely, salty, meaty tints.

▼ FISH AND SEAFOOD

Charles Brickland

📞 01244 346622
✉ 36 Faulkner Street, Hoole, Chester, Cheshire **CH2 3BD**
🕐 Tues–Fri 8am–5pm

Sadly, huge rents pushed this shop out of the centre of Chester into the suburbs, but it is none the worse for that. In spring and summer they get bass, plaice, Dover sole and samphire grass from the local estuary when possible. Much of the rest is sourced from Cornish day boats. They smoke their own cod and haddock, and make hot roast salmon and trout fillet. Game is also available, when in season.

Cheshire Fish ⊙ ⊘

📞 01625 425567
✉ 4 Roe Street, Macclesfield, Cheshire **SK11 6UT**
🕐 Tues–Sat 9am–5pm

A good fish shop with a strong local following, situated in a street with a name that could not be more perfect. The seafood sold here is sourced sustainably when possible and there is a good amount of line-caught fish on sale. I was also delighted to hear that the shop not only sells fresh fillets and whole fish, but does a roaring trade in herring melts and roe, and even monkfish cheeks. Many fishmongers discard these, but they are satisfying little nuggets that can be added to a fish stew.

Furness Fish and Game Supplies (Morecambe Bay Shrimps) ⊙ @ ⦿

www.morecambebayshrimps.
com

☎ 01539 559544

✉ Moor Lane, Flookburgh, Grange-
over-Sands, Cumbria **LA11 7LS**

🕐 The premises are open to
personal callers between 9am–3pm
Monday–Friday

This business changed hands in 2010 but fear not, Les
Salisbury sold it to his niece, Clare Worrall, an employee of
15 years' standing. Worrall, like her uncle before her, is
devoted to peeling and potting Morecambe Bay's famous
brown shrimps. They are peeled by machine although hand-
peeled ones are still available at a premium. The butter used
to pot the shrimps is perfectly spiced or you can buy them
without the butter, too. They also run a thriving game
business, sourcing from local estates. Les has retained his
stall in Borough Market, which is still supplied by his old
company. Furness also attended major county shows and
horse trials (see website for details).

James Baxter & Son ⊙ ⦿

www.baxterpottedshrimps.co.uk

☎ 01524 410910

✉ Thornton Road, Morecambe,
Lancashire **LA4 5PB**

The Baxters have been catching and potting brown
shrimps in Morecambe Bay since the 18th century and make
one of the best versions of this classic and wonderful British
regional dish. They also supply shrimps to the queen and
hold a royal warrant. The rich little brown shrimps, which
are dredged using nets dragged across the flooded
Morecambe sands at high tide, are immediately cooked on
landing, then peeled and potted with spiced butter. Bob
Baxter, patriarch of potted shrimps, died in 2008 and the
company is now in the hands of his son and daughter-in-
law. Little has changed, however, and the Baxters will send
out a minimum quantity if you order by phone. Alternatively,
contact them for your nearest stockist.

Out of the Blue @ ⦿

www.outofthebluefish.com

☎ 0161 881 8353

✉ 484 Wilbraham Road, Chorlton,
Manchester **M21 9AS**

🕐 Tues–Sat 9am–5pm

This is an impressive fishmongers run by David Yarwood in
Chorlton, Manchester's suburban foody district. Here you
will find good, fresh white fish – haddock, cod and plaice –
but also native lobsters and line-caught Cornish fish,
including turbot and monkfish. Cornwall seems a long way

201

from the northern city, I agree, but fast transport via the M5 / M6 means it is still fresh. Sourcing from the inshore day boat fleet is a priority. Commendably, the shop also makes its own sushi by hand, employing a specialist sushi chef. Poultry and game are also available.

Wellgate Fisheries ⊘

www.wellgatefisheries.co.uk
☎ 01200 423511
✉ 5 Wellgate, Clitheroe, Lancashire **BB7 2DS**
🕐 Mon–Sat 8.30am–4.30pm

All the fish in Giles Shaw's delightful and well-stocked shop is responsibly sourced – this is the place to go for brown shrimps (a local speciality), line-caught haddock, cod, sea bass (after May), wild Loon sea trout and salmon. Clitheroe's lucky inhabitants have a great food town with good delis, butchers, a cheese shop and this terrific fish shop.

▼ VEGETABLES AND FRUIT

Dobsons Greengrocers ⊘ € ⊘

☎ 01539 731208
✉ 42 Highgate, Kendal, Cumbria **LA9 4SX**
🕐 Mon–Sat 7am–5pm

Business is booming for Andy and Andrea Dobson's traditional greengrocer's shop, which has a high degree of locally grown produce from Cumbria, including the county's famous damsons, Victoria plums, tomatoes, potatoes and apples. Other British produce and some imported items are also available.

Khawaja Brothers Mini Market ⊘

☎ 0161 881 1818
✉ 63–65 Manchester Road, Chorlton, Manchester **N21 9PW**
🕐 Mon–Sat 8.30am–8.30pm; Sun 9.30am–6.30pm

Ahmed Shabbir's shop has an impressive display of the freshest fruit and vegetables, with a small amount of locally grown produce including leeks and sprout trees (in season). In winter they sell forced rhubarb from Wakefield. The shop will deliver locally, depending on how much you order.

Smithy Mushrooms ⊙ @ ⦿

www.smithymushrooms.co.uk
☎ 01704 840982
✉ 229 Smithy Lane, Scarisbrick,
Ormskirk, Lancashire **L40 8HL**

An impressive fungi business, growing a wide range of exotic mushrooms, including three colours of oyster mushroom, king oysters (excellent firm type for frying), shitake, sticky nameko, enoki (clusters of small fungi), and many more, You can ask for a mixed box and try the whole range. Wild fresh or dried fungi, including cepes (porcini), chanterelles, morels, fairy ring and girolles, are also available (a seasonal chart on the website will tell you when to buy them). An excellent mail order and online service is available.

Unicorn Grocery

www.unicorn-grocery.co.uk
☎ 0161 861 0010
✉ 89 Albany Road,Chorlton,
Manchester **M21 0BN**
🕐 Tues–Fri 9.30am–7pm;
Sat 9am–6pm; Sun 11am–5pm

A food cooperative and shop selling 70 lines of organic and 'in conversion' (from farms not yet fully organically certified) fruit and vegetables from the region around Manchester, this shop is exceptional. Some are grown on the Unicorn Grocery's own 21 acres of land, 14 miles from the shop. Other wholefoods, organic bread and deli items are also available. It is an admirable shop, with strong green principles, offering very good value for money. Take a look at their very informative website.

HONEY ▼

Honey Comb Company ⊙ @ ⦿

www.honeycombco.co.uk
☎ 01524 751347
✉ Stoney Lane, Galgate, Lancashire
LA2 0QY
🕐 Mon–Fri 9am–5pm;
Sat 9am–1pm

Clear and set honeys, plus heather honey, collected from the Midlands and north of England available online, along with some interesting imported honeys including New Zealand Leatherwood, both clear and set. They sell a range of gift packs so you can sample the different flavours.

Northern Ireland

▼ FARM SHOPS

Churchtown Organic ⊙ ⊚ ⊘

www.churchtownfarm
organicproduce.com

☎ 028 4488 1128

✉ 30 Churchtown Road, Strangford,
County Down **BT30 7AT**

🕐 Thurs–Sat 9am–6pm

Owner, Dale Orr, says business is booming ('two record months') at his award-winning farm shop that is leading the way in Northern Ireland, selling fresh organically reared Lleyn lamb and mutton, and Saddleback pork from Dundermotte Farm in Antrim. In early 2009 the shop installed its own smokehouse and is now producing pastrami, smoked lamb, hickory-smoked bacon and smoked salmon.

▼ FOOD MARKETS

Belfast City Food and Garden Market ⊛

☎ 028 9032 0202

✉ St George's Market, 12–20
East Bridge Street, Belfast **BT1 3NQ**

🕐 **Weekly,** Sat 9am–3pm

St George's Market was built between 1890 and 1896 and is one of the city's oldest attractions. The Saturday market offers local, continental and speciality foods including Portavohie fish, pork from Cookstown, beef from Armagh, venison, local organic vegetables, pheasant when in season, wild boar, tapas, cheeses, cured meats, French pastries and teas and coffees from around the world.

▼ DELIS AND SPECIALISTS

Arcadia Deli

www.arcadiadeli.co.uk

☎ 02890 381779

✉ 378 Lisburn Road, Belfast,
Co Antrim **BT9 6GL**

🕐 Mon–Sat 9am–5pm

There has been a fine food shop on this site for over 75 years and Arcadia still stays a step ahead of food trends, with their well-stocked counter housing some beautifully kept artisan cheeses, including many English and Irish favourites. They also sell the wonderful Fermanagh Black bacon, made by O'Doherty's, and other delicious local favourites including some excellent smoked salmon, Clandeboye Estate yoghurt and locally made ice cream.

Deli on the Green

www.delionthegreen.com

028 8775 1775

30 The Linen Green, Moygashel, Dungannon, Co Tyrone **BT71 7HB**

Mon–Sat 8.30am–5.30pm

A shop that exudes passion for food – it opened in 2003 and moved to the current location in 2006 where it sells food from local Northern Irish producers and specialist foods sourced further afield. Run by Claire Murray, the emphasis is on home-made food – salads, tarts, tray bakes – to take home or to be eaten in.

Sawers

www.sawersbelfast.com

028 9032 2021

Unit 7, Fountain Centre, College Street, Belfast **BT1 6ES**

Mon–Sat 9am–5pm

Allegedly Belfast's oldest deli, but certainly timeless, Sawers' reputation for selling almost everything practically rivals Harrods. With the groovy, bright yellow lettering above the shop window, and a lush display outside, you are transported back to the groceries of your childhood. Step inside and buy fresh fish, dulce (an edible sea vegetable), soda bread, free-range eggs, grass-fed beef, rabbit, charcuteries, cheeses, chocolate and a vast store cupboard range from bulgar wheat to anchovies. Sawers are also into selling exotic meats such as crocodile and ostrich. I have tried, but cannot approve of this. Whichever way I look at these foods they remain a gimmick with negligible gourmet credentials.

Yellow Door Deli

www.yellowdoordeli.co.uk

028 9038 1961

427 Lisburn Road, Belfast, Co Antrim **BT9 7EY**

Mon–Sat 8am–5pm

A fabulous-looking deli in Belfast selling home-baked artisan loaves, patisserie and cakes and specialising in Irish produce. There is an excellent cheese counter, housing farmhouse cheeses that have been perfectly matured. Yellow Door also runs an events and catering company, and does parties all over the province. This is a glamorous addition to food in Northern Ireland, and the breads especially are attracting wide praise, made the old-fashioned way, with totally natural ingredients. All eggs in the patisserie are free-range and, as you would expect in Ireland, there's butter galore.

▼ BUTCHERS

Coffeys Butchers

☎ 028 9066 6292
✉ 380 Lisburn Road, Belfast,
Co Antrim **BT9 6GL**
🕐 Mon–Thurs 8am–5.45pm;
Fri–Sat 7am–6pm

A popular Belfast butchery selling much-admired grass-fed, well-hung beef, mutton, lamb and pork, all locally sourced. There is excellent bacon, as you would expect from a Belfast butcher, black pudding and other sausages, plus free-range chickens and ducks, great geese for Christmas and Michelmas, plus some delicious gammon and hams.

David Burns Butchers

www.burnsbutchers.co.uk
☎ 028 9127 0073
✉ 112 Abbey Street, Bangor,
Co Down **BT20 4JB**
🕐 Tues–Thurs 7am–5pm;
Fri 6am–7pm; Sat 6am–5pm

A hard-working butcher's shop, selling award-winning sausages, black pudding, bacon, beef hung for a good four weeks, local lamb, pork and free-range poultry including Christmas geese and turkeys. There's also a range of cooked meats, with boiled ox tongue – always a joy to see – and some good gammon and ham.

Finnebrogue

www.finnebrogue.com
☎ 028 44617525
✉ 23 Finnebrogue Road,
Downpatrick **BT30 9AB**
🕐 Mon–Tues 7.45am–5.30pm;
Wed 7.45am–5.45pm;
Sat 6.45am–5.45pm

Farmed venison divides food lovers. There is no real reason why it should be necessary to farm venison when wild deer are plentiful and in need of being culled to control their numbers. However, venison farmers and their customers disagree, saying that farmed venison is a more consistent product. My view is that the more people that discover venison the better, but I hope they do move on to the many pleasures of wild meat. Finnebrogue's venison comes from deer killed young – under 24 months – and the meat is guaranteed to be tender. Christine and Dennis Lynn source their venison from specially chosen farms all over Ireland, selling a variety of cuts, as well as good sausages. Home delivery available.

T. Knox and Son

028 3835 3713
38b West Street, Portadown,
Co Armagh **BT62 3JQ**
Mon–Sat 8.30am–5.30pm

A butcher and deli combined selling some very good quality Northern Irish meats, including some excellent free-range pork, bacon and poultry, and good well-matured beef, lamb and mutton. In the deli section there is a wide range of cheeses plus some good home-made dishes to take away and reheat. Locals speak highly of Knox and Son.

McCreery's Butchery

www.mccreerybutchers.com
028 906 44911
439 Ormeau Rd, Belfast,
Co Antrim **BT7 3GQ**
Mon–Tues 7.45am–5.30pm;
Wed 7.45am–5.45pm;
Sat 6.45am–5.45pm

Nigel McCreery runs a great traditional butcher's shop, sourcing all his meat from local suppliers; the beef, pork and lamb can be 'traced from birth' he says. The beef, which comes from grass-fed cattle, is hung for at least three weeks or to your requirements. He has won awards for his sausages and home-made pies.

Moyallon Foods

028 926 29790
76 Crowhill Road, Craigavon, Co
Armagh **BT56 7AT**
Thurs–Fri 9am–5pm;
Sat 9am–2pm

In terms of good food, Northern Ireland has been a bit of a backwater for too long but there are some fantastic reports coming out of the province about the smaller producers. One such is Peter Hannon, who has owned this business for more than 20 years and has developed a good reputation. Although mainly a wholesaler they also have a shop where they sell local beef, lamb, poultry and pork. They have won numerous awards, including two for their handmade burgers and sausages. The beef is primarily Irish Short Horn or Hereford.

O'Doherty's Fine Meats ✿ ✿ ✿

www.blackbacon.com
028 6632 2152
3 Belmore Street, Enniskillen,
Co Fermanagh **BT74 6AA**
Mon–Sat 8am–6pm

Bacon heaven, and one of the best cures in the UK, made by real experts. The blackened outside of the rind on the trademark Black Bacon is made to a 100-year-old recipe and is essential when making a real Ulster Fry (full Northern Irish breakfast). Cut into thick slices, it is guaranteed not to leak out white liquid as it cooks and has a lovely intense flavour that is gentle on salt. But that is not all (this is a butcher I would dearly love to have on my doorstep, by the way), there is equally good oak-smoked bacon, nitrite-free bacon (addressing customer concern about health risks of this particular additive), brandy-cured black bacon for a richer breakfast or tea, hams on or off the bone, game and some excellent beef. Minimum order required.

▼ BAKERS AND CONFECTIONERS

Ditty's Home Bakery

www.dittysbakery.com
☎ 028 7946 8243
✉ 44 Main Street, Castledown
BT45 8AB

Robert Ditty is a second-generation artisan baker whose oatcakes win numerous awards and whose bread is hugely popular with locals (who recommended his bakery to be included in this guide). Soft fresh wheaten breads (one of my favourite breads to eat) and small soft white rolls are among the specialities. The bakery was started by Robert's father in the late '70s, with almost immediate success, becoming a wholesale baker and supplying the whole province. In 1976 the bakery was destroyed by a terrorist bomb, but restarted soon afterwards. Robert took over the bakery after his father's death. Latest projects include collaborations with other Irish artisans – oatcakes flavoured with Gubbeen cheese, for example, developed with Andy Rea of the Mourne Seafood Bar in Belfast (www.mourneseafood.com). Contact Ditty's for stockists outside Northern Ireland.

Leslie's Home Bakery

☎ 028 6632 4902
✉ 10 Church Street, Enniskillen,
Co Fermanagh **B74 7EJ**
🕐 Mon–Sat 8am–6pm

A lovely artisan bakery, selling regional favourites such as soda and wheaten bread (a sweetish soda bread packed with wholegrains), but which also makes an excellent sourdough loaf, traditional yeast breads, plus lovely morning rolls and buns. At Easter the hot cross buns are famous. If you are in town, don't miss an opportunity to buy the famous local Black Bacon with which to make an outstanding buttie.

Causeway Cheese Company

www.causewaycheese.com
028 2764 1241
Unit 1, Millenium Centre, Lough
Road, Loughgiel, Ballymena,
Co Antrim **BT44 9JN**

Damien and Susan McClosky make a range of cheeses,
naming them after ancient townlands in Northern Ireland.
Drumkeel is a crumbly, fresh cows' milk cheese (only made
in summer), Castlequarter a cheddar and Ballyveely a hard
cheese made from goats' milk. Coolkeeran is a cheddar type
with added Irish Dulse (seaweed). Home delivery available.

Cuan Oysters

www.cuanoysters.com
028 9754 1461
Sketrick Island, Killinchy,
Newtownards, Co Down

Pacific oysters grown in the cleanest Class A waters in a
marine nature reserve by one of the first commercial oyster
producers in the UK. Cuan are also pioneers of oyster 'seed'
hatcheries. Pacifics are the elongated non-native oysters –
they have slightly less power in their flavour than indigenous
oysters but are delicious all the same, as well as being
cheaper as they grow faster. Home delivery available.

George Cully & Son

028 4277 1463
Princess Anne Road, Portavogie,
Newtownards, Co Down **BT22 1DT**

A shop close to the harbourside in Portavogie, buying
fish landed there by day boats, and that you can absolutely
guarantee to be fresh. George Cully is held in great regard
by locals and others who drive miles to buy his fish, most
of which are local species including cod, whiting, sole, sea
trout (in season), herring and plaice. His refrigerated vans
deliver throughout Northern Ireland. Contact for details.

Glenarm The Northern Salmon Company

📞 028 2884 1691
✉ 8 Caslte Demense, Glenarm,
Ballymena, Co Antrim **BT44 0BD**

This company produces quite simply the best organic salmon. However, in 2007 the company suffered a disaster when the fish cages, which are positioned far out in tidal waters (to allow plenty of exercise for the growing fish), were invaded by a huge shoal of jelly fish, killing all of the salmon. It has taken two years for Glenarm to restock and bring in another harvest and, while you can't buy from the premises direct, I would suggest contacting them to find the nearest stockist of either fresh or smoked fish.

Walter Ewing ✪

📞 028 9032 5534
✉ 124 Shankill Rd, Belfast,
Co Antrim **BT13 2DB**
🕐 Tues–Sat 9am–5pm

Walter Ewing is an esteemed Belfast fishmonger, selling locally sourced fresh fish in the shop his grandfather established in 1911. Now working with his own sons, Warren and Crawford, Ewing sells fish to local restaurants and runs the shop. Most of the fish is sourced from the ports of Portavogie, Donegal and Kilkeel, where he buys from the day boats, guaranteeing that the fish will only be a day or two out of the water. He also sells some from Scotland and a few international species. Cockles, mussels, monkfish, turbot and cod are his customers' favourites, but salmon is also a speciality and his smoked salmon, made to his grandfather's secret recipe, is very highly regarded.

VEGETABLES AND FRUIT ▼

Dolphin Sea Vegetables ✿ ✪

www.dolphinseaveg.com
☎ 028 9061 7512
✉ Unit 54, Glenwood Centre,
Springbank Industrial Estate,
Dunmurray, Belfast **BT17 0QL**

Supplying a new appetite for using sea vegetables in cooking, Gus Heath sells hand-harvested seaweeds to shops (contact for stockists), and will also send his products via mail order. You can buy kelp, kombu, Irish wakame (one of the most delicious), cargageenan moss (to make gelatinous puddings), sea lettuce (another favourite), dulce and many more. Great if you love making Japanese food and want to experiment – and very nourishing, too.

DRINKS ▼

Suki Teahouse ✿ @ ✪

www.suki-tea.com
☎ 028 9033 0938
✉ Unit 6, Twin Spires Business Park,
155 Northumberland Street, Belfast
BT13 2JF

Interesting gourmet teas of every type: try the rare white tea infused with dried sour cherries, the green 'gunpowder' tea (subject to availability), the jasmine flower tea and the impressive organic green tea 'Sencha', which has a clean marine flavour. Added to this is a witty Japanese popcorn tea, made with grassy flavoured Bancha tea leaves and toasted, popped wholemeal rice, and my favourite, the jasmine infused Dragon Pearls, so powerful you can use them more than once.

Scotland

Ardardan Estate and Farm Shop ⊕

www.ardardan.co.uk
☎ 01389 849188
✉ Cardross, Argyll & Bute
G82 5HD
🕐 Tues–Sun 9am–5.30pm

This is quite a big farm shop, perhaps better described as a food hall, featuring a combination of local foods and brought-in items: Aberdeen Angus beef, Inverawe smoked salmon, wild venison and fish from the Summer Isles, olives, antipasti and some English foods. Does it work? Locals certainly appreciate a shop that has more choice yet is not a supermarket. There's a popular tea room, too.

Ardross Farm Shop ⊕ ⊘ ⊕

www.ardrossfarm.co.uk
☎ 01333 331400
✉ Elie, Fife **KY9 1EU**
🕐 Mon–Sat 9am–5.30pm;
Sun 9am–4pm (Oct–Mar,
closed Mon and Tues)

Rob and Fiona Pollock sell beautiful beef from their own herd, and grow over 40 varieties of vegetables through the season, selling them from a shop in a lovely old cart shed. They are also proud honey farmers with their own hives. Their bees thrive on the clover and hawthorn on and around the farm, and produce a pale, delicious honey. Home-made raspberry jam, steak pies, mince rounds and soup are available, plus local artisan foods such as rare-breed bacon and local pork, organic lamb and mutton, venison, wild border game, delicious free-range chickens and turkeys. Ardross is traditionally farmed, using crop rotation to nourish the soil and keep pests down. Cattle are kept in clover-rich fields, or fed from farm-grown feed, which is guaranteed GM free. Hedgerows are left uncut, stubble is left over winter to provide cover for birds and animals, and nesting boxes have been put up for owls. Outstanding – a deserving finalist in the National Farmers' Retail & Markets Association (FARMA) awards, 2010. Local home delivery available.

Blairgowrie Farm Shop ⊕ ⊚ ⊘ ⊕

www.blairgowriefarmshop.co.uk
☎ 01250 876528
✉ 14–16 Reform Street, Blairgowrie,
Perthshire **PH10 6BD**
🕐 Mon–Sat 8.30am–5.30pm;
Sun 11am–3pm

A farm shop in the centre of the Perthshire town most famous for its raspberries and other soft fruits, selling not just the fruit, but organic beef (a bestseller), free-range eggs and fresh chickens, wild venison, Hebridean lamb, plus a range of preserves, honey and other good things all produced locally or on nearby farms. There is also a vegetable box scheme available to locals. The shop has been a welcome addition to the town, which once had a thriving high street, home to many food shops until the opening of a vast superstore on the outskirts. Note that you can often buy soft fruit from stalls on the road, close to the fruit farms. Local deliveries available.

Castleton Farm Shop

www.castletonfarmshop.co.uk
01561 321155
Fordoun, Laurencekirk, Aberdeenshire **AB30 1JX**
May–Oct Mon–Sat 9.30am–6pm; Sun 10.30am–6pm;
Oct–April Mon–Sat 9.30am–5pm; Sun 10.30am–5pm

A farm shop that opened in 2003, which is also home to a soft fruit farm so, as you can imagine, for about six months of the year the shelves are loaded with freshly picked berries. Aside from that, in the large barn-style shop you will find home-cured bacon from Ingrams, Glenbervie Farms Aberdeen Angus beef and free-range chickens from Maryfield Farm. Artisan bread is from the Crannach bakery – take home some Honeyhill Bee Farm honey to spread on it. The farm shop is also a finalist in the FARMA awards for their café-restaurant.

Finzean Farm Shop @ ⏀

www.finzean.com
01330 850710
Balnaboth Steading, Finzean, Banchory, Aberdeenshire **AB31 6PA**
Mon–Sat 9am–5pm; Sun 11am–5pm

This charming farm shop comes highly recommended by friends living north of the border. Situated on the Finzean Estate in Royal Deeside, the former home of the artist Jospeh Farquarson, the shop sells the estate's own game (which you can pre-order during the season), plus other local specialities including oatcakes, farmhouse cheeses, smoked fish, plus fresh, seasonal local vegetables. Online and phone orders for game in season only.

Knowes Farm Shop

www.knowesfarmshop.co.uk
01620 860010
Knowes, East Linton, East Lothian **EH42 1XJ**
Mon–Sun 9.30am–5pm

A shop specialising in home-grown produce, especially unusual varieties of potato and a wide range of salad crops, roots, cabbage family, herbs and much more, which you can view on the website. Aside from this there is a wide range of fresh meat, free-range poultry, haggis, veal, game, plus other strange and useful items such as goose fat and scamorza (fresh smoked) Italian cheese.

217

Loch Arthur Creamery and Farm Shop ✿ @ ✿ ✿

www.locharthur.org.uk
☎ 01387 760296
✉ Beeswing, Dumfries
DG2 8JQ
🕐 Mon–Fri 9am–5.30pm;
Sat 10am–3pm

This is a lovely shop that combines great food with social enterprise, providing jobs for people with learning difficulties, set in the lowlands near Dumfries. Freshly baked artisan bread and some excellent, award-winning, organic cheeses that are handmade on the farm are among the highlights, but also look out for Demeter-certified meat (a standard even more scrupulous than organic), organically grown fruit and vegetables, home-made pies, cakes and preserves. It is the cheese that stars, however.

Try the Crannog, a fresh, sweet unpasteurised cheese; Kebbuck, mellow-flavoured and matured in a cloth bag; Criffel, a semi-soft cheese with a pungent 'washed rind'; or the buttery, smooth Loch Arthur Cheddar. Other dairy food include hand-churned butter, yoghurt and cream. Recently, Loch Arthur farm shop has begun delivering bread to Dumfries Fish and Game, Bank Street, Dumfries. See website for more details.

The Store ✿ @ ✿

www.thestorecompany.co.uk
☎ 01358 788083
✉ Foveran, Newburgh, Ellon,
Aberdeenshire **AB41 6AY**
🕐 Mon–Sun 10am–5pm

This excellent on-farm grocery is run by the enthusiastic gifted retailer Susan Booth, the daughter of the farming family whose great produce is sold in the shop. The farm raises Aberdeen Angus cattle, Suffolks and Texel lambs in small groups, grazing them on open fields. Their diet is mainly grass, but any grain will have been grown on the farm and is therefore guaranteed GM-free. The beef is hung for at least 21 days. Vegetables for the shops are pesticide-free and no artificial fertilisers are used on the farm, where the preservation of wildlife is a priority. The shop also sells a good range of artisan bread, ready-made foods and deli items, including cheeses, pies and preserves. There's a play barn for the children while you shop.

Aberdeen Country Fair ⊕

www.aberdeencountryfair.co.uk

☎ 01224 649000

✉ Belmont Street, Aberdeen
AB10 1JG

🕐 **Monthly**, last Sat 9am–5pm

Aberdeen Angus beef, locally caught fish, fresh fruit during the summer season, vegetables grown on nearby farms, handmade cheeses, Scottish whisky, wines, confectionery and home-baked cakes and biscuits can be found at this monthly market that attracts 30,000 visitors.

Ayr Farmers' Market ⊕

**www.ayrshirefarmersmarket.
co.uk**

☎ 01555 771757

✉ Kyle Centre Shopping Centre
Car Park, River Street, Ayr **KA6 6EN**

🕐 **Monthly**, 1st Sat 9am–1pm

This was one of the first farmers' markets in Scotland and it continues to be committed to providing excellent produce and service. Local chefs and tourists flock here for the amazing range of food on offer – grass-reared Ayrshire lamb, beef, pork, excellent bacon, locally raised chicken, game when in season and west coast seafood. Also a range of cows', goats' and ewes' milk cheeses from Dunlop; award-winning free-range duck and quail eggs; plus farmhouse ice cream, local honey and local fruit and vegetables.

Clarkston Farmers' Market ⊕

**www.lanarkshirefarmersmarket.
co.uk**

☎ 01555 771757

✉ Station Car Park, Clarkston Road,
Clarkston East, Renfrewshire
G76 8NE

🕐 **June–Oct**, 4th Sat 9am–1pm

Locals really rate this farmers' market. It may not be that big, with between 12 and 20 stalls depending on the season, but the produce is great. There's fruit and veg, beef, lamb and pies from Overton Farm, organic meat and poultry from Blackmount Organics, smoked fish from Fencebay fisheries, plus venison and traditionally reared meat from Carmichael Estate.

Dundee Farmers' Market ⊕

**www.scottishfarmersmarkets.
co.uk**

☎ 01382 434548

✉ High Street, Dundee **DD1 1SA**

🕐 **Monthly**, 3rd Sat 9am–4pm

Being so close to the sea, you will find the freshest fish at this good market, which complements the various Angus markets (see website for details of others on alternate weekends). Also available, of course, is the regional

219

speciality, Arbroath Smokies (delicious smoked haddock).
Look out, too, for local soft fruits in late spring, summer and
autumn, some very good beef and lamb suppliers, plus
organic produce.

Edinburgh Farmers' Market 🄯

**www.edinburghfarmersmarket.
com**
☎ 0131 652 5940
✉ Castle Terrace, Edinburgh
EH1 2DB
🕐 Weekly, Sat 9am–2pm

With over 35 stalls this is one of the largest markets in
the UK and a must for central Edinburgh residents each
Saturday. The range of produce is amazing. Stalls vary in
attendance (some are not here every week), but look out for
the Creelers for langoustines and other shellfish, free-range
eggs from Bonnington Farm, cured salmon and trout, free-
range poultry from Gartmorn Farm and organic vegetables
from Bellfield Organic. There is, of course, food typical of
the region, with venison from Fletcher's of Auchtermuchty
and some great beef, haggis and meat pudding producers.
Stallholders at the market have recently set up a
cooperative, sharing marketing costs and involving the
local community.

Forfar Farmers' Market 🄯

**www.scottishfarmersmarkets.
co.uk**
☎ 01382 370203
✉ Myre Park, Forfar, Angus
DD8 3JL
🕐 Monthly, 2nd Sat 9am–1pm

A good market, selling produce from all over Tayside. Not
only is this a good area for fish, but thanks to the milder
climate it is also the main soft fruit growing area in Scotland
so expect to find some of those extraordinary blue-red
raspberries. There is also beef from Braes of Coul, Mrs
Barbara Makie's lovely free-range eggs, traditional oatmeal
from the Alford Mill and J. Batchelor honey. Look out also
for Milton Hough farm shop's stall selling fresh home-grown
vegetables, free-range chicken and home-made meat stock.

Haddington Farmers' Market 🄯

**www.haddingtonfarmersmarket.
co.uk**
☎ 01368 863593
✉ Court Street, Haddington,
East Lothian **EH41 3HA**
🕐 Monthly, last Sat 9am–1pm

A very popular and well-run market with between 20 and
25 stalls selling regional produce, depending on the season.
There's heather honey from Braeside Apiaries, potatoes from
Jock's tattie shed, salad from Cloche, traditionally made

fresh cream and cheese made with Jersey milk from Stichill Farm, and organic bread from Trusty Crust bakery. Look out also for Northwood wild boar, Ballencreiff rare pedigree pork and Monarch venison.

Hamilton Farmers' Market

www.lanarkshirefarmersmarket.co.uk
📞 01555 771757
✉ New Cross, Quarry Street, Hamilton **ML3 7BQ**
🕐 **Monthly**, 3rd Sat 9am–1pm

Another good Lanarkshire market, with an exceptionally good variety of stalls. Look out for free-range pork from Sunnyside Farm, smoked fish from Tarelgin, breads and pastries from Taylor's bakery in Strathaven, sausages from Thompsons in Troon, Fife free-range poultry and artisan cheeses from the Island Cheese Company.

Inverness Highland Food Market 💷

www.highlandfoodmarket.co.uk
📞 07798 934920
✉ Tesco Extra Car Park, 1a Eastfield Way / Nairn Road, Inverness, Highland **IV2 7GD**
🕐 **Monthly**, last Sat 9am–2pm

Organised admirably with the help of Tesco, this farmers' market has established itself in the car park of the giant superstore and is fighting to persuade shoppers to pay a bit more for artisan food. Part of its obvious attraction is the offering of produce that multiples do not have access to, simply because it is not made on a large enough scale. On sale are free-range poultry and eggs, organic produce, good beef, as you would expect, plus hill lamb or mutton, game birds and venison.

Kirkcaldy Farmers' Market 💷

www.fifefarmersmarket.co.uk
📞 01383 730811
✉ Town Square, Wemyssfield, Kirkcaldy, Fife **KY1 1XW**
🕐 **Monthly**, last Sat 9am–1pm

Farmers' markets are held in Fife every weekend in alternate locations (see website). This one, held in the square in Kirkcaldy, comes highly rated – there is an amazing range of produce to choose from (depending on seasonal availability). Breads and cakes from Liz Maxwell at Achray Farm, Ian Spink's Arbroath Smokies, Nelson's ice cream, Gartmorn Farm poultry, venison from Fletcher's of Auchtermuchty, vegetables from John Reid's farm, Puddledub pork and organics from Bellfield Farm. Like all Fife markets, it's well worth a visit, especially if you are holidaying and self-catering in the area.

Montrose Farmers' Market £

www.scottishfarmersmarkets.
co.uk

- 01307 464392
- Town House Car Park, Montrose, Angus **DD10 8PH**
- Monthly, 1st Sat 9am–1pm

This is a lovely farmers' market with a good selection of Angus farmers and producers taking part, including one famous stallholder who smokes his haddock on the spot to make Arbroath Smokies. Vegetable farmer Peter Reid, Puddledub pork, Barbara Mackie (free-range eggs), Brae Farm beef and McDonald's Cheese Shop also attend the market, alongside others.

Paisley Farmers' Market £

www.scottishfarmersmarkets.
co.uk

- 01655 770217
- County Square, Paisley, Renfrewshire **PA1 1BP**
- Twice monthly, 2nd & last Sat 9am–1pm

Set up in the centre of Paisley, and now established for many years, I was originally impressed by this farmers' market not just for the quality of the produce, but because you can get good value for money here, a point not lost on Paisley's student population who report that they love the free-range eggs and organic breads. There are over 30 producers and a good range of produce. See the website to find more farmers' markets in this area.

Perth Farmers' Market £

www.perthfarmersmarket.co.uk

- 01738 582159
- King Edward Street and St John's Place, Perth **PG1 5SZ**
- Monthly, 1st Sat 9am–2pm

This market takes place only once a month, but is nevertheless excellent. It was Scotland's first farmers' market and is still run to the highest principles with a strong local and artisan ethos. There are usually well over 35 stalls and you can buy a wide range. Being in Scotland you can expect excellent meat: look out for Atholl Glens beef, Logiealmond lamb and Puddledub pork. Dairy producers include both Isle of Arran and St Andrews cheeses. There are local strawberries and raspberries in season (this is one of the main Scottish growing areas), and organic produce from Bellfield Farm. Look out also for Hand Made Oatcakes and flour and breads from the lovely Blair Atholl watermill.

Queens Park Farmers' Market (Glasgow) £

www.scottishfarmersmarkets.
co.uk
📞 01738 449430
✉ Queens Park, 520 Langside Road,
Glasgow **G42 9QL**
🕐 **Twice monthly**, 1st & 3rd
Sat 10am–2pm

Established nearly eight years ago, this was the second Glasgow farmers' market. It was set up to complement the Mansfield Park farmers' market which, should it be more convenient for you, is run on alternate weekends at a temporary venue at Dowanhill Primary School, 30 Havelock Street G11 5JE. On offer is some great Scottish produce sold at over 30 stalls: expect good breads and cakes, organic vegetables, game and free-range poultry, naturally reared meat and handmade cheeses.

Stockbridge (Edinburgh) Farmers' Market £

www.stockbridgemarket.com
📞 0131 477 1838
✉ Portgower Place, Stockbridge,
Edinburgh **EH4 1HQ**
🕐 **Weekly**, Sun 10am–4pm

The 30 or so stalls at this Sunday market sell a combination of food and crafts, so you will have to hunt about a bit to get the most out of this for your kitchen. It is a market that is full of charm, however, taking place in an area that is already distinctively food-orientated (nearby Raeburn Place is full of food shops). But locals report that there is good fish and game at the market, and a wonderful coffee stall.

Stornoway Farmers' Market £

www.stornowayfarmersmarket.
co.uk
📞 07810 603188
✉ Point Street, Stornoway
HS1 2XF
🕐 **Weekly**, Sat 9–11.30am
(**Winter**); 8.30am–1pm (**Summer**)

A great farmers' market, which has become an essential outlet for crofters and food producers based in the Outer Hebrides. The organisers insist that visitors to the market arrive early (holidaymakers, take note), because produce sells out quickly. Depending on the season you might find traditional varieties of potato such as red Duke of York and other locally grown vegetables, free-range chicken and duck eggs from various farms and crofts, and even, remarkably, grapes from what is believed to be the most northerly vineyard in Europe, the Poly Croft run by Donald and Jean Hope who also grow peaches and apricots. The clue to how they do this is in the name of the croft! There is also a market on the second Saturday of each month in Tarbert on the neighbouring island of Harris.

A la Carte

www.alacarteedinburgh.co.uk
0131 229 2140
156 Bruntsfield Place, Edinburgh
EH10 4ER
Mon, Fri 9am–5pm;
Tues–Thurs 9am–5.30pm;
Sat 9am–3pm

Superior quality, home-cooked frozen meals are sold from this pretty shop on a high street in Edinburgh. There are many quality frozen food outlets springing up around the UK, leading me to believe it is a growing market. A la Carte's fresh produce is all sourced locally and recipes range from Moroccan lamb stew to Spanish chicken casserole, plus the more prosaic shepherd's pie and lasagne. Each dish comes in returnable ceramic dishes. They also do a range of puddings; and scones and pastries baked on the premises.

Clarks ○

www.clarksfoods.co.uk
0131 656 0500
202 Bruntsfield Place, Edinburgh
EH10 4DF
Mon–Fri 10.30am–6pm;
Sat 9am–5pm; Sun 10am–4pm

Chris Clark's small, specialist food shop sells a well-edited range – Scottish cheeses for those who want to buy locally sourced, and some continental specialities for shoppers who want to bring France, Italy and Spain in to their kitchens. He also sells some superb vegetables (brought from Rungis in Paris) charcuterie, chutneys, pickles and even some beautiful wooden boards to serve it all on. In spite of all this, the locally made cheeses are very popular and Chris pays plenty of attention to keeping the Connage Clava, Dunlop, mould-ripened Brucklay and Sgriob-ruadh cheddar from Tobermory in perfect condition. Good haggis and black pudding are also available.

Deli 173 ○

01556 504880
173 King Street, Castle Douglas
DG7 1DZ
Mon–Sat 8am–5pm

A modern deli selling some of the best locally sourced foods from the south east of Scotland, including lovely cheeses made nearby at Beeswing (Loch Arthur and Criffel), honey, shortbread, marmalade and other preserves. Cakes are made with organic ingredients. For locals who want good things from further afield, there are olives and charcuterie. There is a second branch in Dumfries – call for details.

Delizique ⊙

☎ 0141 339 2000
✉ 70–72 Hyndland Street, Glasgow
G11 5PT
🕐 Mon–Fri 9am–9pm;
Sat–Sun 9am–8pm

Mhari Taylor's bakery and fine food shop has been so successful that it's taken over the Spar shop next door, restoring some of the old architectural features in the process. But I've heard mixed reviews. The produce is excellent and the café is raved about: 'The best meal I've had in Glasgow' was one comment. But when I visited, the staff were neither helpful nor friendly. There was an arrogance about them, which is what others complain of. There is no faulting the produce, though.

Herbie of Edinburgh ⊙ ✿

www.herbieofedinburgh.co.uk
☎ 0131 226 7212
✉ 1 North West Circus Place,
Edinburgh **EH3 6ST**
🕐 Mon–Fri 8.30am–6pm;
Sat 9am–6pm

High quality home-made food and groceries in a charming deli-bakery-café. The shop, and its other Edinburgh branch in Raeburn Place (see website for details), takes care to stock only items that are natural and low in additives and there is an emphasis on artisan food. Bacon and hams are from a butcher in Portobello Road, who has his own farm; chutneys and jams are from the Isle of Bute; there's honey from the west coast of Scotland; and Aberdeen Angus beef, organic vegetables and eggs from local farms. The chicken liver pâté, laced with brandy, is made in Edinburgh. Home-baked bread is also available.

Kember & Jones ⊚ ✿

www.kemberandjones.co.uk
☎ 0141 337 3851
✉ 134 Byres Road, Glasgow
G12 8TD
🕐 Mon–Sat 9am–10pm;
Sun 9am–6pm

Phil Kember and Claire Jones's glamorous café-deli stocks artisan cheeses, cured meats from the Rannoch Smokery near Glasgow, plus cakes, ginormous meringues, chewy cookies and melting pastries, all made on the premises. Other good things include fresh-baked artisan bread, handmade chocolates, preserves, muesli and handcrafted terrines. If you are not shopping, take a seat in the café and eat a lush salad with cheese or a bowl of handmade soup to warm up on colder days. There are usually long queues for tables, which is always a good sign. This lovely, enterprising young couple have a real vision and should be applauded. Visit if you can.

Orient Thai Market

www.orient-edinburgh.co.uk

📞 0131 228 5885

✉ 162–164 Bruntsfield Place,
Edinburgh **EH10 4ER**

🕐 Mon–Sat 10am–6.30pm;
Sun 12–6pm

Opened by Bhunaba Jenyavanija in 2009 and selling everything you need to cook authentic south-east Asian recipes: fresh noodles, baby aubergines, banana leaves, lemon grass, galangal; plus Mae Ploy red, green and yellow curry pastes. Big sacks of Tilda basmati and Thai fragrant rice are also available. Everything you need to prepare a Thai feast and a good range of frozen ready-to-eat meals such as Thai fishcakes and Chinese dim sum.

Peckham's

www.peckhams.co.uk

📞 0131 332 8844

✉ 48 Raeburn Place, Edinburgh
EH14 1HN

🕐 Mon–Sat 8am–12am;
Sun 8am–11pm

A general store with a good bakery open until midnight, selling a wide range, but with a good emphasis on locally produced and Scottish foods. Look out for Mrs Tilly's Tablet from Clackmannanshire, Loch Fyne smoked salmon (welfare-friendly but farmed), Isle of Mull cheese, a lemony flavoured Caboc rolled in hazelnuts and Gruth Dhu rolled in black pepper and pinhead oatmeal. Home-made Simple Simon pies contain Scottish lamb or beef, or fresh fish and Perthshire potatoes. There are further branches of Peckham's in Edinburgh, Glasgow, Aberdeen and other Scotland towns.

Ravenstone Deli

www.ravenstonedeli.com

📞 01988 500329

✉ 61–63 George Street, Newton
Stewart, Withorn, Dumfries &
Galloway **DG8 8NU**

🕐 Tues–Sat 8.30am–5pm

Sara Guild and James Barton's sleek-looking deli interior packs a wealth of locally sourced food. In the butchery you will find meat from local farms, including salt marsh lamb from Wigtown Bay during the summer. The deli's own traditional sausages, black pudding and haggis are also on sale along with fruit, herbs and vegetables grown in the back garden and on a farm nearby, as well as the deli's own honey. Artisan cheeses made by the excellent Loch Arthur creamery and Galloway Dairy are also available, plus home-cooked foods, continental oils, olives, and larder staples.

The Scottish Deli

www.scottish-deli.co.uk

☎ 01796 473322

✉ 8 West Moulin Road, Pitlochry,
Perthshire **PH16 5AD**

🕐 Mon–Sat 8.30am–5.30pm

This shop and mail order service is devoted to Scottish produce and specialities, and has some interesting items on sale. Try the crumbly Anster cheese made in Anstruther using Friesian-Holstein cows' milk, or Carola which was developed in the dairy at Wester Lawrenceton Farm using old crofters' recipes from north-east Scotland. A veg box scheme is also available and there are branches in Dunkeld and Aberfeldy – see website for details.

Valvona & Crolla

www.valvonacrolla.co.uk

☎ 0131 556 6066

✉ 19 Elm Row, Edinburgh
EH7 4AA

🕐 Mon–Thurs 8.30am–6pm;
Fri–Sat 8am–6pm; Sun 10.30am–4pm

The Contini family's historic shop has been Scotland's leading deli for decades, paving the way for an admired food culture in Edinburgh. At heart an atmospheric, classic Italian family-run shop selling the highest quality specialities – charcuterie, breads, antipasti, cheeses – they also sell home-cooked recipes and all the store cupboard ingredients you could possibly want. There is a real feeling of festive abundance evident as you step through the door. There's also a lovely café and a mail order business for anyone who wants a bit of V&C, but lives south of the border. Irresistible – no trip to Edinburgh would be complete without a visit here. In 2008 and 2009, Valvona & Crolla opened in two Jenners stores, one in Edinburgh and the other in Loch Lomond. See website for details.

BUTCHERS ▼

Andrew Gillespie

☎ 0141 959 2015

✉ 1601 Great Western Road,
Glasgow **G13 1LT**

🕐 Mon 7.30am–1pm;
Tues–Thurs 7.30am–5.30pm;
Fri 7am–5.30pm; Sat 7am–1pm

Andrew Gillespie buys meat from Scottish farms, sells it fresh and uses it to make some impressive pies and sausages, including Lorne sausage (a skinless, rectangular meat loaf). Hot soup is also available and very welcome if you visit on a cold, wet day.

Atholl Glens Organic Meat ⊕ @ ✦

www.athollglens.co.uk
☎ 01796 481482
✉ Atholl Glens Ltd, Atholl Estates
Office, Blair Atholl, Perthshire
PH18 5TH
🕐 Mon–Thurs 8am–4pm;
Fri 8am–3pm

A unique and admirable Highland meat business selling organically reared, slow-grown and naturally fed Aberdeen Angus beef and Blackface lamb, bred by a cooperative of tenant farmers on the Duke of Atholl's estate. The meat is hung on the bone and long-matured for flavour.

Ballard Butchers ✦

☎ 01556 502501
✉ 152 King Street, Castle Douglas,
Dumfries and Galloway **DG7 1DA**
🕐 Mon–Sat 7.30am–5pm

This is the place to come for excellent, local Galloway beef, hung for weeks to tender perfection and which has masses of flavour. A new supermarket in Castle Douglas put all of the town's small independent shops under threat, so there is a greater need than ever to support businesses like Ballards and sample their wonderful meat. It may cost a little more, but the whole experience will be superior – and there are always the cheaper cuts.

Blackface Meat Company

www.blackface.co.uk
☎ 01387 730326
✉ Weatherall Foods Limited,
Crochmore House, Irongray,
Dumfries **DG2 9SF**
🕐 Mon–Fri 9am–4.30pm

This farm, run by Ben and Percy Weatherall (both devoted to producing meat with unbeatable flavour) is leading the revival of our taste for mutton, selling both two-year-old and five-year-old ewes. The latter are run on the Scottish hill country for four years, having several sets of lambs, then they come down to lowland pasture in the final year. The resulting meat is astonishingly good, full of flavour and tender after a long slow roast. They also rear Galloway cattle and 'Iron Age' pork. A wide range of high-quality game, sourced from shoots in the north of England and Scotland, is also available. Grouse is a speciality.

W. Christie ♥

☎ 0131 229 3807
✉ 186 Bruntsfield Place,
Edinburgh **EH10 4DF**
🕐 Mon–Fri 7am–5.15pm;
Sat 7am–3.30pm

Just a small, unassuming shop front, but a butchery with a reputation that extends far beyond the attractive residential area of Bruntsfield, where you will find a charming high street packed with good, independent food shopping. All the grass-fed beef is sourced from a farm near Dumfries and slaughtered at a recently opened abattoir near Linlithgow. You will also find useful items such as beef (or other meat) stock, made with leftover scraps and bones, ready to add to stews and gravies. With butchers paying handsomely for waste to be removed, I think this is a great initiative.

Donald Russell ♥ @ ✿

www.donaldrussell.com
☎ 01467 629666
✉ FREEPOST SCO 4131, Inverurie,
Aberdeenshire **AB51 4ZL**

It is hard to know where to begin with Britain's most diverse and dynamic online butchery and specialist food company. Managing Director Hans Baumann has made Donald Russell a favourite service for private individuals who want to take the pain out of buying meat, offering fully traceable meat, poultry, game, fish and other goods. He sells good canapés, smoked salmon, ready-made dishes and continental smoked meat, too. All beef is sourced from dedicated farms, mainly in Scotland. Much attention is paid to hanging and cut: the beef is reliably tender. You can also buy from a vast range of lamb, pork and venison cuts. For economy, choose from a selection of meat boxes.

George Bower ♥ @ ✿

www.georgebowerbutchers.co.uk
☎ 0131 332 3469
✉ 75 Raeburn Place, Stockbridge,
Edinburgh **EH4 1JG**
🕐 Mon–Sat 8am–5pm

Mark Smith makes a better haggis than most for this small butcher's shop on a cheerful Edinburgh high street, using outdoor-reared pork and offal then encasing it in a natural skin. He also makes dry-cured bacon, sells well-hung (four weeks or more) Highland or Aberdeen Angus beef, free-range chickens and ducks reared in Peebles, game birds throughout the season and various breeds most of the year. Lamb and mutton are also available.

J. B. Houston

www.jbhouston.co.uk
☎ 01387 255528
✉ Greenbrae Loaning, Dumfries
DG1 3DQ
🕐 Mon 8am–12pm; Tues–Fri
7.30am–5.15pm; Sat 7am–4pm

Handmade haggis is the speciality here, made by Stuart Houston for a huge number of devoted customers who queue up patiently outside his small Dumfries shop (and who have done so regularly since his grandparents opened it in the '50s). You might like to try his venison haggis as an equally good alternative. But then the meat pies are wonderful, too, with burnished, crisp pastry and juicy insides. There's a good range of fresh meat, some of which is from Houston's own farm nearby.

James Allan Butchers

☎ 0141 334 8973
✉ 85 Lauderdale Gardens,
Glasgow **G12 9QU**
🕐 Mon–Fri 8am–5.30pm;
Sat 7am–5pm

Morton Perrie keeps a regularly updated board on his shop counter identifying the source of the meat he has on display. Usually it will be local from the Highlands and sometimes the islands of Scotland. He's a great cook and baker, too. Try his Lorne sausage, a dish that in other hands can go horribly wrong, and his home-made pies. Sausages are also made with care, not over-spiced.

D. & A. Kennedy

www.kennedybeef.com
☎ 01250 870358
✉ 36 High Street, Blairgowrie,
Perthshire **PH10 6ET**
🕐 Mon–Sat 6.30am–5pm

Alan Kennedy visits Forfar Market every Wednesday to buy livestock from trusted local farms, then takes them back to his butcher's shop in Blairgowrie to mature the carcasses for longer – at least three weeks for beef – to make sure it is always tender and full of flavour. Beef is Limousin Angus cross; lamb is from the Highlands. Ask for game when in season.

MacDonald Brothers

www.macdonald-bros.co.uk
☎ 01796 472047
✉ 6–8 Bonnethill Road, Pitlochry,
Perthshire **PH16 5BS**
🕐 Mon–Wed, Fri–Sat 7am–5pm;
Thurs 7am–1pm

A great Perthshire butcher's, owned and run by the MacDonald family who have been in Pitlochry since 1928, selling the best Scottish meat sourced from local farmers. Beef is farmed organically by Alistair Brewster in Dunkeld and there is a large selection of game, especially red deer venison, shot on local estates. There's good haggis on offer, plus black puddings and a delicious white 'mealy' (oatmeal) pudding in natural skins. On Wednesdays and Fridays MacDonalds sell wet fish from local fishmonger McPhersons.

Mogerleys ✔

www.mogerleys.com
☎ 01387 253590
✉ 49 Friar's Vennel, Dumfries
DG1 2RQ
🕐 Mon–Fri 6am–5pm;
Sat 6am–4.30pm

A small shop that has been here since 1876 (though no longer still in the same family, unsurprisingly) selling good haggis, sausages, bacon and a range of fresh meat that is all sourced from Scottish farms.

Ramsay of Carluke ✪ @ ✔

www.ramsayofcarluke.co.uk
☎ 01555 772277
✉ 22 Mount Stewart Street,
Carluke **ML8 5ED**

When I find a mail order source of great haggis and white pudding, the two most scrumptious foods to emerge from Scotland, I want to weep tears of joy. Grilled or fried white pudding served with scrambled egg and bacon is a favourite in our house, and Ramsay's handy sticks of haggis mean you can slice a piece or two and pop it in a pan for a healthy little lunch. They also sell the puddings ready-sliced in sections of four so you can take a helping from the freezer and use exactly what is needed. Famous for their bacon made with outdoor-reared pork and also for a rather strange fruit and oatmeal pudding that I have not quite got to grips with yet (I am not sure if I like it or not), the current generation of Ramsays, Andrew and John, are keeping up the tradition of great Scottish butchery (they also sell fresh meat) and thankfully making it available nationwide.

Blair Atholl Watermill ❶ ❷

www.blairathollwatermill.co.uk
☎ 01769 481321
✉ Blair Atholl Watermill, Ford Road, Blair Atholl, Perthshire **PH18 5SH**
🕐 1 Apr–31 Oct Mon–Sun 10am–5pm

A hidden-away working watermill (dating back to the 16th century), bakery and café run by Kirsty and Rami Cohen, open only in the summer months. The speciality here is the oat bread, made entirely from grain grown locally and milled by the Cohens, but you can also buy seeded rolls and bagels, gooey cakes and a few other groceries along the Fairtrade and ethically sourced lines. This is also a handy place to stop for lunch; there's a simple menu at the café and most ingredients are locally sourced. I thought this was a great and unusual place with masses of charm in a terrific setting.

Coco Chocolate ❶ @

www.cocochocolate.co.uk
☎ 0131 228 4526
✉ 174 Bruntsfield Place, Bruntsfield, Edinburgh **EH10 4ER**
🕐 Mon–Sat 10am–6pm; Sun 12–4pm

Rebecca Knights-Kerswell uses only single origin chocolate from the Dominican Republic, Venezuela and Madagascar that contains absolutely no vegetable fat or synthetic flavourings. A wide variety of chocolate bars are available, many of them flavoured with spices and herbs – the hand-made chocolate studded with hazelnuts, citrus peel or berries is excellent. The chocolate is all made in Scotland by artisans and twice a month the shop opens its doors for a chocolate school.

Cocoa Mountain Ltd ❶ @ ❷

www.cocoamountain.co.uk
☎ 01971 511233
✉ 8 Balnakeil, Durness, Lairg, Sutherland **IV27 4PT**
🕐 Mon–Sun 9am–6pm

Being the most geographically remote chocolate producers in Europe, owners Paul and James feel the beauty of their surroundings is reflected in the quality of their products. To ensure they are producing the highest-quality chocolate they use premium ingredients from local and organic suppliers where possible. They also avoid using any artificial flavouring. There is a variety of chocolate types on offer, such as gluten free, as well as a selection of products suitable for vegans, vegetarians and those who are lactose intolerant. Truffles are the bestseller, but there is a range of other products such as their own chocolate bars, kids' chocolates, fruit chocolates and many more that you will not be able to resist. Mail order available.

M. Corson ●

☎ 01556 502489
✉ 160 King Street, Castle Douglas, Dumfries and Galloway **DG7 1DA**
🕐 Mon–Sat 7.30am–4.30pm; Sat 7.30am–3pm

You can find lovely buttery oatcakes at this authentic Scottish bakers in the centre of this delightful town full of good food shops – Castle Douglas has been designated as Dumfries & Galloway's 'food town'. Corson's is also a good place to buy a hot pastry, a bacon sandwich, floury baps or a traditional loaf.

Falko Konditormeister ●

www.falko.co.uk
☎ 0131 656 0763
✉ 185 Bruntsfield Place, Edinburgh **EH10 4DG**
🕐 Wed, Fri 8.45am–6pm; Thurs 8.45am–6.30pm; Sat 9am–6pm; Sun 10.30am–6pm

Falko Burkhart specialises in genuine German breads, pastries and cakes made to artisan recipes. Falko was recommended to me by the excellent organic Northumberland grain farmers and flour miller, Gilchesters, who say he makes the best stollen available anywhere that is not home-made. Pretzels, gateaux featuring whatever seasonal fruit is available and chocolates are also on sale and you may occasionally – if you visit at the right time – spot the author and neighbour J. K. Rowling taking her coffee in the shop. There is another shop in Gullane, East Lothian (see website).

Peckham & Rye ●

www.peckhams.co.uk
☎ 0131 229 7054
✉ 155–159 Bruntsfield Place, Edinburgh **EH10 4DG**
🕐 Mon–Sat 8am–12pm; Sun 9am–12pm

The artisan bread in this large family-owned shop selling a wide range of specialist foods is sourced from the Engine Shed, a community bakery in nearby St Leonard's Lane that locals claim to be Edinburgh's best. Much of the food in Peckham's stores (they have other branches in Scotland – see website) has a local or Scottish theme. This is the place to buy Grahams Milk, Ramsay's bacon and the amazing Stornaway black pudding fortified with oatmeal. They also sell wines and spirits.

Tapa Organic

www.tapabakehouse.com

☎ 0141 554 9981

✉ 21 Whitehill Street, Dennistoun, Glasgow **G31 2LH**

🕐 Mon–Fri 8am–6pm; Sat 9am–5pm

If Glasgow resident food fans complain of no artisan baker, this gem is the remedy. Tucked in a small street at the opposite end of the city to Byres Road is the Tapa Bakehouse, well worth a visit to buy loaves of serious quality. Using the most wholesome ingredients, and made slowly so there is plenty of time for the grain and wild yeast to release their flavours, this place is swiftly earning a reputation for being the bees knees of bakeries. Edinburgh-based food expert Joanna Blythman is a fan and I can quite see why. Most bread is organic, some from old family recipes. Try the wholemeal or spelt bread. Coffee brewed in the attached café is Fairtrade. I liked it very much.

The Toffee Shop 💷

☎ 01556 502903

✉ 109 King Street, Castle Douglas, Dumfries and Galloway **DG7 1LZ**

🕐 Mon–Sat 10am–5.30pm; Sun 12–4pm

A shop that is a time machine, transporting one back to the days when you queued to buy sweets by 'the quarter' after school. There are 300 jars in this packed shop – expect to find Jenny's boilings, sugar pebbles, barley sugar, cinnamon balls, and rosebuds, as well as Berrick Cockles (like Ediburgh rock – pink and white stripes, minty flavour), chocolates handmade locally in Twyham, Halloween toffee apples, specialities for Christmas and lots of toffee.

▼ DAIRY

Isle of Mull Cheese 🏠 @ 🍃

www.isleofmullcheese.co.uk

☎ 01688 302235

✉ Sgriob-ruadh Farm, Glengorm, Tobermory, Isle of Mull **PA75 6QD**

Here you can buy a gutsy, cheddar-type cheese made in an idyllic location on the Isle of Mull by Brendan and Shelagh Reade using milk from their own herd. Smooth-textured with a muscular, dusty apple flavour, you should try it with a glass of single malt on the side. It cooks to a beautiful cream – make an Isle of Mull rarebit using a combination of whisky, an egg yolk and a pinch of dried mustard. Contact them for stockists or order from the website.

I. J. Mellis @ ⊘

www.mellischeese.co.uk
☎ 0131 447 8889
✉ 330 Morningside Rd, Edinburgh
EH10 4QJ
🕒 Mon–Wed 9am–6pm; Thurs–Sat 9am–6.30pm; Sun 12am–5pm

I. J. Mellis is to Scotland cheesemongering what Neal's Yard Dairy is to London, selling a large range of perfectly ripened cheeses both from Scotland and the rest of Britain and Ireland. All cheese is artisan-made, much of it from unpasteurised milk, and there is plenty of variety. Helpful and knowledgeable staff will guide you towards some lovely buys – I leave you in their capable hands. Breads, biscuits and some deli items are also on sale. There are six branches throughout Scotland. See website for details.

Wester Lawrenceton Cheese

☎ 01309 676566
✉ Wester Lawrenceton Farm, Forres, Moray **IV36 2RH**

The cheeses are made with raw organic milk from Ayrshire cows and the proprietor, Pam Rodway, has built a formidable reputation as a cheesemaker. She combines an Irish-style cheese with the French Tomme and the result has brought plaudits from far and wide. Her cheeses are available from Elgin and Inverness farmers' markets, as well as a range of delicatessens, specialist food shops and wholesalers (phone for details). But, at the time of writing, there is sadly no mail order or online sales.

FISH AND SEAFOOD ▼

Alex Spink & Sons @

www.arbroathsmokiesonline.
co.uk
☎ 01250 873287
✉ 3 Perth Street, Blairgowrie, Perthshire **PH10 6DQ**
🕒 Mon–Fri 8am–5pm

Norman Spink specialises in Scottish fish, including salmon, lemon sole, shellfish and the local delicacy Arbroath Smokies (whole, undyed, smoked haddock on the bone) from Angus. They're not everyone's cup of tea, but I like them. The other fish here is of a consistently good quality. There are two branches – see website for details.

Arbroath Fisheries ⊕ ⊚ ⊘

www.arbroath-smokie.co.uk
☎ 01241 872331
✉ 5 Seagate, Arbroath, Angus
DD11 5BJ
🕐 Mon–Fri 9am–5pm

A delightful shop, painted a gorgeous sunny yellow, where you can pop in and buy some of the best Arbroath Smokies, plus kiln-smoked salmon, haddock fillet, trout and mackerel. See the website for the nationwide mail order service.

Armstrong's of Stockbridge ⊕ ⊚ ⊘

www.armstrongsof
stockbridge.co.uk
☎ 0131 315 2033
✉ 80 Raeburn Place, Edinburgh
EH4 1HH
🕐 Tues–Fri 7am–5.30pm;
Sat 7am–5pm

A fishmonger who buys from particular Scottish boats with a reputation for high quality, carefully handled fish and who would rather wait for a late boat than buy elsewhere. They sell haddock, sole (lemon, dabs, grey), lobsters, prawns (langoustines), spoots (razor fish) and their own smoked Finnan haddock (on the bone), haddock fillets, mussels and oysters – all subject, of course, to availability. The staff are very helpful and are confident of their product. They will offer you nibbles of salmon and the like before you buy.

Bernard Corrigan ⊘

www.bernardcorrigan.com
☎ 0141 552 4368
✉ 184-200 Howard Street, Glasgow
G1 4HW
🕐 Tues–Sat 7.30am–6pm

A fishmonger and game dealer with a shop on this vibrant high street in Glasgow that also boasts other good food shops. He is a specialist in Scottish shellfish, bought from fleets fishing out of the very north of Scotland. Scallops, langoustines, clams and mussels are bestsellers. Lobsters and crabs should be pre-ordered. His peat-smoked haddock gets good reviews and this is the place for pheasant and partridge, when in season. Venison is available most of the year round.

Clark Brothers

☎ 0131 6656181
✉ 224 New Street, The Harbour,
Musselburgh, East Lothian
EH21 6DQ
🕐 Tues–Fri 7am–5.30pm;
Mon, Sat 7am–5pm

Locals describe this fishmonger, which sells fish and shellfish caught by local boats, as excellent. It also supplies many East Lothian restaurants, who give it a high rating for the freshness of the fish. There is a small smokery, too, producing some delicious kippers and smoked haddock. Wild salmon is available in season along with the great Scottish langoustines, live and cooked crab, farmed mussels, plus unusual items such as razor clams and samphire (an edible succulent weed that grows on the beach in summer).

Cockles Fishmonger

www.cocklesfinefoods.co.uk
☎ 01546 606292
✉ 11Argyll Street, Lochgilphead, Argyll **PA31 8LZ**
🕐 Mon–Fri 9.30am–5.30pm; Sat 9.30am–5pm

Situated at the head of Loch Fyne and buying from the boats that come in there, it is not surprising that this is a place where you can buy incredibly fresh langoustines and other local species. There are also farmed mussels from Loch Etive and a wide range of useful deli items, from artisan cheeses to oils and cured meats, making this a handy and essential place for food lovers in a fairly remote region.

Duncan Fraser & Son Fish & Game

☎ 01463 232744
✉ 8–10 Queensgate Arcade, Inverness **IV1 1DJ**
🕐 Tues–Sat 8.30am–5pm

A popular local fishmonger in Inverness, who also holds a game licence so you can pop in for game birds, rabbit, hare and wild venison, too. Most of the fish is Scottish and you can expect to find fresh herring (including melts and roe), kippers, mussels, haddock, cooked crab, clams, scallops and much more.

Dunkeld Smoked Salmon ◐ @ ◑

www.dunkeldsmokedsalmon.com
☎ 01350 727639
✉ Springwells Smokehouse, Brae Street, Dunkeld, Perthshire **PH8 0BA**
🕐 Tues–Sun 9.30am–5pm

A highly rated smokehouse smoking fish from a sustainable source. One of only a few producers that smoke wild salmon (theirs is sourced from a limited supply that is caught in commercial nets on the west coast of Scotland). Farmed salmon is sourced from RSPCA Freedom Food-accredited Loch Duart and smoked sea trout is also available.

Eddie's Seafood Market ⊘

0131 229 4207

7 Roseneath Place, Edinburgh
EH9 1JH

Tues–Sat 8am–6pm

Eddie's is an interesting shop, specialising in shellfish of all types, selling fresh squid, langoustines, prawns and lobster sourced locally from Scottish suppliers. The lobsters are stored in a tank on display in the shop, so you can pick one out, literally alive and kicking, to take home and cook. Wild sea bass is another speciality and there's a huge variety of other fish from all over – you might like to ask a question or two about the source of some of the more exotic types. I recommend that you arrive early on busy Saturdays and in the run up to Christmas.

George Hughes & Son ◑ @ ⊘

www.freshfishdaily.co.uk

0131 447 1183

197 Bruntsfield Place, Edinburgh
EH10 4DQ

Tues–Fri 7am–5.30pm;
Sat 7am–3pm

Specialising in the freshest fish from Scottish fishing ports, George Baxter's fishmonger's shop is very popular with locals shopping on this high street in residential Edinburgh. It sells good shellfish – it is the place to come for Scottish lobsters and enormous scallops – excellent fresh haddock and lemon sole, plus some unusual, less familiar wild species. There was a rockfish on the counter the day I visited. The undyed smoked haddock and on-the-bone Finnan's haddock are a must; smoked salmon is from the welfare-friendly Loch Fyne farms.

Hebridean Smokehouse ◑ @ ⊘

www.hebrideansmokehouse.com

01876 580209

Clachan, Locheport, Isle of North
Uist **HS6 5HD**

A special smokehouse on the remote island of North Uist in the Hebrides, smoking over peat fires salmon that has been reared in the island's sea lochs in a sustainable system. The fish itself is remarkable in that it is an indigenous species (dubbed 'Hebridean' by Fergus Granville who runs the business) and not the Norwegian variety that is reared in all other Scottish fish farms. The Hebridean salmon's suitability in this environment means it is less vulnerable to disease (so needs the minimum of chemical treatments), and it is no threat to wild salmon if it escapes from the cages. The taste of the smoked fish is intense and earthy, thanks to the peat. The fish are hand sliced. The smokehouse also produces smoked sea trout, scallops and lobster, and also makes a blend of butter and their smoked fish to eat with boiled potatoes, on toast, pasta or risotto. If you are on the island, pay them a visit, but check ahead for opening hours. Alternatively, everything is available online.

Ken Watmough

☎ 01224 640321
✉ 29 Thistle Street, Aberdeen
AB10 1UY
🕐 Tues–Fri 9am–5pm;
Sat 7.15am–1pm

A great place for fresh and ethically sourced Scottish fish including razor clams, crab, haddock, wild salmon (in season), sardines, wild bass, various sole species and wild samphire (an edible beach weed delicious to eat with fish). Ken Watmough buys from the market at Aberdeen, but is known for his care in only buying from boats that fish responsibly. There is also a smokehouse and Watmough's Arbroath Smokies (smoked whole haddock) are some of the best you can buy.

VEGETABLES AND FRUIT ▼

Andersons

☎ 0141 357 4944
✉ 190 Byres Road, Glasgow
G12 8SN
🕐 Mon–Fri 8.30am–7pm;
Sat 8am–6.30pm; Sun 9am–6pm

Andersons is a traditional greengrocer's shop, selling wonderfully fresh top quality produce mostly sourced via Glasgow's wholesale market. Sometimes there's rhubarb, watercress and tomatoes from local allotments and in summer there are plenty of Scottish-grown strawberries and raspberries. Organic fruit juice, Scottish honey, Galloway Lodge jams, mustards and pickles are also available.

Pittormie Fruit Farm 🍂

www.pittormiefruitfarm.co.uk
☎ 01334 870233
✉ Dairsie, Fife **KY15 4SW**

This is a truly charming farm run by Jackie and Gillian Cameron, selling all its own home-grown fruit and vegetables, from potatoes to asparagus, soft fruits, salad and brassicas. The range is great and the shop a delight – a small, stone-built cottage behind a wall, with flower-filled pots outside the door. Not to be missed if you are in the area. Call for opening times.

Scot-herbs

www.scotherbs.co.uk
☎ 01382 360642
✉ Longforgan, Near Dundee
DD2 5HU

While there is no shop front or mail order this Perth farm deserves inclusion in this guide for the sheer excitement of the variety it offers and for innovation. A former Farmer of the Year in the BBC Radio 4 Food & Farming Awards, Robert Wilson branched out of dairy farming into growing herbs when he spotted that increasing health concerns were pointing towards the arrival in the UK of the Mediterranean diet and a greater use of more herbs in cooking. Wilson is now one of the UK's larger suppliers, supplying the multiples and also farm shops in the area. The range is too numerous to list, but aside from the standard favourites there is chervil, sorrel, purple basil, lemon grass and spearmint. He also grows salad leaves and microleaf. Contact Scot-herbs for details of your nearest stockist.

Wester Hardmuir Fruit Farm

☎ 01309 641259
✉ Auldean, Nairn, Nairnshire
IV12 5QG
🕐 Jun–Dec Mon–Sun 9am–6pm

It's always nice to see outdoor-grown strawberries, especially in Scotland. When they ripen slowly they taste amazing. This is a good fruit farm with berries grown at table height for those who find bending to pick them hard work. The farm shop sells other produce grown on the farm, including a good variety of vegetables, other soft fruit, rhubarb and apples. The freezer is stacked with the surplus berries so you can eat them through winter, too. There are also free-range eggs, home-baked items, jams and chutneys.

Brookes Honey ◐ @ ◑

www.brookeshoney.com
☎ 01250 881200
✉ Woodend Cottage, Enochdhu,
Perthshire **PH10 7PW**

Jenny and David Brookes produce outstanding heather honey in Scotland, placing their hives near the moors where the purple flowering plant flourishes. David is the beekeeper who cares for the bees; Jenny is in charge of selling the honey, which is available via mail order. Heather honey has a unique, semi-granular texture with a slight gelatinousness. Its flavour is herby with a hint of mint. Many believe it to be the best of the honeys produced in the UK.

Scarlett's Honey

www.scarlettshoney.co.uk
☎ 01828 640821
✉ Meigle, Blairgowrie, Perthshire
PH12 8QX
🕐 Mon–Fri 7am–6pm

Special, glutinous, heather honey made by a reasonably large-scale honey producer (1000 hives) run by policeman-turned-beekeeper John Scarlett. The hives are placed and moved around farms and soft fruit growers in eastern Scotland. The actual production of the honey is undertaken in a state-of-the-art plant, but it remains a very natural high-quality honey. Scarlett does not have a shop, but his honey is widely available at farm shops, grocers and farmers markets in Scotland (the first and third Saturday of every month at Edinburgh farmers' market – see page 220). Contact Scarlett's for stockists.

The Bean Shop 🏠 @ ❂

www.thebeanshop.com
📞 01738 449955
✉ 67 George Street, Perth **PH1 5LB**
🕐 Mon–Sat 9.30am–5.30pm

A small but special shop selling tea and coffee with its own roastery in the centre of Perth. Much trouble is taken to source the coffee, some of which is Fairtrade and / or Rainforest Alliance accredited. Run by John and Lorna Bruce (John has the perfect credentials as he was born on a tea plantation in Darjeeling), it sells a large variety, including single origin and blended coffee; white, green and black tea; plus herbal and floral infusions. You can buy online.

Edinburgh Tea & Coffee Co ❂ @

www.edinburghteacoffee.co.uk
📞 0131 669 9222
✉ 15/G 214 Sir Harry Lauder Road, Edinburgh **EH15 2QA**

Fully accredited by the Fairtrade Foundation, this roastery specialises in good quality coffee, although they are mainly bulk sellers so it makes sense to order a good amount. They are also specialists in equipment for making coffee, especially traditional espresso machines. If you want to buy their coffee in small quantities, contact them for stockists.

Equal Exchange @

www.equalexchange.co.uk
📞 0131 554 5912
✉ Suite 1, 2 Commercial Street, Edinburgh **EH6 6JA**

An ethical trading company that was ahead of most: an idea of three former aid workers who realised in 1979 that the answer to the unfairness (on coffee and tea farmers) of the world-wide commodities markets was in fair-trading direct with the producers. The first product (an instant coffee) they dubbed Campaign coffee, but Equal Exchange have moved on since then launching Fairtrade-accredited coffee and tea from all over the world, now beautifully packaged and in many sophisticated blends. They incidentally make a delicious Rooibos tea, and also sell Fairtrade sugar, cocoa, nuts and nut butters. Contact them for stockists.

Matthew Algie ⊙ ⊘

www.matthewalgie.com

☎ 0800 263333

✉ 16 Lawmoor Road, Glasgow
G5 0UL

A professional coffee merchant who also runs a Barista
(coffee training) school in Islington, London (see website)
and sells espresso machines. The coffees, which have
inspired names such as Darwin, Elevator and Source of the
Nile, can be roasted to order and some are accredited
Fairtrade and / or organic. They also sell Rosie's Fairtrade tea
– as in Rosie Lee, they add helpfully (yep – we get it).

South East

The BarnYard

www.the-barnyard.com
☎ 01634 235059
✉ Oak Lane, Upchurch,
Sittingbourne, Kent **ME9 7EZ**
🕐 Sun–Thurs 8.30am–5pm;
Fri–Sat 8.30am–late

A delightful fruit farm run by the Goatham family, selling apples, pears, strawberries, cherries and plums. Juices are made with the orchard fruit, and the on-site pastry chef makes lovely scones, cakes and muffins. The meat in the farm shop comes from Mulberry Farm nearby in Newington and includes free-range, rare-breed pork, beef and lamb. The BarnYard was a finalist in the National Farmers' Retail & Markets Association (FARMA) awards, 2010.

Boathouse Organic Farm Shop

www.boathouseorganicfarmshop.
co.uk
☎ 01273 814188
✉ The Orchards, Uckfield Road,
Clayhill, Lewes, East Sussex
BN8 5RX
🕐 Mon–Sat 8am–6pm;
Sun 10am–2pm

A great-looking shop in a simple wooden building, with produce displayed outside and a wealth of good things within. Run by Martin Tebbut and his family, the shop is Soil Association-certified, a guarantee that all produce on sale is naturally produced and traceable. Beef is from red-coloured, Sussex breed cattle, supplied by a local farm. Dairy, eggs, fresh seasonal fruit and vegetables are also available. This is a place with plenty of charm and integrity.

Cobbs Farm Shop 🅿️

www.cobbsfarmshop.co.uk
☎ 01488 686770
✉ Bath Road, Hungerford,
Berkshire **RG17 0SP**
🕐 Mon–Sat 9am–6pm;
Sun 10am–5pm

A good all-round farm shop recommended by locals, housing its own butcher and with a market garden supplying seasonal vegetables and fruit (ready-picked or PYO). Expect to find soft fruit in the summer, including tayberries, red currants, strawberries and raspberries. Broad beans, chard, beetroot and squash are among the vegetables on offer. Also a strong supporter of local produce, the shop sells locally made cheeses, pies and ham.

Copas Farms 🔵

www.copasfarms.co.uk
☎ 01753 652727
✉ Calves Lane Farm, Billet Lane,
Iver, Buckinghamshire **SL0 0LU**
🕐 April–Sept Tues–Fri 10am–6pm;
Sat–Sun 10am–5pm

A pick-your-own and farm shop run by a family who are more famous for the excellent free-range turkeys they rear for Christmas (see page 270). In spring there is asparagus, then soft and orchard fruit throughout the summer. Other veg includes runner beans, French and broad beans, spinach, beetroot, courgettes and marrows. This is not an organic farm, but it operates under the conservation grade LEAF scheme, which aims to encourage wildlife back on to conventional farms by using agricultural chemicals with care and creating ideal habitats in hedgerows and woodland.

Cowdray Farm Shop

www.cowdrayfarmshop.co.uk
☎ 01730 815040
✉ Cowdray Park, Midhurst, West
Sussex **GU29 0AJ**
🕐 Mon–Sat 9am–6pm;
Sun 10am–4pm

A handsome farm shop housed in a half-timbered building on the Cowdray Estate. It sells, as you might expect, beef and lamb from the Cowdray farms, butchered on site by Vic May. Venison, cereals and dairy foods are also from the estate. Pork and turkey comes from the Smith family, farmers at nearby Great Garnetts; chickens from not-so-near Creedy Carver farms in Devon. Home-grown vegetables and an in-house bakery – plus a café – make this a lovely shop to visit.

Dews Meadow Farm 🔵 🟢

www.dewsmeadowfarm.co.uk
☎ 01235 868634
✉ Oxford Road, East Hanney,
Wantage **OX12 0HP**
🕐 Mon–Sat 8.30am–5.30pm

Dews Meadow started rearing additive-free pork in the '80s, a long time before it became fashionable. Run by Andy and Jane Bowler, the shop, and particularly the pork and bacon, has a fabulous reputation. Locals rave over it. It was recommended to me by former Grand National winning jockey and local resident, Marcus Armytage ('It's the place to go for pork.'). They do very good black pudding and a delicious old-fashioned hazlet. The shop has a full range of cooked food and a well-stocked deli section, but it's the pork that is the star here.

Foxbury Farm ✍

www.foxburyfarm.co.uk

☎ 01993 867385

✉ Foxbury Farm, Burford Road, Brize Norton, Oxfordshire **OX18 3NX**

🕐 Tues–Sat 9am–6pm; Sun 10am–4pm

In November 2009 this successful farm shop, run by Di and Colin Dawes with their daughter Rebecca, reopened in a new roomy food hall. The state-of-the-art meat counter is impressive, with all pork, beef and lamb coming from the farm. The range of cuts is amazing; butchers are at work all the time behind the counter – do not be surprised to see a magnificent whole leg of well-hung, wine-coloured beef on display. Free-range chickens are from a supplier in Lechlade, who only started rearing poultry because the Dawes provided the market. That is the kind of people they are. I am not a wine buff (only an enthusiastic consumer), but I liked the display of wines in their boxes. Vegetables are seasonal and mostly local; jams are supplied by an allotment holder; flour is from Matthews and Wessex Mills, both local firms. A great farm shop run by nice 'driven' people selling competitively priced meat. Bravo.

Goodwood Farm Shop

www.goodwood.co.uk

☎ 01243 755154

✉ Home Farm, Goodwood, Chichester, West Sussex **PO18 0QF**

🕐 Tues–Sat 9am–6pm; Sun 10am–4pm

The Goodwood Estate has recently been revitalised by the son and heir to owner Duke of Richmond & Gordon, Lord March, and is now farmed organically. The Estate's farms rear organic Sussex / Dairy Shorthorn beef, Saddleback pork and Southdown lamb to Soil Association standards, guaranteeing excellent welfare. Environmental standards on the farm have seen the return of many songbirds and wildlife now flourishes. Most of the week the shop will have meat in the freezer, but by Wednesday a fresh supply will be on the shelves. The Goodwood dairy (see page 279) supplies the shop's other star – lovely, golden-coloured non-homogenised milk and cream. You can also buy raw, unpasteurised milk. On race days, burgers, sausages and roasts made with Estate meat are on sale at the racecourse.

Harewoods Estate Sussex Fowl

www.brooklandwhite.co.uk
☎ 01342 893967
✉ Brookland White, Lodge Farm, Lower South Park Road, South Godstone, Surrey **RH9 8LF**

Farmer Mike Pinard has been breeding traditional Sussex fowl on his farm for many years, rearing chickens in a traditional way that goes back to the 19th century. They have 24-hour access to the outdoors and are fed on a diet of oats harvested from the farm and milk. The birds are like no other – they lose none of their volume during cooking. The white breast meat has a dense texture and good length of flavour; the leg meat is dark and yet more intensely flavoured. Try it and you will realise how chicken used to taste. The chickens are sold directly from the farm, through local outlets and at London's Borough Market. Award winner of the National Trust's 2010 Fine Farm Produce awards. Home delivery available.

Hazeldene Farm

www.hazeldenefarm.com
☎ 01494 783501
✉ Asheridge Road, Chesham, Buckinghamshire **HP5 2XD**
🕐 Thurs–Sun 10am–4pm

Breeding traditional Hereford cattle, Oxford Down sheep, British Lop pigs and Marsh Daisy chickens, Hazeldene is a farm committed to preserving native and rare breeds. The farm shop stocks the farm's own free-range beef, lamb, pork, home-made sausages, home-cured bacon, eggs, chicken and locally sourced organic vegetables. It is in a wonderful location and the animals have a relaxed and comfortable life. The website is updated weekly, detailing exactly what is available to buy and encouraging customers to buy seasonal produce and avoid the need to buy-in produce from elsewhere. Hazeldene products benefit from thoughtful rearing and butchery, producing a wonderful result.

Hunts Hill Farm

☎ 01483 811840
✉ Normandy Common Lane, Normandy, Guildford, Surrey **GU3 2AP**
🕐 Thurs–Fri 9am–6pm, 2–5pm; Sat 9am–5pm

You can order native breed beef; Saddleback, Tamworth and Middle White pork; and hogget, mutton and lamb from Whiteface Woodland and Norfolk Horn sheep; hen and duck eggs; honey; and poultry (including turkeys for Christmas) all from the farm. There is no mail order so you need to collect.

Hurstwood Farm ⬡ @ ✎

www.cobnutoil.co.uk

☎ 01732 88 5050

✉ The Hurst, Crouch, Borough Green, Sevenoaks, Kent **TN15 8TA**

I was excited to hear that a British farm had made cold-pressed 'virgin' Kentish cobnut oil; for too long we have had to rely on nut oils from anywhere but the UK. The oil itself is rich and has a delicate flavour of the cobnuts – recommended on watercress salads with shavings of British cheese. Cobnuts have been grown on this Kent farm since 1985. The Dain family experimented with several varieties in order to find the most suitable for their area, and planted 780 trees, including the Butler, Spanish Longre, Lara and Broadview types. Fresh cobnuts are available in season, also roasted, as well as, of course, the wonderful oil. Bravo, to a great new and innovative producer. Home delivery available.

Invicta Natural Meats & Court Farm Quality Butcher

www.courtfarm.org

☎ 01634 240547

✉ Court Farm, Halling, Rochester, Kent **ME2 1HR**

🕐 Mon–Sat 8am–5pm; Sun 9am–1pm

An on-farm butchery run by Andrew Lingham and his family, selling home-produced beef, lamb and venison. Invicta have also diversified into selling fresh produce, some of it local. Good bread is supplied by a local baker in Strood, Chris Beeney, who also makes pies.

Kingfisher Farm Shop

☎ 01306 730703

✉ R. Coe & Son, Guildford Road, Abinger Hammer, Dorking, Surrey **RH5 6QX**

🕐 Mon–Sat 9am–6pm; Sun 10am–4pm

A small farm shop selling local watercress, vegetables, bread and meat and which is vital in an area, that is, in spite of its wealth, something of a food desert. Bear in mind that the local old market town, Guildford, has next to no independent shops, so anything in the area is a bonus.

King's Manor Farm Shop

www.kingsmanorfarm.co.uk
☎ 01983 754401
✉ Kings Manor Farm, Copse Lane,
Freshwater, Isle of Wight **PO40 9TL**
🕐 Mon–Sat 9.30am–5pm;
Sun 10am–4pm

Kings Manor Farm Shop's mission statement is to supply sustainable, affordable farm produce of the highest quality to customers who care, as the owners do, about the welfare of the environment and the animals. The stars of the show are the Aberdeen Angus and salt marsh lamb, bred on the farm itself and hung for a minimum of three weeks. The results are fantastic and various traditional cuts are available to buy in the shop. In addition, the shop stocks produce from several local producers, ranging from seasonal vegetables to free-range poultry and freshly made bakery items.

Laverstoke Park Butchers ❶ ⓐ ✿

www.laverstokepark.co.uk
☎ 0800 334 5505
✉ Laverstoke Park Farm, Overton,
Hampshire **RG25 3DR**
🕐 Tues–Sat 9.30am–5.30pm;
Sun 10am–3pm

An extraordinary farm shop selling mostly home-produced meat, poultry, vegetables, plus the farm's own buffalo milk and very nearly authentic mozzarella. Rather immodestly, Jody Schecter, the millionaire owner, has dubbed his place the 'University of Organic', referring to his newly built lab on the farm. I wait to see how this claim will be backed up. Meanwhile the meat tastes good, there's some decent home-grown veg, plus more from other organic farms and micro-brewed ale. See also page 272.

Leckford Farm Shop

www.waitrose.com
☎ 01264 810585
✉ New Farm, Leckford,
Nr Stockbridge, Hampshire
SO20 6DA
🕐 Mon–Fri 9am–12.30pm,
1.30–5pm; Sun 2–4.30pm

Owned by the John Lewis Partnership, Leckford is a seasonal shop selling Leckford Farm's own produce from its 4000 acres. Crunchy English apples and pears, apple juice from different varieties, mushrooms, eggs and honey are all on offer, but that is about it. Leckford is a working farm producing arable crops, including high quality breadmaking wheat, which is used to make a range of Leckford label flour for sale in some Waitrose outlets. Phone ahead to check opening times.

Millets Farm Shop

www.milletsfarmcentre.com

☎ 01865 392200

✉ Millets Farm Centre, Kingston
Road, Frilford, Abingdon, Oxfordshire
OX12 0JX

🕐 Mon–Sun 9am–5pm

Originally a pick-your-own, this is now a substantial farm
shop run by the enthusiastic Tony and Nigel Carter, which
houses a bakery, deli, butchery, fish counter and, of course,
a fruit and vegetable shop. Very impressive – even the bread
is made with the farm's own flour. A finalist in the National
Farmers' Retail & Markets Association (FARMA) awards,
2010 – you must visit.

Newlyns Farm Shop

www.newlyns-farmshop.co.uk

☎ 01256 704128

✉ Lodge Farm, North Warnborough,
Hook, Hampshire **RG29 1HA**

🕐 Mon–Fri 8am–6pm; Sat 8am–
4pm; Sun 9am–12pm

A farm shop with its own butchery, specialising in well-hung
beef and ready-to-eat meals made with the farm's own
meat. On the deli counter you will find local cheese (such as
Barkham Blue, which is delicious) and there's a large selection
of different fresh eggs including quails', ducks' and hens'.

Renhurst Farm Shop ○

☎ 01892 852168

✉ Mark Cross, East Sussex
TN6 3NR

🕐 Thurs 9am–5pm; Fri 9am–
6.30pm; Sat 9am–5pm

This is a farm shop with a strong animal welfare ethos.
The Padfields are fourth-generation farmers rearing native
breeds. The animals are mainly grass-fed, supplemented by
home-grown (GM-free) cereals. Pigs are bought as weaners
from free-range rare breed sows and loose-housed in straw
yards. All go to slaughter at an abattoir six miles from the
farm. Beef is hung for 21 days minimum, lamb for 10 days
and you can buy any fresh cut, although some is made into
meat pies, sausages and bacon.

Rookery Farm, Flansham

www.rookeryfarm.com

☎ 01243 583583

✉ Rookery Farm, Flansham, West
Sussex **PO22 8NN**

🕐 Mon–Wed 8am–1pm; Thurs
8am–3pm; Fri 8am–5pm

Free-range chickens producing free-range eggs in the countryside
of West Sussex, Rookery Farm is a no-nonsense, quality
producer. The team ensure that their chickens have a happy,
relaxed life and feed them an organic diet. The eggs are
collected daily and sorted on the farm ready for purchase, ensuring
they travel no further than they need to and taste fantastic.

Roundhurst Farm ⊙ @ ⊘

www.roundhurstfarm.com
☎ 01428 656455
✉ Lower Roundhurst Farm,
Tennysons Lane, Roundhurst,
Hazlemere, West Sussex
GU27 3BN
🕐 Thurs–Sat 9am–5pm

A delightful shop, selling Moya and Richard Connell's home-reared organic beef from their herd of Sussex cattle, a local rare breed. Good value meat boxes are available via mail order or to collect. The farm also produces eggs and lamb, and sources vegetables, fruit and dairy foods locally. You can also eat in the charming café on Friday and Saturday – as you've guessed, all food served is made using the Connell's own ingredients. Well worth visiting – a real pleasure.

Secretts of Milford ⊙

www.secretts.co.uk
☎ 01483 520500
✉ Hurst Farm, Chapel Lane,
Milford, Surrey **GU8 5HU**
🕐 Mon–Sat 9am–5.30pm;
Sun 10am–4pm

This famous farm shop near Godalming is best known for its salad leaves and vegetables. However, it also sells a wide range of natural foods and flowers, and houses a wet fish counter run by Rex Goldsmith, who sources the freshest seafood sustainably. Secretts has a big wholesale operation supplying London restaurants, but don't let that put you off. The quality is very high and this 100-year-old traditional salad farm has a fascinating history.

Sharnfold Farm ⊛

www.sharnfoldfarm.co.uk
☎ 01323 768490
✉ Hailsham Road, Stone Cross,
Pevensey, East Sussex **BN24 5BU**
🕐 Mon–Sun 9.30am–5.30pm

A farm shop and PYO selling the farm's own soft fruit, including blackberries, black and red currants, loganberries and strawberries. Vegetables include pumpkins, marrow, mangetout, broad beans and much more. The farm's own free-range pork is also available in the shop, which gets a very good write-up from local devotees.

Sherbourne Farm ⊙

www.sherbourne-farm.co.uk
☎ 01483 202586
✉ Shere Road, Albury, Guildford
GU5 9BW
🕐 Sat–Sun, Bank Hol Mon 11am–6pm

Tiny Dexter beef cattle, Gloucester Old Spot pork and lamb are all reared on the farm and slaughtered locally. Based in the Surrey Hills, a gem of a location, this is not really a shop, but they do sell by mail order and are a small, worthy outfit. You can visit to look round the farm (fees apply – see website).

Silcocks Farm Shop ⊕ ⊘

www.silcocksfarm-organics.co.uk
☎ 01580 763351
✉ Grange Road, St Michaels,
Tenterden, Kent **TN30 6TL**
🕐 Thurs, Fri 9am–4pm;
Sat 9am–1pm

Opened only five years ago, this farm shop has earned a strong following of customers who flock to buy the organically reared meat. Beef, lamb, pork and veal is reared on the farm, and the latest development is a cheese room, where two organic soft cheeses are made, along with organic double cream. Home delivery available.

Village Greens ⊕

www.vgfarmshop.com
☎ 07792 211457
✉ Coles Lane, Ockley, Dorking,
Surrey **RH5 5LS**
🕐 Mon–Sat 9am–6pm;
Sun 11am–4pm

A good local shop with a tremendous community feel. James and Catherine Dampier have not been open for long, but have already established themselves as one of the top shops in the country. Supporting local produce is a first principle, although they also grow their own greens on a smallholding across the road from the shop. They hold food fairs from time to time so you can meet the producers. It is not an enormous shop, which is refreshing, but you can buy all you need. Free-range meat is supplied from Ruckman Farm and naturally reared chickens from Etherley Farm; locally grown rare-breed tomatoes, lovely jams and jellies are from Ouse Valley; and there is great artisan bread. I am a fan, as you can see.

Windsor Farm Shop ⊘

www.windsorfarmshop.co.uk
☎ 01753 623800
✉ Datchet Road, Old Windsor,
Berkshire **SL4 2RQ**
🕐 Mon–Sat 9am–5pm;
Sun 10am–5pm

There is much in this Royal farm shop to praise, in spite of the rather obvious opportunity it seizes to sell gift box-wrapped confectionery and jams to eager tourists. The beef (from Sussex cattle, a red-coated local breed), pork, lamb, poultry and game hail from the Royal farms. There are also dairy products (the gluey cream is excellent) and remarkable honey gathered from the bees that forage for pollen among thousands of exotic plants in the gardens of the Royal Lodge. Organic vegetables are from Hampshire and on my visit I spotted sacks of potatoes grown in Berkshire.

Worton Organic Farm and Farm Shop

www.wortonorganicgarden.com
☎ 07718 518964
✉ 3 Rectory Farm Cottage, Worton, Near Cassington, Oxfordshire **OX29 4SU**
🕐 Fri 10am–5pm; Sat 10am–12pm

Established eight years ago, this organic produce garden is worshipped by locals, who enthuse about the extraordinary flavour of the fruit and vegetables. Old and rare varieties (from the UK and around the world) are a speciality, chosen for their stronger aromas, and the farm also grows flowers – not just for pleasure but because they encourage wildlife on to the farm. Their green credentials are sound, with as much on the farm as possible being recycled to keep the carbon footprint low. Eggs are also available in the weekend shop, as well as other produce from the farm (it is all clearly marked). There's a café on site, too.

FOOD MARKETS ▼

Beaconsfield £

www.tvfm.org.uk
☎ 01865 820 159
✉ High Street, Hungerford, Berkshire **RG17 ONF**
🕐 **Monthly,** 4th Sun 9am–1pm

Beaconsfield Old Town is a historic market town providing a charming setting for this popular market, which is seven years old. There is very good local produce and other non-foodie items on offer. Angus and Longhorn beef and lamb from Wykham Park Farm Shop, free-range eggs from Bloomfield Hatch Farm, Bakers Basket's hand-moulded breads, cakes and savoury goods, Mapleleaf Watercress and Moreton Mushrooms are just a few examples of what is on offer. Well worth a visit, and you can explore the old town to appreciate the historic architecture – very atmospheric.

Deddington Farmers Market

www.deddington.org.uk/commun ity/farmersmarket
☎ 01869 338 532
✉ The Market Place, Deddington, Oxfordshire **OX15 0SB**
🕐 **Monthly,** 4th Sat 9am–12pm

This market in a delightful village spot is loved by its customers for the sheer range of produce on offer, including artisan bread, fresh vegetables and fruit, wet fish, meat, honey, locally made mustard and preserves and home-made soups. The market is held in the square, with some stalls inside the church. Villagers report that its arrival has been a great boost to the economy and has spawned other community events such as the annual village show.

Future Farms @ 🍃 ⓔ

www.futurefarms.org.uk
☎ 07005 805519
✉ Village Hall, Martin, Hampshire
SP6 3LA
🕐 **Twice weekly**, Sat 9.30am–12.30pm; Mon 9–11am, 5–6pm

Martin is a very special little village in Hampshire. In 2004, the residents started Future Farms, a cooperative run by a group of eight Martin residents. The eight run the farm and hire in a bit of casual labour. They breed chickens, cows, pigs and lambs and grow all sorts of vegetables. Then every Saturday morning and Tuesday afternoon they sell their goods in the village hall along with local cheese, honey and bread. The idea ultimately is to make the village self-sufficient. The produce is superb: the big, leggy, well-formed chickens are a must, as are the amazingly fresh vegetables and home-baked bread. Already more than 100 of the 200 residents are members of the cooperative. The great thing is that anyone can join so you don't need to be a Martin resident. A truly inspiring venture.

The Goods Shed ⓔ

www.thegoodsshed.net
☎ 01227 459153
✉ Station Road West, Canterbury, Kent **CT2 8AN**
🕐 Tues–Sat 9am–7pm; Sun 10am–4pm

Winner of the Best Market category in the 2009 BBC Radio 4 Food & Farming Awards, The Goods Shed is first of all unusual in that it is a collection of individual stalls, permanently housed – rather like traditional market halls you see in every good-sized French town. Founded by Susannah Saite, who put her own money into the venture, it is a remarkable place both in terms of ethos and the sheer delectability of the food on sale. Every stallholder is truly excellent. The fishmonger, Simon the Fish (see page 285) sells glisteningly fresh seafood from the south coast; the butcher makes wonderful sausages and sells only locally sourced meat and game; and Patrick's Kitchen makes *traiteur* food to take away and the finest sausage rolls. There's an artisan bakery, a store-cupboard essentials stall, a cheesemonger and a stand selling organic and locally grown vegetables. The Goods Shed also has a well-reviewed café. A must if you are in the area.

Hungerford Farmers' Market ●

www.tvfm.org.uk/markets
☎ 01628 670272
✉ Windsor End, The Old Town,
Beaconsfield, Buckinghamshire
HP9 2JJ
🕐 Monthly, 4th Sat 9am–12.30pm

Hungerford's long high street is home to a few good food shops including a decent (if pricey) independent fruit and veg shop and a well-stocked butcher. Presumably to avoid upsetting them, the farmers' market is held on the same street on the fourth Sunday of every month. The market is part of the Thames Valley Cooperative, and features various stalls from its members, which include 4 fish suppliers, 17 cheesemongers / makers, 20 butchers and much more. Obviously not all are present at each market in the area, but you will always find a good variety when you visit.

Olney Farmers' Market ●

www.olneytowncouncil.co.uk
☎ 01234 711679
✉ Market Place, Olney,
Buckinghamshire **MK46 4EF**
🕐 Monthly, 1st Sun 9am–1pm

I grew up near Olney and remember shopping at the high street shops with my mother. Of course there was no farmers' market then. The one that comes here monthly has more than 30 stallholders selling a great selection of food and drink. There is venison from the Woburn estate, locally grown herbs, seasonal home-grown vegetables and cut flowers, artisan bread, honey from local apiaries and wonderful poultry from Franklins (see page 19).

Oxford Farmers' Market ●

www.sketts.co.uk
☎ 01789 267000
✉ Gloucester Green, Oxford
OX1 2BL
🕐 Twice monthly, 1st & 3rd
Thurs 9am–3pm

Started in 2006 on a temporary basis, this market proved to be such a hit that it is now held twice a month. The dairy stalls star, selling delicious locally made goats' cheese and fresh goats' milk. Another stall sells unpasteurised milk and there is a baker whose loaves are very reasonably priced. There are a range of meat producers selling both organic and naturally reared beef, pork and lamb, plus heaps of seasonal vegetables. A market with a good atmosphere.

Shoreham Farmers' Market 💷

01243 454628
East Street, Shoreham, West Sussex **BN43 5ZD**
Monthly, 2nd Sat 9am–1pm

Set up in 2001, this market boasts over 70 stalls and recently won Best Farmers' Market in Sussex at the Sussex Food & Drink Awards 2009. It attracts many visitors and has played a part in the town's renaissance over the last few years. This is one of the largest markets in Sussex and offers all the quality produce you would expect to find in the region.

St Giles Farmers' Market 💷

01732 355325
St Giles Church, Stumble Hill, Shipbourne, Kent **TN11 9PF**
Weekly, Thurs 9am–11am

In 1285 Edward I granted the village of Shipbourne permission to hold a weekly market. In 2003 the market was re-inaugurated and today the farmers' market, held inside and outside the 11th-century church, has over 20 stalls offering seasonal fruit and vegetables, breads, meat, mushrooms, smoked fish, pickles and cheeses.

Tunbridge Wells Farmers' Market 💷

www.tunbridgewells.gov.uk
01892 554244
Town Hall, Royal Tunbridge Wells, Kent **TN1 1RS**
2nd and 4th Sat 9am–2pm

A good market in a town dominated by too many superstores. Look out for Rob Bookham who makes fresh pasta; Twineham Grange cheese (the only British 'parmesan' to get close to the real thing); asparagus in season from Birchden Farm; Kate Kent's biscuits from the Battle Bake House; and biodynamic organic vegetables, salads, beef and flour from Perry Court Farm near Canterbury (see page 293).

West Malling Farmers' Market 💷

www.westmallingfarmersmarket.co.uk
01732 876077
High Street, West Malling, Kent **ME19 4LZ**
Monthly, 4th Sun 9.30am–1.30pm

Street trade has been in this area since the Roman times. Now this ever-busy farmers' market sells a great supply of farm-raised fruit and vegetables, hand-made breads, jams, English wines, beers and sloe gins. Some of the regulars include Love Chilli, selling around 30 chilli varieties and chilli plants; Far Acre Farm free-range eggs; Meopham Valley Vineyard's red, white, rosé and sparkling wines; and Octopussy, a family-run business based in Whitstable supplying fresh and cooked fish.

Winchester Farmers' Market £

www.hampshirefarmersmarkets.org
☎ 01420 588671
✉ Middle Brook Street and Middle Brook Street car park, Winchester, Hampshire **SO23 8DQ**
🕐 **Twice monthly**, 2nd and 4th Sun 9am–2pm

This is one of the biggest, if not the biggest, and most professional farmers' market in the UK. Sponsored and organised by Sustainable Winchester, there is an astonishing number of stalls, though some have travelled quite far (but within the distance permitted).

DELIS AND SPECIALISTS ▼

A Cena

www.acena.co.uk
☎ 020 8940 0414
✉ 23 Friars Stile Road, Richmond, Surrey **TW10 6NH**
🕐 Mon–Sat 8.30am–7pm; Sun 9.30am–3.30pm

I have been following the career of cook Paul Hughes since tasting his wonderful pies and potted meats at the Ginger Pig in Marylebone (see page 77). Paul is now cooking at A Cena, and is on top form with a wider range of delicious things. Do visit, and also find great olive oils, cheeses, pasta and wines. There is a café/restaurant attached and more recently a second shop, the Hill Bakery, in the same street.

Added Ingredients

www.addedingredients.co.uk
☎ 01235 537 405
✉ 14–16 Stert Street, Abingdon, Oxfordshire **OX14 3JP**
🕐 Mon–Sat 9am–6pm

A popular deli with a good range of cold meat, charcuterie, di Gustibus breads (made in Abingdon though there are bakeries in London, too), wines from a local vineyard, fresh meat reared nearby, and some lovely food made with quince from a producer down the road in Aston Rowant. The shops own home-made tapenade (olive paste) with pesto is an award winner.

Arte Bianca ⓞ ⊘

www.artebianca.co.uk
☎ 01892 510554
✉ 1 Chapel Place, The High Street, Tunbridge Wells, Kent **TN1 1YQ**
🕐 Mon–Fri 9am–5.30pm

This Italian specialist food shop has been open for over a decade. It is run by the Battelli family and stocks all the usual Italian favourites. They sell almost any shape of dried pasta, but the last time I visited there were some good, fresh stuffed tortellini and ravioli, too. Home-made sauces (pesto, tomato), olives, olive oil, air-dried prosciutto, cheeses, jars and tins of vegetables, wine and grappa are also available, along with a few ready-made dishes, pizzas and sandwiches.

Bill's Produce Store

www.billsproducestore.co.uk
01273 692894
The Depot, 100 North Road, Brighton **BN1 1YE**
Mon–Sat 8am–10pm; Sun 9am–10pm

The theatricality of the surroundings in Bill's Brighton establishment is matched by the kaleidoscope of goods on offer. The old bus garage is packed to the rafters with local fruit and vegetables as well as exotic imported offerings. Home-made cakes, desserts, quiches, sandwiches and pizzas can be made to order and eaten in the midst of the store in the café area. The shop looks exciting, the foods taste wonderful – it really is an inspiring place to shop, eat or just look around. In addition, the friendly, high-energy staff are helpful and clearly know their stuff when it comes to provenance. There is another store in Lewes, East Sussex, and although it lacks the theatre of the Brighton set-up, it is just as thoughtfully stocked.

Cadogan & Company ○ @ ●

www.cadoganandcompany.co.uk
01962 877399
31a The Square, Winchester, Hampshire **SO23 9EX**
Mon–Sat 9.30am–5.30pm

A good deli in a pretty Winchester street selling good food: pasta and sauces, cooked meats and continental charcuterie / specialities. Cheeses include a cheddar-type made in the New Forest called Winchester Cheese and soft Tunworth, also made nearby.

East Boldre Post Office

01590 612936
Aerodrome Cottage, Main Road, East Boldre, Brockenhurst, Hampshire **SO42 7WD**
Mon–Fri 8am–6pm; Sat 8.30am–6pm; Sun 8.30am–1pm

If only all village shops / post offices were like this one. Ian Evans presides over his shop selling all the essentials and a little bit more. He sources fresh foods locally from the New Forest area. Fresh poultry and meat are from nearby Ferndown Farm, vegetables are from Hampshire market gardens not far from East Boldre, honey is from local hives and the bread is made in Poole, about 40 minutes drive away. He will not sell eggs from caged hens, preferring to stock barn-reared and free-range eggs, both again from local farms. You can also buy a day licence to fish locally, and perhaps buy hardwood charcoal (made in traditional kilns from the New Forest Charcoal company) and barbecue your catch.

Elanthy Olive Oil 🏠 @ 🪙

www.elanthy.com
☎ 08001 696252
✉ PO Box 227, Chipping Norton, Oxfordshire **OX7 9AH**

Elanthy's olive oil is made with 100 per cent Greek olives harvested and pressed in the Peloponnese. The production supports a network of small-scale farmers. It is pressed close to the farms within hours of the olives being picked, blended – purely for reasons of consistency – near Athens and then imported into the UK by road. Packed in 3-litre cans, it is a low acidity, extra virgin olive oil with a nice colour and a good robust flavour, suited equally to dipping and cooking. Critics have voted it the best value oil for the price. Elanthy is an online shop with free delivery; it makes sense to buy in bulk – as its many fans will testify.

High Barn Oils 🏠 @ 🪙

www.highbarnoils.co.uk
☎ 01403 730326
✉ Muntham Home Farm, Barns Green, Horsham, West Sussex **RH13 0NH**
🕐 Mon, Wed, Sat, 7am–1pm; Tues, Thurs, Fri 7am–4.30pm

Cold-pressed rapeseed oil now joins olive oil as a healthy salad oil and – up to a point – cooking oil, and it has the added advantage of being British. The flavour takes some getting used to, being powerfully fruity, but if you are a fan, farmer Durwin Banks of High Barn Oils will send you virgin oil pressed on the same farm that grows the rapeseed crop.

Huckleberry's of Sussex @

www.huckleberrysproducestore.
co.uk
☎ 07805 754898

Preserving the local tastes and recipes of Sussex and surrounding areas, Huckleberry's is an online store that places particular emphasis on good quality local produce. Home-made flavours and handmade quality run across their plentiful range of goods, which include chutneys, biscuits, cheeses, jams and cordials. Both their hand-packed butter and extra virgin rapeseed oil come from the Sussex Downs and have a delicate taste. Particularly delicious is their Olde Sussex cheese: tangy and creamy it is a wonderful alternative to regular cheddar.

Infinity Foods

www.infinityfoodsretail.co.uk
01273 603563
25 North Road, Brighton,
East Sussex **BN1 1YA**
Mon–Sat 9.30am–6pm;
Sun 11am–5pm

A workers' cooperative as well as a top-ranking supplier of almost every bean, grain and pulse that exists. Their 500g of good-quality ethically sourced wholefoods are available in many independent shops. The range is enormous: every type of lentil and pea, whole groats, cracked wheat, nuts and dried fruit, plus some stranger ancient grains such as millet and sorghum. Many are organic and Fairtrade – this is infinity, all right. Sadly they do not do mail order, but contact them for your nearest stockist. If you live near their HQ in Brighton, however, visit the shop, which also sells fresh fruit and vegetables from four different organic farms, including Hankham organics. They also bake naturally leavened bread daily on the premises, sell wine from local vineyards, Sussex artisan cheese, vegan sushi made on-site and organic milk or yoghurt. There's also a vegetarian café next door.

John Robinson & Son

01264 810609
Marsh Meadow, High Street,
Stockbridge, Hampshire **SO20 6HF**
Mon–Fri 7.30am–1.00pm,
2.00pm–5.30pm;
Sat 7.00am–2.00 pm

Robinson's is a Test Valley institution. Their sausages are rightly fabled and people travel miles to buy them. Made from pork shoulder and sage, they are as masterful as they are reliably good-tasting. My own children say they are the best they have ever eaten and I agree. But beware: they do not contain preservatives, so need to be used within a week if refrigerated or frozen. Bacon smoked in an onsite smokehouse is sliced in front of you (so you decide the thickness) and there is a good selection of cheeses, some local. Robinson's also have a bulging game larder with pheasant, partridge, hare, rabbit, grouse and several types of venison all available. The lamb is sourced locally and the (predominantly) Aberdeen Angus beef comes down from Scotland. It is testimony to their success that they are still recruiting apprentices. This shop is well worth a detour. Ask about the outside catering, particularly the hog roasts.

Leckford Village Stores

☎ 01264 810514
✉ Leckford High Street, Leckford, Stockbridge, Hampshire **SO20 6JG**
🕐 Mon 7am–6pm; Sat 7am–1.30pm

Apples from the nearby, John Lewis owned, Leckford Estate, as well as locally grown vegetables, apple juice, honey, cold-pressed 'virgin' rapeseed oil and marmalade. The shop is beautifully run by Vin Marmur.

Little Shop

☎ 01797 226384
✉ 9 High Street, Winchelsea, East Sussex **TN36 4EA**
🕐 Mon–Sat 8am–5.30pm; Sun 9am–4.30pm

This is a not-for-profit, 'mutual' village shop where every one of the 300 shareholders (town residents) has one share and a vote. It sells locally grown Appledore salad in season, Korkers sausages, ice cream from Willet's Farm, vegetables, fruit (including strawberries picked within a mile), bread from Rye and honey. They will deliver to within walking distance from the shop. Every village should have one.

Macknade Fine Foods ⊘

www.macknade.com
☎ 01795 534497
✉ Selling Road, Faversham, Kent **ME13 8XF**
🕐 Mon–Sat 9am–5.30pm; Sun 10am–4pm

This is a food hall that began as a pick-your-own on a farm that formerly grew hops for the breweries. The shop now sells the farm's own vegetables, although they also buy from London's Covent Garden market presumably in an effort to take on the superstores that have flourished all over Kent. This place does not have much of a farm shop feel – the range of food on offer makes it seem more like a deli – but seek for local produce and you will find it here. A second, much smaller, branch can be found in the centre of Faversham. See website for details.

No. 2 Pound Street

www.2poundstreet.com
☎ 01296 585 022
✉ Pound Street, Wendover, Hampshire **HP22 6EJ**
🕐 Mon–Thurs 10am–11pm; Fri–Sat 10am–midnight; Sun 10am–5pm

A buzzy deli run by the enthusiastic partnership of Neil Irvine and Nicola and James Grant, selling high quality British produce. Cured meats, cheeses with an emphasis on those from the surrounding counties, foraged treats, seasonal fruit and vegetables, with a wine shop and café attached. It only opened in the autumn of 2010 but signs are good – no doubt I will be saying more about this shop in the next edition. Your comments will be very welcome.

Pallant of Arundel ● ●

www.pallantofarundel.co.uk
☎ 01903 882288
✉ The Square, 17 High Street, Arundel, West Sussex **BN18 9AD**
🕐 Mon–Sat 9am–6pm; Sun 10am–5pm

Pallant's shop front is stage-set pretty and has been the site of a grocer's shop for over a century. Mark Robinson and Jonathan Brantigan took over Pallant in 2007 on a mission to sell not just good, but 'interesting' food. It's a good ethos. They seek out local specialities, but also stock items from around the world. This is a well-edited shop. Cheeses include Sussex Slipcote and Lord of the Hundreds (one of my favourite hard cheeses). There is bread for every taste, whether you like conventional yeasty bread, a robust sourdough, a healthy spelt loaf or a rustic French stick. You'll also find pickled fruit, Sussex Higgidy pies, smoked fish, charcuterie and excellent juicy ham, carved from the bone. Wines are also a big draw here.

Pieminister ● ● ●

www.pieminister.co.uk
☎ 01865 241613
✉ 56–58 The Covered Market, Oxford **OX1 3DX**
🕐 Mon–Sat 10am–5pm; Sun 11am–3pm

Jon Simon's pies are now available in many outlets and he has a string of shops in the UK (see website). His shop in the covered market in Oxford is hugely popular, and not surprisingly. The pastry is excellent, made with real butter and baked to a proper crisp shell. Under the crust all the ingredients have integrity. Judging the flavour of pies is subjective stuff – I urge you to try a couple and decide which of the large range you like best.

Plenty Food & Provisions

www.plentyprovisions.co.uk
☎ 01424 439 736
✉ 16 Grand Parade, St Leonards on Sea, East Sussex **TW37 6DN**
🕐 Mon–Sat 10am–6pm; Sun 12pm–4pm

A range of local, organic and fairtrade groceries, store cupboard essentials and bread is delivered daily from the wonderful Lighthouse Bakery located nearby. In order to cut down on their carbon footprint they endeavour to source not only locally but from suppliers that already deliver in the St Leonards, Hastings and Rye area.

Pollen True Taste Ltd ⊙ @

www.pollentruetaste.com
☎ 01428 608870
✉ Three Firs House, Bramshott
Chase, Hampshire **GU26 6DG**
🕐 Mon–Fri 7am–6pm

Pollen specialises in bottled sauces made with natural ingredients. Mayonnaise (made with free-range eggs) is their speciality, but it is their pesto made with Hampshire watercress that I have enjoyed the most. See website for stockists or buy online.

The Real Eating Company

www.real-eating.co.uk
☎ 01273 221444
✉ 86–87 Western Road, Hove,
East Sussex **BN3 1JB**
🕐 Tues–Sat 9am–11pm;
Sun–Mon 9am–5pm

This is a café-deli company that is gradually expanding to open other outlets – mainly cafés – in the south and as far afield as Oxfordshire (see website). The Hove store, however, seems best to pull off the original ethos, selling local cheeses from Sussex, freshly baked bread, milk, yoghurt and home-made cakes, plus a range of deli foods including charcuterie, preserves and pickles, honeys, jams and biscuits.

Rye Spice Co Ltd ⊙ @ ⊘

www.ryespice.co.uk
☎ 01797 225015
✉ Rye Harbour Road, Rye,
East Sussex **TN31 7TE**
🕐 Mon–Fri 8am–5pm

Brothers Robbie and Glen Holland sell more than 170 different herbs and spices, all from fully traceable sources. If you visit their shop you can buy anything from a pinch to a ton; alternatively there is an online shop.

Spice Store ⊘

☎ 01892 524068
✉ 70 Grosvenor Road,
Tunbridge Wells, Kent **TN1 2AS**
🕐 Mon–Sat 9.30am–6pm;
Sun 11am–4pm

A specialist Asian store run by Dee Patel, selling spices from India, Thailand, Africa and the Philippines, occasional home-made curries (depending how busy she is) and store cupboard items, such as lentils and pulses. This is the only store of its kind in this area of Kent. They also stock pig's blood and offal, which is very popular with Filipinos living nearby. Most of the food in the store is of Indian origin, however.

Taj Natural Foods ✪ @ ⊘

☎ 01273 735728

✉ Western Road, Brighton, East
Sussex **BN1 2L13**

🕐 Mon–Sun 9am–6pm

Taj Natural Foods is a large, brightly lit supermarket packed to the beams with every possible type of food you need to make authentic Indian and other Asian-style dishes. Spices come in every pack size and are very good value for money. There are sacks of rice, chestnut or gram (chickpea) flour, lentils, chickpeas and beans, big bags of poppadums, cans of ghee, coconut milk and fresh produce. There is also a range of organic muesli, porridge oats and dried fruits.

The Weald Smokery ✪ ⊘ @

www.wealdsmokery.co.uk

☎ 01580 879601

✉ Mount Farm, Flimwell,
East Sussex **TN5 7QL**

🕐 Mon–Sat 9am–5.30pm;
Sun 10am–4pm

Andrew Wickham smokes award-winning, smoked, dry-cured bacon over 'open' smoking oak logs; cold-smoked fish is also available. Standards here are exceptional and produce a very impressive, subtle smoke. The bacon is especially good and I urge you to visit or order via the internet – there is a very well-stocked deli on site and an efficient mail order service for those who live further afield. They also smoke fish and sell an impressive range of cheeses, wines and cooked meals.

Yum Yum ⊘

☎ 01273 606777

✉ 22–23 Sydney Street, Brighton,
East Sussex **BN1 4EN**

🕐 Mon–Sat 10am–6pm;
Sun 12pm–5.30pm

In the basement below this noodle bar there is a popular mini market selling an amazing variety of Asian and Chinese foods – fresh, dried, bottled and frozen – some familiar, some peculiar. You can even buy the blue and white china bowls to eat your creations from.

A. E. & M. Alcock ⊘

☎ 01865 515658
✉ 273a Banbury Road, Oxford
OX2 7JF
🕐 Tues–Fri 8am–5pm;
Sat 8am–1pm

You can choose between meat carrying the 'Real Meat Company' logo, which comes with guarantees regarding high standards of animal welfare, feed and breed, or conventional meat, which will be the more economical, but less traceable, of the options. Expect the usual butcher's offering of beef, pork and lamb, game in season and free-range poultry, but also a range of wet fish and other food items, making this a one-stop shop in many respects.

Armstrongs Family Butchers

☎ 020 8940 1833
✉ 205 Lower Mortlake Road,
Richmond, Surrey **TW9 2LP**
🕐 Mon, Tues, Thurs–Sat 7am–6pm;
Wed 7am–1pm

A good, old-fashioned butcher's shop for suburban Richmond residents, selling British meat sourced from Scotland, Wales, Devon and Cornwall. Really well-hung, traditionally reared beef, home-made bacon and sausages, free-range chicken and pork, plus cheese and preserves.

Ashbee & Son ⊘ ⊕

☎ 01797 223303
✉ 100 High Street, Rye, East Sussex
TN31 7JN
🕐 Mon, Wed, Thurs 8am–5pm;
Fri–Sat 7.30am–5pm; Sun 8am–4pm

A picturesque shop (est 1850) on the High Street of the town made famous by the novels of E. H. Benson (Mapp and Lucia), which still has the original front with brass plates and hooks on which carcasses would have once hung. Paul and Jayne Dengate have been here for 20 years, selling British pork and beef plus, best of all, local lamb from Romney Marsh. The plain pork sausages are good, having a straightforward, gentle seasoning. Wood pigeon, partridge, wild ducks and pheasant are abundant during the shooting season (pigeons all year round). You can buy good free-range Bronze turkeys at Christmas. Milk and cream from nearby Hinxden dairy are other admirable buys.

Barkaway's Butchers ○ ◎

www.ajbarkaway.co.uk

☎ 01795 532026

✉ 6 West Street, Faversham,
Kent **ME13 7JF**

🕐 Mon 7am–12pm;
Tues–Fri 7am–5pm;
Thurs 7am–4.30pm; Sat 7am–4pm

Chris Barkaway's popular sausages are always made with locally sourced free-range pork, and his salt marsh lamb is utterly delicious. He visits the farms that supply his shop and picks out the animals he wants – a sign of a very good butcher. All the livestock he chooses is slaughtered locally at Marden, between the farm and Faversham. He is a good baker, too, making popular steak and ale pies using locally brewed beer made with real hops and barley by Shepherd Neame.

Bastable Brothers of Kitbury ◎

www.bastablebrothers.co.uk

☎ 01488 658 537

✉ Thatcher's Yard, 2 Church Street,
Kintbury, Berkshire **RG17 9TR**

🕐 Tues–Fri 8.30am–5.30pm;
Sat 8.30am–1.30pm

A traditional village butchery run by Jonathan and Simon Bastable who farm in Berkshire grazing 1000 sheep (and a smaller flock of organically reared Llleyn sheep) that keep the shop supplied with lamb. They also have a beef suckler herd fed predominantly on grass.

The Best Butchers Ltd ○ ◎

www.thebestbutchers.co.uk

☎ 01908 375275

✉ Unit 5, Lower Rectory Farm,
Great Brickhill, Milton Keynes,
Buckinghamshire **MK17 9AF**

🕐 Wed 8am–12pm;
Thurs–Fri 8am–5pm; Sat 8am–2pm

A farm-based butcher selling from a shop on the farm and also to local shops (contact for stockists). The lamb is from farmer Alan Forsyth who also works here as a butcher. The butchery specialises in pork: making bacon, hams and an impressive, air-dried Italian-style coppa (cured pork shoulder) and bresaola (air-dried beef). If you buy fresh beef you can ask for a joint to be hung as long as you like. This is a place well worth seeking out, despite being in a remote spot, and is highly recommended and popular with locals.

Broughton Water Buffalo ○

www.broughtonwaterbuffalo.co.
uk

☎ 01794 301031

✉ The Log Cabin, Manor Farm,
Broughton, Stockbridge, Hampshire
SO20 8AN

Here you can buy slow–grown, naturally reared water buffalo from a herd that now numbers 230. Dagan and Jessy James say that each animal has a hectare of grassland to itself during the warmer months (in winter they go into open barns). Various cuts are available, but be aware when roasting that buffalo is an almost fat-free meat so cook the joints carefully, barding with a strip of pork or other fat to keep it juicy. Their burgers are terrific. You need to phone to make an appointment to call in.

Brownrigg Poultry ⊘ ⊕

www.brownriggpoultry.co.uk
☎ 01983 840978
✉ Sheepwash Farm, Sheepwash Lane, Godshill, Ventnor, Isle of Wight **PO38 3JP**
🕐 Mon–Fri 9am–5pm; Sat 9am–1pm

Paul and Sue Brownrigg run a free-range poultry farm producing chickens, ducks and eggs all year round, plus turkeys, geese and game birds in the run-up to Christmas. Feed is natural, with no antibiotics and as much as possible of the farm's home-grown wheat. The birds are plucked then hung non-eviscerated for a few days to allow flavour to develop. The produce is on sale at Newport farmers' market every Friday or you can phone in advance and collect from Sheepwash Farm.

Challow Hill Meats ⊘

www.challowhillmeats.co.uk
☎ 01235 765792
✉ Challow Hill Farm, East Challow, Wantage, Oxon **OX12 9PD**

Lyn Blackwell and her family have been farming at Challow Hill since 1919. They now have a single suckler Dexter herd and kill between four to five a month. The cattle graze over 300 acres. 'We love our cows and are very welfare minded,' says Blackwell. The majority are pedigree with three stock bulls at the farm. They also do limited supplies of lamb and pork. Challow Hill was runner-up at the Oxfordshire Livestock Farmer of the Year. The family attend eight farmers' markets a week – see website for details. They also supply A. R. Handley, a butcher in nearby Grove. Freezer packs are from £50. They welcome visitors, but do ring first, and they can arrange local delivery within a 10-mile radius.

Charles Baynham ⊙ @ ⊘

www.charlesbaynham.co.uk
☎ 01962 869877
✉ 65A High Street, Winchester, Hampshire **SO23 9DA**
🕐 Mon–Fri 7am–5pm; Sat 7am–4pm

This is a British butcher's shop with a South African flavour and one of five branches (see website for details). You can buy boerewors, biltong and droewors made from British meat. They may not be to everyone's taste but the sausages are great on the barbecue. The shop helpfully sells British hardwood charcoal for the purpose and will even take over total organisation of a braai (South African-style barbecue) for you. Fresh Gloucestershire Old Spot pork is also available.

Clive Miller ✦

www.sussexbutcher.co.uk
☎ 01273 832256
✉ 2 Cuckfield Road, Hurstpierpoint, West Sussex **BN6 9RU**
🕐 Mon–Fri 8am–5pm;
Sat 8am–4pm

I found Brighton to be surprisingly short on butcher's shops, so it was a relief to find Clive Miller and his delicious Sussex-breed lamb, sourced from the Danny estate nearby. There are also some unusual, less English cuts for variety, including kleftico lamb, chicken paupiettes stuffed with thyme and parsley and Italian-style meatballs. Miller also boasts a huge range of sausages – 45 varieties! The chickens are from Lewes and you can buy welfare-friendly English veal.

F. Conisbee & Son

www.fconisbee.co.uk
☎ 01483 282073
✉ Park Corner, Ockham Road South, East Horsley, Surrey **KT24 6RZ**
🕐 Mon and Wed 8am–1pm; Tues and Thurs 8am–1pm, 2pm–5pm; Fri 7.30am–1pm, 2pm–5.30pm; Sat 7.30am–1pm, 2pm–3.30pm

It is the meat pies that gets everyone flocking to this traditional butcher's shop. With their thin, crisp pastry, baked dark for extra flavour, containing generous helpings of beef and other fillings, they have been worthy multiple winners of the National Trust Fine Farm Produce awards. Neil Conisbee (along with his sons James and Stephen) also sells fresh meat, both here and at the family's other branch on Station Parade, Ockham Road South, East Horsley, Surrey (Tel: 01483 283391) – most of which is sourced from livestock reared naturally at the Trust's Polesden Lacey Estate and Chapel Farm.

Copas Traditional Turkeys ⬢ @ ✦

www.copasturkeys.co.uk
☎ 01628 499980
✉ Kings Coppice Farm, Grubwood Lane, Cookham, Maidenhead, Berkshire **SL6 9UB**

The Copas family (who also have a farm shop – see page 247) specialise in Christmas poultry, especially turkeys, and do a roaring mail order trade throughout December. The turkeys are the Bronze variety, with dark brown feathers. They graze in cherry orchards and water meadows, giving the meat a wonderful depth of flavour. Contact for stockists or Copas will arrange home delivery, sending the turkeys neatly packed in a box with cooking instructions.

David John 🖋

01865 200922
93–97 The Oxford Covered Market, Oxford **OX1 0DY**
Mon–Sat 7am–5pm

Working from a stall in the covered market is old-fashioned butcher David John. He makes his own pies, savoury tarts and sausages, and specialises in home-cooked meats. There are helpful staff here who will take an order for almost any type of pie. All meat is locally sourced.

Dunsbury Farm 🏠🖋

www.dunsburyfarm.co.uk
01983 740152
Brook, Isle of Wight **PO30 4EL**
Every other Sat 10am–2pm

Here you'll find grass-fed, pure-bred Poll Dorset lamb reared on a farm dedicated to conservation situated between the chalk downland and South Wight seashore. Susannah Seeley hangs the meat for at least 10 days to develop flavour and tenderness. Good value, boxed, whole and half-butchered lambs are available, plus a roast and chop selection. Mutton (from animals over two years of age) can be bought throughout the year. Note the infrequent opening times; delivery by arrangement.

Farmer Guy 🏠@🖋

www.farmerguy.com
07796 696653
Wallend Farm, Upstreet, Canterbury, Kent **CT3 4DF**

An online shop selling hams made with pork from the farm's own free-range pigs using traditional recipes, including one that has been used on the farm for four generations. The meat remains juicy and succulent, but not too salty, even after a long cure. Choose between smoked, breaded and glazed hams, on or off the bone.

M. Feller Son & Daughter 🏠🖋

www.mfeller.co.uk
01865 251164
54–55 The Oxford Covered Market, Oxford **OX1 3DY**
Mon–Sat 6am–5pm

An accredited organic butchery selling great quality organic lamb, pork and beef from Wales (so the principle of short journeys / low fuel consumption is watered down somewhat). His shop is very popular, though, and there are local items available, including snipe, partridge and woodcock in season. Wild duck and venison, too.

271

The Isle of Wight Bacon Company

www.isleofwightbacon.co.uk

☎ 01983 840210

✉ Moor Farm, Godshill,
Isle of Wight **PO38 3JG**

🕐 Mon–Tues, Thurs–Fri 6am–1pm,
2–5pm; Sat 6am–1pm, 2–4pm

David Harvey says that there is no better place than the warm climate of the Isle of Wight for rearing pigs. Born and reared outside at Moor Farm near the pretty village of Godshill, his happy pigs are destined to become some of the best bacon and ham I have tried. Most notable was the lack of shrinkage after cooking compared to more commercial products. Harvey also makes sausages, and fresh meat is available direct from the farm.

Jamie Wickens Family Butchers

www.jwickens
familybutchers.co.uk

☎ 01797 226287

✉ Castle Street, Winchelsea,
East Sussex **TN36 4HU**

🕐 Mon–Sat 8am–5pm;
Sun 10am–5pm

This is a small, family butcher's shop in a pretty town overlooking the East Kent salt marshes that specialises in the beautiful lamb that grazes there. Beef is sourced from Sussex (very close by) and pork is from Berkshire pigs. There are lots of nicely made kebabs and burgers for a quick dinner, and look out for meat from some interesting breeds, including White Park, Belted Galloway, Middle White and Gloucester Old Spot pork, and Shetland and Torwyn lamb. There is a good local artisan cheese range, too, including Tournegus, Lord of the Hundred's and Harbourne Blue.

Laverstoke Park Butchers

www.laverstokepark.co.uk

☎ 0800 334 5505

✉ Laverstoke Park Farm, Overton,
Hampshire **RG25 3DR**

🕐 Tues–Sat 9.30am–5.30pm;
Sun 10am–3pm

Laverstoke produce is a wonder. I first came across the chicken around 10 years ago and it was saintly, succulent and made fantastic, gelatinous stock. A lot of the meat is from rare breeds, although some is supplied from other organic farms. Consistency is sometimes a problem. Jody Scheckter, a former Formula One world champion, is passionate and has invested millions in his vision and applied science to his method, with a research centre in-situ. Some think he's too elitist but I say taste the produce and you'll be convinced that his fervour is worth every penny. See also page 251.

Manor Farm Game /
Richard Waller Poultry ○ @ ◑

www.manorfarmgame.co.uk
☎ 01494 774975
✉ Long Grove Wood Farm,
234 Chartridge Lane, Chesham,
Buckinghamshire HP5 2SG

As their name would indicate this is a game dealer. Among the good foods they can deliver to your door, however, are Richard Waller's amazing slow-grown genuine Aylesbury ducks. These are the last broodstock of the original Aylesbury duck, a breed that is derived from a Mallard with the most delicious dark meat. Reared in Waller's cherry orchards, a few yards down the lane from Manor Farm Game headquarters, they are killed on the farm, dry-plucked and hung non-eviscerated for a few days (a major factor in their flavour). They are seasonal and only available from May to October. Aside from the ducks, Waller breeds turkeys and geese for Christmas, and some capon-sized chickens

V. F. Montgomery's Traditional
Butchers ○ ◑

www.vfmontgomery.com
☎ 07899 917604
✉ 3 The Post Office Vaults,
Market Place, Wantage, Oxfordshire
OX12 8AT
🕐 Mon–Fri 7am–5pm;
Sat 7am–3.30pm

Vincent Montgomery is a brave man. He opened his butcher's shop 18 months ago, with the country in the teeth of recession. It is a much-needed addition to this grisly market town. When I visited, the quality of the beef looked excellent. They had Stornoway black pudding on sale and they make their own faggots and sausages, as well as curing their own bacon, and they will deliver within a 10-mile radius. Sadly, on the day of my visit, they had run out of their own cure and I was sold some pretty average packet bacon with the giveaway 'product of the EU' sticker on it – meaning that it is anything but British. There are hundreds of local meat producers locally, many of them excellent. I am sure Montgomery's would be even more popular if they used them. But on the whole they must be applauded – particularly considering there is a Waitrose within yards of them. I hope they succeed.

Petworth Butchers ⊘

☎ 01798 345148
✉ Saddlers Row, Petworth,
West Sussex **GU28 0AN**
🕐 Mon–Fri 8.30am–5.30pm;
Sat 8.30am–5pm

This popular butcher's shop in the centre of town sells beef and wild boar from butcher Roland Kenny's own farm. There are also 14 types of sausage on sale at any one time, plus free-range chickens reared near Portsmouth and excellent lamb from the South Downs.

Rother Valley Organics ⊙ @ ⊘

www.rothervalleyorganics.com
☎ 01730 821062
✉ Sandilands Farm, Rogate,
Petersfield, Hampshire **GU31 5HU**
🕐 Mon–Thurs 9am–4.30pm;
Fri 9am–2pm

Organic beef farmers Shon and Simon Sprackling farm on the South Downs producing Aberdeen Angus beef, as well as pork and lamb. The animals are grazed on certified organic pasture, which includes clover-rich herbage on the hills in the winter and lush, river bottom pasture and sea frontage marshland in the warmer months. Such a varied diet, which includes wild plants such as sorrel, rosemary and garlic, gives the meat an exceptional flavour. Supplement feed is grown on the farm, so is guaranteed GM-free.

Southborough Butchers ⊘

☎ 01892 529757
✉ 60a London Road,
Southborough, Tunbridge Wells,
Kent **TN4 0PR**
🕐 Mon–Fri 6.30am–5pm;
Sat 6.30am–1pm

Pork and lamb from Romney Marsh sold by a butcher trying his hardest to compete in what can only be described as Tesco heartland. But there is a terrific effort here, not least because this butcher sells some of the most delicious sausages and bacon I have tried, much better than any sold in a supermarket. Beef is well-hung and full of flavour – this is a shop deserving of your loyalty.

S. J. Suter ⊘

☎ 01798 872441
✉ 54 Lower Street, Pulborough,
West Sussex **RH20 2BW**
🕐 Mon–Wed, Sat 8am–1pm;
Tues, Thurs–Fri 8am–5pm

Friendly butcher brothers Steve and Martin Suter sell superb, well-hung, traditionally reared beef and lamb from farms on the South Downs and make their own sausages from local free-range pork. They are next to an excellent greengrocers and wine merchant making this a delightful street to visit.

Village Butchers ⊘

☎ 01590 623208
✉ 74 Brookley Road, Brockenhurst,
Hampshire
SO42 7RA
🕐 Mon–Fri 7am–5pm;
Sat 7am–4pm

This butcher's in the heart of the New Forest sells locally produced free-range chickens and ducks, game including rabbits, pigeons and partridge, and wonderful local beef from farms where the cattle roam the New Forest, grazing on ancient pasture and wild plants. There are various cuts of venison, including burgers, plus a wide range of sausages – the plain pork, pork and leek, and venison are recommended.

BAKERS AND CONFECTIONERS ▼

The Bridge Patisserie ⊕

www.thebridgepatisserie.co.uk
☎ 01962 890767
✉ The Bridge Patisserie,
20 Bridge Street, Winchester,
Hampshire **SO23 9BH**
🕐 Mon–Fri 8am–7pm;
Sat 8am–6pm; Sun 10am–4pm

Moira Windsor runs a pretty, traditional tea room and bakery selling sumptuous cakes and chocolates, handmade on the premises, along with savoury cheese pastries and tarts. She sources as many organic ingredients as possible for the bakery and some certified Fairtrade, too.

Judges Bakery ⊙

www.judgesbakery.com
☎ 01424 722588
✉ 51 High Street, Hastings,
East Sussex **TN34 3EN**
🕐 Mon–Thurs 8.15am–5.30pm;
Fri–Sun 9am–5pm

All you could wish for from a baker: organic breads including great sourdoughs, fruit breads, rolls and croissants all made on the premises by Emanuel Hadiandreou. Children will love the jam doughnuts and sticky buns, all free of hydrogenated fat. The Rock-a-Nore rolls, devised by the Green & Black originator Craig Sams, are truly good – well-seasoned herring certified by the Marine Stewardship Council (MSC) are wrapped in buttery pastry – and lovely with mulled white wine or ale.

Lighthouse Bakery ☉

01580 831 271
Ockham, Dagg Lane, Ewhurst
Green, Robertsbridge, East Sussex
TN32 5RD

A superb artisan bakery and baking school run by Rachel
Duffield and Liz Weisburg. Both used to be neighbours of
mine when they ran a bakery in Battersea selling the best
bread in south London. Their move to Sussex was
devastating for us – but lucky for East Sussex locals.
Bestselling breads include Pane Pugliese (an open-textured,
slow-made white), white or rye sourdough, traditional
farmhouse and wholemeal breads. Flour for the bread is
sourced from independent British mills including the lovely
Cann Mills in Dorset and Shipton Mill. You can also book a
breadmaking course here – highly recommended. Home
delivery available.

Mapledurham Water Mill ☉ @ ✦

www.mapledurham.co.uk
01189 723350
The Estate Office, Mapledurham,
Nr Reading, Berks **RG4 7TR**
Easter Sat–end Sept, Sat–Sun
(plus Bank Hols) 2–5pm

Mildred Cookson is the only female water-miller in the
country. She produces high quality stoneground flour from
English wheat from nearby Basingstoke. Wholemeal flour is
the speciality and another flour called 81%, which is much
whiter in colour, lighter in texture and can be used to make
sponges, cakes and pizza bases. A by-product of the 81%
is bran, but also semolina that is a lovely creamy colour, not
the garish yellow you find in supermarkets. The three are
sold at local farm shops and other outlets. See website for
details. Mildred produces just 40 tons a year and locals rave
about it.

Oscar's Bakery ✦ £

01795 532218
3 Limes Place, Preston Street,
Faversham, Kent **ME13 8PQ**
Tues–Sat 8am–1.30pm

Martin and Carolyn Flynn bake traditional loaves and rolls
on the premises of their popular Faversham shop, turning
out a wholesomely delicious Kent Cob made from malted
multigrain flour, a mixed grain and oat Sussex Supper
bread, and Irish 'batch' loaves.

Real Patisserie ⊕ @

www.realpatisserie.co.uk
☎ 01273 570719
✉ Real Patisserie, 43 Trafalgar Street, Brighton, East Sussex **BN1 4ED**
🕐 Mon–Sat 6.30am–5.30pm

The emphasis here is on French patisserie and traditional breads, but all is made in Brighton for two branches (see website) and for a wholesale and catering service. Breads range from a rustic baguette, proudly made with English flour, various mixed grain and sourdough loaves and rolls. Cakes are the spectacular glazed perfection you expect from a French patisserie and there is a range of pretty, squishy bite-sized macaroons in a dozen flavours. Their croissants and pain au chocolat do not disappoint either.

Simply Cakes ⊘

www.simplycakes.co.uk
☎ 01932 858888
✉ 58 Baker Street, Weybridge, Surrey **KT13 8AL**
🕐 Mon–Fri 9am–5.30pm; Sat 9am–4pm

Jonathan Woodgate designs some of the cleverest, wittiest celebration cakes in Britain, building and icing them in front of enthralled onlookers passing by his shop window. Many designs can be viewed on his website. Testimonials are awesome and, as this part of the world is something of a foodie desert, it is well worth a visit.

Slindon Bakery

www.slindonbakery.com
☎ 01243 814369
✉ The Old Bakery, Slindon Top Road, Slindon, West Sussex **BN18 0RP**

Andy Turner-Cross bakes traditionally using wholemeal flour from the Lurgashall watermill at Singleton, or from Calbourne Mill on the Isle of Wight. Many of his loaves are made using a long 12-hour fermentation. Try the Sussex Kibble wholemeal loaf, or Roman Army bread made with spelt flour. Buy Andy's bread at Sussex and Hampshire farmers' markets – contact him to find your nearest one.

Winchester City Mill £

www.nationaltrust.org.uk/ main/w-winchestercitymill
☎ 01962 870057
✉ Bridge Street, Winchester, Hampshire **SO23 0EJ**
🕐 Wed–Sun 11am–5pm Opening times vary throughout the year; see website for details.

This lovely watermill on the River Itchen with its own shop has recently been revived by its owner the National Trust. Flour is milled on site and sold alongside locally gathered honey. You may even have a hand in the milling, if you ask.

Boho Gelato

☎ 01273 727205
✉ 6 Pool Valley, Brighton
BN1 1NJ
🕐 Mon–Sun 11am–7pm

Modern and stylish, Boho Gelato is a brilliant new venture and the product of Seb Cole's hard work and vision. His flavours range from classic vanilla, to the more avant-garde mojito, avocado, violet and olive oil. All of the concoctions use local Sussex milk and are made on the premises. The attractive array of ice creams made in the Italian gelato style is constantly changing and Seb's ability to conjure up new combinations is admirable. Different and surprising, Boho Gelato is becoming a firm favourite with visitors and locals alike.

The Cheese Gig

www.thecheesegig.com
☎ 01264 861385
✉ Little Warden, Winchester St, Chilbolton, Stockbridge, Hampshire
SO20 6BQ

For fans of West Country cheeses, this is the ideal online shop. Specialising in the beautifully made artisan cheddars of Somerset, they also sell a seemingly endless number of modern British cheeses from Dorset, Devon, Cornwall, Wiltshire and Gloucestershire, bringing home what a rich area this is for specialist dairies. Favourites on their online shop catalogue include nettle-wrapped Yarg, Dorset Blue Vinney, Devon Blue, Devon Oke, rich creamy Elmhurst, Heligan from Cornwall, Woolsery from Dorset and a rustic pebble-shaped cheese called Ceris made in Wiltshire.

The Cheesebox

www.thecheesebox.co.uk
☎ 01227 273711
✉ 60 Harbour Street, Whitstable, Kent **CT5 1AG**
🕐 Mon, Wed 10am–4pm; Thurs 10am–5pm; Fri 10am–8pm; Sat 10am–5.30pm; Sun 11am–3.30pm

Dawn Hackett was once a travelling cheese 'gypsy', taking her well-stocked Citroen H van from place to place in the south east and selling cheese via mail order. She now has a shop in Whitstable and sells a great range of well-kept handmade cheeses, including Ashmore (now made in Kent), Celtic Promise, Golden Promise, Keen's Cheddar from the West Country and the zesty blue Two Hoots from Wokingham. The van, which Dawn refers to as 'she', still goes to Faversham and Herne Bay on a regular basis (call for information). Dawn is one of my favourite cheesemongers – she's a real enthusiast who is in love with her trade.

Corbin's Deli ⚙

www.corbinsdeli.co.uk

☎ 01825 766670

✉ 23 High Street, Uckfield,
East Sussex **TN22 1AG**

🕐 Mon–Sat 8.30am–5pm

Specialising in cheese, this Sussex deli sells a vast range, but also stocks local cheeses such as Flower Marie (a sweet bloomy-rinded goats' cheese that I like to cook with when under-ripe and eat with bread when mature and runny inside). Look out also for Ashdown Forrester's (pressed cows' milk cheese with a firm texture) and Wigmore (an unusual and flavoursome ewes' milk cheese with a thick white cream inside). It has a sister cheese, Waterloo (made with cows' milk); both are made in Berkshire. Good artisan Stilton, cheddar and Cheshire cheeses are also available along with continentals.

Goodwood Estate

www.goodwood.co.uk

☎ 01243 755154

✉ Goodwood Estate Farm Shop,
Home Farm, Goodwood, Chichester,
Sussex **PO18 OQF**

🕐 Tues–Sat 9am–6pm;
Sun 10am–4pm

Goodwood Farm Shop (see also page 248) is one of the few places you can still get raw (untreated) milk. All of the milk is produced on the estate from Dairy Shorthorn cows. Goodwood is also experimenting with making butter, which I tasted on my last visit there in summer 2009, and cheese that will be made on the farm. None of the milk is homogenised and they have a good, if limited, selection of local cheeses. But it is the untreated milk that you should head here for – it is so rare that it's worth making a detour.

Hampshire Cheeses

www.hampshirecheeses.co.uk

☎ 07880 738470

✉ Hyde Farm, Herriard,
Basingstoke, Hampshire **RG25 2PN**

Tunworth, which as far as I know is the only cheese that Hampshire Cheeses produces, is worth hunting high and low for. Handmade and unpasteurised, it is more like a continental cheese than anything I have tasted, although more subtle. It is made in a converted cowshed in Hampshire and is available through retail outlets detailed on the website. This is a stunning soft cheese with a bloomy rind and gentle, beautifully balanced taste. Hunt it down.

High Weald Dairy ⚘ @ ✿

www.highwealddairy.co.uk
☎ 01825 791636
✉ Tremains Farm, Horsted Keynes,
West Sussex **RH17 7EA**

Here you'll find a range of artisan cheeses made from cows' and ewes' milk certified by the Soil Association. Sarah and Mark Hardy are famous in the cheesemaking world for their Sussex Slipcote (a soft, fresh cheese that comes plain or flavoured with herbs), Duddleswell (a hard ewes' milk cheese) and Ashdown Forresters (a lovely looking round cheese with an open texture) – the list goes on. All are available mail order or contact for stockists.

Minghella ⚘ @ ✿

www.minghella.co.uk
☎ 01983 883545
✉ Minghella Centre, High Street,
Wootton, Isle of Wight **PO33 4PL**
🕐 Mon–Fri 9am–5pm

Traditional ice creams made on the Isle of Wight by the family that also gave us 'The English Patient' film director, Anthony Minghella. The Ventnor shop is a treat, every child's fantasy of what an ice cream parlour should be: plenty of chocolate in the chocolate, strawberry in the ripple, and buckets of fresh cream in all of it. Situated on the esplanade, it is rarely without a patiently waiting queue. You can even order your own flavour to serve at a party (ask about minimum order), but give a fortnight's notice.

Nut Knowle Farm £

www.nutknowlefarm.com
☎ 01825 872214
✉ Worlds End, Gun Hill, Horsham,
East Sussex **TN21 0LA**

Nut Knowle Farm produces 13 different types of goats' cheese from its creamery in East Sussex. Reports are good for the hard cheeses and some of the more straightforward soft cheeses. They sell mainly at farmers' markets in London and the south east and you should consult their website or ring for details of stockists.

Winterdale Cheesemakers

www.winterdale.co.uk
☎ 01732 820021
✉ Winterdale, Platt House Lane,
Wrotham, Sevenoaks, Kent
TN15 7LX
🕐 Saturday 11am–1pm

The Betts family has had a dairy farm for over 60 years, and has been making cheese since 2006. Using fresh milk from the farm, their cheese is made in traditional cheese vats, moulds and wooden presses. By creating a cave, dug into the North Downs of

Kent, Winterdale has endeavoured to cut its carbon footprint considerably, bypassing the need for electrically controlled maturation rooms. The cheese is unpasteurised and there are two types: Winterdale Shaw and Winterdale Oak Smoked. These are hard, creamy cheeses with a deep flavour and wonderful texture.

FISH AND SEAFOOD ▼

Brighton and Newhaven Fish Sales 🅐

www.brighton-fish-sales.co.uk
🕿 01273 430646
✉ Basin Road South, Portslade,
Brighton, East Sussex **BN41 1WF**
🕐 Mon–Sat 8am–4pm

A great-looking fish shop, right by the quayside on Hove Lagoon, selling fish caught by the shop's own fleet of boats. You can also buy some locally sourced deli foods and store cupboard items to go with the fish. Fresh fish includes south coast specials such as cuttlefish, lemon sole, squid, scallops, mussels, sea bass and cod. There is also a good range of frozen seafood including crab meat, langoustines, soft shell crab, scallops of all sizes and prawns.

The Fish Society 🅞 🅐 🅐

www.thefishsociety.co.uk
🕿 01428 687768
✉ Unit 1, Coopers Place, Wormley,
Surrey **GU8 5TG**

An amazing mail order company that only sells frozen fish, proof that when fish is blast frozen having just been caught it will, once defrosted, biologically be as fresh as if it were landed only a couple of hours beforehand. The other great virtue of this efficient mail order service is the variety. There is almost nothing they cannot get, from raw anchovies to superb, large-sized Scottish langoustines. It is impressive stuff – ask for next day delivery and the fish will arrive on dry ice. Spectacular.

Fisherman's Yard 🅐 🅐

🕿 07970 896143
✉ Oare, Faversham, Kent
ME13 0PY
🕐 Fri–Sat 9am–3pm

Specialities here are fresh fish from the south coast straight off the boat. The Fisherman's Yard also smoke their own fish and have their own oyster beds. You can also buy a selection of game, when in season, from Leeds Castle or other local shoots. Locals love this shop and it comes highly recommended.

George Botterell ⊘ £

01797 222875
Seafarers, Rye Harbour Road,
Rye, East Sussex **TN31 7TT**
Mon–Fri 8am–5pm

A father-and-son business established by John Botterell over 25 years ago in Rye Harbour, which gives the chance to buy direct from the boat or at local farmers' markets – call to ask for dates and your nearest. He and his son George sell (subject to availability) shrimps from Camber Sands, sardines, haddock, brill, crab and lobster. They are generally a wholesaler, so call before you visit.

Griggs of Hythe ♠ @ ⊘

www.griggsofhythe.com
01303 266410
The Fisherman's Landing Beach,
Range Road, Hythe, Kent **CT21 6HG**
Tues–Fri 7am–3pm;
Sat 7am–12pm

Two fishing boats will pull up outside this shop on Hythe beach delivering fresh fish to Andrea Edwards and Andrew Cook. You can buy from the shop or Griggs will deliver. They specialise in supplying fish to chefs, but are happy to take orders from private customers, too. The emphasis is on selling sustainable seafood, and you will find local specialities such as herring (and kippers), crab, brill, wild bass, fresh prawns in season, red mullet, Dover sole and live or cooked lobsters.

Hales & Moore Fishmongers

01634 372782
13 Station Road, Rainham,
Gillingham, Kent **ME8 7RS**
Tues–Sat 7am–5pm

This is the place for fresh herring, plus their melts (spleen) and roes, and some other good south coast specialities. The shop's own boat, the Osprey, brings in some of the fish and the rest is sourced from the market. The shop will not open on Sunday or Monday, because they cannot guarantee the freshness of the fish. Look out also for oysters, Dover soles and fresh brown or rainbow trout.

Jack & Linda Mills Traditional Fish Smokers £

201 Kings Road Arches,
Brighton, Sussex **BN1 1NB**
Mon–Sun 10am–5pm

Visiting this tiny shop, a finalist in the 2009 BBC Radio 4 Food & Farming Awards, is an extraordinary experience. The Mills (Jack is a former fisherman) smoke fish over apple wood and oak chippings in a small smokehouse right on the beach opposite the shop, which is under the arches supporting the esplanade. Inside the shop, the brickwork is bare and there is a makeshift kitchen. Jack and Linda source fish from the boats that fish out of Brighton and some from the market, but much care is taken to buy only from a sustainable source. Not only do they sell the smoked fish for you to take home, they also grill kipper fillets and mackerel and put them in a fresh roll, making one of the most delicious sandwiches I have ever eaten. There's home-made gooseberry sauce to eat with the mackerel (made with berries from the Mills's garden), fresh-picked crab and other delights, depending on season and availability. Note that they cannot be telephoned in advance.

Market Fisheries Rye 🕐 ⓔ

☎ 01797 225175
✉ Unit 1, Simmons Quay, Rock Channel (East), East Sussex **TN31 7HJ**
🕐 Mon 9am–12.30pm; Tues–Fri 9am–5pm; Sat 10am–2pm

An East Sussex family business (Suzanne and Russell Drew) that specialises in hand-dived scallops and other shellfish, plus a good variety of local fish landed by a cooperative fleet of approximately 30 boats fishing out of Rye on short trips – which is usually a guarantee of freshness. Hot- and cold-smoked fish is also available.

O'Driscoll's 🕐

☎ 01753 832735
✉ 69 St Leonard's Road, Windsor, Berkshire **SL4 3BX**
🕐 Tues–Sat 8.30am–6pm

Joe O'Driscoll sells an unusually diverse range of seafood. Sprats, octopus, scabbard, razor clams, mussels, squid, Dover sole, brill and oysters were on the counter the day I dropped in.

M. & M. Richardson 🕐 🕐

www.dungenessfish.co.uk
☎ 01797 320789
✉ Battery Road, Dungeness, Romney Marsh, Kent **TN29 9NJ**
🕐 Mon 9am–5.30pm; Tues–Sun 8am–5.30pm

Mark Richardson buys-in all his fish from five local day boats (short-trip boats that always have the freshest fish). A finalist in the BBC Radio 4 Food & Farming Awards, Richardson's shop is a magnet for both locals and customers from much further afield who love traditional south coast fish, including herring, Dover sole, crab, scallops and cod. During summer and autumn there is samphire on the counter picked from local beaches, and at the back of the shop is a smokehouse. The undyed smoked haddock, cod and kippers are a triumph. His jellied eels also have a wide following, with people travelling from London regularly to stock up. The shop also sells locally made honey. You can buy online.

River Test Smokery Ltd ○ ○

www.rivertest.net
☎ 01264 860 813
✉ Watch Estate, Coley Lane,
Chilbolton, Hampshire **SO20 6AZ**
🕐 Mon–Fri 8am–4pm

A smokery that was set up originally in 1987 by Jeff Hounslow to smoke the fish of local anglers; they now smoke thousands of trout from the River Test, salting then cold-smoking so the flesh remains red. Smoked eel is also available. This place is a real gem and well worth a visit.

Rock-a-Nore Fisheries ○ @ ○

www.rockanore.co.uk
☎ 01424 445425 / 461912
✉ 3 Rock-a-Nore Road, Hastings,
East Sussex **TN34 3DW**
🕐 Tues–Sat 8.30am–5pm;
Sun 9am–4pm

Right beside the extraordinary, wooden 'skyscraper' buildings where fishing nets are stored by the beach at Hastings' Old Town is Albert and Lilly Elliott's busy and enterprising shop famed for its smoked fish. The natural (undyed) smoked haddock, kippers (herring) and mackerel are excellent, the latter two used in delightful pastries by Judge's organic bakery, just up the street. Look out also for fresh Hastings Dover sole certified by the Marine Stewardship Council.

Seasalter Shellfish ○ ○

www.oysterhatchery.com
☎ 01227 363359
✉ Old Roman Oyster Beds, Reculver,
Herne Bay, Kent **CT6 6SX**
🕐 Mon–Fri 9am–5pm

A supplier of native and rock (Gigas) oysters that owns its own oyster beds, which include the Pollard Ground, two square miles near Whitstable, and the Ham Ground, a Crown fishery off the Isle of Sheppey. I am always struck, when buying oysters, by a great sense of their history. These grounds were once the source of oysters for the monasteries affiliated with Canterbury Cathedral and Seasalter and are one of the last Whitstable oyster producers in an area that once employed over 500 people and ran 100 boats for harvesting the shellfish. Find out more on their website.

S. & J. Shellfish ⊘ ⓔ

01590 688501
Snooks Farm, Snooks Lane,
Lymington, Hampshire
SO41 5SF
Mon–Fri 8am–3pm

Joan Mitchell buys just-landed crab and lobster from local fishing boats on the Solent. She also leases part of the Beaulieu River where she rears native oysters. Her crabs are glorious and the processing is done daily with nothing added so they're very fresh. This is a lovely outlet and worth seeking out.

Sid's Fresh Fish ⊘

01273 603625
18 Open Market, Marshalls Row,
Brighton **BN1 4JS**
Mon 7am–1pm; Tues–Thurs
7am–5pm; Fri–Sat 7am–6pm

A long-established stall originally run by Sid, but now run by Sid's son Dave who maintains a varied supply of fresh fish on every working day. It would take me too much space to list all the different varieties of seafood, but if you cannot find it fresh here, you are unlikely to find it fresh anywhere else in Brighton. Much is landed from local day boats and crab comes from Selsey.

F. Silverthorne

01903 200854
145 Montague Street, Worthing,
West Sussex **BN11 3BX**
Tues–Sat 8am–4.30pm

Frank Silverthorne and family specialise in fresh fish sourced from boats fishing off the south coast. There is a strong emphasis on sustainability, and in season you will be able to buy brown shrimps netted on local tidal beaches; also scallops, Dover sole, rock oysters, grey mullet, wild sea bass and crab.

Simon the Fish

www.thegoodsshed.net
01227 459153
The Goods Shed, Station Road
West, Canterbury, Kent **CT2 8AN**
Tues–Sat 9am–7pm;
Sun 10am–4pm

A really good fishmonger housed within The Goods Shed food hall, a permanent 'farmers' market' set up in 2002 by Suzannah Atkins (see page 256). Simon has been at the fish stall for nearly two years and latest reports are that the freshness of the fish and effort made to source sustainably are outstanding. You will find some interesting species beautifully displayed here: cuttlefish, brill, ling, pollock, pouting, eel, mirror carp and pike lie alongside brown shrimps, cockles, razor clams and sea urchins. If you are anywhere near Canterbury, do not miss a chance to visit The Goods Shed, have some lunch in the restaurant and buy from the stallholders, all of which are excellent.

Smelly Alley Fish Company ⚬ @ ✦

www.smellyalleyfishcompany.
com
☎ 0118 939 3076
✉ 11a Union Street, Reading,
Berkshire **RG1 1EU**
🕐 Mon–Fri 9am–5.30pm;
Sat 9am–4pm

Not just a shop, but also renowned as an efficient mail order service, sending fish all over the UK. The range is enormous and the fish very fresh. There is plenty that is sourced from British ports and fisheries, including sole (Dover, lemon and Torbay), mackerel, sprats, sardines, whiting, plaice or grey and red mullet. Smelly Alley (not the most attractive brand name I have come across, but certainly intriguing) also sell a lot of international species, some of which are air-freighted, so do ask about provenance if you have issues with this. I would welcome your feedback.

Southern Head Fishing ✦

www.southernheadfishing.com
☎ 01323 646366
✉ The Fishing Station, Royal Parade,
Eastbourne, East Sussex **BN22 7LD**
🕐 Tues–Sat 8.30am–4pm;
Sun 8.30am–2pm

This is an outstanding fishmongers run by Bob Page, a former fisherman who now buys from local boats that land their catch within yards of the shop. There is a very strong sense of the place of this shop in the community. When Page started selling fish he employed the wives of fishermen to serve behind the counter. Locals cannot believe the freshness of the fish, and while he sells a range of international species, you will be able to buy locally caught fish (as long as the weather permits) that has been landed the day before. South coast species are obviously a speciality – so expect Dover sole, brill (the next best fish to a turbot), grey and red mullet and sardines when in season. Shellfish and smoked fish also available.

Terry's Fisheries

☎ 01273 487268
✉ Unit 7, Riverside Food Hall,
Cliffe High Street, Lewes, East Sussex
BN7 2RE
🕐 Mon–Sat 9am–5.30pm

Buying fish directly from boats that come into Newhaven, you can expect to find all the south coast favourites gleamingly fresh on the counter at this shop in the Riverside Food Hall. You might see dabs, Dover or lemon sole, herring, scallops, red mullet, bream and bass, brill and turbot, plus some of the less familiar types such as gurnard and huss. In season there is wild salmon, and the shop also sells undyed smoked haddock, salmon and kippers.

Thyme & Tides

www.thymeandtidesdeli.co.uk
01264 810101
Thyme & Tides, The High Street, Stockbridge, Hampshire **SO20 6HE**
Tues–Fri 9am–6pm; Sat 9am–5pm; Sun 11am–4pm

Sally and Iain Hemming have created a thoroughly enjoyable shopping experience at their new deli-bistro-fishmonger in the vibrant high street of Stockbridge. Their food is eclectic and balanced: artisan breads and organic pastas are thoughtfully matched with individually sourced cheeses and charcuterie, chutneys and sauces from local producers in the Test Valley; and their smoked trout from the River Test is outstanding. Their regular tasting days are popular and equally well conceived. The bistro serves wonderfully fresh, tasty dishes, sourcing produce from local farms and allotments. Ashley, the on-site fishmonger with 17 years of experience, sources fish for the bistro from the day boats in Poole and Cornwall, or from sustainable line and pole sources, so the fish is particularly good.

Ventnor Haven Fishery

01983 852176
Eastern Esplanade, Ventnor, Isle of Wight **PO38 1JR**
Mon–Sun 11am–4pm

When I first visited the Blakes they sold fish from a small wooden shed on the esplanade, but since a much-needed government grant built a new safe haven harbour for the Ventnor fishermen and crabbing boats, Geoff and his wife Cheryl have moved their premises on to the newly built Eastern Esplanade. Here they continue to process and sell the wonderful Ventnor brown crab that has been the mainstay of the South Wight longshoremen's income for centuries. Hand-picked crab and freshly cooked lobster are always available – as long as the weather is not too terrible – and there are other fresh fish that creep in to the pots on sale, too.

Wheeler's Crab Shed ⚓

www.steephillcove-
isleofwight.co.uk
📞 01983 852177
✉ Steephill Cove, Ventnor,
Isle of Wight **PO38 1AF**
🕐 **Apr–Nov** Mon–Sun
12pm–3.30pm

Mandy Wheeler and her fisherman husband Jim live in a tiny cottage on Steephill Cove. He catches and she cooks during the summer season only. Find your place on the beach – you cannot drive here so be prepared for a short 15-minute walk down to the cove – then tap on Mandy's door for delicious crab pasties or whole-cooked lobster and crab salads. You can also take away oven-ready pasties to bake at home. Call for availability if the weather is looking dodgy.

Whitstable Shellfish Company ⬆ ◐

www.whitstable-shellfish.co.uk
📞 01227 282375
✉ Westmead Road, Whitstable,
Kent **CT5 1LW**
🕐 Mon–Fri 8.30am–5pm;
Sat 9am–12pm

One of just a few Whitstable firms still harvesting native oysters from the clean, grade A waters of Whitstable, using their own boat. After harvest, the oysters are put in tanks to be further purified. The company also sources rock oysters from Scotland, and both can be bought either from the outlet in Whitstable or via mail order. There is a definite difference between the two types. Native oysters have a much 'longer' flavour and can actually make your mouth tingle; rocks have a wonderful, but more fleeting taste. Oysters, by the way, travel very well and you can buy oyster knives, should you need one. There are good instructions on the website showing you how to open them if you have never tried it before.

▼ **VEGETABLES AND FRUIT**

Bill's Produce Store ◐ ⬡

www.billsproducestore.co.uk
📞 01273 692894
✉ The Depot, 100 North Road,
Brighton, East Sussex **BN1 1YE**
🕐 Mon–Sat 8am–10pm;
Sun 9am–10pm

A fantastic-looking shop run by Bill Collison, who opened his first of two branches in nearby Lewes in 2001 (see website for details of the second branch). The shop is stacked with vegetables and fruit – all delivered daily so they are as fresh as can be – and much is local as Collison is a keen supporter of local growers and market gardens. If you live nearby he will deliver a vegetable box to your door and there is also a huge choice of other good larder foods, such as oils, biscuits and teas, plus artisan bread.

Bourne Valley PYO

www.bournevalleypyo.co.uk
☎ 01264 738888
✉ Breach Farm, Egbury Road,
St Mary Bourne, Nr Andover,
Hampshire **SP11 6DQ**
🕒 **Jun–Oct** Mon–Fri 9am–6pm;
Sat–Sun 9am–5pm

Here you can pick red fruit including black, red and white currants, gooseberries and raspberries in season. Vegetables, which are grown on the farm, harvested and sold in the shop, include courgettes, squash, pumpkin, sweetcorn, potatoes, broad beans and cabbage. Well worth a visit.

Brogdale Farm

www.brogdalecollections.co.uk
☎ 01795 536250
✉ Brogdale Road, Faversham,
Kent **ME13 8XZ**
🕒 Mon–Sun 10am–5pm

The National Fruit Collection is a major Kent tourist attraction and gives you the opportunity to taste the apple varieties that Henry VIII would have eaten, the nuts Columbus would have carried to America, and the varieties of plum the Victorians loved so much. They make juices, too. With nearly 4000 varieties of fruit, this is an education in historic plant species and a delicious voyage of discovery. Throughout the year there are tours around the orchards, plus an annual cherry festival, a plum day and both a cider and apple festival.

Chegworth Valley

www.chegworthvalley.com
☎ 01622 859272
✉ Water Lane Farm, Chegworth,
Harrietsham, Kent **ME17 1DE**

Organic apples, pears and juices, soft fruit and fruit compote, direct from David and Linda Deme's Kent farm, where they specialise in growing British varieties, including Egremont Russet and Cox. The 5-litre apple juice boxes are great value for money. You can buy online or at various farmers' markets in the south east. Check on their website for the markets and stockists.

Copas Farms

www.copasfarms.co.uk
☎ 01628 529511
✉ Lower Mount Farm, Long Lane,
Cookham, Berkshire **SL6 9EE**
🕒 Tues–Sun 10am–5pm

A pick your own and farm shop run by the same farming family, who sell excellent free-range turkeys at Christmas (see page 270). There are two farms, both substantial in size, with 81 acres devoted to PYO. The season begins with asparagus in April, and moves on to soft fruits, which run on through the summer into the autumn. Other seasonal vegetables are available. The farm operates under the LEAF scheme, dedicated to returning wildlife to farmland. Opening times do depend on the season, so please check before visiting.

Durleighmarsh Farm Shop 🅟🅞

www.durleighmarshfarmshop.
co.uk
☎ 01730 821626
✉ Rogate Road, Petersfield,
Hampshire **GU31 5AX**
🕐 Mon–Sun 9am–5pm

A lovely farm shop and PYO growing unusual crops such as blueberries, tayberries, mangetout and herbs. The farm shop sells free-range eggs, naturally reared meat, poultry, game, home-made jams, ice cream and local honey. Opening is seasonal and PYO times vary so it's best to check ahead of visiting.

Dyke Farm and Farm Shop

☎ 01798 872447
✉ West Chiltington Road,
Pulborough, West Sussex **RH20 2EE**
🕐 Mon–Fri 8.30am–5pm;
Sat 8.30am–4pm

A farm shop selling vegetables grown on the farm by Richard and Lynne Martin, who also run the Four Seasons Fruit & Vegetables in Pulborough (see below). As well as the outstanding produce grown by the family or sourced as locally as possible, you can also buy hen and duck eggs, cheeses, milk, home-made cakes and deli foods.

Four Seasons Fruit & Vegetables

☎ 01798 875522
✉ 56 Lower Street, Pulborough,
West Sussex **RH20 2BW**
🕐 Mon–Tues, Thurs–Fri 9am–5pm;
Wed, Sat 9am–1pm

A lively shop on a high street that also boasts a great butchery, selling produce from Dyke Farm (see above). Depending on the season you will find a wealth of good, fresh market garden produce, some from the farm, others locally sourced and a few imports (citrus, bananas, exotic fruits). On the day of my visit the shelves were loaded with marrows, runner and bobby beans, apples, cobnuts, sweetcorn, bunched carrots and Horsham-grown blueberries. You can also buy hardwood charcoal made in kilns in Sussex woods.

The Fruit Basket

www.thefruitbasket.net
023 9250 2923
339 Forton Road, Gosport,
Hampshire **PO12 3HF**
Mon–Sat 7am–5.30pm

A greengrocers that is loyal to local growers, selling fresh produce, milk, herbs, eggs and flowers. There is also a small range of natural snack foods on sale. A second branch can be found in Fareham, Hants, at 10 Stubbington Green. Local delivery available.

Fundamentally Fungus

www.fundamentallyfungus.com
0800 9804784
Meon Hill Farm, Stockbridge,
Hampshire **SO20 6HA**

Jane Dick and Sue Whiting grow some extraordinary fungi in specially acclimatised sheds on their Hampshire farm and also buy in both wild and various cultivated varieties from elsewhere. Among the types grown on the farm are the extraordinary pom pom or monkey head mushrooms, which can be sliced and fried. They also grow or supply shitake, enoki, nameko, various oyster mushrooms, wood blewits and king oyster. A 'chef's mix' is available so you can try the range. Note that some fungi is organically grown and some not; also that some are imported from Europe, but from specially chosen suppliers that meet the high standards set by Dick and Whiting.

Garsons Esher

www.garsons.co.uk
01372 464778
Winterdown Road, Esher, Surrey
KT10 8LS
Mon–Sat 9am–5pm;
Sun 11am–5pm

There are so few old, established salad farms or market gardens left in the area around London (most were closed down by the arrival of the multiples in the late '70s), that when you do find one still working it is a cause for celebration. Garsons has two sites, one in Esher and one not far away in Titchfield (see website for details) where you can pick your own fruit and vegetables in season or visit the farm shops on both sites and buy locally produced food (they are very proud of their cheese counter), bread baked fresh every morning and other deli foods.

Godshill Organics @ ✪ ✪

www.godshillorganics.co.uk
☎ 01983 840723
✉ Newport Road, Godshill,
Isle of Wight **PO38 3LY**
🕐 Mon–Sat 9am–6pm;
Sun, Bank Hols 10am–5pm

An organic box scheme and farm shop selling its own
produce and other food items. Order regular boxes or have
one tailor-made to suit your needs. The farm grows produce
out in its 12 acres of fields or in 14 acres of polytunnels so
there is always a good supply throughout the year. All is
Soil Association-registered.

Goodall's Strawberry Farm ✪ ✪ ✪

☎ 01590 679418
✉ Bampton's Farm, Lisle Court
Road, Lymington, Hampshire
SO41 9SG
🕐 May–Jul Mon–Sun 9am–5pm

Call in at Brian and Pauline Goodall's PYO for strawberries
and raspberries that are truly ripe, plus newly planted
cherries and apricots. Brian Goodall says the south-facing
slope, plenty of muck and well-guarded family growing
techniques are the secret of his great strawberries. Flowers,
broad beans and potatoes are also available.

Horti Halcyon @ ✪ ✪

www.hortihalcyon-organic.co.uk
☎ 01483 232095
✉ Heath Mill House, Heath Mill
Lane, Fox Corner, Worplesdon, Surrey
GU3 3PR
🕐 Thurs–Fri 9am–4pm

Surrey growers Miranda and Halcyon Broadwood sell their
own 'real' broadleaf spinach, sorrel, Italian dandelion and 60
other varieties of fruit and veg. Other UK-grown produce is
also sold, plus some European organic. They will tailor-make
boxes to suit your needs – see the website for details.

Johnson's the Fruiterers ✪ ✪ ✪

☎ 01797 222133
✉ 29b High Street, Rye,
East Sussex **TN31 7JG**
🕐 Mon–Sat 8am–5pm

The Johnsons sell plenty of locally grown produce in their
traditional greengrocers. On my winter visit I was impressed
by the beautiful leeks, beets and brassicas. Locally made jam
and pickles, milk from Northiam and organic grape juice
from Sedlescombe vineyard are also on sale. They will make
up boxes for local delivery.

McCarthy Brothers ⓛ

mccarthy-bros@btinternet.com
☎ 01865 246975
✉ 18–19 The Covered Market,
Oxford **OX1 3DU**
🕐 Mon–Sat 6.15am–5.15pm

Local fruit and vegetables are the main objective of this greengrocer in the covered market. The coriander, chillis, peppers, marrows, onions and shallots are grown by an Abingdon Road allotment-holder not far from the market; purple sprouting broccoli and cabbage hails from Hinton Waldrist; and the strawberries and raspberries come from Rectory Farm (see page 294).

C. H. Mears & Sons ⓛ

☎ 01273 670711
✉ 33 Open Market, Marshalls Row,
Brighton East Sussex **BN1 4JS**
🕐 Mon 7am–1pm; Tues–Thurs
7am–5pm; Fri-Sat 7am–6pm

The Mears family have been in the Open Market since 1948. Today Pat, Cyril and their sister Mary run the stall, buying produce from local farms and market gardens that grow especially for them. You might find Sussex rhubarb, apples, parsnips and cauliflowers, all of them vibrant and fresh. Good value for money, too, so drop in here in advance of a supermarket trip to see what you can pick up.

Perry Court Farm Apple Crisps

www.perrycourt.com
☎ 01233 812408
✉ Bilting, Ashford, Kent **TN25 4ES**
🕐 Mon–Sun 8.30am–6pm

Fruit farmer Martin Fermor explains that while he is not an organic farmer, he operates a traditional system of rotation and keeps pigs (great for fertiliser) so he never (or very rarely) needs to spray. He grows over 100 varieties of pears and apples, plus a wide range of other produce all sold in the farm shop. He also makes apple crisps, a healthy alternative to potato snacks, available via mail order.

Peterley Manor Farm ⊕

www.peterley.co.uk
☎ 01494 863566
✉ Peterley Lane, Prestwood,
Great Missenden, Buckinghamshire
HP16 0HH
🕐 Tues–Sat 8.30am–5pm;
Sun 9am–1pm

A fabulous-looking farm shop with wooden counters piled with banks of vegetables and fruits from the farm. You can also pick your own – either soft fruits (lovely blackberries and strawberries) or orchard fruits such as apples and plums. Other produce includes local ice cream and cheeses. Later in the year keep in mind that they grow Christmas trees.

Pips of Petworth @ ⊘ ⊕

www.pipsofpetworth.co.uk
☎ 01798 342115
✉ Unit B, The Old Bakery, Golden
Square, Petworth, West Sussex
GU28 0AP
🕐 Mon–Sat 8am–5.30pm

A greengrocers with the smart idea of selling fresh produce, sourced either locally or from London's wholesale market, in one half of the shop (with a box delivery service, too) and a takeaway in the other. They make juices, smoothies and sandwiches helping to offset the waste that can be the downfall of fruit and veg selling. Locally grown produce might include strawberries, lettuce, beetroot and potatoes.

Rectory Farm ⊘ ⊕

www.rectoryfarmshop.co.uk
☎ 01223 860374
✉ Stanton St John, Oxford,
Oxfordshire **OX33 1HF**
🕐 Mon–Sat 9.30am–5pm;
Sun 10am–4pm

Rectory Farm specialises in soft fruit, but also has vegetables, such as asparagus (from the beginning of May). It claims to have something available every day of the year whenever it is in season so you may find raspberries, strawberries, carrots, cucumbers, tomatoes, artichokes, beetroot or runner beans. See their website.

Roundstone Farm Shop ⊕

☎ 01903 783817
✉ Littlehampton Road, Ferring,
Nr Worthing, West Sussex
BN12 6PW
🕐 Mon–Sat 9am–5pm;
Sun 10am–4pm

Locals love this PYO, praising the quality and – oddly – the size of the vegetables, and also the tractor that will take you from field to field if you do not fancy a walk. It is open all year – when the PYO veg and fruit runs out, there's a farm shop selling local food. PYO times vary so it's best to phone to check before visiting.

Village Veg ⊙

☎ 01590 622234
✉ 72 Brookley Road, Brockenhurst,
Hampshire **SO42 7RA**
🕐 Mon–Fri 8am–5.30pm;
Sat 8am–5pm

In the centre of the New Forest National Park you will find this good, straightforwardly stocked greengrocer's selling locally sourced produce when in season, plus more sourced from local wholesale markets. The free-range hens' eggs on sale are also from a New Forest farm.

Worton Organic Garden and Farmshop

www.wortonfarms.co.uk
☎ 01865 881247
✉ 3 Rectory Farm Cottage, Worton,
Near Cassington, Oxfordshire
OX29 4SU
🕐 Thurs, Fri 10am–5pm;
Sat 10am–2pm (Jun–Oct only)

A small shop stocked with organic vegetables grown in two one-acre fields. Sixty fruit trees are planted in another 2.5-acre site, with the harvest also sold here. There are over 40 vegetable varieties grown through the seasons, and a wide range of herbs and soft fruit. Eggs, honey and flowers are also available.

HONEY ▼

English Honey ⓞ @ ✿

www.pyrford.com
☎ 01932 349828
✉ 8 Lincoln Drive, Pyrford,
Woking, Surrey **GU22 8RL**

A very small-scale producer, but one with an online shop selling delicately flavoured honeys from hives distributed in the Hampshire / Surrey heathland and operated according to organic regulations. The honey is sometimes lightly crystalised, but the flavour and texture changes throughout the spring and summer season.

Gum Tree Apiary

www.gumtreeapiary.com
☎ 01227 261507
✉ 60b Cromwell Road,
Whitstable, Kent **CT5 1NN**

At the time of writing, Gum Tree Honey was setting up a network of farm shops and delis across the UK through which to distribute its Australian honey. Gum Tree is a family-owned concern located in Sawyers Valley, Western Australia. The six different gourmet honeys are harvested from hives in the bushland and shipped to the UK. The Jarrah (Eucalyptus) honey is particularly fine. Although these are Australian honeys, their production supports many honey farmers as well as the local environment. Finding a market in the UK offers much-needed support and gives us the chance to taste some exciting varieties. See webiste for details.

Homestall Honey 🅞 🅛

📞 01580 765055
✉ Homestall House, Shoreham Lane, Tenterden, Kent **TN30 6EG**

Ben Turner's uncle, George Jewell, started keeping bees at age 15 and worked for 40 years inspecting hives around the country for the Ministry of Agriculture. George is now 70 and his nephew Ben took over five years ago. He now has 120 hives all over Kent and keeps meticulous records about yield. 'You have three good years and three bad, unfortunately we've just had three bad ones,' says Turner. His most famous customer was the Queen, but he no longer delivers to London so she has to make do elsewhere. It's a pity, because the honey is so varied. Hives are started in apple orchards for the first batch, then moved to broad bean fields, then they harvest the clover and finally move to the Kent coast – so a true eclectic taste of honey, depending on what batch you chance upon. The honey is available from local butchers, farm shops and small retailers, as well as mail order. Ring for further details.

Howat's Hives

www.howatshives.co.uk
📞 023 8090 7850
✉ 8 Oliver's Close, West Totton, Southampton, Hampshire **SO40 8FH**

Honey from hives in the New Forest National Park promising extraordinary variety throughout the year, depending on which forest and heathland wild flowers are in season. Howat's are developing their online ordering, but in the meantime you can buy their honey from a number of local stockists – see their website or phone them for details.

Paynes Bee Farm ✿ @ ✪

www.paynesbeefarm.co.uk
☎ 01273 843388
✉ Bentley Cottage, Wickham Hill,
Hassocks, West Sussex **BN6 9NP**
🕐 Mon–Fri 9am–5pm;
Sat 9am–1pm

Here you can buy English honey from a working bee farm, other locally produced flower and heather honeys and some imported honeys. Honey is made throughout the spring and summer and the flavour changes depending on various seasonal blossoms. This is a working farm so it is better to call ahead to check opening times before you drop in.

DRINKS ▼

Char

☎ 01962 868760
✉ 156 High Street, Winchester
SO23 9BA
🕐 Mon–Sat 10am–5.30pm;
Sun 11am–4pm

Every wall in this shop is devoted to tea. Whether you are popping in for basics such as Earl Grey or Darjeeling (though, as you will discover, there are a number of choices even with these teas) or looking for something exotic harvested from a single estate, it will be here. Aside from the teas there is a vast number of other infusions to discover, such as teas made with flowers, herbs and spices offering multifarious health benefits. I could spend happy hours here.

Darvilles of Windsor ✿ @ ✪

www.darvillesofwindsor.co.uk
☎ 01753 861481
✉ Kardelton House, Vansittart
Estate, Arthur Road, Windsor,
Berkshire **SL4 1SE**

Traditional tea blenders who have been established for over 140 years, based in Windsor, which I suppose must be the capital of afternoon tea. The boxes and caddies are faintly twee, but there is absolutely no doubt that these teas are top quality. They sell the finest Indian and China tea, but also some good quality green teas and herb infusions. A lovely business and one to support.

Eve Coffee Company ✿ @ ✪

www.evecoffee.co.uk
☎ 07825 738828
✉ 10 Caselden Close, Addlestone,
Surrey **KT15 1PS**

Here are coffee experts with a huge range in their catalogue, all of which can be bought online. A nice touch is the offer of taster packs so you can find a coffee you love and want to buy regularly. The emphasis here is on ethical, and coffees are accredited by either the Fairtrade Foundation or the Rainforest Alliance. The single estate origin coffees are fascinating, offering coffee from Brazil, Sumatra, Sidamo, Guatamala and Columbia. Prices are competitive, too.

Fireside Coffee ◐ @ ◑

www.firesidecoffee.co.uk
☎ 01865 243834
✉ 103–104 St Clements St, Oxford
OX4 1AR

A company that is deservedly proud of its principled stance on selling a variety of teas and coffees that are accredited with the Fairtrade mark and are organically produced. Strict criteria means that there is not a huge number of varieties sold, but they are good quality and wide ranging in origin with coffees from Sumatra, Costa Rica, Peru and Ethopia; green tea from India and black tea from India and China. Good chocolate is also on offer from Zotter, Maestrani and Organic Seed & Bean.

Qi Teas ◑

www.qi-teas.com
☎ 01580 713613
✉ Herbal Health Ltd, PO Box 114,
Sissinghurst, Cranbrook, Kent
TN17 2QX

A Kent-based tea company that works with mountain tea-growing communities in China producing green and white tea. All the teas sold are single estate, accredited Fairtrade and certified organic. At present the mail order service is limited only to wholesale quantities, but contact this interesting company for stockists and see what you think of their infusions. I am a fan, having tried two white teas, enjoying the fresh flavours and imagining all those good health benefits.

Whole Earth

www.wholeearthfoods.com
☎ 01428 685100
✉ Coopers Place, Combe Lane,
Wormley, Godalming, Surrey
GU8 5SZ

You have to thank Whole Earth for making a good first of producing an organic cola and various other fizzy drinks to satisfy childrens cravings, while not tasting too worthy. These are drinks, however, to give them before they taste the somewhat more addictive real thing because they are otherwise unlikely to make the switch. It's not a bad effort, although a dentist will still not approve.

South West

▼ FARM SHOPS

Allington Farm Shop

www.allingtonfarmshop.co.uk
☎ 01249 658112
🌐 Chippenham, Wiltshire
SN14 6LJ
🕐 Mon–Sat 9am–6pm;
Sun 10am–5pm

Tim and Naomi Reynolds's shop is hugely popular, not least for its position on the main road out of Chippenham. Inside there's a large butchery counter, selling the farm's own meat, including some specialities, namely goat and rose veal. Organic fruit and vegetables, nicely displayed in wooden boxes, are labelled as to whether they are local, British or imported. Otherwise look out for lovely asparagus in season, local hardwood charcoal, golden-coloured milk from Jersey cattle from nearby Ivy House Farm and freshly cut watercress from the local beds. Online ordering is planned for 2011.

Ansty Pick Your Own and Farm Shop ⓨ

www.anstypyo.co.uk
☎ 01747 829072
🌐 Ansty, Salisbury, Wiltshire
SP3 5PX
🕐 Jan–start Aug: Tues–Sat 9.30am–5.30pm Start Aug–mid-Sept: Sun and Mon 10am–4pm Mid–Sept–Dec: Tues–Sat 9.30am–5pm
Mid–Apr–May: Sun 10am–1pm

Ansty began as a dairy farm in 1988 but gradually expanded into a market garden and popular local pick your own, selling a wide variety of fruit and vegetables. You can also buy home-made cakes and puddings in the shop, plus locally produced milk, eggs, bacon, organic meat, apple juice and bread.

Britford Farm Shop ⓞ ⓞ

www.britfordfarmshop.co.uk
☎ 01722 413400
🌐 Bridge Farm, Britford,
Salisbury, Wiltshire **SP5 4DY**
🕐 Mon 9am–6pm; Tues closed;
Wed–Sat 9am–6pm; Sun 10am–4pm

The shop changed hands in 2010, but the new owners have continued the tradition of selling over 80 per cent locally sourced produce. There's organic vegetables from five miles away plus beef, pork, lamb and poultry from Manor Farm at Burkham, just outside Salisbury. Other specialities include smoked fish from Fjordling Smokehouse; goats' milk and butter, plus pickled walnuts made from the trees in the orchard near the shop.

Cedar Organic @

www.cedarorganic.com
01929 481393
Rempstone Farm, Corfe Castle,
Wareham, Dorset **BH20 5JH**
Fri 9am–7pm; Sat 9am–12pm

I met Claire and Andrew Gead at a food festival in Dorset and was immediately intrigued by their commitment to organic farming and good food. On their idyllic farm near the sea they produce organic poultry and eggs, lamb and beef. They rear rare breeds, including Ruby Red North Devon cattle, whose meat is some of the best you will try, and Lleyn sheep. They have not been going that long, but this will be a lovely place to visit and see how organic farming fits so well on the heritage coast.

Darts Farm Shop

www.dartsfarm.co.uk
01392 878200
Darts Farm, Topsham, Exeter,
Devon **EX3 0QH**
Mon–Sat 8am–5.30pm; Sun
9.30am–4.30pm

This really is an exceptional shop. In 40 years it has evolved from a small hut selling fruit and vegetables into a lively hub that provides those lucky enough to pass through with fresh, seasonal, local produce of the highest standard. The Fish Shed sources its produce in Lyme and the River Exe each day, ready to be bought or tastily cooked there and then. The farm's Ruby Red Devon beef is delicious and expertly butchered on site, and the fruit and vegetables are grown outside the door – both feature in the restaurant's thoughtful and tasty menu. Hosting tastings, barbecues and Salamander dinners, the Dart brothers aim to bring food and community together and to inspire others with their palpable passion and ambition. I am rather ashamed that I had not spotted this shop earlier – it is a delight and sets a benchmark.

Daylesford Organic Farm Shop

@

www.daylesfordorganic.com
01608 731700
Near Kingham, Gloucestershire
GL56 0Y
Mon–Sat 9am–6pm;
Sun 10am–4pm

The organic farm shop in Gloucestershire that has raised the bar for all others, housed in a set of beautifully refurbished farm buildings on the Daylesford estate in the North Cotswolds. The brainchild of Carole Bamford (who has family farms at Daylesford and in Staffordshire), the shop and supply chain has obviously had the benefit of some very substantial investment. Organic rare-breed beef, park venison, pork, lamb and poultry is of exceptional quality and well priced. An abundant supply of vegetables comes from the estate's own market garden throughout the year. Bamford has hired talented bakers to make some of the best bread mentioned in this guide, and also has several excellent cheeses made at Daylesford's own dairy, including Daylesford Organic Cheddar, Single and Double Gloucester made with milk from genuine Gloucester cattle and a soft cheese called Pennystone. Milk (sold in biodegradable chalk cartons), yoghurt, fruit juice and eggs are the farm's own. Deli items are carefully chosen: you will find the best charcuterie from Italy and Spain; there's oil and apple juice from the family's estate in France; plus plenty of ready-made puddings, cakes, chocolates, pies, soups and sauces. Daylesford has been a good influence on the organic market and pricing is sensitive, with many fresh foods. The shop has been rebuilt after a fire, and is now even more beautiful. A cookery school has also opened.

East Farm Shop

www.eastfarmshop.co.uk
☎ 01258 880 642
✉ Winterbourne Whitechurch, Blandford Forum, Dorset **DT11 9AW**
🕐 Mon–Wed 10am–5pm; Thurs–Sat 9am–5pm

The beef sold here is produced on the farm, and the rest of the fresh meat sold is local. Free-range chickens are from Creedy Carver in Devon, and are excellent value. With game, pork, vegetables (from East Farm) and artisan bread, this is a thoroughly honest shop with a good local following. Highly recommended.

Everleigh Farm Shop ⬆ @ ✦

www.everleighfarmshop.co.uk
☎ 01264 850344
✉ Everleigh, Marlborough, Wiltshire **SN8 3EY**

David Hammerson is about as passionate over food and his wide-ranging mail order service as it is possible to be. He is a busy game dealer and processor, a butcher selling some wonderful, free-range local meat including excellent poultry (the Christmas turkeys come highly recommended) and a delicatessen. The food you can buy here has star status: venison is perfectly hung and you can ask about specific breeds, seasonal game birds are in tidy nick, trussed and oven-ready, and wild trout are as fresh as can be. You may even be able to buy Signal crayfish, caught in local chalk streams. One to get to know – I am a fan, as you can see.

Eversfield Organic @

www.eversfieldorganic.co.uk
☎ 01837 871 400
✉ Ellacott Barton, Bratton Clovelly,
Okehampton, Devon **EX20 4LB**

Mark Bury is passionate about organically reared produce and achieved full organic status in 2004. In addition, Eversfield cattle are the only herd in the country preserving the 'Presteign' bloodline, which is directly traceable back to the native Aberdeen Angus. Based on the Eversfield Estate in Devon, provenance and quality matter to the Burys, and this can be seen and tasted across their range of products. When in season, their wild venison and game comes from the estate itself, and all year round they provide a wide range of beef, lamb and pork products via their online shop.

Farrington's Farm shop

www.farringtons.co.uk
☎ 01761 452266
✉ Farrington's Farm Shop Limited,
Home Farm, Main Street, Farrington
Gurney, Bristol **BS39 6UB**
🕐 Mon–Sat 8am–7pm;
Sun 10am–4pm

This is a good, honest farm shop that stocks a wide range of locally grown and reared produce. Well worth a visit on a Wednesday, Friday or Saturday when fresh fish, landed daily in Cornwall, is sold from the wet fish stall at the front of the shop. Artisan rolls and breads, pickles and preserves give the shop a wonderful homely feel. That said, the quality of the produce is excellent and the care taken in its preparation and presentation is notable. If you're keen to try before you buy, sample some of their home-made cakes in their elegant café.

Fermoy's Garden Centre and Farm Shop ✪

☎ 01803 813022
✉ Totnes Road, Ipplepen, Newton
Abbot, Devon **TQ12 5TN**
🕐 Mon–Sat 9am–5.30pm;
Sun 10.30am–4.30pm

This farm shop near Newton Abbott in Devon currently sells locally grown vegetables and fruit, locally reared meat, bread and a range of cooked foods including pies, pasties and cakes. Fermoy's is gradually expanding so please let me know what you think. You can order over the phone for local delivery only.

Gear Farm Shop

☎ 01326 221150
✉ Gear Farm, St Martin, Helston, Cornwall **TR12 6DE**
🕐 **Winter** Wed–Sat 9.30am–4.30pm; **Summer** Mon–Sat 9am–5pm

Right down on the Lizard you'll find this popular organic farm shop recommended by local good food devotees who say the home-produced organic meat is outstanding. They also pop in here regularly for home-grown vegetables and fruits, as well as locally sourced fish landed by day boats. This is also the place to come and buy award-winning honey from Gwenen Apiaries.

Goldhill Organic Farm

www.goldhillorganicfarm.com
☎ 01258 861916
✉ Ridegway, Child Okeford, Blandford, Dorset **DT11 8HB**
🕐 Wed–Sat 10am–4pm; Sun 10am–2pm

A brilliant, eco-friendly shop run by Maria Timperley, selling the farm's own organic vegetables and rare British White beef, as well as White Lake goats' cheese, Manna Organic ready-meals, Dorset blueberry jam, and pork from Pampered Pigs. Owners Andrew and Sara Cross are passionate about their vegetables grown on site and welcome school visits. There is also a delightful café on site called The Cake Tin Café.

Goldy's Farm Shop ✿ @ ✦

www.goldys.co.uk
☎ 01202 625777
✉ Bere Farm, Lytchett Matravers, Dorset **BH16 6ER**
🕐 Mon–Sun 8am–7pm

Goldy's is an acclaimed farm shop, housed in a tall barn, selling its own organically reared beef and even milling home-grown wheat to make flour, bringing the farming activity close to the shop. The wheat and rye flour is used to make bread in an in-house bakery, using the traditional technique of slow fermentation. Each day a piece of mother dough is 'fed' and used in the next day's bread, rolls and buns. If that were not enough, there is a market garden supplying potatoes, salad crops, strawberries, asparagus, tomatoes and root vegetables to the shop. An awesome example of a farm shop – tell me if you agree.

Higher Trenowin Farm Shop

www.highertrenowin.co.uk
☎ 01736 362439
✉ Nancledra, Penzance, Cornwall
TR20 8BE
🕐 Wed–Sat 9am–6pm;
Sun 9am–1pm

A good straightforward farm shop – a great proportion of what you find here is grown on the farm. Seasonal herbs, salad and vegetables, free-range hens' and quails' eggs. Farmer's wife Bridgette make all her own jams and bakes cakes for the shop. There is ice cream from Zennor and you can buy the farm's wonderful beef. Highly recommended.

Hindon Organic Farm ❍ @

www.hindonfarm.co.uk
☎ 01643 705244
✉ Hindon Organic Farm,
Nr Seaworthy, Exmoor, Minehead,
Somerset **TA24 8SH**

Part of the National Trust's Holnicote Estate, the farm is run by Roger and Penny Webber. It is a typical 'mixed stock' hill farm looking over the Bristol Channel, best known for its lamb. Penny believes that it is the quality of the breed, a Swaledale/Cheviot cross, and the slow natural way the sheep are reared that makes their lamb so good. Eating nothing but natural forage as they graze on Exmoor adds to the deliciousness of this meat. Available online, from the farmers' market in Minehead and also the Bristol Slow Food Market, the Webber's lamb was a winner of the National Trust's 2010 Fine Farm Produce awards. Home delivery available.

Holme for Gardens ❷

www.holmeforgardens.co.uk
☎ 01929 554716
✉ Holme For Gardens, West Holme
Farm, Wareham, Dorset **BH20 6AQ**
🕐 Mon–Sun 9am–5.30pm

With a pick-your-own area on site and a farm shop full of locally grown and reared produce, Holme for Gardens is achieving its goal of 'putting local food first'. There is a good range of hand-reared beef, lamb and pork, as well as freshly caught local trout on offer. Particularly tempting is the range of locally grown and brewed ciders – from the very dry to the lovely and sweet, there is one to suit each individual taste. The home-made cakes available in the tea room are a welcome treat after an intensive PYO session, and the jams and preserves that are served are made with Holme's own fruit. This business has taken a holistic view of growing and selling and has achieved a happy balance while maintaining a lovely local feel.

Home Farm

www.homefarmshop.co.uk
☎ 01258 830083
✉ Tarrant Gunville, Blandford
Forum, Dorset **DT11 8JW**
🕐 Tues–Sat 9am–5.30pm;
Sun 10am–4pm

Farmer Rodney Belbin is something of a cattle expert. He's been farming since he was in short trousers. The beef, (wonderful) lamb and duck are produced on the farm. The butchery is superb and the butcher, Ray Lewis is a master of his craft. They sell very good home-cooked pies and quiches with local breads and cheese, plus some very good frozen meals, and a range of good hot foods are served in the small café. Home Farm is off the beaten track and it's a testimony to Rodney's wife Marlene's enthusiasm that people come here from far and wide.

Killerton Estate

www.nationaltrust.org.uk/
killerton
☎ 01392 881345
✉ Broadclyst, Exeter, Devon **EX5 3LE**
🕐 11am–5.30pm (seasonal
opening times apply, see website)

The National Trust's Killerton estate has been milling their own flour at Clyston Mill for over 10 years. Two years ago, the estate began employing tenant farmer John Kittow to grow a traditional variety of wheat on the estate. The Maris Widgeon flour is sold at the estate shop and the mill. Killerton honey is also a speciality. The hives are set in the middle of the orchards and the honey the bees produce is uniquely flavoured, with a real sense of the place where it is produced. The estate has also been making charcoal from their woodlands for the last six years; seek it out – it's a much greener choice than opting for the imported stuff at the nearest garage. Killerton is a deserving award winner of the National Trust's 2010 Fine Farm Produce awards.

Kimbers Farm Shop ❻

www.kimbersfarmshop.co.uk
☎ 01963 33177
✉ Higher Stavordale Farm, Barrow
Lane, Charlton Musgrove,
Wincanton, Somerset **BA9 8HJ**
🕐 Tues 9.30am–5.30pm;
Thurs–Fri 9am–6.30pm;
Sat 10am–4pm

Kimbers has a very good local reputation. It rears its own Angus and Devon beef and welfare-friendly, milk-fed veal. They also have a milking herd and unpasteurised milk is available in the shop. Paul and Ruth Kimber try to keep things simple and local: short journeys to the abattoir, and milk delivered to the local Wyke Farms creamery (young children particularly love the Wyke's butter). Good cheeses, Stoates flour and a good range of beer and wine make this a must-visit shop.

Lifton Strawberry Fields

www.liftonstrawberryfields.co.uk
☎ 01566 784605
✉ Lifton, Devon
PL16 0DE
🕐 Mon–Sat 8am–6pm; Sun 8am–5pm (seasonal opening times apply)

Jo and Roger Mounce are prolific growers of strawberries between May and October, along with other produce. They rear their own South Devon beef, sell pasties, saffron buns, pies, preserves, free-range eggs and clotted cream. A much-loved place and a finalist in the National Farmers' Retail & Markets Association (FARMA) awards, 2010. Local delivery available.

Lobbs Farm Shop ♠ @ ✿

www.lobbsfarmshop.co.uk
☎ 01726 844411
✉ Heligan, St Ewe, St Austell, Cornwall **PL26 6EN**
🕐 Mon–Fri 9.30am–5pm

A popular farm shop selling home-reared beef and lamb, plus an imaginative range of Cornish and West Country produce, including canned Cornish sardines (pilchards, really, but good all the same), smoked salmon from the excellent Dartmouth smokehouse, strawberry jam from Boddington's Berries, Cornish sea salt, freshly made sausages and bacon, game birds in season and some of the farm's own home-made hog's pudding and boiled ox tongue.

Long Close Farm Shop ♠ @ ✿

www.tregewfarm.co.uk
☎ 01326 373706
✉ Tregew Farm, Flushing, Falmouth, Cornwall **TR11 5UQ**
🕐 Mon–Sat 8.30am–5pm; Sun 10am–2pm

The Newton family grow mainly vegetables, such as asparagus, beetroot, squash and purple sprouting broccoli, selling them all year round in their shop. Here you'll also find locally made ice cream, clotted cream, apple juice, freshly baked bread, preserves and cheese.

Marr Green Farm Shop

☎ 07900 952152
✉ Collingbourne Road, Burbage, Wiltshire **SN8 3RT**
🕐 Mon–Fri 9am–6pm; Sat 9am–5pm; Sun 10am–3pm

You hear better and better things about this farm shop. The smallholding attached to the shop is home to some very spoilt Saddleback and Large White pigs, reared in a small number to high standards of welfare. The young pigs are brought in if the weather is cold, otherwise they can roam outside. Other than the pork there is organic beef, lamb and free-range chicken, (excellent) Sandridge bacon, organic eggs, bread from the baker in Great Bedwyn, Chad's honey, plus fresh produce delivered every day.

Millers Farm Shop ●

www.millersfarmshop.com
☎ 01297 35290
✉ Axminster, Devon **EX13 7RA**
🕐 Mon–Fri 7am–6.30pm;
Sat 7am–6pm; Sun 8am–1pm

A shop that sells itself as 'Devon's favourite' should be an immediate turn-off, but at least two locals, including the chef Mark Hix who has a restaurant in nearby Lyme Regis, rate Miller's Farm shop highly. There are always just-harvested vegetables grown on the farm, fresh meat reared by neighbours, and also, uniquely, a wet fish counter serving fish caught in Lyme Bay or not far away. Once a week a van comes packed with good things from France. This may seem slightly bizarre, considering farm shops are all about local marketing, but it is nice to be able to pick up good quality deli items when popping in for potatoes that have been grown in the next field.

Modbury Organic Farm

www.modburyfarm.co.uk
☎ 01308 897 193
✉ Burton Bradstock, Bridport,
Dorset **DT6 4NE**
🕐 Mon–Sun 7am–7pm

An enterprising farm shop devoted to Channel Island cattle, selling both organic milk and cream from a small Jersey herd reared on the farm, plus organic beef produced from a dairy cross of Aberdeen Angus and Jersey. In summer the shop sells home-grown organic vegetables; there is also a range of local foods and cheeses made from Channel Island milk, including Exmoor Blue, Sharpham Rustic and Channel Island Brie. Jersey ice creams are also available.

Occombe Farm @ ●

www.occombe.org.uk
☎ 01803 520022
✉ Preston Down Road, Paignton,
Devon **TQ3 1RN**
🕐 Mon–Sat 9am–5.30pm;
Sun 9.30am–4.30pm

This is a principled farm shop that puts the emphasis on local, Fairtrade and organic produce. The butchery sells meat from both locally reared and organically farmed cattle, sheep and pigs; bacon is cured on the premises. Bread is baked daily at Occombe's organic bakery and the range includes plain white, wholemeal, malthouse and sourdough loaves. West country cheeses, preserves, pies, cooked meats and pasties are also on sale, plus some deli items. Produce is clearly labelled so that customers know exactly where the food comes from.

The Organic Farm Shop

www.theorganicfarmshop.co.uk
01285 640 441
Abbey Home Farm, Burford Road, Cirencester, Gloucestershire **GL7 5HF**
Tues–Thurs 9am–5pm;
Fri 9am–6.30pm; Sun 11am–4pm

A dairy that has its own pasteurisation plant, selling the farm's own organic milk, yoghurt, cheese and cream; and a farm that produces naturally reared chicken, organic vegetables, fruit, flowers and herbs. Award-winning, with a miniscule carbon footprint – bravo.

Pitney Farm Shop

www.pitneyfarmshop.co.uk
01458 253002
Glebe Farm, Woodsbirdshill Lane, Pitney, Langport, Somerset
TA10 9AP
Mon–Tues, Thurs–Sat 9am–5.30pm

Lizzie and Rob Walrond sell their own home-reared Saddleback organic pork, free-range poultry, beef and lamb. Welfare is paramount and all livestock is slaughtered locally to reduce stress. Other good products include ice cream, apple juice and cider from Ermie & Gerties (see page 366) in the village, apples from Charlton orchards (when in season) and flour from Burcott Mills.

Primrose Vale Farm Shop and Pick Your Own 🅿🅈🅞

www.primrosevale.com
01452 864592
Shurdington Road, Bentham, Cheltenham, Gloucestershire
GL51 4UA
Jun–Oct Mon–Sat 9am–6pm;
Sun 10am–5pm. **Nov–May** Mon–Wed, Sat 9am–5pm; Thur–Fri 9am–6pm; Sun 10am–4pm

A wide-ranging PYO, now with a good farm shop. This was originally A. & A. Farms run by Mr Alexander and Mr Angell, two pig and poultry farmers who took to growing strawberries in the '70s. It changed its name to Primrose Vale in 2007. Aside from the soft fruit you will find the farm's vegetables in the shop all year round, as well as meat, game, plus local artisan cheeses and breads.

Pythouse Kitchen Garden 🟠 🟡

www.pythouse-farm.co.uk
☎ 01747 870444
✉ West Hatch, Tisbury, Wiltshire
SP3 6PA
🕐 Mon, Wed–Sun 8.30am–5.30pm

Henry and Holly Rumbold's farm shop is in one of the UK's prettiest locations, within the walls of an old kitchen garden with glorious views. You can pick your own bouquet of flowers from the garden or buy vegetables just moments after they have been pulled from the ground. In summer the fruit cages bulge with tayberries, raspberries and red, white or blackcurrants. Organic or naturally reared meat and poultry are also on sale, along with larder items, apple juice and locally made cheeses from nearby Wyn Green dairy. There is also a café and catering service.

Richards of Cornwall

www.cornishflowerbulbs.co.uk
☎ 01736 757888
✉ Carwin Farm, Loggans, Hayle,
Cornwall **TR27 5DG**
🕐 Mon–Sat 9am–5.30pm

The Richards's farm shop near Hayle is a good and useful all-rounder, selling the farm's own fresh produce (plus some sourced from nearby farms), free-range poultry, naturally reared meat, local cheeses and bread. Carwin Farm is also a flower farm (you will be able to pick up bulbs when visiting) and the great soil here enables a huge range of salad crops to be grown, plus vegetables throughout the year, soft fruit in summer and asparagus in the spring.

River Cottage 🟠 @ 🟢

www.rivercottage.net
☎ 01297 631715
✉ The Square, Axminster, Devon
EX13 5AN
🕐 Mon 10am–5pm; Tue–Sat 9am–
5pm; Sun 10.30am–4pm

This is TV chef Hugh Fearnley-Whittingstall's shop and restaurant in the centre of Axminster, and which has a good reputation (though I confess I have not visited; I admire Hugh, however, and think his various TV campaigns raise awareness in the right way). The shop sells charcuterie, Aberdeen Angus beef, local seasonal vegetables and drinks (both soft and alcoholic). There are also regular visits and demonstrations by local producers. You'll find another branch in Bath and you can buy a limited range online.

Riverford Farm Shop ⊙⊙

www.riverford.co.uk
☎ 01803 762059
✉ Staverton, Totnes, Devon
TQ9 6AF
🕐 Mon–Fri 8.30am–6pm;
Sat 9am–5pm

Riverford have been farming organically under Soil Association rules since 1987. Their excellent and earthily robust shop stocks not only their own vegetables but some imports, which are clearly labelled. They have a butchery and bakery on site (the ham and leek pies are wonderful) and sell many locally made foods including Luscombe drinks (arguably the best organic apple juice in the UK), Posbury goats' cheese (good) and Tideford soups (OK). Their veg box delivery scheme, a separate business to the farm shop, delivers across England from local hubs. On the organic spectrum Riverford is no minnow, but as an organic supplier you cannot fault them. They also have a small shop in Totnes town centre, which is well worth visiting (see website).

Rumwell Farm Shop

www.rumwellfarmshop.com
☎ 01823 461 599
✉ Wellington Road, Rumwell,
Nr Taunton, Somerset **TA4 1EJ**
🕐 Mon–Fri 9am–5.30pm;
Sat 8.30am–5pm

An award-winning, family-run shop owned by Anne and David James, with Jack Mitchell selling fruit and vegetables grown on the farm, plus free-range eggs and Aberdeen Angus beef. The home-baked fruit pies are bestsellers.

Source at Cholderton

www.choldertonfarmshop.co.uk
☎ 01980 629894
✉ Cholderton Farm Shop, Tidworth
Road, Cholderton, Wiltshire **SP4 0DR**
🕐 Mon–Sun 9am–4pm

A working organic farm and estate near Salisbury, with a farm shop housed in an old Smithy, run by the Edmunds family. Inside you will find meat from Tamworth pigs, Aberdeen Angus cattle and Hampshire Downs sheep – breeds that have been reared on this farm for over 100 years. Organic milk from the dairy is not only sold in the shop but Bryony Edmunds makes cream (including clotted cream), ice cream and a lovely creamy custard. There is also a bakery with attached café. This is a principle place, run by a passionate team, and well worth visiting.

St Kew Harvest Farm Shop ⓨ❶ ⓔ

www.stkewharvest.co.uk
☎ 01208 841818
✉ St Kew Highway, Bodmin,
Cornwall **PL30 3EF**
🕐 Mon–Sat 10am–6pm,
Sun 10am–4pm

A vegetable farm and farm shop: either pick your own soft fruit and seasonal vegetables from a wide range in the fields around the shop or buy ready-picked. Expect typical Cornish produce grown to the highest standards – potatoes, greens of every sort, strawberries and more. The farm's own pork and bacon are also on sale.

Stevens Farm Shop

www.stevensfarmshop.co.uk
☎ 01305 889216
✉ Martinstown, Dorchester, Dorset
DT2 9JR
🕐 Mon–Sat 8.30am–5.30pm;
Sun 10am–4pm

A farm shop devoted to Dorset produce, with beef, pork and lamb reared by owners and farmers Norman and Liz Barnes. Chickens are local, as are the fruit and vegetables; dry-cured hams and sausages are made on site along with the cakes (which are bestsellers). There are dairy foods from Ostington, and additional items from the surrounding counties. Now in its fourth year, this shop has been a valuable addition to the Dorset food trail.

Stourhead Farm Shop ❶ @ ⓓ

www.stourhead-farm-shop.co.uk
☎ 01747 841164
✉ High Street, Stourton, Wiltshire
BA12 6QF
🕐 Mon–Sun 10am–5pm

Stephen Harris and Nick Hoare run this farm shop on the Stourhead estate, which is supported by landlords The National Trust. The shop was opened as a place to sell food, mainly meat, produced on the Stourhead estate or produced locally. Beef is from a continental cross, not my favourite since I prefer native breeds, but if hung properly it can taste delicious. Pork is produced by farmer Gerald Maltby near Dorchester, and lamb is a Texel cross. Game birds are available in season, and venison for most of the year. Dorset Blue Vinney cheese and West Country cheddars are usually in stock, plus free-range eggs and trout from local farms.

Stream Farm ⊙ @ ∅

www.streamfarm.co.uk
☎ 01823 451191
✉ Broomfield, Bridgwater, Somerset
TA5 2EN
🕐 Mon–Fri 9am–5pm;
Sat 9am–1pm

A remarkable farm that sells rare-breed Dexter beef, Saddleback, Gloucester Old Spot and Berkshire pork, and organic chickens reared in an exemplary system. Added to this they produce 'stream-fed' rainbow trout from two trout ponds, which are sold fresh or hot-smoked over oak, cherry, or alder wood. Contact them if you want to visit.

Taste of the West Country ⊙ @ ∅

www.tasteofthewestcountry.
co.uk
☎ 01579 345 985
✉ Fore Street, St Cleer, Liskeard,
Cornwall **PL14 5DA**
🕐 Mon–Sat 8am–6pm;
Sun 10am–6pm

A self-service farm shop (meaning everything is already weighed and priced) popular with holidaymakers who can whizz in here and pick up what they need. I am not sure that I feel cheered by this, but this is a nice shop, selling the farm's own free-range rare-breed pork, and vegetables, too. Basic larder items encourage shoppers away from supermarkets. The farm is a few miles from the shop, which is more conveniently situated in a village. Chris and Sunshine Bolton and Rachel Cole took over in June 2010.

Trevaskis Farm Shop ⊙

www.trevaskisfarm.co.uk
☎ 01209 714009
✉ Gwinear, Hayle, Cornwall
TR27 5JQ
🕐 Mon–Sun 9am–5pm

Vegetables have been grown on this farm for 30 years. You can pick your own or visit the stunningly good-looking new Trevaskis Market, a shop that houses a butchery and wet fish counter, and also sells freshly baked artisan bread from Tom's bakery a few miles up the road. Reviews of this shop have been very good. Go there for free-range poultry, south Devon beef, home-made sausages and hams that have been cooked on the premises. Out in the fields there is a huge range of vegetables including peas, mange tout, broad beans, carrots, lovely waxy potatoes typical of the region, and strawberries.

Trudgian Farm Shop

www.trudgianfarm.co.uk
☎ 01726 883946
✉ 1 Church Terrace, Probus, Truro, Cornwall **TR2 4JN**
🕐 Tues–Fri 9am–5pm; Sat 9am–4pm

A farm shop, beloved of locals, where you get a real feel of Cornwall's farming history. The family has been here rearing livestock since 1901 and farmer John Richards now runs an on-site butchery and sells his own South Devon beef (one of my favourite breeds for flavour and its lovely tight grained meat), lamb and pork. The family also grow their own vegetables and fruit, picking and harvesting every day so that all is extraordinarily fresh. Add to this the Richardson's efforts to keep prices down and you have a perfect farm shop, selling fresh and naturally produced food that is good value for money.

Washingpool Farm Shop ✪

www.washingpool.co.uk
☎ 01308 459549
✉ North Allington, Dottery Road, Bridport, Dorset **DT6 5HP**
🕐 Mon–Sat 8.30am–4pm; Sun 10am–3.30pm

My Dorset friends recommend this shop highly, impressed by the range of food inside including the farm's own potatoes, vegetables, salad crops, orchard and soft fruits all piled appetisingly on to cool wooden shelves. Some extra produce is sourced locally from Riverford Organic and Dorset Down Mushroom Farm. Beef, pork and lamb is sourced from local farms – the beef from Goodfellows Farm, ham from Denhay and Dorset Farms and pies from Bridport Pies – which are excellent. There are some imported fruits and veg (bananas, lemons), plus deli foods, but overall there is a good local flavour to the contents of this place. I especially loved to see the Dorset chillies, and tomatillos from Sea Spring Farm in nearby West Bexington. Note that seasonal times apply in summer so do check before visiting.

Witheridge Farm Shop ✪

www.witheridgefarmshop.co.uk
☎ 01884 860313
✉ West Yeomoor Farm, Witheridge, Tiverton, Devon **EX16 8QA**
🕐 Tues–Sat 8.30am–1.30pm; Fri 8.30am–6pm

The farm has stood here at Witheridge since the 17th century, remaining unaffected by modern intensive farming methods. The farm's own naturally reared beef, lamb, free-range pork and chicken is sold in the shop, along with home-made sausages and bacon. Game is sourced from local shooting estates. Home-grown salad, local cheeses –

including the beautiful Keen's Cheddar, Devon Blue and Vulscombe – plus pickles and chutney from Ottervale preserves are also for sale. Home delivery available.

Wotton Farm Shop ®

www.wottonfarmshop.co.uk
☎ 01453 521546
✉ Bradley Road, Wotton-under-Edge, Gloucestershire **GL12 7DT**
🕐 Mon–Sat 9am–5.30pm;
Sun 10am–4pm

Popular, well-run PYO and farm shop offering a wide range of soft fruits (including strawberries grown on tables so no bending) plus vegetables, including broad beans, runner beans, asparagus and courgettes. The farm shop sells the farm's own free-range pork, free-range chicken from Devon, plus other produce made and grown in the south west.

Wyld Meadow Farm ® ®

www.wyldmeadowfarm.co.uk
☎ 01297 678318
✉ Monkton Wyld, Bridport, Dorset **DT6 6DD**
🕐 Tues–Fri 10am–2pm

The Sage family has farmed sheep and beef at Monkton Wyld for generations. They use traditional methods of rearing their livestock and take great pride in their animals, which are all reared naturally, grazing on prime Dorset meadowland. The sheep are mostly Dorset Poll although no provenance is given for their beef. The lamb is available throughout the year as individual cuts or quarters, half and whole beasts, and they also sell wild venison, either at the farm gate or for home delivery.

FOOD MARKETS ▼

Bath Farmers' Market ®

www.bathfarmersmarket.co.uk
☎ 01761 490624
✉ Green Park Station, Green Park Road, Bath, Somerset **BA1 1JB**
🕐 **Weekly**, Sat 8.30am–1.30pm

Home to one of the earliest farmers' markets when the movement took off in the '90s, Bath's market is still excellent, selling apple juice, home-made pastries, organic beef, artisan bread, organic cereals, farmhouse cheeses, organically reared pork, lamb, chickens and ducks, plus free-range eggs. You can also buy fresh wet and smoked fish, English cut flowers, wild venison and game birds in season, and fruit and vegetables.

Bristol Slow Food Market £

www.slowfoodbristol.org

☎ 0117 904 1530

✉ Corn Street, Bristol **BS1 1JQ**

🕐 Monthly, 1st Sun 10am–3pm

Slow Food Bristol was set up in 2004 and its aim was to offer an excellent weekend food market to complement the existing farmers' market. Today it is recognised as the first regular Slow Market in the world; it is the largest food market in Bristol and it recently won a Soil Association award. International stallholders now sell next to local producers – fresh fish and local sausages; local beer, cider and perry; shellfish; buffalo and other cheeses; plus fruit and vegetables, handmade bread, honeys, apple juice, plants and herbs.

Broadstone Farmers' Market

www.dorsetfarmersmarkets.co.uk

☎ 01258 454510

✉ Broadstone First School, Tudor Road, Broadstone, Dorset **BH18 8AA**

🕐 Monthly, 3rd Sat 9am–1pm

Broadstone, a suburb of Bournemouth, came into being in 1890 following the building of its first railway station in 1872. Before then the area was farmland and home to a thriving lavender oil business. You will not find the perfumed oil at the farmers' market, but you will find around 20 producers, including fantastic award-winning Gourmet Pies from Bridport, vegetables from Enford Farm Organics, home-made 'Manna' ready meals, smoked trout and pâté from Mere Fish Farm, pork from Pampered Pigs, Oxfords Bakery and Sopley Fruit Farm. Regulars advise arriving early.

Buckfastleigh Farmers' Market £

www.local-farmers-markets.co.uk

☎ 01803 762674

✉ Near Globe Inn, Town Centre, Buckfastleigh, Devon **TQ11 0DD**

🕐 Weekly, Thurs 10am–1pm

In a gorgeous setting, near the Abbey and its unusual monastic produce shop (see page 316), this is a great weekly market with plenty of stalls selling free-range, home-reared beef, lamb and pork, poultry and game, meat pies, bacon and sausages. There is fresh local fish and smoked fish, shellfish and ready-made fish dishes, such as fishcakes. This is an important cheesemaking area and you will find West Country cheddars, goat and ewes' milk cheese, farmhouse butter and free-range eggs, home-made cakes and puddings, plus vegetables, salad, herbs and fruit. Everything, basically.

Cullompton Farmers Market £

www.cullomptonfarmersmarket.com
☎ 07866 241343
✉ Station Road Car Park, Cullompton, Devon **EX15 1AG**
◷ **Monthly**, 2nd Sat 9.30am–12.30pm

The oldest farmers' market in the south west (since 1998) with a huge following of devoted shoppers and producers from a strict 30-mile radius. The produce is great (Ellises Farm Old Spot pork, Culm Valley organic vegetables, Charlton Orchard apples/juices to name a few), although this market should also be commended for the way it works with the town of Cullompton. The arrival of the farmers' market has regenerated the town centre, encouraging new shops, whose owners say that business is booming since the arrival of the market.

Gloucester Country Market £

www.gloucestercountrymarket.co.uk
☎ 01452 522021
✉ Northgate Hall, St John's Lane, Gloucester **GL1 2AT**
◷ **Weekly**, Thurs 8.30am–12.30pm

Previously known as the WI Country Market, Gloucester Country Market is a non-profit-making organisation. All the seasonal fruit and vegetables are grown locally and picked as close to market day as possible; home-baked cakes, pies and biscuits are available with jams, preserves, honey and free-range eggs. Foodie gift parcels can also be delivered locally or, if arranged through another Country Market, parcels can be sent nationwide.

Liskeard-St Neot Farmers' Market £

www.stneot.org.uk
☎ 01579 326048
✉ The Village Hall, St Neot, Liskeard, Cornwall **PL14 6NG**
◷ **Monthly**, 1st Sat 9am–12pm

A great small-scale farmers' market with some high quality stalls, including Bocaddon veal selling welfare-friendly milk-fed veal from a local dairy farm near Looe. Everything at the market comes from within a 35-mile radius – look out for stalls selling typical Cornish vegetables. There is an extra-early asparagus season here, the new potatoes are just as good as Jersey Royals and it is a great area for soft fruit.

Lostwithiel Local Produce Market ⓛ

www.cgos.co.uk
☎ 01840 250586
✉ Lostwithiel Community Centre, Liddicoat Road, Lostwithiel, Cornwall **PL22 0HE**
🕐 **Fortnightly**, Fri 10am–2pm

Everything on sale is produced within a 35-mile radius of Lostwithiel and only the producers themselves are allowed to sell – no goods are sold by middlemen, sticking to the original FM principle that it is an opportunity for growers and producers to meet and be accountable to their customers (if that does not sound too horrendously authoritarian). Expect to find artisan bread, cakes, cheeses and ice cream, free-range meat, poultry and eggs, hand-made sausages, ham, bacon, vegetables, fruit and fruit juices, and herbs.

Plymouth Farmers' Market ⓛ

☎ 01725 306552
✉ Nr Lower George Street, Plymouth, Devon **PL1 1PS**
🕐 **Twice monthly**, 2nd & 4th Sat 9am–4.30pm

With 25 stalls setting up twice a month selling a wide variety of local produce, the city centre farmers' market is a lively and bustling place to visit. Situated by the sundial in the heart of the city centre, here shoppers can source produce that has been reared, grown or made by local farmers. Visitors to the market can expect to find locally reared ostrich meat (not my favourite, but if you like that kind of thing . . .), free-range pork, naturally reared beef and lamb, locally grown strawberries and vegetables. There is also a stall selling locally made artisan cheese, home-made chutney and preserves, pies and pasties.

Sherborne Farmers' Market ⓛ

www.dorsetfarmersmarkets.co.uk
☎ 01258 454510
✉ Cheap Street, Sheborne, Dorset **DT9 3AB**
🕐 **Monthly**, 3rd Fri 9am–1pm

The farmers' market in this beautiful market town is held at the bottom of Cheap Street. Here you can expect to find good strong Dorset cider, a stall selling smoked fish and meat, locally roasted coffee, venison, rabbit and game birds sourced from local shoots. You'll also find an organic butchery and a local mushroom farm.

St Ives Farmers' Market ⊕

www.stivesfarmersmarket.co.uk

☎ 01736 795387

✉ Backpackers, Lower Stennack,
St Ives **TR26 1RS**

🕐 **Weekly**, Thurs 9.30am–2pm

St Ives farmers' market is run by a local not-for-profit group called GULP (Great Tasting Unbeatable Local Produce). They have a rule that all food must be either grown or reared within a 30-mile radius of the market location and they especially encourage free-range and organic producers, too. The Cornish Smokehouse has a stall selling smoked fish, a visit to Jim's Bakery is a must, there is a vegetable stall selling seasonal produce, a sprouting seed and bean outfit, even a stall selling freshly made Indian takeaway food.

St Nicholas Market, Bristol ⊕

www.stnicholasmarketbristol.
co.uk

☎ 0117 922 4015

✉ St Nicholas Market, Bristol
BS1 1JQ

🕐 Mon–Sat 9.30am–5pm

Bristol's historic covered market, housed in a beautiful stone building, is just a few paces away from the site where the award-winning Slow Food market and weekly farmers' market takes place. The food outlets in the various arcades have a global theme, but the council market authority team (led by the inspirational Steve Morris) have been proactive in encouraging the use of local fresh ingredients in their cooked food. At Spice Up your Life, Bill and Suki Wagay use local lamb and vegetables in their Punjabi curries; Abdul Naimi sources meat from local Halal butchers for his beautifully decorated Moroccan café Bab Mansour; and Jennie Reid uses ingredients bought in local shops on St Mark's Road for her Caribbean wraps. Added to this are some actual grocers, including Trethowan's Dairy shop, run by the cheesemakers who make Gorwydd Caerphilly; Bakery Agnes; the Bristol Sausage Shop; and Kalahari Moon, an interesting shop selling ingredients and potjes (pots) to cook them in. You can also eat Portuguese and Italian food, sup home-made soup or visit Dr Burnorium's Hot Sauce Emporium (slogan: 'Your pain is our pleasure').

Stroud Farmers' Market ⊕

www.fresh-n-local.co.uk

☎ 01453 758060

✉ Cornhill Market Place, Stroud
Gloucestershire **GL5 2HH**

🕐 **Weekly**, Sat 9am–2pm

This was Gloucestershire's first farmers' market and it continues to be one of the busiest in the UK. There are around 60 stallholders, depending on the season, with as many as 10 stalls specialising in organic food and drink. Organic burgers and free-range sausages are cooked on-site, a market café serves hot drinks and snacks, and look out for Katie Lloyd's shitake mushroom-growing kits and Annette Eaton's smoked garlic. This award-winning market is worth a visit.

Taunton Farmers' Market

www.lot2do.co.uk
☎ 01823 412979
✉ High Street, Town Centre, Taunton, Somerset **TA1 3SX**
🕐 **Weekly,** Thurs 9am–3pm

A large range of local produce is on offer at this farmers' market that takes place at the traditional market place conveniently each week. With Somerset packed full of outstanding producers, the pies, apple juice, cider, fish, meats, potted herbs, cheeses, breads and honey sold by the stalls will be of the best quality.

Wimborne Market 🄯

www.wimbornemarket.co.uk
☎ 01202 841212
✉ Wimborne Market, Wimborne, Dorset **BH21 1QA**
🕐 **Weekly,** Fri 8am–2pm

Wimborne is a particularly nice market town in north Dorset, with a beautiful market square where you will find a branch of the Long Crichel Bakery. The market is on the edge of town, a big crowded affair with a huge number of stalls, both inside the hall and outside on the concourse. You can shop well here, but you will have to be picky and see beyond the usual high number of stalls selling very large underwear and bargain socks. The market is strong on fruit and vegetables, quite a good deal of which will be locally sourced (especially in summer), and there are some good meat and egg stalls, too. Outside I have bought potted herbs. There are a couple of vans selling meat of questionable provenance. A friend claimed, many years ago, to have bought horsemeat from this market, as well as wild boar meat from an escaped beast found wandering in local woods.

Ashburton Deli ⊘

01364 652277
16 North Street, Newton Abbot, Devon **TQ13 7QD**
Mon–Sat 9am–5pm

Ashburton is one of those lucky towns with a couple of good butchers, a fish shop and this deli selling local cheeses including Sharpham 'Brie' and 'rustic' varieties, plus Devon Blue, among a wider range of British and continental types. It also sells a huge number of global ingredients and spices, plus local honeys, jams and pickles.

Bird & Carter ✿ @ ⊘

www.birdandcarter.co.uk
01722 417908
3 Fish Row, Salisbury, Wiltshire **SP1 1EX**
Mon–Sat 8.30am–6pm; Sun 10.30am–4pm

Annie Bird specialises in local produce but also stocks deli foods from France and Italy. Among the West Country foods are New Forest Blue Cheese, Old Seram, home-made beef dishes with meat from Shrewton and hams from Sandridge Farm. Regulars love the chocolate mousse cake.

Bridfish Smokery

www.bridfish.co.uk
Unit 1, The Old Laundry Industrial Estate, Sea Road, North Bridport, Dorset **DT6 3BD**
Mon–Fri 9am–5pm; Sat 9am–4pm

A good company specialising in smoking all sorts of fish, meat and cheese; it looks to be a thriving concern. There's a plethora of different smoked fish available, ranging from salmon to eel, cod roe, haddock and kippers. They also sell white fish, shellfish and fish soup (mostly frozen). There are also marinated herrings and anchovies – in fact just about everything for the seafood aficionado. They will also smoke fish and game for customers who drop in with their own catch or bag.

Bridport Gourmet Pies

www.dorset-pies.co.uk
01308 420244
Gore Cross Business Park, Bridport, Dorset **DT6 3UX**

I first met Martin and Janet Aldridge when I was judging best producer for popular local freesheet, the *Blackmore Vale Magazine*. Tipped off by the magazine's knowledgeable and legendary editor, Fanny Charles, I hurried down to the unprepossessing site in Bridport's industrial park. The workshop was a revelation: Martin Aldridge, a former award-winning butcher from Oxfordshire, makes affordable, scrumptious pies with local pork and proper lard or butter pastry. Everything is right about these pies – the seasoning, the ratio of gravy/jelly to content. I loved the pork and chutney pie and the economical Dorset sausage plaits. Give them a call if you have a large order, otherwise the pies are stocked in many shops – just ask.

Brown & Forrest ○ @ ○

www.smokedeel.co.uk
☎ 01458 250875
✉ Bowdens Farm Smokey, Hambridge, Somerset **TA10 0BP**
🕐 Mon–Sat 10am–4pm

Many will tell you that Brown & Forrest make the best hot smoked eels in Britain and I have to admit I agree. The Pattissons learned to smoke fish in Germany and use a method where the raw fish is first roasted over a wood fire then the flames are 'killed' with a covering of sawdust creating the smoke that will then flavour the eels. The result is a juicy perfumed flesh with none of the dryness that is sometimes associated with hot smoking. They also cold-smoke salmon and trout, and the result is also exceptional. You can turn your visit into a whole day out and book to eat in their popular restaurant.

Buckfast Abbey Monastic Produce Shop ○ @ ○

www.buckfast.org.uk
☎ 01364 645570
✉ Buckfast Abbey, Buckfastleigh, Devon **TQ11 0EE**
🕐 Mon–Fri 9.30am–5pm; Sun 12pm–5pm

A treat for the curious – a shop selling food items produced in convents and monasteries all over the world. Headed by Fr Bennett from the attached Buckfast Abbey, the shop sells the Abbey's own honey alongside many others. There are mellow apple juices from Notre Dame des Dombes in France, boiled sweets in various iconic shapes flavoured with natural essences, cough sweets, cold-pressed olive oil from Sant'Apollinare, red and white wine from an Austrian abbey, meat pâtés from a Normandy order, syrups from Eyguebelle, flower-infused jams, crème de cassis and much more.

Dartmouth Smokehouse ● @ ●

www.dartmouthsmokehouse.
co.uk
☎ 01803 833123
✉ Nelson Road Dartmouth,
Devon **TQ6 9LA**
🕐 Mon–Fri 8.30am–5.30pm

This smokehouse overlooks the port of Dartmouth and specialises in smoking locally sourced fish, especially the mackerel which has an appetising juiciness. Kippers, kiln-roasted salmon, hot-smoked trout and smoked duck are also above average.

De-Liz Delicatessen @ ●

www.deliz.co.uk
☎ 01747 871771
✉ High Street, Tisbury, Wiltshire
SP3 6HA
🕐 Mon–Fri 8.30am–5.30pm;
Sat 8.30am–3pm; Sun 9am–2pm

Liz Crossleys's well-established and popular deli and catering service sells locally baked bread from Panary at Can Mills (where the bread is baked using Stoates Flour, milled on site), West Knoyle charcuterie, sourced a few miles away, and plenty of good, strong, artisan West Country cheddar among a selection of continental larder foods (parmesan, prosciutto, pesto, etc). There's a butcher and greengrocer in the village, too.

Di's Deli & Pantry ● @ ●

www.disdairyandpantry.co.uk
☎ 01208 863531
✉ Rock Road, Rock, Wadebridge,
Cornwall **PL27 6NW**
🕐 Mon–Sat 8am–8pm;
Sun 8.30am–6pm

This is a useful shop, especially if you are on holiday nearby and want to buy good quality deli food, such as salamis, cheeses (many from Cornwall), locally grown vegetables and ice cream, but also need a bottle of shampoo. This well-stocked grocery will save a trip to a superstore and the food is anyway much more interesting. Handy for those who really want to take time off from cooking are the home-made pies (shepherd's, fish, fruit and many more), and soups for those inevitable wet days. Local delivery is available and there is an online shop. Seasonal changes apply to the opening hours so do check before visiting.

Effings ● £

www.effings.co.uk
☎ 01803 863435
✉ 50 Fore Street, Totnes, Devon
TQ9 5RP
🕐 Mon–Sat 9am–5pm

A popular deli on the main shopping street in Totnes, which was packed with locals having coffee when I popped in. I was especially impressed with the quality of the meat terrines. The kitchen sources meat from Totnes butchers – a good sign. Also brilliant is the local honey, plus the tarts and cakes. A good, old-fashioned deli.

The Good Food Store

01297 442076

21 Broadstreet, Lyme Regis, Dorset **DT7 3QE**

Mon–Sat 9am–5pm (**Winter**)

Louise and Pete Atkinson took over this former mini supermarket in August 2008. It has been recommended to me by numerous Lyme locals, particularly for the cakes that are baked on the premises and pasties from Chunk, an award-winning Devon pastie producer. They also have organic fruit and veg from Riverford, local Lyme Regis honey and Moores biscuits. Cheeses include Dorset Blue Vinney, Denhay, Quickes and Village Oak. Free-range meat comes from Colyton Butchers – bacon, sausages, chicken, and numerous cuts of beef. Then there's cooked ham from Gatcombe Farm just three miles away, and Dorset coffee, which you can take away to make at home or have a cup brewed on the premises. The Atkinsons have put a lot of hard work into this venture and deserve to succeed. Summer opening times vary so ring beforehand.

Gusto Deli @ ✪

www.gusto-deli.com

01242 239111

12 Montpellier Walk, Cheltenham, Gloucestershire **GL50 1SD**

Mon–Fri 9am–5.30pm; Sat 8.30am–5.30pm; Sun 10am–4pm

Rachel Capuccini and Gavin Thompson have a hit with this acclaimed café and food shop where you can buy freshly cooked Italian-inspired foods and a wealth of high quality larder items. You'll find traditional breads, polenta cakes, ribollita soup (twice boiled with bread), and antipasti, including olives from Villanova, roasted artichokes, and charcuterie from top importers Vallebona (see page 72).

Kalahari Moon ✪ ✪

www.kalaharimoon.co.uk

07886 887523

Shop 86, The Covered Market, St Nicholas Market, Corn Street, Bristol **BS1 1JQ**

Mon–Sat 10am–5pm

This is a haven for homesick South Africans with springbok, kudo and beef biltong accounting for a third of everything sold from this shop. You can buy Wors and Iwisa maize meal and even potjes to cook them in. Mail order is also available.

Kingsley Village Food Hall

www.kingsleyvillage.com
☎ 01726 861111
✉ Penhale, Fraddon, Cornwall
TR9 6NA
🕐 Mon–Sat 9am–6pm;
Sun 10.30am–4.30pm

An impressive food hall in this shopping 'village' on the A30, which encompasses a butchery selling locally sourced meat, a fishmonger (as you would expect in Cornwall) selling really fresh fish, locally grown fruit and vegetables (including strawberries, potatoes and asparagus), and a deli. The emphasis here is to support local producers and showcase them so passing holidaymakers will be inspired and choose to cook with local meat (sides of beef and lamb displayed in an amazing, glass-fronted built-in fridge), or spend a little extra on fish landed by a small day boat. Hopefully they will fall for this place, which was recommended by a trusted local food enthusiast. See the website for a long list of Cornish deli items, cheeses and specialities.

Maples Delicatessen @ ✪

www.maplesdeli.com
☎ 01225 862203
✉ No 4 The Shambles, Bradford-on-Avon, Wiltshire **BA15 1JS**
🕐 Mon–Fri 9am–5.30pm;
Sat 9am–5.15pm

A beautiful deli in the centre of the old market town of Bradford-on-Avon, dedicated to local produce, selling milk and other foods from the Bowles family at Beckington Farm, organically grown vegetables from Tallywacker Farm, wonderful rustic bread from Hobbs House Bakery (phone and ask for your favourite to be set aside), potatoes and eggs from South Wraxall, and ready-made cakes and pies, baked on the premises. There is also a comprehensive range of store cupboard foods, from pulses to pickles – some of the latter made by reliable Wiltshire producer Tracklements (see page 328).

Olives Et Al ✪ @

www.olivesetal.co.uk
☎ 01258 474300
✉ 1 North Dorset Business Park, Sturminster Newton, Dorset
DT10 2GA
🕐 Mon–Thurs, Sat 9am–5.30pm;
Fri 9am–6.30pm

Lucky Dorset to have a source of naturally preserved olives that retain a proper crunch, sold with various imaginative marinades. These are sold in a shop attached to the building where they are produced and there is a good range of salads, cheeses, coffee, bread and biscuits on sale, too. If you can't visit Olives Et Al you can order their products online. This is a cheerful, socially responsible small business deserving support. They also supply a growing array of other local food shops and delis, and the owner Giles Henscher is planning to open a bigger, covered food market in Sturminster Newton within the next year or two.

Purely Cornish

www.purelycornish.co.uk
☎ 01503 262680
✉ 18 Fore Stret, East Looe, Cornwall **PL13 1DT**
🕐 Mon–Sat 9am–8pm; Sun 11am–7pm

Packed to the rafters with local produce, Purely Cornish of East Looe is a treasure trove of traditional and modern Cornish fare. Cheeses, vegetables, meats and traditional breads are all available, not to mention the huge variety of cider, ale and apple juice to wash it all down. The Kernewek range of chutneys and relishes on the shelves are some of the best and the home-made saffron cake is of equal note. This establishment gathers together the best of Cornwall under one roof, and also runs a hamper service via their online shop.

The Real Boar Company ⊙ @ ⦿

www.therealboar.co.uk
☎ 01249 782861

Simon Gaskell, who runs this unusual farm, explains that, as dangerous wild boar are kept penned in woodland here, it is best that the location of the farm is not revealed. The boar are eastern European pure bred and the sight of them moving around in the woodland in their family groups is formidable. The 18-stone males are awesome and their stripy boarlets quite adorable. They are slow-grown – it takes almost 18 months to rear a boar ready for slaughter (three times the time it takes to rear a domestic pig). Gaskell turns most of the meat into a good salami (I like the simple one with red wine the best) and sells the fresh meat cuts, too. A real treat. Mail order is available or contact him for stockists.

The Real Olive Co ⦿

www.therealolivecompany.co.uk
☎ 0117 909 9587
✉ St Nicholas Market, The Glass Arcade, Bristol **BS1 1LJ**
🕐 Mon–Sat 9am–5pm

All the olives you could want, plus hummus and pesto from this plucky company's original shop. There's even bread, baked on the premises, to complement takeaway foods, which include individual lunch boxes. There are two branches of Karin Andersson and Ben Flight's shop in Bristol – see website for details.

Relish

www.relishwadebridge.co.uk
01208 814214
Foundry Court, Wadebridge,
Cornwall **PL27 7QN**
Mon–Sat 9am–5pm

A lovely deli housed in an old stone house in this pretty Cornwall town, selling good quality deli foods (cheeses, smoked fish, charcuterie and cakes), and which also has a café serving exquisitely made cappuccino and latte. Stop here to buy picnic food before heading for the great surfing beaches of the north and west coast. Highly recommended by locals.

Severn & Wye Smokery

www.severnandwye.co.uk
01452 760 190
Chaxhill, Westbury on Severn,
Gloucestershire **GL14 1QW**

I really love this smokehouse, wet fish shop and home delivery service for a number of reasons. Richard Cook is a second-generation fisherman and expert curer of fish. He is currently involved in a project to protect the local, endangered Severn eel, catching elvers (glass eels) to ranch and return to the wild once they have grown, or sending them to eel farms – he will not use wild eel in his own smokehouse. He makes a wonderful job of smoking the farmed stuff, however, along with some of the best salmon you can eat. Wild salmon is also available, caught sustainably in the Severn using almost Medieval fishing methods. The shop is fabulous, packed with some of the best West Country foods I have eaten, along with great basics, too, such as eggs, bacon, butter and bread. On the wet fish counter, everything glistens with freshness. This is also a very green smokehouse: Cook uses off-cuts, including those from his own trees; he has recently planted a further 250 deciduous trees to replenish. Water is not wasted but retained and treated on site, and the shop has put in an application for a wind turbine. At Cook's right hand is the knowledgeable and passionate Dai Francis, seeking out new products to sell and liaising with the extensive number of famous chefs – such as Mark Hix – who buy from here. If you have time, stop by for lunch in the restaurant – the fish and chips, and the grilled smoked eel, are unbelievably good. Home delivery available.

Speciality Farm Foods ⬤ @ ◐

www.specialityfoods.org.uk
☎ 0845 8120128
✉ Cleave Farm, East Down,
Barnstaple, Devon **EX31 4NX**
🕐 Mon, Wed, Sat, 7am–1pm,
2–5pm; Tues, Thurs, Fri, Sat,
7am–1pm, 2–5pm

A new and unusual specialist selling extraordinary foods sourced from all over the world. Just when you think that you know every food that exists, Alan Porter finds something rare and hitherto unseen. Aromatic and hot Indonesian 'long' peppercorns, Nepalese tea, raw cashews, Bali beach salt crystals, salt 'diamonds' from Tibet and some lovely sugars made from coconut palm and maple, flavoured with vanilla, ginger and cinnamon. Lovely for gifts as well as for your own kitchen.

The Spicery @

www.thespicery.com
☎ 01225 426309
✉ Unit 2, Roseberry Place, Bath,
Somerset **BA2 3DU**

James Ransome established The Spicery in 2005 and has steadily grown the business year on year. His own background as a high-end chef took him all over the world, and on his travels he picked up a taste for the exotic and aromatic. Deciding that the scents and fragrances of India and the Middle East should be available wherever you are, he began sourcing and creating his own blends, endeavouring throughout to retain as much authenticity as is possible in the UK. The range now includes blends such as chermoula and berbere, whole spices such as cardamom and tamarind, as well as recipe kits and spice boxes. The quality of the spices is excellent and the blends are deliciously transporting. See their website for ordering information.

Tracklements ⬤ @ ◐

www.tracklements.co.uk
☎ 01666 827044
✉ Whitewalls, Easton Grey,
Malmesbury, Wiltshire
SN16 0RD

Always a principled company, started by William Tullberg and now run by his son Guy. Until recently they only wholesaled to independent shops, but you can now buy direct from them. Famous for their range of excellent mustards, made from seed grown in the UK (unlike almost all others), they also make many chutneys, marmalade, mayonnaise and other sauces. The recipes are generally good, tried and tested versions of old favourites.

Turnbulls

www.turnbulls-deli.co.uk
01747 858575
9 High Street, Shaftesbury,
Dorset **SP7 8HZ**
Mon–Sat 8.45am–5.30pm

Charlie and Corinne Turnbull's lovely deli-café sells local pâtés, hams, pickles, smoked cheeses (Dorset Blue Vinney, Woolsery, Ashmore) and other Dorset goodies. For Apple Day they make apple and blackberry pie piled with Blackmore Vale Dairy clotted cream. This is also a great place for lunch.

Wild Thymes @ ✿ £

01672 516373
2 Hughenden Yard, High Street,
Marlborough, Wiltshire
SN8 1LT
Mon–Sat 9am–5.30pm

A good wholefoods shop selling the usual extensive range of dry store cupboard goods including pulses, rice, beans, nuts, seeds and cereals. Organic vegetables are also on sale, plus a few cooked foods. The shop is owned by Christopher Markham, who owns an artisan cheese shop, La Petite Fromagerie, a few yards away (see page 346).

William's Fish Market & Food Hall

www.williamsfoodhall.co.uk
01453 832240
3 Fountain Street, Nailsworth,
Gloucestershire **GL6 0BL**
Mon–Fri 7.30am–5pm;
Sat 7.30am–4pm

Begun as William's Kitchen, this is a long-established deli and a decent fish shop that I have known since childhood when my parents would buy the odd ready-to-bake pie. Now a food hall and as busy as ever, it is still a great deli selling a vast range, including fresh vegetables, cheeses, charcuterie, artisan bread and, of course, the pies.

BUTCHERS ▼

Bilsand Butchers ✪

01258 452846
11 Market Place, Blandford
Forum, Dorset **DT11 7AF**
Mon–Fri 8am–5pm;
Sat 8am–4pm

John Bilsand's shop in Blandford's beautiful market square is a reliable place to buy every cut of locally sourced beef and lamb. He also sells some good free-range poultry, though you need to get there early on a Saturday before he sells out of the chickens – I speak from experience. Also recommended are the gammons and bacon, plus some of the local cheeses. A good, straightforward traditional butchers run by charming and helpful staff.

Bocaddon Farm Veal 🔵 ⏣ 🔵

www.bocaddonfarmveal.com
☎ 01503 220995
✉ 1 Bocaddon Cottages,
Lanreath, Looe, Cornwall
PL13 2PG

Jonanthan and Vicky Browne produce welfare-friendly milk-fed veal on Vicky's parents' dairy farm, offering an alternative to imported Dutch and continental veal, and that is not cruelly reared. The Browns take the unwanted bobby (male) calves from the dairy mothers (farmers will often destroy what they perceive as useless livestock at two days old) and rear them in small groups of eight in open barns on a diet of milk with some roughage. The veal calves are slaughtered at six months, by which time they are a fairly hefty size. If this does not convince you to try this delicious meat, keep in mind that these animals would either have no life at all or that simply by eating cheese there is a responsibility to eat veal, which is a by-product. The veal chops are recommended and you can buy shin for braising, loin for roasting, escalopes and mince, as well as kidneys and liver. Visit the farm by appointment (see website).

W. S. Clarke & Sons ⏣

☎ 01725 552328
✉ 55 High Street, Sixpenny Handley,
Salisbury, Wiltshire **SP5 5ND**
🕐 Mon 9am–1pm; Tues–Fri
8am–1pm, 2.15–5pm; Sat 8am–1pm

A butcher's shop with a small abattoir attached. It is beloved not only of its huge following of customers, but also local farmers who can take their animals the short distance to be slaughtered in a quiet place where stress to the animal is kept to the absolute minimum. The meat, which is almost all home-killed, is expertly hung and butchered, and there are good deli items and a range of cheeses on sale.

Dibble Direct ⏣ 🔵

www.dibbledirect.co.uk
☎ 01793 762196
✉ Eastrop Farm, Highworth,
Swindon, Wiltshire **SN6 7PP**

Guy and Liza Dibble milk a dairy herd and also organically rear around 130 cross-bred British Friesians each year as beef cattle. The beasts are grass-fed and all are reared from within a 'closed' herd of just eight or nine beasts. They are advocates of local food for local people so they don't sell mail order. 'We don't want to see the countryside cluttered up with polystyrene boxes,' says Liza. They will, however, deliver locally. Reports are good and the beef is well-priced. You can drop in anytime, but preferably ring first.

Dorset Charcoal 🥕

www.dorsetcharcoal.co.uk
☎ 01258 818176
✉ Tudor Cottage, Pidney,
Hazelbury Bryan, Dorset **DT10 2EB**

The only non-food item in this guide has a place in this chapter because I want to draw attention to barbecue fuel. The most popular summer cooking method has its issues, namely that huge quantities of wood from rainforests are used for making frankly inferior fuel. In the UK, however, there has been a revival in the tradition of making charcoal from hardwood left over from the timber business. It burns hotter and longer and is a totally sustainable product. Dorset Charcoal is sold all over the south west but www.bioregionalhomegrown.co.uk has contact details for other sources of 'green' charcoal. Ask your local butcher to stock it. It may cost a bit more than typical garage forecourt charcoal, but it performs better so the discrepancy is balanced in the end and you can enjoy barbecuing your meat with a clear conscience.

Exmoor Finest Meats ⊙

☎ 01643 862502
✉ Woodcocks Ley Farm, Porlock,
Minehead, Somerset **TA24 8LX**

A new venture, this one. Here's a place to buy amazing, full-flavoured beef from naturally reared, native Red Devons. The Dunkery herd are farmed on Exmoor by Simon and Tracy David, National Trust tenant farmers, where they graze on ancient grasslands and forage among wild plants. The Davids also farm Exmoor Horn sheep on the same pasture. All this is evident in the flavour of the meat, which is fully traceable. The couple should have a website up and running by the time this guide is published (check on the internet). Otherwise ring for details of the county shows they'll be visiting or place an order over the phone.

Field & Flower ○

www.fieldandflower.co.uk
☎ 07843 388939
✉ Home Farm, The Gordano Valley, Clevedon, North Somerset

James Mansfield and James Flower set up Field & Flower in 2009, offering boxes of grass-fed Hereford beef for delivery straight to the consumer's door. The cattle have an enviably beautiful environment in which to breed and grow, and they only travel four miles to a local abattoir, ensuring a stress-free life. Expertly butchered into various cuts and also made into fantastic sausages, the meat is hung for a minimum of four weeks. The online service offers standard as well as customised boxes of meat. The quality is truly remarkable. Their burgers are rich and juicy and the spicy beef sausages are a tasty alternative to pork.

S. J. Harvel Butchers ○

☎ 01747 811229
✉ The Chalk, Iwerne Minster, Dorset **DT11 8NA**
🕐 Mon 8am–1pm;
Tues–Fri 2–6pm; Sat 8am–1pm, 2–5pm

Simon Harvel's is a very high quality butcher's shop in this grand little village between Blandford Forum and Shaftesbury. Famous for his perfectly matured beef (occasionally from rare breeds), he also makes excellent sausages and sells a wide range of other carefully sourced meat. The free-range duck I have bought in the past from Harvel was among the best I have eaten. On Saturdays you can expect a queue, but everyone is happy to wait and once it is your turn, you will be on the receiving end of Mr Harvel's legendary courtesy and professional service. Visiting this shop is like a trip back in time and is not to be missed if you are in north Dorset. Cheeses, pickles, olive oil and other store cupboard items are also on sale.

Jesse Smith & Co ●

www.jessesmithbutchers.co.uk
☎ 01672 519915
✉ 4 High Street, Marlborough, Wiltshire **SN8 1AA**
🕐 Tues–Fri 8am–5pm;
Sat 8am–4pm

One of a chain of Cotswold butchers selling great quality, but not necessarily locally sourced, meat. Much of the beef is Scottish, supplied by Buccleuch & Macduff, but you will find traditional Hereford-breed beef here, too. Pork is free-range from Plantation Pigs in Surrey and there will often be some Gloucestershire Old Spot on the counter that is reared locally, plus lamb from nearby farms. Chickens are from Wooley Park Farms near Wantage in Berkshire. There's also a deli counter selling cheeses, charcuterie and olives.

John Robinson & Sons ⊘

jrbutchers@btconnect.com
☎ 01264 810609
✉ Marsh Meadow, High Street,
Stockbridge, Wiltshire **SO20 6HF**
🕐 Mon–Fri 7.30am–1pm,
2–5.30pm; Wed 7am–1pm;
Sat 7am–2pm

Robinson's numerous customers will tell you that their sausages are the best in Britain. It depends on your preferences, but the perfect balance of meat and fat (only belly and shoulder cuts are used), subtle seasoning and fresh Hampshire sage make the chipolatas and bangers great all-rounders. The pork for the sausages is locally sourced, the lamb in the butchery is from nearby Andover and the beef, well-hung for a good long time, is brought from the Scotch Premier Beef company. Run by Paul, Peter and Jonathan Robinson, this is a butcher offering a great service – many staff have worked here a long time and they are still recruiting apprentices. Frozen pies, smoked fish from the River Test, artisan cheese and pickles are also available. Ask about the catering service and hog roasts.

Jurassic Coast Meats

www.jurassiccoastmeats.com
☎ 07770 770476
✉ Fossil Farm, Winfrith Newburgh,
Near Dorchester, Dorset
DT2 8DB

Although sounding at first like a supplier of dinosaur meat this is a family-run farm close to Dorset's fragile fossil-filled cliffs, which specialises in slow-reared, naturally fed meat. It is a mixed dairy and beef farm, rearing dairy-bred bull calves for veal, and is also the finishing unit for mainly Aberdeen Angus beef cattle. Meat is sold in local butchers' shops (contact for stockists) or to private customers in good-value boxes. Home delivery available.

Lower Washbourne Geese ⌂ @

www.gribblesbutchers.co.uk
☎ 01752 893030
✉ 15 / 16 Fore Street, Ivybridge,
Devon **PL21 9AB**
🕐 Mon–Thurs 8am–5pm;
Fri 8am–5.30pm; Sat 8am–2pm

Here you can buy traditionally reared geese from a small Devon farm, fed only a natural diet of grass, corn and straw, and free to run around the fields during the day. Being slow-grown they have strong bones and the dark, tight-grained meat has real depth of flavour. Order well in time for Christmas.

Montbeliarde Beef ⊕ @ ⊘

www.lordswoodfarms.co.uk

☎ 01373 836160
✉ Lordswood Farms Ltd, Walk Farm, Witham Dairy, Frome, Somerset **BA11 5EX**
🕐 Mon–Tues, Thurs–Fri 6am–1pm, 2–5pm; Sat 6am–1pm, 2–4pm

An interesting beef supplier with a fascinating history. Montbeliarde are dual purpose cattle that originated in the foothills of the French Alps where their milk is used to make the Vacherin Mont d'Or cheese. The breed can also be reared for beef, solving the age-old problem of what to do with unwanted bobby calves born in a dairy herd. Neil Darwent, a Nuffield Farming Scholar, runs a large-scale dairy farm and owns one of the few British herds of the hardy and beautiful Montbeliarde cattle. He has started to produce beef – I have tried it and was deeply impressed. Who would have thought a dairy breed could taste like that? Local delivery is available if you live in the area.

Pampered Pigs

www.pampered-pigs.co.uk
☎ 01929 472327
✉ Rye Hill Farmhouse, Rye Hill, Bere Regis, Wareham, Dorset **BH20 7LP**
🕐 Mon 10am–4pm; Tues–Fri 8.30am–6pm; Sat 9am–5pm; Sun 10am–1pm

As the name suggests, the welfare of the animals at Rye Hill is a top priority. British Saddleback and Large White crosses are kept free-range, and the beef herd consists of traditional breeds as well. The meat is hung for a minimum of three weeks and then carefully butchered and moved just a few yards to the farm shop, which also stocks local vegetables and fruit. Their gammon steaks and pork chops are particularly fine and they also stock a good range of offal. Care for the animals from field to farm shop is paramount, and this makes for a fantastic product.

Partridge Farm ⊕ ⊘

www.partridgefarmtiverton.com
☎ 01884 242651
✉ Partridge Farm, Templeton, Tiverton, Devon **EX16 8BN**
🕐 Mon–Fri 9am–5pm; Sat 9am–1pm

The pork and bacon that you can buy direct from this small Devon farm is either Saddleback or Large Black, a breed that originated in the West Country. Both are reared in a free-range system, locally slaughtered and then hung to mature – something not all pork producers do but which does wonders for crackling! Farmers Peter and Wendy Bates also sell beef, either pure-bred or 'three quarters' Aberdeen Angus, grazing outside for most of the year then brought indoors and fed hay through the winter. The cattle are grown slowly, slaughtered locally and then hung for three weeks. All cuts are available.

Philip Warren ○ ✦

www.philipwarrenbutchers.co.uk
☎ 01566 772089
✉ 1 Westgate Street, Launceston,
Cornwall **PL15 7AB**
◷ Mon–Fri 8am–5pm;
Sat 7.30am–1pm

This butcher's shop in Launceton, with a second branch in Liskeard across Bodmin Moor, is run by the Warren family, who also farm in the area. They sell their own meat and source from other small and organic farms in Cornwall. Pork is from whey-fed pigs on Quickes Farm and eggs are supplied by Mrs Allerton in Pensilva.

Piper's Farm ○ @ ✦

www.pipersfarm.co.uk
☎ 01392 881380
✉ Cullompton, Devon
EX15 1SD

Peter and Henrietta Greig's mail order butchery is among the best. Devon Ruby beef, Saddleback pork (both hung for tenderness and, in case of the pork, to make the crispest crackling), free-range chicken, venison and lamb are produced by them and neighbouring farms to an exact standard, all buying feed from the same mill, all using the same local abattoir. Greig supervises the butchery and both he and Henrietta have devised some excellent recipes for ready-made foods, which are also a notch above the competition. There are some good value meat boxes, especially the barbecue boxes.

Pritchetts the Butcher ✦

www.pritchetts.co.uk
☎ 01722 324346
✉ 5 Fish Row, Salisbury, Wiltshire
SP1 1EX
◷ Mon, Wed 7am–4pm;
Tues, Thurs–Sat 7am–5pm

Butcher Mark Aldridge has run Pritchetts for 10 years now and has a large, loyal following in a town that is more or less hemmed in by superstores – quite an achievement. He sources beef grazed on Salisbury's water meadows, lamb from Shrewton, local venison and makes wonderful sausages and faggots. The sausages are made in front of you and are excellent. Tripe, chitterlings and Bath chaps (cured pig cheeks) are there for traditionalists, and I hear that Aldridge is also supplying local schools – cheering news.

Sandridge Farmhouse Bacon ⊕ ⊘ ⓛ

www.sandridgefarmhouse
bacon.co.uk
☎ 01380 850304
✉ Sandridge Farm, Bromham,
Chippenham, Wiltshire **SN15 2JL**
🕐 Thurs–Sat 9.30am–5pm

Sandridge is an excellent producer with a giant reputation,
who was curing naturally reared pork long before the new
wave of ethical producers. The pigs are loosely housed in
barns and slow-grown. You are welcome to see them when
you visit and witness their contentment. Most are Large
Whites or Landrace pigs crossed with rare breeds to produce
pork perfect for a traditional cure. The bacon cooks to a
crisp (if that is how you like it) with minimum shrinkage. The
gammons and hams are juicy with the right amount of salt.
Sandridge specialises in the Wiltshire cure, a process that
produces a milder, less salty bacon and ham.

Sheepdrove Organic Butcher ⊕ @ ⊘

www.sheepdroveshop.com
☎ 0117 973 4643
✉ 3 Lower Redland Road, Bristol
BS6 6TB
🕐 Mon–Sat 8am–6pm

Established in 1997 by Peter and Juliet Kindersley,
Sheepdrove farm is a homage to high organic standards
of animal welfare and care for the wild environment. They
produce pork, beef and lamb (from native breeds), plus
chickens that are slaughtered in the farm's own abattoir.
There are two shops – their second is in London at 5 Clifton
Road, Maida Vale. See website for details.

W. G. Smith & Sons

☎ 01364 652250
✉ 42 East Street, Ashburton,
Newton Abbott, Devon **TQ13 7AX**
🕐 Mon, Wed, Sat 7am–1pm; Tues,
Thurs–Fri 7am–1pm, 2–5pm

This Ashburton butcher's shop is run by Arthur and John
Smith, who took over from their father who bought the
butchery in 1955. All meat is sourced from a farm just
outside town and the brothers are well-known for their
sausages, which are made on the premises. Plain pork is
available all year round, but there are seasonal specials,
including pork and leek or pork with peppers and garlic.
I liked them, but sausage appreciation is very subjective
so I will leave it to you to decide.

Somerset Ducks Cuisine @ ✪

www.somersetducks.co.uk
☎ 01278 662656
✉ Greenway Farm, Moon Lane,
North Newton, Bridgewater,
Somerset **TA7 0DS**

I met Jonathan and Jenny Pepper at the Bath & West Show in 2009 where they were doing a roaring trade in hot duck sausages. The sausages had to be among the best I'd ever had, with perfect levels of fat, meat, breadcrumbs and seasoning. The ducks are reared in a free-range system and the Peppers also produce smoked duck breast, whole-boned and stuffed duck for a festive roast, and duck burgers – a great idea and one really worth trying. Let me know what you think of the sausages. Find them at Somerset farmers' markets (see website for details).

Sumbler Brothers ✪

☎ 01672 512185
✉ 11 London Road, Marlborough,
Wiltshire **SN8 1PH**
🕐 Mon–Tues 7am–5pm;
Wed 7am–1.30pm; Thurs–Fri
7am–5.30pm; Sat 7am–2.30pm

John Sumbler has worked in this shop since he was a boy – for over 50 years – and is devoted to buying the best that Wiltshire has to offer and using his considerable butchery skills to make a wonderfully appetising display. Beef is Aberdeen Angus sourced from Rectory Farm near Ashbury and he also sells rare breeds such as the delightfully woolly Belted Galloway. He hangs beef sides for a minimum of three weeks. Fresh pork is Wessex Saddleback and he makes good home-made sausages, pies and faggots. The bacon and hams are from Sandridge Farmhouse Bacon (see page 336); the lamb is the Wiltshire Horn breed from Home Farm, Devizes. That's not all. You will often find mutton, venison and rabbit on the counter, plus free-range duck bought from a supplier in Bradford-upon-Avon.

The Thoroughly Wild Meat Company ❂ @ ✪

www.thoroughlywildmeat.co.uk
☎ 01963 824788
✉ The Royal Bath & West
Showground, Shepton Mallet,
Somerset **BA4 6QN**

Remarkable lamb and beef from small farms on the Somerset Levels, including those that border Bridgewater Bay (on the Severn Estuary), which produce salt marsh lamb and mutton. Andrew Moore is the brains behind TWM and is responsible for the butchery and distribution. The lamb and mutton is truly extraordinary. The sheep feed on a diet of wild grass washed daily by the tide and this manifests itself in the herby flavour of the meat. Moore has also developed Brewhamfield beef, a mature cross between a Jersey cow and Aberdeen Angus bull – the beef is hung for over a month and is unimaginably good. If this is not enough Moore has also launched yearling beef, a veal-like product but from beef animals that live longer (one year) and combine a milk diet with cereal. Not disappointing, and good for osso buco and other favourite veal recipes. A great and dedicated producer, deserving of praise.

Torbay Turkeys

01803 872278
Compton Holt, Compton, Paignton, Devon **TQ3 1TA**
Mon–Fri 8am–4.45pm; Sat 8am–3.30pm

This Devon poultry farm specialises in free-range turkeys and, oddly enough, potatoes. The turkeys roam over grassland on their farm situated in a beautiful location on land owned by the National Trust.

Twelve Green Acres

www.twelvegreenacres.co.uk
01929 460017
Roebuck Farm, Highwood, Wareham, Dorset **BH20 6AR**
Mon–Fri 7am–6pm

Dan Green rears his pigs, beef cattle and lambs on a smallholding in Dorset to exemplary standards and will pack a box of cuts and send via home delivery. He is well known on the farmers' market circuit (contact for details of your nearest) and has expanded to producing cooked and cured meats, plus eggs (the latter obviously not suitable for home delivery). There is no question about the quality of the meat and the enthusiasm of this young farmer. Definitely well worth supporting, so do try one of the boxes.

Tywardreath Butchers

www.thelocalbutcher.co.uk
01726 812051
41 Church Street, Tywardreath, Par, Cornwall **PL24 2QQ**
Mon–Fri 9am–5pm; Sat 9am–4pm

Charlie Harris's butcher's shop has a formidable reputation in Cornwall, especially for his award-winning sausages, which are all made on the premises. Harris has developed over 30 recipes, from plain pork to the more eclectic leek and ginger. Fresh meat cuts, including beef and lamb, game and poultry, are all sourced locally and there is now a mail order service so you can try Charlie's sausages no matter where you live. His home-cured bacon is also excellent.

The Well Hung Meat Company
🏠 @ 🌿 🏵

www.wellhungmeat.com
☎ 0845 230 3131
✉ Tordean Farm, Dean Prior,
Buckfastleigh, Devon **TQ11 0LY**
🕐 Mon–Fri 9am–4pm

This is an exemplary organic farm selling superb meat. During the recession they have made sterling efforts to come up with mixed boxes of Soil Association organically certified meat that is affordable, choosing it on the premise that not every day should be a meat-eating day, but when you do eat meat, eat the best. Their beef is tender and intensely flavoured, thanks to a long maturation (as suggested in their name). But it is not just the fresh meat that impresses; their gammons have won prizes and the bacon is great, not too salty and cooks to a delicious crisp.

Wild Beef 🏠 @ 🌿

www.wildbeef.co.uk
☎ 01647 433433
✉ Hillhead Farm, Chagford,
Devon **TQ13 8DY**

So-called because Richard and Lizzie Vines's Welsh Black and South Devon beef animals graze over ancient untouched pasture, feeding on the wild plants and grasses that have existed there for centuries. More and more evidence is emerging that backs up the theory that animals that forage on natural grassland contain higher degrees of nutrients. Either way, this is delicious meat, perfectly hung and butchered, too. You can also find them at Borough Market in London on Fridays and Saturdays. Contact for availability.

▼ BAKERS AND CONFECTIONERS

Chococo The Purbeck Chocolate Co @

www.chococo.co.uk
☎ 01929 421777
✉ Cocoa Central, Commercial Road, Swanage, Dorset **BH19 1DF**
🕐 Mon–Sat 9am–6pm

Claire and Andy Burnet's chocolates are all handmade using the best raw materials including some Fairtrade chocolate and locally sourced essentials such as butter, cream and Somerset cider brandy (some see this as essential anyway). They come packed in eye-catching tutti frutti-hued boxes that cannot fail to grab attention. Luckily the contents will have chocolate lovers drooling – whether filled with gooey creams or studded with nuts. Visit their Swanage shop or order from them online.

Figgy's Puddings ✿ @ ✦

www.figgys.co.uk
☎ 01392 459488
✉ 20 East Avenue, Exeter, Devon **EX1 2DY**

Jo and Richie Evans's properly made Christmas puddings are delivered to your home in a traditional, cloth-covered ceramic pudding basin (in three sizes) and are amazing value for money. Inside the bowl is a rich mix of fruit, a soaking of Port Stout from O'Hanlon's brewery in Devon, and absolutely no nasties like hydrogenated suet.

Hobbs House Bakery ✿ @ ✦

www.hobbshousebakery.co.uk
☎ 01453 839396
✉ 4 George Street, Nailsworth, Gloucestershire **GL6 0AG**
🕐 Mon–Sat 7.30am–5pm

A Gloucestershire-based bakery, run by three generations of one family and now employing 120 people. Yet despite its growth Hobbs House retains its artisan feel. There are three shops (others in Tetbury and Chipping Sodbury) and they also wholesale bread, selling in various other outlets in the west of England and at farmers' markets. You can even buy bread from Hobbs House online, though in a minimum quantity of 10 kg. All the flour used to make the dough is from Shipton Mill and the bread is made slowly, some with wild yeast (producing a sour dough). Among the bestsellers is the spelt soda bread, the rustic 'petit baguette ancienne' and white Sherston bread. The shops also have cafés (with different opening hours), serving tempting cakes and confectionery, which are also on sale in the shops.

Honeybuns ⊙ @ ⦿

www.honeybuns.co.uk
☎ 01963 23597
✉ Naish Farm, Stony Lane, Holwell,
Sherborne, Dorset **DT9 5LJ**

Emma Goss Custard bakes with anxious parents in mind, using natural ingredients, some organic, no hydrogenated fat and free-range eggs. Her idea has been a hit – growing from a one-family-band to quite a significant regional employer. They make flapjacks, brownies and other chocolate cakes, shortbread and cookies; many come wrapped individually. A good-hearted company with much charm. Order online or see website for stockists.

Lavender Blue ⊙ ⦿ ⓔ

☎ 01747 821333
✉ Unit 42 Brickfields Business Park,
Gillingham, Dorset **SP8 4PX**
🕐 Mon–Fri 9am–4pm

Lavender Blue has a good local reputation. Samantha Ross's lovely company specialises in handmade fruit cakes and sponges. The cakes are made with butter and the range includes a gamekeeper's cake made with the addition of sloe gin. Christmas puddings are available by mail order (phone for details). I would welcome more reader feedback on this business.

Long Crichel Bakery

www.longcrichelbakery.co.uk
☎ 01258 830 852
✉ Long Crichel, Nr Wimborne,
Dorset **BH21 5JU**
🕐 Tues–Fri 9.30am–5pm;
Sat 9am–5pm

The bakery was started in 2000 by Jamie and Rose Campbell who also run their architect practice in the grounds. To say this is a food shop from heaven is understating it. The baking in a wood-fired oven is superb. Locals rave about the slow-fermented bread, and the sourdoughs are crunchy to bite and have a wonderful spongy texture. Whenever I come here I buy large batches and freeze the bread. The baker, Robert Schultz, is ably assisted by co-owner Jamie Campbell, and Jenni Channon is brilliant behind the counter – she has a great knowledge of all the different types of bread. Organic vegetables grown in the grounds are always on sale, as are home-made jams and chutneys, pasta, store cupboard essentials and a good selection of wines. So successful has their venture been that a café and bakery have been opened in the nearby town of Wimborne. This has to be one of the best bakeries ever as such.

Sharpham Park

www.sharphampark.com
☎ 01458 844080
✉ Walton, Nr Street, Somerset
BA16 9SA

One of the few UK farms growing the ancient wheat breed spelt, which is then milled and processed into breakfast cereals and muesli, biscuits and groats (for making 'speltotto' or risotto-type dishes). Roger Saul's farm also produces some excellent white and brown flour. Order online or see website for stockists.

Stoates Flour

www.stoatesflour.co.uk
☎ 01747 852475
✉ Cann Mills, Shaftesbury, Dorset
SP7 0BL
🕐 Mon, Wed–Fri 8.30am–1pm, 2–5pm

If you like flour, you'll love Michael Stoate (a fifth-generation miller) and his certified organic Cann Mills operation. The flour is all stoneground and the mill is powered by the River Sturkel, a tributary of the Stour. Stoate sells a range of flours, all milled on the premises, including malt star, real wholemeal and an amazing sifted white. You can buy Stoate's flour at numerous outlets nationwide and he welcomes callers to the mill where flour is sold from the door. You won't be disappointed. He also runs a wide range of breadmaking courses.

Winterborne Bakery

www.winterbornebakery.co.uk
☎ 01929 472948
✉ The Old Stables, North West Farm, West Street, Winterborne Kingston, Dorset **DT11 9AT**

Established in 2009, Winterborne Bakery provides the local community with handmade breads, cakes and pastries, freshly baked every day. The bakers create a wide range of artisan and sourdoughs as well as traditional yeasted loaves and cakes. Their Blue Vinne sourdough is particularly delicious: a large crusty loaf studded with the wonderfully salty and fragrant Dorset blue cheese – a real treat. Their products are attractive and tasty and it's wonderful to see traditional methods being practised and appreciated.

Barford Farmhouse Ice Cream

www.barford-icecream.co.uk
☎ 01258 857 969
✉ Cowgrove Road, Sturminster Marshall, Wimborne, Dorset **BH21 4BY**
🕐 Tues–Sun 11.30am–5.30pm (from April until October)

Chris and Wendy Pope have a great little company here. The milk for the ice cream comes from their own cows that graze the lush meadows of the famous National Trust-owned Kingston Lacey Estate. As well as having their own shop on the premises Barford ice cream is available from a wide variety of farm shops and small retailers. They source locally as far as possible (blueberries from the Dorset blueberry company, eggs from local farms). Barford has a growing band of fans and is also available in a wide variety of restaurants and hotels in the area. One criticism is the extraordinarily long list of different flavours – I wonder whether Coca Cola sorbet is really necessary? Home delivery available.

Brown Cow Organics 🌱 @ 🍃

www.browncoworganics.co.uk
☎ 01749 890298
✉ Perridge Farm, Pilton, Shepton Mallet, Somerset **BA4 4EW**

What I like most about this dairy is the way that the wider picture of cattle farming is addressed. Farmer Judith Fearne, a worthy nominee for a Women in Ethical Business Award, produces milk from her 100-strong Guernsey herd and rears beef cattle from the group as well so that the normally unwanted bobbys (boys) will produce good quality meat rather than be slaughtered or sent to market when young (as is the norm, I am afraid). You can even buy the cow skins, and luggage made from the hides. The yoghurt, packed in glass jars and marketed under the River Cottage brand, is not my favourite, but lots of people love its silky texture. Fearne's business sets a great example to other farmers.

Cerney Cheese 🍃 🥛

www.cerneycheese.com
☎ 01285 831312
✉ The Dairy, Chapel Farm, North Cerney, Cirencester, Gloucestershire **GL7 7DE**

Cerney makes around 700 small cheeses a week for distribution to local shops and restaurants. The inspiration came when owner, Lady Angus, went on a trip to France and learned about Valencay goats' cheese. The goat milk, gathered from local farms, is made into pyramid-shaped cheeses then covered in salt and ash as a preserver. It's a very creamy, wholesome cheese, lovely eaten alone or with salad, and great as a cooking cheese, too. You can also buy honey, jam and organic eggs here.

The Cheese Shed ○ @ ∅

www.thecheeseshed.com
☎ 01626 835680
✉ 81 Mary Street, Bovey Tracey,
Devon **TQ13 9HQ**

A highly regarded online shop specialising in West Country cheeses, set up by James Mann and Ian Wellens. Mann runs a deli in the same town, but the idea for the cheese shed was born when he wondered if cheese lovers in the north of England had access to the best cheddars and so on. It has been a great success, the cheeses are well cared for and the service efficient. Cheddars include Keen's (my favourite,) Montgomery, Denhay and Westcombe. Other hard and semi-soft cheeses include Sharpham Rustic, Ducket's Caerphilly, Curworthy and Devon Oke. Soft cheeses include Bath Soft Cheese and Heligan. Among the goat varieties are Dorstone, White Nancy and Ticklemore. And finally the blues – the great Dorset Blue Vinney, Harbourne Blue and Blissful Buffalo. The wonderful aspect of this business is the way it showcases the incredible achievements in just one region. I particularly like the 'wall of cheese' on the web page – just like looking at an appetising shop window!

The Cheeseworks ○ @ ∅

www.thecheeseworks.co.uk
☎ 01242 255022
✉ 5 Regent Street, Cheltenham,
Gloucestershire **GL50 1HE**
🕐 Mon–Fri 9.30am–5.30pm;
Sat 9am–5.30pm

A popular specialist cheese shop run by Ben Axford, selling a huge number of British and continental artisan cheeses. Many of the West Country cheeses are represented, in particular the excellent Stinking Bishop (made in Gloucester), some great double and single Gloucesters and farmhouse cheddars. There is also a mail order service and several deli items, such as charcuterie and olives, on sale.

Cornish Cheese Company ○ @ ∅

www.cornishcheese.co.uk
☎ 01579 363660
✉ Knowle Farm, Upton Cross,
Liskeard, Cornwall **PL14 5BG**
🕐 Mon–Fri 8am–4pm

It was in 2001 that Philip and Carol Stansfield started producing their blue cheese. Like many farmers they were looking for a way to diversify and at the same time add some value to their own milk. They decided to make a blue cheese that could compete with Stilton and continental cheeses of the ilk. Their cheese has won several awards and all reports have been good. Designed to be eaten young, it has a very creamy texture and a poignant, sharpish flavour.

The Dorset Blue Soup Company

dorsetblue.moonfruit.com
☎ 01963 23133
✉ Woodbridge Farm, Stock Gaylard, Sturminster Newton, Dorset **DT10 2BD**
🕐 Mon–Fri 9am–5pm; Sat 9am–1pm

Makers of the famous Dorset Blue Vinney cheese – a powerful, densely veined cheese made from unpasteurised milk that, when perfectly ripe, is among the best British cheeses you can eat. I once bought half a cheese and cut thin slices horizontally from it for over two months (never cutting a wedge) and it kept beautifully in the fridge. The farm has now branched out to making rich soups, adding the cheese to vegetable bases. Soups are widely available. Call or see website for stockists.

Jess's Ladies Organic Milk

www.theladiesorganicmilk.co.uk
☎ 01452 720343
✉ Hardwicke Farm, Hardwicke Lane, Hardwicke, Gloucestershire **GL2 3QE**

If you live in the Gloucestershire area, seek out Jess Vaughan's organic milk. Contact her and she will tell you your nearest stockist. It will be well worth it in order to buy milk that is not only from cows cared for under Jess's strict code of good welfare, but which graze on untreated pasture. The milk is pasteurised and bottled at the farm, but not homogenised so there is a nice plug of cream floating on top of each bottle. There are no farm gate sales.

Keen's Cheddar

www.keenscheddar.co.uk
☎ 01963 322286
✉ Moorhayes Farm, Verrington Lane, Wincanton, Somerset **BA9 8JR**

George Keen's family have been at Moorhayes Farm for more than 100 years. They make all their cheeses by hand. Keen's is one of my favourite hard cheeses: creamy and nutty without the sharpness or acidity that some have. The cheese is available in Waitrose, Neal's Yard, some farm shops and at the farm gate (but do ring first). They come in truckles, anywhere between 27 kg and 1.5 kg, and are matured for between 10 and 18 months. Keen's, justifiably, has a stack of awards for their cheese and stick to what they know best – producing superb cheddar. They are also a member of a Slow Food presidia, a producer group whose members use only raw milk to make their cheddar.

La Petite Fromagerie 🄴

01672 514321
6 Old Hughenden Yard,
High Street, Marlborough, Wiltshire
SN8 1LT
Mon–Sat 9am–5.30pm

Christopher Markham's increasingly popular shop in Marlborough does well to compete with a Waitrose 'flagship' store across the high street. But he deserves to be successful considering the standard of the artisan cheeses he sells and the high number of local cheeses on offer. Sourdough and rye breads, made locally by Italian baker Dolcepani, biscuits for cheese, pickles, relishes and sauces are also for sale.

Lyburn Cheese 🄳

www.lyburnfarm.co.uk
01794 390451
Hamptworth, Salisbury, Wiltshire
SP5 2DN
Tues–Fri 11am–4.30pm

Mike and Judy Smales make cheese and grow pumpkins on their farm. They are regulars at many of the south west's farmers' markets and have a farm shop. They make four cows' milk cheeses, two of which I believe are excellent: the pressed, delicately flavoured Lyburn Gold that has a slight creamy texture though it is technically a hard cheese, and Old Winchester, a drier harder cheese with a flavour of nuts that is a good British-made alternative to grana padano or even parmesan. Call in during the autumn and you will also see a fabulous display of pumpkins and squash.

Lynher Dairies 🄰 @ 🄳

www.lynherdairies.co.uk
01872 870789
Pengreep Dairies, Ponsanooth,
Truro, Cornwall **TR3 7JQ**

Lynher Dairies is home to the nettle-wrapped, semi-hard Cornish Yarg cheese. Yarg has its detractors, but I am not one. Immensely creamy, the cheese tastes almost lemony and it stands out from the crowd. Lynher has added a wild garlic-wrapped cheese to the range and they must be doing something right as they sell over 200 tons of cheese a year.

Martins Dairy

01503 262525

Martins Dairy, Fore Street,
East Looe, Cornwall **PL13 1HH**

Mon–Sun 8.30am–6pm

Thick, gooey cooked cream – a speciality of the region and made with the gorgeous yellow cream from Channel Island dairy breeds – is made here on the south coast by the appropriately named Butters family. Having been heated and cooled, the cream is a surprisingly easy mail order purchase – it travels well and has a long shelf life.

Montgomery's Cheddar

**www.farmhousecheesemakers.
com**

01963 440243

Manor Farm, North Cadbury,
Yeovil, Somerset **BA22 7DW**

Jamie Montgomery has a closed herd of 220 Holstein-Friesian X and every last pint they produce goes into making the 2500 kg of cheese each week. There are no farm gate sales and even wholesalers have a quota, such is the popularity of this mild, yet nutty, cheddar. It is available through good retail outlets. Phone to find out your nearest stockist.

Newhouse Farm Milk Deliveries

www.themilkman.co.uk

01747 822700

Cole Street Lane, Gillingham,
Dorset **SP8 5JQ**

Totally traceable milk and other dairy foods produced on a 650-acre Dorset farm, delivered to your door if you live within a 10-mile radius. Farmer Richard Pike took matters into his own hands when the local processing plant was taken over by one of the dairy 'giants'. Along with some other disgruntled farmers, Pike began taking his milk to the Blackmore Vale Dairy for processing and then set up a team of milkmen to deliver to doorsteps in the area. The milk is fresher than any sold in supermarkets, has a longer shelf life and buying it supports the local farming economy. Order from the website.

Pengoon Farm 🏠 @ 🌿

www.pengoon.co.uk
☎ 01326 561219
✉ Nancegollan, Helston, Cornwall
TR13 0BH
🕐 Mon–Sun 8.30am–9.30pm

Jim East milks 17 Jersey cows at Pengoon Farm and has been doing so for 25 years. He says his clotted cream is 'different, it's yellow, has a good head and it's tastier than most'. It's pasteurised, but not sterilised. He welcomes visitors and is open for a whopping 13 hours every day. He does mail order and online sales, too, and his cream will keep for seven days in the refrigerator.

Quickes Cheddar 🏠 @ 🌿

www.quickes.co.uk
☎ 01392 851222
✉ Home Farm, Newton St Cyres,
Exeter, Devon **EX5 5AY**
🕐 Mon–Sat 9am–5pm

Quickes is quite simply one of four or five outstanding cheddars produced in the UK. It is made on the farm using milk from the 300-plus head of cows. Such is the demand there are now nine cheesemakers and a lovely farm shop where you can buy it, along with other delicacies. Quickes, which is matured for more than a year in muslin wraps, has a nutty, round flavour. They make other cheeses, too, but for me this one is outstanding.

Rodda's 🏠 @ 🌿

www.roddas.co.uk
☎ 01209 823300
✉ The Creamery, Scorrier, Redruth,
Cornwall **TR16 5BU**

Rodda's is the biggest of the clotted cream producers, which is available through hundreds of outlets. The cream is delicious and they still supply small farm shops – hence their inclusion in this guide. A fifth-generation concern, you can order either online or by phone and if the order is large enough, such as for a village fete or a Buckingham Palace Garden Party perhaps, they welcome callers to the creamery, 'but not for small orders, please,' says Rodda.

Simon Weaver Cotswold Organic Dairy

www.simonweaver.net
☎ 01451 870852
✉ Kirkham Farm, Upper Slaughter,
Gloucestershire **GL54 2JS**
🕐 Mon–Fri 9am–5pm

The Weavers have been following traditional, organic farming methods in the Cotswolds for three generations, but have been farming in the south west since the 16th century. As a result, the land, the animals and the product are all looked after with great care. Each of the 180 Friesians is known to Richard, the herdsman, by name and he walks them on their short journey to the parlour each morning. The milk travels all of five metres from the milking shed to the creamery, and it is here that the artisan cheese-makers begin the process of creating their product. Three types of brie are produced at the creamery: Blue-veined, Herb and Cotswold Brie. Each cheese is organic and the herb variety combines the soft, buttery quality of the brie with organic herbs – a fresh, fragrant mix.

Town Mill Cheese

www.townmillcheese.co.uk
01297 442626
Mill Lane, Lyme Regis, Dorset
DT7 3PU
Fri–Sat 10.30am–5.30pm;
Sun 11am–4pm

Local Lyme restaurateur and chef Mark Hix rates this new cheese shop, run by former publisher Justin Tunstall, which largely sells expertly matured artisan cheeses from the West Country. Hix is rarely wrong about these things and I was impressed by the list that includes Blue Vinney and Woolsery cheese (both made in Dorset) Beenleigh Blue, Montgomery Cheddar and a number of other good cheeses. Tunstall has also found some new local cheeses, including St Alhelm's Blue and Original (fresh) cheese from The Windswept Cow Cheese Company in Dorset. He also sells the excellent Barford Farmhouse ice cream, also made in Dorset. Opening times vary according to the season.

Woefuldane Organic Dairy

www.woefuldaneorganics.co.uk
01453 886855
3 Market Square,
Minchinhampton, Gloucestershire
GL6 9BW
Tues–Fri 8.40am–1pm,
2–5pm; Sat 9am–2pm

All the dairy produce in this shop is originally produced on their own farm. They have been artisan cheesemakers for nearly 15 years now and their glorious cheeses have won Gold, Silver and Bronze at the British cheese awards. Their selection of cheeses include the wonderful local Double Gloucester, oak-smoked cheese and both fresh and blue cheeses. It is said that going to their shop is like a 'step back in time' as they sell milk in litre bottles and refillable containers. As well as stocking their own milk and cheese they sell their own cream, home-made salad dressings and free-range eggs. Mail order available.

Bells Fish ◐

🕿 01202 885338

✉ 1 The High Street, Wimborne,
Dorset **BH21 1HR**

🕐 Tues–Sun 7am–1.30pm

John Bell is the fourth generation to run this wet fish shop in Wimborne. Most of the fish comes from day boats. Brill, gurnard, haddock, sea trout – the range is wide and for the more unusual fish Bell gives tips on cooking. They also smoke their own salmon, which has a good local reputation. Local deliveries plus mail order for smoked salmon.

The Blue Sea Food Company ◐

www.theblueseafood
company.com

🕿 01803 555777

✉ South Quay, The Harbour,
Paignton, Devon **TQ4 6DT**

🕐 Mon–Fri 7.15am–5.30pm

David Seabourne is a local fish specialist and is highly recommended by his devoted customers who visit his shops in Penryn and Falmouth. He also has three vans delivering over much of Cornwall to private homes, and operates a mail order service, too. You can buy almost everything – depending on seasonal availability – fresh anchovies, wild sea bass, live lobsters (by arrangement), grey mullet, sea trout, seaweed and samphire, various sole, fresh turbot and whitebait. Seabourne also supports the South West Handline Fishermens Association, so do ask for line-caught mackerel, pollock and sea bass.

The Cornish Fishmonger – Wing of St Mawes ◐ @ ✪

www.thecornishfishmonger.co.uk

🕿 01726 861666

✉ Unit 4, Warren Road, Indian
Queens Industrial Estate, Indian
Queens, Cornwall **TR9 6TL**

Rob Wing is a fish supplier with a formidable reputation. He has supplied restaurants in the area for many years, buying the freshest fish from Cornish day boats. Now he has launched a well-organised mail order service so that anyone in the UK can buy his wonderfully fresh fish. I have had an awesome box of it myself recently and cannot recommend the service enough. Specialising in crab and lobster, he will also send boxes of mixed fish or shellfish. I suggest that if you are embarking on mail order fish for the first time, to save on the cost of delivery, buy a number of types and freeze what you are not using.

Cornish Native Oysters ⊕ @ ◐

www.cornishnativeoysters.co.uk
☎ 07791 378503
✉ Admiralty Quay, Mylor Harbour,
Falmouth, Cornwall **TR11 5UF**

Beautiful, discus-shaped native oysters from a new oysterage in a region where the ancient tradition is being revived in several locations. Traditional harvesting by sailing boat yields some of the best oysters I have tried – with such a long, long, tingling flavour, I can hardly bear to sip a glass of wine with these in case it washes away the experience. Oysters travel well, so buying via home delivery is practical and good value.

David Farquar Smoked Products ⊕

☎ 01249 740488
✉ Elvaston House, Foxham,
Wiltshire **SN15 4NQ**
🕐 Mon–Tues, Thurs–Fri 6am–1pm,
2–5pm; Sat 6am–1pm, 2–4pm

Perfectly cured, cold-smoked, wild Scottish salmon, wild sea trout and organically farmed Scottish salmon available by post. David Farquar also makes a good hot-smoked 'roast' salmon, hot-smoked trout, kippers, cod's roe and duck breast. I first tasted Farquar's smoked salmon at a market and was struck by the outstanding flavour of the smoke and the quality of the fish (not too fatty, not too dry). It is also great to come across wild salmon, though be assured it is sustainably sourced.

Dorset Oysters ⊕ ◐

www.dorsetoysters.com
☎ 01202 666057
✉ 13 Benson Road, Nuffield Trading
Estate, Poole, Dorset **BH13 0GB**
🕐 Mon–Fri 7am–6pm

Fisherman and restaurateur Pete Miles started this company only recently, when he realised that almost all oysters in the Othneil Oyster beds in Poole Harbour were being exported. He has established a purifying plant in Poole and now will send these oysters and other local shellfish (clams, cockles, crab) via courier anywhere in the UK. I have tried my first dozen and can report they are wonderful (there are no native oysters harvested in Poole Harbour, at least not commercially). Among these I tried were a couple of size 1's – a giant treat. Visit Pete's restaurant, Storm, while in Poole www.stormfish.co.uk.

The Fish Deli ♥ @ ✇

www.thefishdeli.co.uk
☎ 01364 654833
✉ 7 East Street Ashburton, Devon
TQ13 7AD
🕐 Mon–Sat 9am–5pm

The Fish Deli is an amazing shop, selling fish that has been locally caught by short-trip boats when possible. No deep-sea or pair net trawled – sustainability is taken very seriously here. Buy fresh fish and shellfish (mussels are from the River Teign estuary) or one of Michele and Nick Legg's wonderful ready-made dishes.

The Fish Plaice

☎ 01803 526595
✉ 1 Victoria Street, Paignton, Devon
TQ4 5DH
🕐 Mon–Sat 7.30am–4pm

Locals love the quality of the seafood sold at The Fish Plaice. Last year it was awarded Best Fishmonger by *The Independent* newspaper. Freshness is paramount, and you can expect to find all the south coast favourites, depending on the season and availability. The only grumble, sadly, has been about the service, which my Devon spies have warned can be arrogant and frosty. Let's hope this can be put right because this is clearly otherwise a terrific place to buy fish.

The Fish Stall ✇

www.mudefordfishstall.co.uk
☎ 01425 275389
✉ Mudeford Quay, Christchurch, Dorset **BH23 4AB**
🕐 Mon–Sun 9am–4pm

A very popular fish stall right beside the quay close to where the boats land their fish, buying from local fishermen or from the market. Ask for locally produced oysters (from the beds at Brownsea Island in Poole Harbour), fresh herring, octopus, red and grey mullet, sea trout (in summer only), Dover sole and squid.

Flowers Farm Lakes

www.flowersfarmlakes.co.uk
☎ 01300 341351
✉ Hilfield, Nr Cerne Abbas, Dorchester, Dorset **DT2 7BA**

Alan Bastone would like nothing more than not to have any fresh water American Signal crayfish to sell. Having escaped from crayfish farms some years ago, these pests have overtaken many streams and lakes in the UK where trout, their favourite meal, are prevalent. Bastone catches them live in traps and sells at the farm gate. Call ahead for availability. To eat you must boil live ones for about five minutes in salty water.

There is meat in the tail and body, which can be delicious, but if you are used to seawater prawns it may take time to acknowledge that the flavour is delicate rather than weak.

Fowey Fish

www.foweyfish.com
☎ 01726 832202
✉ 37 Fore Street, Fowey, Cornwall **PL23 1AH**
🕐 Mon–Wed, Sat 9am–4pm; Thurs–Fri 9am–5pm

A good fish shop and long-established, efficient online shop, selling very fresh fish sourced from local Cornish day boats fishing out of Looe Harbour and a few boats from Fowey itself. There is no end of variety (the south coast of Cornwall sees cold water merge with sub-tropical so there is always an extraordinary diversity of fish on offer). Expect excellent crab (live and cooked), line-caught mackerel and wild sea bass caught by hand-line fishermen, luxurious treats such as turbot, and humble yet delicious fish such as sardines.

Hand Picked Shellfish Company

www.handpickedshellfish.com
☎ 01305 820651
✉ The Esplanade, Chesil Cove, Portland, Dorset **DT5 1LN**
🕐 Mon–Sun 10am–4pm

Weymouth diver fishermen Steve Hall and Matt Baldwin began selling fish at West Country markets, but they have now opened a little café on the sea wall by Chesil Cove in Dorset selling squid, turbot, less familiar dabs and red gurnard, plus hand-dived scallops and crab, alongside sticky cakes. They still sell at local markets – call for details.

Houghton Springs Fish Farm

☎ 01258 880058
✉ Winterbourne Houghton, Blandford Forum, Dorset **DT11 0PD**

Hans Hoff is doing something exceptional in aquaculture – rearing Arctic char. This fish, which has white or pale pink flesh, is found both in the sea (in the Atlantic but not in British coastal waters) and in land-locked lakes in Europe, notably Windermere in England, where it is thought to have naturalised after the ice age. It is a delicious fish with a delicate flavour. Hoff has found farming it successful and is now supplying restaurants in the area and can be contacted should you want to order and collect the fish. When cooking, treat it as sea trout (it grows to about 40 cm), poaching or baking the whole fish, and prepare to enjoy an unusual banquet.

353

Martins Seafresh – Fish for Thought

www.martins-seafresh.co.uk

01637 806103

St Columb Business Centre, Barn
Lane, St Columb Major, Cornwall
TR9 6BU

Jeff and Barbara Martin have been selling fish online almost
since the technology came into existence. They have their
own boats, the *Resolute* and the *Manx Ranger*, and also buy
from a few small day boats that fish off the Cornish coast.
The emphasis here is on sustainability, and they buy only
from boats who fish responsibly. Shellfish are a speciality,
especially lobster, but they also buy from some of the south
coast's excellent shellfish farms, such as the Duchy Oyster
Farm at Port Navas and Sue and Dave Hancock of Fowey
Seafarms. The range of fish they sell is enormous, and I
recommend (for the sake of good value) ordering a box
packed with as much fresh fish that will fit in it and freezing
what you do not need. All the south coast favourites are
available, from sardines to sea bass and gurnard to megrim
soles. Good quality frozen fish is also available.

Matthew Stevens & Son

www.mstevensandson.co.uk

01736 799392

Back Road East, St Ives, Cornwall
TR26 1NW

Mon–Fri 8am–5pm;
Sat 8am–12pm

A remarkable online shop selling all the freshest Cornish
fish, bought from short-trip boats that come into St Ives
harbour, and day boats and responsible trawlers that fish
out of Newlyn. Matthew operates a strong sustainable
fishing policy. Line-caught bass and cod are available and he
buys only male lobsters (returning berried or fertile females
to the lobster hatchery in Padstow). He sells the familiar and
the unfamiliar, such as megrim soles, ling, cockles and
gurnard. He never sells skate, but will supply the more
sustainable ray. Locally farmed mussels, native and Gigas
oysters from the Fal and Helford Rivers are also available.
The mail order service is very efficiently run. He also runs a
fish shop, just behind the harbour in St Ives. There are few
better people to buy fish from.

Mevagissey Wet Fish ✪ ✪ ✪

☎ 01726 843839
✉ The West Quay, Mevagissey,
Cornwall **PL26 6QU**
🕑 **Winter** Mon–Sun 11am–5pm;
Summer Mon–Sun 10am–6pm

Kim Wigmore buys from the day boats that come in to the small port at Mevagissey in south Cornwall. Depending on season and availability there can be a huge selection to choose from. On the day I called, her wet fish counter boasted cod, pollack, monkfish, lemon sole, plaice, haddock, hake, red mullet, gurnard, whiting and a range of shellfish including whole and dressed crab, plus rock oysters.

Mere Fish Farm ✪ ✪ ✪

☎ 01747 860461
✉ Ivymead, Mere, Wiltshire
BA12 6EN
🕑 Mon–Fri 9am–5pm;
Sat 9am–1pm

I have known the Mere Fish Farm for many years as this charming family supply many village shops and delicatessens all over the Dorset and Wiltshire area. They rear their own fish in two farms in ponds fed by spring water originating from the Wiltshire Downs. There is also a smokery and the trout are either cold-smoked and sliced thinly or hot-smoked and sold as fillets or made into a delicious pâté. Roulades of cold-smoked trout and trout mousse are also available and make delicately delicious canapés. Larger roulades are ideal starters or picnic food. Fresh fish is also available, but contact for stockists.

New Wave – The Fish Shop ✪ @ ✪

www.new-wave.co.uk
☎ 01285 651 751
✉ 3 Market Place, Cirencester,
Gloucestershire **GL7 2PE**
🕑 Tues–Fri 10am–7pm;
Sat 9.30am–5.30pm

When my mother lived in the Cotswolds she used to visit this fishmonger in Cirencester regularly, buying some superbly fresh fish. Considering how 'landlocked' the area is the resourcefulness of fishmonger Timothy Boyd is amazing. Primarily a catering supplier, he has a processing workshop in Fairford where the mail order service is run from. Fish is bought mainly from the south coast, from Plymouth fishmarket and day boats from lovely Looe Harbour. He aims always to buy from dayboats, but this is not possible in bad weather when the only fish landed will have been from larger vessels. You can buy everything – from grand fish such as turbot, to less familiar species such as slip soles, flounder, megrims and gurnard.

355

Pengellys Fish Shop ✪ ✪

☎ 01579 340777
✉ 2 The Arcade, Fore Street,
Liskeard, Cornwall **PL14 3JB**
🕐 Mon–Fri 8.30am–4pm;
Sat 8.30am–1pm

Angela Harrison and her daughter Jackie run a fish shop, started by her grandparents, which is hugely popular with the locals. All fish is from small day boats and none is beam-trawled using large nets. 'Day boat fish is always fresher', says Angie. Line-caught mackerel (a Looe speciality), Dover sole, lobsters and large cock crabs are all good. Harrison is also an expert on picking out turbot from the market and selling the finest specimens – good value for money. There is also a branch of Pengellys in Looe on the quay by the fish market (tel: 01503 262246).

River Exe Shellfish Farms ✪ ✪

☎ 01626 890133
✉ Oak Farm, Kenton, Nr Exeter,
Devon **EX8 8EZ**

David Jarrad is an experienced shellfish producer who farms Pacific (rock or Gigas) oysters and harvests mussels in the fertile waters of the River Exe. You can buy mail order or call in advance and make an arrangement to collect the shellfish. A very highly rated producer, St Ives fishmonger Matthew Stevens recommends the Exe shellfish. They also supply many restaurants in the south west.

The Rockfish Grill & Seafood Market @ ✪

www.rockfishgrill.co.uk
☎ 0117 973 7384
✉ 128 Whiteladies Road, Bristol
BS8 2RS
🕐 Tues–Sat 9am–5.30pm

Mitchell Tonks's combined fishmonger and seafood grill sells fish sourced mainly from Brixham boats who, he says, he 'works closely with'. Expect to find typical white fish favourites – cod, haddock and so on – and some less familiar types, such as pollock (getting a lot more familiar since restaurants began serving this cod cousin with slightly greyer flesh), plus sandsoles and dabs. You can call or email an order in advance for collection, but there is no mail order service yet.

The Scallop Shell

www.thescallopshell.co.uk

☎ 01373 831641

✉ White Row Farm, Beckington, Nr Frome, Somerset **BA11 6TN**

🕐 Tues–Fri 9am–6pm; Sat 9am–5pm; Sun 10am–2pm

Fresh fish is delivered to this long-established fishmonger every morning from south Devon and Cornwall. Garry Rosser and his team are highly trained and passionate about food – they are committed to working with conscientious fishermen and treat their produce with utmost respect. Fresh crab and lobster are available every day and by 11am every morning some of the shellfish has been cooked in a wooden barrel, hand-picked and dressed, ready to be enjoyed.

Seabourne Fish 🅞 🅥

www.seabournefish.co.uk

☎ 01326 378478

✉ The Fish Shop, Unit 1, Islington Wharf, Penryn, Cornwall **TR10 8AT**

🕐 Tue–Fri 9am–5pm; Sat 7am–1pm

A smokery that was set up originally in 1987 by Jeff Hounslow to smoke the fish of local anglers, Seabourne Fish now smoke thousands of trout from the River Test, salting then cold-smoking so the flesh remains red. Smoked eel is also available. This place is a real gem and well worth a visit.

Smiths Fishmongers

www.smithfish.co.uk

☎ 0117 973 1666

✉ 23 North View, Westbury Park, Bristol **BS6 7PT**

🕐 Tues 8am–4.30pm; Wed 8am–4pm; Thurs 8am–4.30pm; Fri 8am–5pm; Sat 8am–1pm

Despite the annoyingly complicated opening hours you have to take your hat off to David and Matthew Smith who have been on the same site for 30 years – even more so when you realise that they are bang next door to Waitrose. But you can't keep a good fishmonger down and the shop engenders a real sense of community. The Smiths know their customers and have a detailed product knowledge. The fish come mainly from West Country boats, but also from Scotland, Grimsby, Hull and from as far away as Norway and Iceland. Because of the wide catchment area the fish range is comprehensive. Bestsellers are mackerel, lemon sole, plaice, hake, squid, skate, bass bream and herrings.

Ticklemore Fish Shop

☎ 01803 867805
✉ 10 Ticklemore Street, Totnes, Devon **TQ9 5EJ**
🕐 Mon–Sat 9am–5.30pm

A popular fishmonger in Totnes, a town with a strong sustainability ethos in all its shops and this place reputedly is no exception. Being so close to the coast, there is a wide range of fresh fish typical of the regional waters, from turbot to economical types such as sardines and grey mullet (a very underrated, delicious white fish) to superb shellfish including crab, mussels, langoustines and oysters. You can also buy some unusual things such as samphire (a succulent beach weed) and freshwater crayfish.

William's Fish Market & Food Hall

www.williamsfoodhall.co.uk
☎ 01453 832240
✉ 3 Fountain Street, Nailsworth, Gloucestershire **GL6 0BL**
🕐 Mon–Fri 8am–5pm;
Sat 7.30am–4pm

Willam's Food Hall is a long-established shop selling a wide range of foods, but I have included them as a seafood supplier because they have a great reputation in the area for stocking some wonderfully fresh fish, most sourced from Cornish day boat (short trip) fisheries. Great for crabmeat, langoustines, lobsters, Dover sole, trout, turbot and rock oysters. (See also page 329).

▼ VEGETABLES AND FRUIT

Abbotts Greengrocers ✔

☎ 01747 853424
✉ 9 Bell Street, Shaftesbury, Dorset **SP7 8AR**
🕐 Mon–Sat 8am–5pm

Paul and Ruth Rowe's well-stocked traditional high-street greengrocer has a huge following and is surviving in spite of the arrival of an enormous Tesco in Shaftesbury three years ago. Locally sourced produce is positioned right by the door, so you are much more likely to notice it and pick it up. Everything, including fruit and vegetables from further afield, is wonderfully fresh.

Annies Fruit Shop @ 🌀 🌀

01803 867265

Unit 11, Totnes Shopping Centre,
Ticklemore Street, Totnes, Devon
TQ9 5EJ

Mon–Fri 6am–5.30pm;
Sat 6am–3pm

If only all traditional greengrocers had Annies' vision, offering not only a great shop filled with everything you need and with a huge emphasis on locally grown, but a delivery service backed up by a clever internet shopping site. Delivery is mainly local, with the nearer addresses benefiting from daily deliveries and those further away being able to get Annies' veg once a week. Eggs and fruit juice are also on sale. You can tailor-make your box of vegetables – the online shop will point out any produce that is local or organic. This is the way forward for high street shops: stop complaining and widen your horizons!

Bake Farm 🌀

www.bakefarm.com

01722 568167

Coombe Bissett, Salisbury,
Wiltshire **SP5 4JT**

Jun–Aug Mon–Sun 10am–6pm

A PYO fruit farm, open between June and August, that is a must-visit place. Salisbury GP Roger Jowett and his wife Rachel farm 10 acres just outside the city of Salisbury, throwing off a wide variety of strawberries, raspberries, gooseberries and all sorts of currants (black, white and red). Rachel makes lovely jellies and jams from her fruit. There's a tea room, too, but opening hours are a bit hit and miss, so ring first.

Beddoes Arcade Fruits 🌀

01579 348680

1 Fore Street, Liskeard, Cornwall
PL14 3JA

Mon–Sat 8am–5pm

Andrew Beddoes' shop, next to one of my favourite fishmongers Pengelly's (see page 356), provides everything you need to sit on the plate or serving dish beside a turbot steak, local lobster or wild sea bass. Cornish potatoes, greens, salad, tomatoes and aparagus – everything is labelled clearly and local foods are grouped together in a display outside the door under the arcade.

Buttervilla ⊘ ⊙

www.funkyleaves.co.uk
☎ 01503 230315
✉ Buttervilla Farm, Polbathic,
St Germans, Torpoint, Cornwall
PL11 3EY

Buttervilla Farm is run by Robert Hocking, an inspirational grower who has got together with two other farms, Keverel and Skyegrove, to grow a range of extraordinary and diverse plants including heritage tomatoes, edible flowers and microleaf (infant food plant leaves to scatter over salads and grills). The produce is organic and, in the case of Skyegrove, ultra-green since all ploughing is actually done using draughthorses. By visiting the website, you can make contact with each farm and sign up to a box scheme or find your nearest stockist. The quality of the vegetables, and the variety, is awesome.

Continental Fruits ⊘ ⊛ ⊙

☎ 01579 342770
✉ 17 Bay Tree Hill, Liskeard,
Cornwall **PL14 4BG**
🕐 Mon–Sat 8am–5pm

A small, but locally minded, fruit and vegetable shop selling Cornwall's amazing seasonal produce. The soft summer fruits are picked ripe and kept out of the fridge so taste as if they came from your own back garden; there are yellow Cornish potatoes that possess an extraordinary buttery sharpness; asparagus in spring comes that bit early thanks to the warmth of the county; and there's good quality, fresh salad, herbs and vivid greens. Other nice West Country items include elderflower cordial, apple juice and honey, plus milk and cream from Trewithen dairy.

Hayles Fruit Farm ⊛

☎ 01242 602123
✉ Winchcombe, Cheltenham,
Gloucestershire **GL54 5PB**
🕐 **Jun–Sept** Mon–Sun 9am–6pm;
Oct–May Mon–Sun 9am–7pm

Soft red fruits are available for picking during the summer and autumn months, along with apples and plums. The farm shop also sells free-range eggs, meat, locally baked bread and the farm's own apple juice.

Hollom Down Growers ⊛ ⊛

☎ 01264 781087
✉ Testwood Farm, Hollom Down,
Lopcombe, Salisbury, Wiltshire
SP5 1BP
🕐 Mon–Sat 10am–5pm

Carol Saunders grows soft fruit in summer and specialises in the most delicious, fully ripe tomatoes. She also grows potatoes, courgettes, beetroot, carrots and squash, and you can cut lovely crisp, fresh lettuces straight from a trough outside the shop door. Sometimes there's a box of plums or apples from Carol's orchard. This is a delightful, traditional market garden, and very good value for money.

Living Food of St Ives ⊕ @ ⊘

www.livingfood.co.uk
☎ 01736 791981
✉ Pier House, Quay Street, St Ives, Cornwall **TR26 1PU**
🕐 Mon–Sat 10am–5pm

Sprouting pulses and seeds, including alfafa and lentils, are available by post or from this shop full of healthy foods just by the harbour in St Ives. A greater range would be welcome than the small one that is currently available. You can also buy equipment so you can farm your own sprouts on your windowsill if you wish.

South Devon Chilli Farm ⊕ @ ⊘

www.southdevonchillifarm.co.uk
☎ 01548 550782
✉ Wigford Cross, Loddiswell, Kingsbridge, Devon **TQ7 4DX**
🕐 Mon–Sun 10am–4pm

Jason Nichols and Steve Waters started growing chillies on a small scale in 2003, and have been so successful that they have 10,000 plants growing, mainly under glass / plastic tunnels on their Devon farm. You can visit to buy fresh chillies, choosing from a seemingly endless variety; taste and buy home-made hot sauces; or take a walk around the farm. Among the varieties are Padron peppers (delicious fried and salted as a snack, but watch out, some are mild and some not), hot Jalapeno, mild Hungarian Hot Wax (which are good raw in salads) and classic, all-purpose red Serrano. Dried and smoked chillies are also available.

Trevathan Shop ⊕ £

www.trevathanfarm.com
☎ 01208 880248
✉ St Endellion, Port Isaac, Cornwall **PL29 3TT**
🕐 Mon–Sun 10am–dusk

Call ahead to see what is growing on this little farm with holiday cottages that also sells free-range hen's eggs, clotted cream from a local dairy (to eat with the strawberries), herbs, ice cream and cheeses. The Cornish growing season begins early when you should be able to buy their lovely yellow-fleshed potatoes. Asparagus follows soon after, then soft fruit, green beans . . . A sweet place selling the freshest possible produce.

Woodland Fruit & Vegetables

01803 813760

Moorfoot Cross, Denbury,
Newton Abbot, Devon **TQ12 6EQ**

A seven-acre organic smallholding, typical of this area, which is rich in good food producers and small-scale, organic farms, growing fruit, vegetables and salad for a local, home-delivery box scheme. Organic free-range eggs are also available. Call for details.

▼ HONEY

Basterfield Honey

www.basterfield.com/theapiary

01404 815885

Westcott, Gerway Lane,
Ottery St Mary, Devon **EX11 1PW**

Pure Devon honey, honey fudge, honey marmalade and beeswax, made by producer Ken Basterfield, who began keeping bees as a hobby in 1974. Recently his son Daniel has joined the business to revive the number of hives, which Ken had scaled right down after years of part-time beekeeping. You can order online or check the website for details of stockists and local farmers' markets where you can buy Basterfield products.

Chettle Honey

01258 830223

Chettle Village Shop, Chettle,
Nr Blandford, Dorset **DT11 8DB**

Mon–Tues, Thurs–Fri
8am–5.30pm; Wed 8am–1pm;
Sat 9am–5pm;
Sun 9.30am–12.30pm

Chettle in north Dorset is a remarkable village that has an atmosphere of being set in aspic – 50 years ago. The village shop has been in the same family for centuries and it is testament to the 90 or so villagers that they are able to keep the store alive. It is here that you can purchase honey that has been reaped from the hives located on the chalk and flint downland and from ancient woodlands around this 1200-acre estate. The runny honey is very liquid, tooth-achingly sweet and the set honey is crunchy to the bite.

Hudnalls Apiaries ⌂ @ ✿

www.hudnallsapiaries.co.uk
☎ 01594 530807
✉ The Hudnalls, St Briavels, Lydney, Gloucestershire **GL15 6RT**

Very classy honey gathered in the broadleaf woodlands of the Forest of Dean and on pasture in the region of the Welsh Marches. This mix of tree and blossom pollen makes a very distinctive honey. Honey-nut spreads, honey mustard and honeycomb are also available. See website for details.

Maisemore Apiaries ⌂ @ ✿

www.honey-online.co.uk
☎ 01457 700289
✉ Long Road, Maisemore, Gloucestershire **GL2 8HT**
🕐 Mon–Fri 9am–5pm; Sat 9am–4pm

A large-scale honey producer selling both fragrant English heather and English clover honey processed on the site of the shop. Established in 1953, Maisemore apiaries also supply beekeeping and honey-making equipment to anyone keen to try their hand at keeping bees.

Quince Honey Farm ⌂ @ ✿

www.quincehoney.co.uk
☎ 01769 572401
✉ North Road, South Molton, Devon **EX36 3AZ**
🕐 Mon–Sun 9am–5pm

A family-run honey farm, established by George Wallace in 1949, with over 1500 hives distributed over the Devon hills and moors. There are dozens of honeys based on various blossoms, the heather is especially recommended and for special occasions you can buy a 2 kg complete comb.

Sedgemoor Honey Farm

www.sedgemoorhoney.co.uk
☎ 01823 442734
✉ 53 West View, Creech St Michael, Taunton, Somerset **TA3 5DU**

Exquisite borage, heather, runny and set honeys made near the orchards of Taunton in Somerset. There is no online shop or farm gate sales, but the honey is widely available in the region – see their website for details or phone to find a stockist near you.

▼ DRINKS

Bensons

www.bensonsapplejuice.co.uk
☎ 01451 844134
✉ Sandy Hill Farm, Sherborne,
Gloucestershire **GL54 3DS**

Jeremy and Alexia Benson originally started selling their apple juice at music festivals. At their first WOMAD festival the juice sold out before the music had stopped playing and they knew they were on to a winner. They have now outgrown their premises twice and the juice is gaining in popularity. They hand-press apples from the Cotswolds and this particular juice is a favourite with my children. It is now also available in a large range of independent shops, pubs and restaurants (contact for stockists). They also do frozen 'ice pole'-style lollies made with apple juice, called Chilly Billies.

Bridge Farm

☎ 01935 862387
✉ East Chinnock, Yeovil, Somerset
BA22 9EA
🕑 **May–Sep** Mon–Sun
10.30am–6.30pm

Though selling predominantly cider, they also do a roaring trade in a raft of single variety apple juices. The apples are sourced from the orchards at Bridge Farm and nearby farms and are available at the gate, as well as at local events in the south west, including farmers' markets. The farm also sells a range of cakes and chutneys.

Burrow Hill

www.ciderbrandy.co.uk
☎ 01460 240782
✉ Pass Vale farm, Burrow Hill,
Kingsbury Episcopi, Martock,
Somerset **TA12 6BU**
🕑 Mon–Sat 9am–5.30pm

Julian Temperley is something of a legend in the West Country and is a pure artisan. He is a pioneer who became one of the first farmers to start buying up orchards (going into heavy debt) to rescue them from being grubbed up and becoming arable land after UK entry into the EC. He produces award-winning cider and highly regarded cider brandy, but the reason he is in this book is for his apple juice. The farm has a nice feel to it: laid back, congenial and friendly (you can even land your helicopter on the lawn, should you so wish!). The juice is produced on the farm using delicious Russet, Cox and Bramley varieties.

Charlton Orchards ⊕◎⊘⊕

www.charltonorchards.com
☎ 01823 412959
✉ Charlton Road, Creech St
Michael, Taunton, Somerset
TA3 5PF
🕐 **Mid Aug-Feb**, Mon–Fri
9am–5pm; Sat 10am–5pm

A charming place that has been producing traditional varieties of apples for more than 60 years. Four partners (and apparently the farm's dog) run the enterprise which sees them producing 35 different apple varieties for sale at the farm's apple shed (not shop). The juice is coarse-filtered and then pasteurised, giving it a shelf life of 18 months. From very sweet Egremonts to the sharper Bramley, there are 14 varieties of juice in all (subject to availability). Charlton Orchards juice is also available at a variety of farmers' markets in the area – contact them for locations and dates.

Clipper Tea ⊕◎⊘

www.clipper-teas.com
☎ 01308 863344
✉ Broadwindsor Road, Beaminster,
Dorset **DT8 3PR**

Mike and Lorraine Brehme began this stylish ethical tea company over 25 years ago and it is now one of the most prominent Fairtrade-accredited brands. What is more, the teas are not just feel-good drinks, they taste good and are also affordable. There are, as with all artisan tea companies, many exciting types to choose from. The Brehme's stand by their claim that their Everyday tea bags are the best conventional tea on the market and it is not an outrageous claim. Coffee and herb infusions are also available. Stockists nationwide – see website for details.

Cornish Orchards ⊕◎⊘

www.cornishorchards.co.uk
☎ 01503 269007
✉ Westnorth Manor Farm, Duloe,
Liskeard, Cornwall **PL14 4PW**
🕐 **Apr–Oct** Mon–Fri 10am–5pm

Westnorth Manor Farm belongs to the Duchy of Cornwall (aka, the property of the Prince of Wales). Andy Atkinson moved there in 1992 after selling his dairy farm. In 1999 he turned to apple juice and cider production. The business has boomed and he now employs 20 people. Four hundred tons of apples are processed each year and everything sold is produced on the farm. The Collegett Pippin, Tommy Knight and Pigs Nose are all native Cornish apples that are among some of Atkinson's favourites. They also make elderflower pressé, cider vinegar and honey from hives in the orchards. The juice is mainly sold locally to pubs and restaurants, but they do have customers as far away as Dundee. You can visit

the farm, but check opening times as they vary seasonally.
See website for stockists and how to order.

Daylesford Organic Farm Shop

www.daylesfordorganic.com
0800 0831233
Daylesford, Near Kingham,
Gloucestershire **GL56 0YG**
Mon–Sat 9am–5pm;
Sun 10am–4pm

Daylesford (see also pages 54 and 301) must be given
a cheer for their recent launch of a range of Fairtrade
accredited coffees. The Ethiopian coffee is sourced from a
producer group of smallholder farmers from the Yirgacheffe
cooperative and the Mexican coffee is grown by the
indigenous people of Sierra Madre of Motozintla.
Daylesford also sell many delicious teas, both herbal
infusions and a good black tea. I must also add, because this
is the drinks chapter, that they make a number of their own
juices, including an English apple juice, plus both grape and
apple juice from France. See website for other shop
branches and stockists.

Day's Cottage Apple Juice

www.dayscottage.co.uk
01452 813602
Day's Cottage, Upton lane,
Brookthorpe, Gloucestershire
GL4 0UT

Days Farm pasteurise their apple juice, which is sold very
locally at farmers' markets and small retail outlets in the
Gloucestershire area. The fruit comes from unsprayed
orchards only and dozens of varieties are used, some unique
to the county, such as Taynton Codlin, Flower of the West
and Underleaves. They produce single varieties and also
blend their juices. Feedback has been good. They are
passionate about orchards and apple trees and run courses
on pruning and grafting – as well as wigwam-making!

Ermie & Gerties

www.ermieandgertie.com
01458 252308
Pitney House, Pitney, Langport,
Somerset **TA10 9AR**

Named after two Guernsey cows who live on the farm. The
business was set up in 2000 selling principally ice cream, but
also meat and apple juice, as well as honey. The orchard
where the apples are picked contains varieties from Hoary
Morning, Harry Masters Jersey and Tom Putt to the more

mundane Bramley and Russet. The juice is pressed on the farm and new trees are planted every year, but the farm is open by appointment only, which seems a pity. There are lots and lots of local outlets, though, and the juice is definitely worth seeking out. See website for details.

Essential Trading ○ @ ●

www.essential-trading.co.uk
☎ 0117 958 3550
✉ Unit 3, Lodge Causeway Trading Estate, Fishponds, Bristol **BS16 3JB**

A worthy trading company who source all their products ethically and sell a huge range of teas and coffees from all the different Fairtrade producers, including Hampstead Tea and Coffee, The Natural Coffee Company, Café Direct, Qi, Pukka Organic and Traidcraft. You can also shop for juices and bottled water. See website for details of stockists.

Helford Creek ○ @ ●

www.helfordcreek.co.uk
☎ 01326 231341
✉ Mudgeon Vean, Nr Helston, Cornwall **TR12 6DB**

Helford Creek are very special. They care passionately about their orchards and apples and promote old Cornish varieties such as Pigs Snout and John Broad. They press their apple juice using more conventional apples such as Cox, Bramley and Russet and they will press and bottle customers' apples for them at a cost of around £1 per bottle, although there is a minimum 200 kg of fruit needed. Their own juice is wide-ranging, some sour, some sweet and medium, too. The range is excellent and it is stocked at local outlets as well as farther afield (at the National Gallery, London, for example).

Heron Valley Organic Drinks ○ @ ●

www.heronvalley.co.uk
☎ 01548 820111
✉ Crannacombe Farm, Hazlewood, Loddiswell, Kingsbridge, Devon
TQ7 4DX
🕐 Mon–Fri 9am–5pm

Natasha Bradley's apple juice enterprise has won a clutch of awards. The organic farm was originally started by her parents in the '70s following their rush from London life. The apples come from 40 or so local growers, the juice is bottled by hand, pasteurised and has a drop of vitamin C added to help preserve colour. It has a good reputation that is growing quickly. They supply, among others, Riverford, so should really be up to the mark.

Luscombe

www.luscombe.co.uk
☎ 01364 643036
✉ Dean Court, Lower Dean,
Buckfastleigh, Devon **TQ11 0LT**

Luscombe drinks are wonderful and there's a wide selection. Ranging from apple, elderflower and pear to apricot, lemonade, lime and blueberry and a mixture of most. They are all made with fresh ingredients – no concentrates, additives or preservatives and all have an attractive, unfiltered cloudy appearance. All the drinks are handmade in Devon, even the lemonade, which includes real Sicilian lemons. They are all organic, too, and can be found in a wide range of outlets (contact them for stockists).

Magic Monkey ○ @ ●

www.magic-monkey.co.uk
☎ 01202 772185
✉ PO Box 5947, Bournemouth
BH11 0AA

Pomegranate juice has been hailed as one of those wonder-foods yet you have to be selective over your reasons for drinking it. If it is purely the health benefits, which are apparently numerous, avoid because there is scant evidence to support the claims. But if you like pomegranates and that watery, refreshing taste then this is for you. Magic Monkey distributes this juice, which is organic and processed from the fruit, not from concentrates. It's available in restaurants and small stores, mainly in the south of England.

Miles Tea & Coffee Specialists ○ @ ●

www.djmiles.co.uk
☎ 0800 387948
✉ Porlock House, Stephenson Road,
Minehead, Somerset **TA24 5EB**

Derek Miles has been in the tea trade since the early '50s, beginning as a dealer in London. He bought a shop in Minehead in 1961 and discovered a talent for blending tea. D. J. Miles is now considerably larger, blending dozens of teas, including a Fairtrade-certified type, and also selling coffee. I had a fascinating tour of the premises once, conducted by Mr Miles, and marvelled at the extraordinary world of this so English, yet so un-English, drink. My favourite is the 'Original' blend, a good powerful, yet mellow, everyday tea. Miles' teas are sold in plenty of local shops, so contact for stockists.

The Orchard Pig 🏠 @ 🍴 🏵

www.orchardpig.co.uk
☎ 01458 851222
✉ West Bradley Orchard, West
Bradley, Nr Glastonbury, Somerset
BA6 8LT
🕐 Mon–Fri 8am–6pm

Neil Macdonald and Andrew Quinlan started producing apple juice and cider five years ago as a hobby. Three years later they were producing 20,000 bottles a year so decided to turn it into a business. They admit they don't know a great deal about apple juice or cider: 'It's all been a bit hit and miss,' says Quinlan. More hit than miss, I'd say. All the juice is pressed at the farm and importantly there are no additives or sugar added. Farm shops, restaurants and festivals are forming an orderly queue to stock it. Ring before visiting as it's just a porch with an honesty box. PYO in September only.

Origin Coffee 🏠 @ 🍴

www.origincoffee.co.uk
☎ 01326 340320
✉ Trewardreva Mill, Constantine,
Nr Falmouth, Cornwall **TR11 5QD**

This is a very unusual coffee company that pursues the highest standards when it comes to flavour, combing the coffee producing regions of the globe for the most interesting varieties. You can buy whole beans or three grades of ground, choosing from a wide range including Sumatran Indonesia Aceh Takengon, Kenyan Gethumbwini Estate or Finca el Carmen from El Salvador. The coffee is supplied seasonally so throughout the year there are variations in availability. Origin's Tom Sobey also promises that the coffee he sells is produced meeting high standards of environmental and economic (Fairtrade) responsibility. He has his own roastery, and also a coffee school where you can learn the handy skills of a barista and find out how to make the most delicious espresso and latte.

Real Drink Ltd 🏠 £

www.realdrink.co.uk
☎ 01803 782217
✉ Broad Path, Stoke Gabriel,
Devon **TQ9 6RW**

Paul Jack and his family manage roughly 20 acres of apple orchards around their home and when they bottle their apple juice they identify each and every one. The company is relatively new having started in 2004, but it is doing well. They sell to local farm shops and National Trust properties as well as from their own back door. The one proviso is that stockists must be within a 25-mile radius of their home.

They are passionate about apple juice and there's a nice touch on the website where they give instructions on how to make it. This is a tiny artisan outfit that deserves every success. Opening times are flexible so ring before visiting.

Richs Farmhouse Cider ❶ @ ✿

www.richscider.co.uk
☎ 01278 783651
✉ Mill Farm, Highbridge,
Watchfield, Somerset **TA9 4RD**
🕐 Mon–Sat 9am–6pm;
Sun 10am–6pm

Cider is the speciality here and they are quite commercial, too, with a farm shop, restaurant and museum. Richs has been going for 50 years and is still a family-owned and run operation. Their apple juice, produced from their own orchards and pressed on the farm, is available in Russet, Cox, Bramley and a blend of the whole lot.

Roast & Post ❶ @ ✿

www.realcoffee.co.uk
☎ 01454 417147
✉ Bridgeview House, Redhill Lane,
Elberton, Bristol **BS35 4AE**

This is a well-established and good value mail order coffee company selling a great variety of blends, single origin, organic and accredited Fairtrade coffees. You can even buy green coffee beans to roast and blend at home, should you want to experiment. Of the blends offered, I recommend the Mocha Mysore and the After Dinner coffees – but this is a very subjective area and I suggest you buy a few types in a small quantity and find your very own favourite.

The Somerset Cider Brandy Company ❶ @ ✿

www.ciderbrandy.co.uk
☎ 01460 2400782
✉ Pass Vale Farm, Burrow Hill,
Kingsbury, Episcopi, Martock,
Somerset **TA12 6BU**
🕐 Mon–Sat 9am–5pm

This is not a guide to alcoholic drinks, but pioneer Julian Temperley is the British apple farmer who turned around the decline of orchards in the '70s. Rescuing acres and acres of orchard due to be grubbed to make way for more profitable arable farming, he started a cider business. After this, and much persuasion of the authorities, came the distillery where he now makes the best Calvados taste-alike in the UK. Oh, and he also makes delicious apple juice – which allows his entry into the guide. But do make a present to yourself of his amazing brandy. Home delivery available.

Wales

Bethesda Farm shop

www.fresh-welsh-meat.co.uk
☎ 01437 563124
✉ Rose Villa, Bethesda, Narberth,
Pembrokeshire **SA67 8HQ**
🕐 Mon–Sat 8am–6pm

Sian and Geraint Bowen founded this charming farm shop six years ago as a result of the foot-and-mouth crisis, converting their cow shed into a shop with the aim of selling local produce to local people. A few years on and the business has grown but still retains the feel of a traditional farm shop, selling home-made sausages, burgers, pies and pasties to great acclaim. Using their own smoker on site and their own pigs, they produce wonderful smoked bacon; this can be enjoyed as part of a breakfast in their café, which looks out on the farm itself. Their pies are definitely worth tasting as the high quality of the meat gives the pie a wonderful texture and taste. The shop rewards the curious passer-by with a friendly welcome and tasty produce sourced just a stone's throw away in the stunning Pembrokeshire countryside.

Cwmcerrig Farm Shop and Grill

www.cwmcerrigfarmshop.co.uk
☎ 01269 844 405
✉ Gorslas, Llanelli, Carmarthenshire
SA14 7HU
🕐 Mon–Sat 8.30am–5pm;
Sun 10am–4pm

The Watkins family has been here since 1952 and they are now locally famous for their pedigree beef. The shop has grown to a magnificent 8000 sq ft, housing a butchery, deli and grill where customers enjoy the roast beef, faggots, rissoles (there's a blast from the past) and pies. Lamb is also a speciality – naturally, being in Wales – and there's plenty of other local produce. Bring the family – there's lots here to enjoy. A finalist in the National Farmers' Retail & Markets Association (FARMA) awards, 2010.

Derwen Farm Shop ⬤ ⓐ ⬤ ⬤

☎ 01938 551586
✉ Derwen Garden Centre,
Guilsfield, Welshpool, Powys
SY21 9PH
🕐 Mon–Sat 9.30am–5.30pm;
Sun 11am–5pm

A blossoming farm shop and mail order service based within a garden centre in South Wales, run by the talented Rachael Joseph. Passionate about good ingredients, she has gone to much trouble to source the best. It is good, for example, to see Wenlock Edge pancetta from a great dry-cured meat company over the border in Shropshire. But Welsh produce abounds, from fresh organic fruit and vegetables grown by the

Welsh Food Co-operative to locally reared fresh meat, organic Caerphilly and bread from Llandysill Bakery. Chocolates, ice cream, dairy, fish and continental deli foods are also available.

Glasfryn Parc

www.siop-glasfryn.com

☎ 01766 810004

📧 Glasfryn Fawr Farm, Pencaenewydd, Pwllheli, Gwynedd **LL53 6RD**

🕐 Mon–Sun 10am–6pm

An enterprising farm on the Llyn peninsula, with all sorts of activities going on (such as karting), but also housing a good, very well-stocked farm shop. If I lived in the area I would be very grateful to have this place. Specialising in the great Welsh breeds including Welsh Black beef (meat that is up there with the best pedigree English South Devon, Red Poll and Hereford), but also delicious Lllyn lamb, a very local breed that is now becoming popular with farmers all over the UK. Look out for the farm butchery's own dry-cured bacon, smoked over Welsh oak, free-range eggs from Llaniestyn 12 miles away, Edern wildflower honey from a farm 10 miles away and other good Welsh things such as Bara Brith and Caws Cenarth cheese.

Hawarden Estate Farm Shop

www.hawardenestate.co.uk

☎ 01244 533442

📧 Chester Road, Hawarden, Flintshire **CH5 3FB**

🕐 Mon–Thurs 9am–6pm; Fri 9am–7pm; Sat 8.30am–5.30pm; Sun 10am–4pm

This is a large and beautifully designed farm shop that has received some substantial investment and is providing a number of jobs in a remote part of North Wales. In the centre of the floor is a large, antique table loaded with artisan breads. Elsewhere you will find vegetables grown on the farm's own 20-acre market garden and a huge range of foods from Wales and Cheshire. There is a fantastic display of cheeses in a specially designed fridge and a good café is attached. The estate is also involved in various community projects connected with food. Call for details.

Llwynhelyg Farm Shop

www.llwynhelygfarmshop.co.uk

☎ 01239 811079

📧 Llwynhelyg Farm Shop, Sarnau, Ceredigion **SA44 6QU**

🕐 Mon–Sat 9am–6pm; Sun 9.30am–1pm

The modest size of this friendly farm shop belies the wide range of products it offers those lucky enough to visit. Home-grown potatoes, vegetables, salads and seasonal fruits sit alongside over 80 different Welsh artisan cheeses. Provenance matters to Teifi and Jenny Davies, and helpful notes around the shop clearly label where the products have come from. Over 85 per cent of their stock is Welsh. Visit on a Thursday to pick up fresh fish, caught only a few miles away, or pop in any day of the week for a freshly made organic loaf, baked in a clay oven. The farm kitchen produces delicious pies and quiches made from local fare – the smell of baking permeates the whole shop and is utterly tantalising. The shop also runs a hamper scheme for holidaymakers and will make up gift hampers to order. Friendly, knowledgeable, committed staff take their cue from the Davies who value their customers as highly as the quality of their stock.

Thornhill Farm Shop

www.thornhillfarm.co.uk

☎ 029 2061 1707

✉ Capel Gwilym Road, Thornhill, Cardiff **CF14 9UB**

🕐 Mon–Fri 10am–5pm; Sat 9am–5pm

Just outside Cardiff, Andrew and Carol Philips have established Thornhill, an inviting and attractive farm shop with locality and quality at its heart. Their own lamb and beef take pride of place on the extensive meat counter, and everything is butchered on site and to the customer's specifications. Locally grown fruit and vegetables are clearly labelled and every effort is made to ensure that the customer knows where specific products are made, and by whom. Their selection of Welsh beer, ales and wines is fantastic; along with the range of Welsh cheeses and deli products, which are a real treat. Home-made cakes are available to buy whole, or can be enjoyed a slice at a time in the café or on the sun terrace that overlooks stunning Cardiff Bay and the farm itself. The lemon drizzle cake is particularly fine. Home-made sweets are also sold. Visitors may also be treated to a hands-on meeting with donkeys, pigs and three reindeer, all of which live on the farm.

Yerbeston Farm Shop

www.farmshopfood.co.uk

☎ 01834 891637

✉ Yerbeston, Nr Cresselly, Pembrokeshire **SA68 0NS**

🕐 Tues–Sat 9am–6pm; Sun 9am–12pm

Situated right on the farm itself, Yerbeston Farm Shop is a traditional establishment selling honest products of excellent quality. The finest Saddleback pigs, bred on the farm, provide the meat for their home-made sausages, pork pies, pork belly, sausage rolls and home-cooked hams – all of which are excellent. They sell beautifully perfumed honey harvested from the four guest hives on the farm and their own free-range eggs as well. Andy and Debbie Eastwood have worked tirelessly to ensure that the produce in the shop is traceable and of a high standard, making as much as possible on site and closely monitoring that which is provided by local producers. The shop also stocks a range of Welsh whiskys and wines.

FOOD MARKETS ▼

Abergavenny Farmers' Market

**www.abergavennyfarmers
market.co.uk**
☎ 01873 860271
✉ Market Hall, Cross Street,
Abergavenny **NP7 5HD**
🕐 **Twice monthly**, 4th
Thurs 9.30am–2.30pm

There is a traditional weekly produce (fruit and vegetables) market in Abergavenny's graceful market hall, but twice a month there's a larger farmers' market with a good range of stalls. Look out for Philip Watkins's organically grown local potatoes, Gothi Valley goats' cheeses and Black Mountain honeys.

Anglesey Farmers' Market

www.fmiw.co.uk
☎ 01248 490213
✉ David Hughes School, Menai
Bridge, Anglesey **LL59 5SS**
🕐 **Monthly**, 3rd Sat 10am

In spite of its remote location on Anglesey, this market has grown, and locals are devoted. There is some great local produce here, including fresh fish, organic vegetables, naturally reared beef, lamb and poultry. I was disturbed to hear grumblings, published in the local press, from local farmers and small producers who have not managed to get a stall at the market – surely in a place like Anglesey there is room for everyone providing they match the market criteria?

Brecon (Brecknock) Farmers' Market

**www.breconfarmersmarkets.
wordpress.com**
☎ 01874 636169
✉ Market Hall, Brecon, Powys
LD39AH
🕐 **Monthly**, 2nd Sat 9.30am–2pm

A very popular and famously good market held in the town's traditional market venue, with a large number of stalls (up to about 35). Depending on the time of year you can expect to find hill lamb from Castle Lands and Elan Valley, or Welsh Black beef from Pen-Min-Cae farm. There are eggs from Roger Little's hens, smoked fish from the Organic Smokery, the excellent artisan-made Teifi cheese, Cardigan Bay honey, pastries from Love Patisserie, beers from the Breconshire Brewery and locally grown fruit and vegetables (including organic) from a number of stalls. Being near-ish to the Welsh border, you will also find food from Herefordshire at the market.

Colwyn Bay Farmers' Market ©

www.fmiw.co.uk
☎ 01492 680209
✉ Bayview Shopping Centre, Sea View Road, Colwyn Bay **LL29 9LJ**
🕐 **Weekly**, Thurs 9am–3pm

Expect to find some delicious local foods in this farmers' market. This is the region for salt marsh lamb and Welsh Black cattle, and the area's shellfish is famous. Depending on the season you will be able to find both fresh fish and meat, honey from a nearby apiary, handmade cakes and breads, farmhouse cheese, plus jams and chutneys.

Fishguard Farmers' Market ©

www.fmiw.co.uk
☎ 01348 873004
✉ Town Hall, Fishguard, Pembrokeshire **SA65 9HA**
🕐 **Twice monthly**, alternate Sat 9am–2pm

A well-stocked market featuring produce sourced from within 30 miles of the coastal town. Depending on availability you can expect to find some great hill-bred lamb, fresh trout from a local fishery, breads, free-range poultry, locally and organically grown vegetables, local honey, soft fruit and even sheepskins. Check the website for the market dates.

Haverfordwest Farmers' Market ©

www.fmiw.co.uk
☎ 01437 776168
✉ Riverside Shopping Centre, Riverside Quay, Haverfordwest, Pembrokeshire **SA61 2LJ**
🕐 **Twice monthly**, alternate Fri 9am–3pm

On average around 24 stallholders sell their best produce at this market that opened in 1999 (the second farmers' market to open in Wales). Real heather honey, locally caught fish, free-range duck, guinea fowl and geese, home-reared meats, organic, rare-breed Oxford and Sandy Black pork, crab and lobster sandwiches, bread and locally milled flour, bara brith (a traditional sweet tea bread), Welsh cakes, Lanboidy farmhouse cheese, laver bread, ewes' milk cheese and smoked game can all be found at this popular market.

Mold Farmers' Market £

www.celynfarmersmarket.co.uk
☎ 01745 561999
✉ St Mary's Church Hall, King Street, Mold, Flintshire **CH7 4LN**
🕘 **Monthly**, 1st and 3rd Sat 9am–2pm

I know Mold quite well and have seen how local initiatives to develop a good food culture have taken off. There are lots of fantastic producers based in this area of North Wales close to the border. This market is one of three in the Celyn Farmers' Market group (details of Belgrave and Northrop markets are on the website). Among the producers at the market you will find (depending on season and availability) beef and lamb from Bryncocyn Organic farm, organic eggs from Castell Farm, handmade loaves baked by Jane Tomlin (who has a formidable reputation), vegetables from J. H. Jones, bara brith and eggs from Nant Ucha Farm, pork from Orchard Pigs and authentic pasta dishes made by Nonna (Grandmother) Teresa.

Monmouth Farmers' Market £

www.fmiw.co.uk
☎ 0845 6106496
✉ Monmow Street, Monmouth, Monmouthshire **NP25 3EG**
🕘 **Monthly**, 4th Sat 10am–1pm

The local council in Monmouth had the flair and imagination to permit this market a position on the bridge that crosses the River Monmow. It makes for a great sight, especially in winter when the December market is illuminated. The produce matches the venue, with Trealy Farm's superb Welsh charcuterie (see page 379), Diana Smart's artisan-made Single and Double Gloucester cheese, hams and bacon made using pork from her whey-fed pigs, Cothi Valley goats' cheese, Welsh Black beef and hill lamb from Pen-Min-Cae farm, and some delicious, Indian ready-made food made by Tiffy Kabir at K. K. Ventures.

Porthcawl (Bridgend) Farmers' Market £

www.bridgendfarmersmarket.co.uk
☎ 01656 658963
✉ Awel y mor, Porthcawl, Bridgend **CF36 5TS**
🕘 **Monthly**, 4th Sat 10am–1pm

You will find some interesting and delicious things at this market including Bethesda butter, hand-churned at a local farm, Hillside's fresh wet fish, laverbread plus cockles from Penclawydd, artisan loaves from Stuart's Hot Bread Shop in Swansea, milk from Ty Tanglwyst Dairy bottled on the farm (see page 385), home-grown vegetables, eggs and honey from Crickton Farm, good value whole and half pig boxes from Caermynydd Piggery, plus naturally reared meat from Morgan's Farm and Butchery.

Riverside Farmers' Market 🏷️

www.riversidemarket.org.uk
☎ 029 2019 0036
✉ Fitzhammon Embankment,
Riverside, Cardiff, South Glamorgan
CF11 6AN
🕐 **Weekly**, Sun 10am–2pm

Every week over 30 producers, many of them award-winning, sell the best in local Welsh and organic food that best represents the variety Cardiff has to offer. Cardigan Bay honey, goat sausages, Sugarloaf wine, award-winning cheeses, plus baked goods, meat, fruit and vegetables are all available, plus many more seasonal items.

Ruthin Produce Market 🏷️

www.ruthinproducemarket.co.uk
☎ 07798 914721
✉ Old Gaol Courtyard, St Peter's
Square, Ruthin, Denbighshire
LL15 1HP
🕐 **Monthly**, last Sat 10am–3pm

Deep in the North Wales countryside the area around Ruthin is becoming well-known for good food. At this charming market you will find some good producers. Look out in particular for Bryn Cocyn Organics who rear lamb and beef, but who are also getting into producing juice from their new orchards and growing vegetables. There is also another stall selling organic Aran lamb, preserves from Goetre Farm and Rosie's Triple D cider.

Usk Farmers' Market 🏷️

www.uskfm.co.uk
☎ 0845 6106496
✉ Memorial Hall car park,
Maryport Street, Usk, Monmouthshire
NP15 1LH
🕐 **Twice monthly**, 1st and 3rd Sat
10am–1pm

A very good farmers' and produce market featuring some unusual suppliers. Try the cured meats from Trealy Farm, fresh fish from Choices, Thomas's Welsh Black beef, organic vegetables from Whitebrook and Ty Mawr farms, Italian meals made with (mainly) Welsh ingredients at A Presto and fresh goats' cheese from Cothi Dairy.

▼ DELIS AND SPECIALISTS

Siop Y Gornel

www.siop-y-gornel.co.uk
☎ 01678 520423
✉ 21 Tegid Street, Bala, North Wales
LL23 7EH
🕐 Mon, Tues, Thurs, Fri, Sat
8.30am–4.30pm; Wed 9am–2pm

Adam and Feline took over a small corner shop three years ago, though to walk into the rustic, whitewashed, elegant premises they have now, you would not know it. The deli and bakery counters feel as though they have always been there – and this is what makes Siop Y Gornel so special. Six or seven different breads are baked every day on site, and the range of quiches, salads, sandwiches, pies and pasties on offer are also all home-made, often to order or on request. In a short space of time, this deli-bakery has become a local favourite: hearty homemade soup or an excellent roasted vegetable salad can be enjoyed with a hunk of fresh bread and rounded off with excellent coffee and a locally made cake – all of it is made with care for the produce and an eye for quality. They also stock local fresh produce, and much of this is used in the deli section as well. The shop and café area feel like an extension of the owners' kitchen and this welcoming, generous atmosphere translates into food that is enticing, delicious and of an excellent standard.

Trealy Farm Charcuterie

www.trealyfarm.com
🕿 01600 740705
✉ Mitchell Troy, Monmouth
NP25 4BL
🕐 Mon, Wed, Sat 7am–1pm, 2–5pm; Tues, Thurs–Fri 7am–1pm, 2–5pm

Not every effort to make a continental style, air-dried salami or prosciutto works when a UK producer tries it, but Trealy have succeeded where others fail with hams and yeasty cured sausages that would hold their own in Italy. The ham has a lovely elasticity and gentle saltiness, and the salamis come in many varieties – fennel, wild boar, venison and game. Call to place an order. (See page 382.)

BUTCHERS ▼

Alan P. Young Family Butcher

🕿 01446 792356
✉ 10 Church Street, Llantwit Major, Cardiff **CF61 1SB**
🕐 Tues 8.30am–3pm; Wed 8.30am–1pm; Thurs 8.30am–4.30pm; Fri 8am–5pm; Sat 7.30am–4pm

A picturesque village butcher's shop, with a huge following of devoted locals, specialising in Welsh lamb and beef, organic Oakland chicken, home-made 'farmhouse' faggots, hand-made sausages and organic eggs. It is well worth seeking out – a trip to this little shop is a delightful step back in time.

H. J. Edwards & Son ⊙ ⊘

www.hjedwards.co.uk
☎ 01873 853110
✉ 1–3 Flannel Street,
Abergavenny, Gwent **NP7 5EG**
🕐 Mon–Sat 7am–5pm

A butcher's with a strong local sourcing policy. The beef, pork and lamb in this Abergavenny shop is sourced from farms no more than 22 miles from the shop and quite often you will see a label by the meat showing the actual farm. The fresh meat is superb quality, especially the beef, and the dry-cured bacon, sausages and pies, all of which are made on the premises, are good (the bacon excellent).See website for other branches

Elwy Valley Welsh Lamb ⊙ @ ⊘ £

www.elwyvalleylamb.co.uk
☎ 01745 813552
✉ Gwern Elwy, Henllan, Denbigh
LL16 5BA

Daphne and David Tilley's lamb runs on the high hills of North Wales near Denbigh and is sold via mail order all over the UK. Their lamb, mutton and naturally reared beef is also popular with London chefs including Jamie Oliver, Anthony Demetre (Arbutus) and Jeremy Lee (The Blueprint Café). Daphne rounds up her beloved sheep riding her horse – a mounted shepherd whose special flock has all the flavours of hillside herbs and grasses.

Glanrafon Farm Free Range Saddleback Pork ⊙ @ ⊘

www.glanrafonfarm.co.uk
☎ 07917 667663
✉ Waen, St Asaph, Denbighshire
LL17 0DY

Cisa Borsey's blissfully happy, registered rare-breed Saddleback pigs have the run of her orchards where they can glean apples, damsons, wild garlic, acorns and bracken. Taste the meat and all the flavours of the seasons seem to be there. There is extra fat on a Saddleback, which intensifies the flavours further. Welfare is paramount on the Borsey's farm. To start with the sows are 'serviced' naturally by Carl the boar, so unlike in the pork 'factory' farms, no artificial insemination is used. The pigs only travel five miles to slaughter to keep stress to the minimum. You can order any cut, but I recommend (if you have a freezer or party to give) ordering a half pig butchered to your requirements. Discuss with Cisa, who will advise.

North Wales Buffalo @ 🦮 £

www.northwalesbuffalo.co.uk
📞 01352 781695
✉ Midlist Farm, Halkyn, Holywell,
Flintshire **CH8 8DH**

A welfare-friendly family farm, rearing water buffalo on a mainly grass diet. Young animals are kept with their mothers, suckling for as long as possible. The livestock is slaughtered locally so no animal travels more than 15 miles. John Sigsworth has set up a butchery on the farm, which also produces pork and lamb. You can order direct or buy their meat from local farmers' markets (see website for details). A catering service is also available.

Poyntons 🦮

poyntonsbutchers@aol.com
📞 01492 515377
✉ 417 Abergele Road, Old Colwyn,
Colwyn Bay, Clwyd **LL29 9PR**
🕐 Mon–Thurs 7am–5pm;
Fri 7am–5.30pm; Sat 7am–4pm

Richard Poynton is a sixth-generation butcher with a strong local following selling free-range Saddleback pork from Nant-Yr-Efail Farm, Betws-Yn-Rhos and Welsh Black beef from a farm in Dolwyn. Sausages are made with free-range pork and the range runs from plain pork to some pretty wild flavours, including asparagus and stilton or tomato and basil. While I agree the standard of the fresh meat is hard to beat, I'd like feedback on the more esoteric stock here.

Rhug Estate Organic Farm 🏠 @ 🦮

www.rhug.co.uk
📞 01490 413000
✉ Rhug Estate, Corwen,
Denbighshire **LL21 0EH**
🕐 Mon–Sat 8am–6pm;
Sun 8.30am–6pm

A large organic farm near the Berwyn mountains, owned by Lord Newburgh, producing beef, pork and lamb, which seems to be growing in scale each year. I hear that Rhug (pronounced 'reeg') is now selling to London restaurants and is set to expand yet further. But back in Wales there is indeed a more organic feel to this producer. The pedigree beef, hung for at least four weeks, is sold not only in the farm shop but also in the estate's burger stop at the edge of the Rhug estate on the A5. Poultry, including good Christmas turkeys, and game are also available.

Rob Rattray Butchers

01970615353
8 Chalybeate Street,
Aberystwyth, Ceredigion **SY23 1HS**
Mon–Wed 8.30am–5pm;
Thurs–Fri 8.30am–5.30pm;
Sat 8.30am–4pm

Rob Rattray has been rearing and butchering sheep, cattle and pigs on his farm just outside the busy market town for nearly 20 years and his shop bears the wonderful fruits of his considerable experience and skill. The stunning window display will draw you into a perfect, friendly little butcher's shop situated down one of Aberystwyth's lovely side streets. Not only does the shop stock fantastic free-range meats, expertly butchered on site, but it also sells the very best pork products. Far from the anaemic, mean offerings found elsewhere, the home-made pork pies have a rich and crumbly pastry, housing a deliciously meaty filling encased in a good layer of tasty jelly. The scotch eggs are just as delightful: large local free-range eggs nestle in a generously thick sausage casing, which tastes as hearty as it looks. The wide variety of sausage flavours, developed by Rob's wife Sheila, the treacle-cured bacon and the home-cured ham are all irresistible. The business prides itself on local produce of excellent quality; hand-reared, hand-picked and treated with the skill and care it deserves, the produce in this establishment is truly something special.

Slade Farm Organics

www.sladefarmorganics.com
01656 880048
Pitcot Farm, Wick Road, St Brides Major, Bridgend **CF32 0TE**
Wed, Sun 10am–5pm;
Thurs–Sat 10am–6pm

Traditional lamb, beef and pork breeds, organically reared on this staggeringly beautiful piece of land right on the coast at Southerndown, Vale of Glamorgan. Standards of animal welfare are exceptional with animals transported just a short distance to the abattoir, keeping stress to the minimum.

Trealy Farm Charcuterie

www.trealyfarm.com
01600 740705
Trealy Farm, Mitchel Troy,
Monmouth **NP25 4BL**
Mon–Fri 7am–6pm

This is an impressive business doing what is often seen as impossible and producing a range of continental style dry-cured ham that could hold up its head in Parma. James Swift, Graham Waddington and John Standerwick studied the art of charcuterie-making in Europe and now make an amazing range that includes air-dried chorizos, air-dried hams, loins and pancetta and a wide range of salamis including a nice, child-friendly, lightly smoked 'snack salami' and cabanos. The free-range pork used is reared at Trealy Farm and other local farms on a natural diet. The breeds used are primarily Gloucester Old Spot, Welsh and Saddleback. Braesaola (air-dried beef) is also available.

Ty-Talgarth Organics ⊕ @ ⊘

www.tytalgarthorganics.co.uk
☎ 01656 840436
✉ Nanty Moel, Bridgend
CF32 7NR
🕐 Thurs–Fri 10am–5.30pm; Sat 10am–3pm

This is a lovely farm with a shop attached, high on the hills near a former mining village. The animals are reared organically and include the wonderful native breed Welsh Black (some of the most delicious beef available), and hill-bred lamb whose meat carries all the flavour of the region's natural wild grassland.

The Welsh Venison Centre ⊕ ⊘

www.welshvenisoncentre.com
☎ 01874 730929
✉ Middlewood Farm, Bwlch, Brecon, Powys **LD3 7HQ**
🕐 Mon–Fri 8.30am–5pm; Sat 8.30am–12.30pm

The farmed venison is reared in the Brecon Beacons National Park close to the village of Bwlch in Powys. Animal welfare is paramount, say the Morgan family who have run this business since 1985 and who sell every cut through their shop, where you can witness the butchers at work, and via an efficient mail order service.

Williams & Son ⊘

☎ 01978 761078
✉ 14–16 High Street, Caergwrle, Wrexham **LL12 9ET**
🕐 Mon–Fri 9am–1pm, 2–5.30pm; Sat 9am–3pm

Justin Williams's small shop specialises in the best regional meat, including beef from Welsh Black cattle and small, yet exceptionally good, locally bred hill lamb. Newcomers to grass-fed Welsh Black are in for a treat. This is a tight-grained beef with a marbling of fat and real depth of flavour. The lamb is wonderful, too. It is best to buy a butchered half or whole one and freeze what you do not need. Other fresh cuts are on sale, plus home-cured bacon, pies and ham.

▼ BAKERS AND CONFECTIONERS

Cocoa and Company ⊙

www.cocoaandco.co.uk
☎ 01446 775729
✉ Cocoa and Company, Verity's
Court, Cowbridge,
Vale of Glamorgan **CF71 7AJ**
🕐 Mon–Sat 9.30am–5pm

This is a bespoke chocolate maker with a loyal clientele, making traditional-style chocolates in this small Glamorgan town using Fairtrade chocolate. One handy aspect of Mary Roberts's business is the mini 'goody bag' chocolate boxes and bags that she designs for weddings and parties.

The Tipyn Bach Chocolate Company ⊙

www.tipynbach.co.uk
☎ 01492 879000
✉ 6 Trinity Avenue, Llandudno
LL30 2NQ

Mona and Paul Davies' business is a bright light in the Welsh food produce scene. Fairtrade chocolate filled with ganaches made with locally produced cream, Welsh liqueurs and British made syrups. From chocolate-coated coffee beans to Welsh Vodka truffles and nutty pralines to fruit-filled white chocolate bars. Please let me know what you think. Buy online or see website for stockists.

▼ DAIRY

Gorwydd Caerphilly ⊘

www.gorwydd.com
☎ 01570 493516
✉ Gorwydd Farm, Llanndewi Brefi,
Tregaron, Ceredigion **SY25 6NY**

Gorwydd Caerphilly is a very creamy, golden-coloured cheese that is made at Trethowan's dairy on the farm. The venture was established in 1996 by Todd Trethowan. This is the Caerphilly to beat all Caerphilly's – a really superb artisan cheese with a slightly loose texture and sweetish fresh flavour. It's available at various outlets including Borough Market, London and St Nicholas Market, Bristol. See website for details.

Heavenly @

www.orchardweb.co.uk/heavenly
☎ 01558 822800
✉ Heavenly, London House,
Rhosmaen Street, Llandeilo,
Carmarthenshire **SA19 6EN**
🕐 Mon–Sat 9.30am–5.30pm;
Sun 11.30am–4.30pm

Paul and Tracey Kindred opened this fantastic shop in 2005 after personally researching chocolate and ice cream-making in Britain and on the continent. Using local organic milk, their ice cream is made in the Italian gelato style and they have created a tantalising range of flavours. Their lavender ice cream is made with local lavender and is wonderfully perfumed, without being overwhelming. Alongside the frozen delights is a dazzling array of home-made, hand-crafted chocolates and cakes in a myriad of shapes, sizes and flavours. The shop mixes a European boutique-patisserie style with traditional English retro-sweetshop warmth, and the staff are extremely knowledgeable about the ingredients and processes that go into each product. This little gem is wonderful and the Kindreds deserve full credit for creating a fantastic establishment and modern, tasty products that use as much local fare as possible.

Ty Tanglwyst Dairy ⚡ 🧀

www.tytanglwystdairy.com
☎ 01656 745635
✉ Pyle, Bridgend, Vale of
Glamorgan **CF33 4SA**
🕐 Mon–Fri 7am–6pm

Three generations of the Lougher family are involved in milking and processing milk from their small herd of pedigree Holstein cattle. The dairy cows graze the family's 125 acres of grassland on their small farm near Bridgend. The milk is processed on the farm, bottled and sold to either neighbouring shops, restaurants, pubs and fuel stations, or you can have it delivered to your door if you live within approximately five miles of the farm (in the Vale of Glamorgan). Double cream is also made on the farm, but the minimum order is two litres – great if you are thinking of making ice cream for a party. The milk is competitively priced, about the same as that sold in supermarkets, but the point here is that it is local and buying it supports the local farming economy. If you live near, sign up if you can.

Wild Fig @ ✿ ⓟ

www.fruitgarden.co.uk
☎ 01446 760358
✉ Groes Faen Road, Peterston-
Super-Ely, Vale of Glamorgan
CF5 6NE
🕐 Mon–Thurs 9.30am–5.30pm;
Fri–Sat 10am–5.30pm
Sun and Bank Hols 10am–4pm

This is a PYO and an ice cream shop on the farm where the fruit is grown. The ice cream is made on the farm and flavours include caramelised fig (and, yes, it is made with figs from their own garden!), vanilla, strawberry, chocolate, stem ginger, blueberry, gooseberry and cherry. Sorbets include blackcurrant and strawberry. Local free-range beef, lamb, pork and chicken are also available along with oven-ready meals, made using local ingredients.

▼ FISH AND SEAFOOD

Billy Fish ○ ✿ ₤

billythefish08@bt.com
☎ 01745 855067 / 07932 166845
✉ 29 Perbeck Avenue, Llandudno,
LL19 7UP
🕐 Tues, Thurs–Sat 9am–1pm

A fisherman-cum-fishmonger, selling whatever can be caught using a small fishing boat off the North Wales coast. Sea bass, plaice, red and grey mullet and crabs are among the regular catch. Billy is also a keen shrimp fisherman – call in advance to see what he has brought in.

Coakley-Greene Fishmonger

www.coakleygreene.food-
passion.co.uk
☎ 01792 653416
✉ Stall 41c, The Market, Oxford
Street, Swansea **SA1 3PF**
🕐 Mon–Sat 8.30am–5.30pm

The lucky people of Swansea can rely on this great stall with its fabulous display and reputation for fresh fish mainly sourced from local boats. In season you will be able to buy local mussels, squid, sea bass, crab or lobster and smoked fish including salmon, kippers and haddock.

Hive on the Quay

www.hiveonthequay.co.uk
☎ 01545 570599
✉ Cadwgan Place, Aberaeron
SA46 0BU
🕐 Tues–Sat 10.30am–4.30pm
(Thurs–Sat in low season)

The display of fish on ice in Will Willis's attractive fish shop in Aberaeron is always stunning, with all sorts of species looking their absolute freshest and best. Flat fish (sole and plaice) jostle for room among scallops, brown crab, lobster, eel and some less typical types such as spider crab. If you are not in the mood for shopping there is a good café next door selling fish soups and seafood platters.

Mermaids Seafoods ○ ●

www.mermaidseafoods.co.uk
☎ 01492 878014
✉ Builder Street, Llandudno,
Gwynedd **LL30 1DR**
🕐 Mon–Fri 8.30am–4.30pm;
Sat 8.30am–12.30pm

Malcolm Wright and Margot Pilling's small but exceptional fishmongers in North Wales sells the catch of the day from local fishermen. Crab, lobster and flat fish are Mermaid's forte, but contact them for availability of Conway river mussels and oysters from the Menai Straits.

New Quay Fresh Fish Shop

☎ 01545 561011
✉ South John Street, New Quay,
Ceredigion **SA45 9NP**
🕐 Mon–Fri 9.30am–3pm
(In season open every day of the week)

A tiny fish shop close to the entrance of New Quay's harbour specialising in crab and lobster brought in by the still thriving small fleet of boats that fish out of this lovely location. Housed in a former lifeboat station, the shop has a great following not only among the locals, but also the many holidaymakers who visit in summer. The shop also sells other species, all subject to season and availability.

Selective Seafoods ○ @ ●

www.selectiveseafoods.com
☎ 01758 770397
✉ Ffrid Wenn, Tudweiliog, Pwllheli,
Gwynedd **LL53 8BJ**

Gareth Griffiths and Mary White supply fresh lobster, crab and sea bass to a plethora of restaurants and hotels in North Wales and operate an efficient mail order business. The shellfish is sourced from local fishermen who put down pots in the nearby coastal waters. All the fish is processed on the premises and the home-made crab soup is wonderful. Opening times vary seasonally, so it's best to ring first.

Welsh Seafoods

www.welshseafoods.co.uk
☎ 01646 692 331
✉ The Docks, Milford Haven,
Pembrokeshire **SA17 3AE**
🕐 Mon–Fri 6am–3pm

A chance to buy superbly fresh fish and shellfish from the last two remaining Welsh-owned trawlers in Milford's docks. Expect to find sea bass, red mullet, ray wings, sole, squid – depending on season – plus fish bought from small boats off the coast of South Wales. With Milford Haven and the Bristol channel ever more threatened by industrialisation (it is destined to become a huge shipping port) it is great to see that the fishermen are standing their ground, keeping sustainable fishing going in these parts. Sean Ryan and Chris Davies' business was shortlisted in the BBC Radio 4 Food & Farming Awards in the Best Local Retailer category. As a judge, I visited them myself and was impressed.

▼ VEGETABLES AND FRUIT

Hooton's Homegrown 🏠 ⬤ 🐾

www.hootonshomegrown.com
🕾 01248 430344
✉ Gwydryn Hir, Byrnsiensyn, Anglesey **LL61 6HQ**
🕐 Mon–Sat 10am–5.30pm

There are two PYO sites on this beautiful farm that looks across Anglesey towards the mountains of Snowdonia. From June you can turn up and pick from a huge range of soft fruit or vegetables, or simply go to the shop (year round) and buy the farm's own or local produce, plus Welsh Black beef, free-range eggs, chicken and duck. At Christmas you can buy the farm's own larger-sized chickens, geese or turkeys. This is a great enterprise, with nicely chosen goods in the shop – not too gift-orientated like many in tourist areas. Worth a detour. There is a second shop in Fron Goch Garden Centre, Llanfaglan, Caernarfon LL54 5RL. See website for details.

Pencoed Growers ⬤ 💷 ⬤

🕾 01656 861956
✉ Felindre Nurseries, Pencoed, Bridgend, Mid Glamorgan **CF35 5HU**
🕐 Mon, Wed, Sat, 7am–1pm; Tues, Thurs, Fri 7am–4.30pm

A great vegetable box scheme run by John Roberts and Yvonne Leslie from their 34-acre market garden / smallholding specialising in herbs, including dill, chervil, parsley and basil, salad leaves and whole lettuces, spinach, soft fruit, cut flowers and much more. Phone ahead and they will pick to order and pack a box for you to make an appointment to collect (no deliveries). This is a scheme that guarantees absolute freshness.

Strawberry Fields 💷

🕾 01446 772675
✉ 6b Penny Lane, Shopping Precinct, Cowbridge, Glamorgan **CF71 7EG**
🕐 Mon–Sat 8am–5.30pm

There are some good-looking, fresh locally grown vegetables in this shop run by Paul and Joel Preece. Most are loosely stacked so there is little packaging to unwrap at home after a visit. Look out for the fine Gower peninsular cauliflowers – a local crop with a steadfast following. Goose, duck and chicken eggs from a local farm are also available.

Tredilion Fruit Farm ⊘ ⓕ ⊛

01873 854355
Villa Salerno, Llantillo, Pertholey, Abergaveny, Monmouthsire
NP7 8BG
Mon–Sun 9am–5pm

An Italian-run market garden and fruit farm that has a considerable following among the locals who recommended it for this guide. Drop in to the farm shop for a wide range of seasonal, just-picked produce, or pick your own strawberries and raspberries, plus other produce, in season.

Ty Mawr Organic @ ⊘ ⓕ ⊕

www.ty-mawr-organic-veg.co.uk
01873 0796
Great House Farm, Penpergwm, Abergavenny, Monmouthshire
NP7 9UY
Fri 3pm–6.30pm

Organic growers Philip and Josie Bevan operate a box scheme and run farm gate sales, selling their outstanding Soil Association-certified produce. The range, which obviously changes through the seasons, is huge, from kohl rabi to raspberries, pumpkins to purple sprouting broccoli, Sweet Florence fennel to herbs. They also attend local markets – see website for details. Note the very limited opening times.

HONEY ▼

New Quay Honey Farm ⊙ @ ⊘

www.thehoneyfarm.co.uk
01545 560822
Cross Inn, New Quay, Ceredigion
SA44 6NN
Mon–Sun 10am–5.30pm

Really lovely honeys from west Wales made on the farm that is open to visitors curious to learn all about bees and how honey is made. The honeys are sold in the shop and include the light and floral-flavoured borage honey, a more robust-tasting wildflower honey and a scented, almost minty-tasting heather honey. Mead, honey mustards and chutneys are also available. A must if you are in the area. Seasonal changes apply to opening times so check the farm is open before you visit.

Seasonal food calendar

These days you can buy most foods all year round, but there's nothing like eating fabulous, fresh local produce when it is at its best. Here is a selection of the huge variety of great food produced in the UK and the best time of year to buy it.

* variable

	January	February	March
Meat	Hare Partridge Pheasant Venison (English and Welsh)	Guinea fowl Venison	Hare Rabbit Spring lamb
Fish	Haddock John Dory Langoustines Line-caught cod Mackerel Monkfish Red mullet Scallops Sea bass UK Oysters Whiting	Cockles Hake Mussels Turbot	Brown trout Crab Hake Lemon sole Lobster Sea trout Wild brown trout * Wild salmon *
Vegetables	Celeriac Chicory January King cabbage Jerusalem artichoke Kale Rosemary Sage Swiss chard Turnips	Brussels sprouts Chervil Cornish new potatoes Jersey Royals Kale Onions Purple sprouting broccoli Red chicory Spring cabbage Shallots Swede	Cauliflower Chicory Green celery Fennel Morelles Parsley Parsnips Purple sprouting broccoli Salad onions Sorrel Swedes Turnips
Fruit	Rhubarb (forced)	Rhubarb (forced)	

	April	May	June
Meat	Spring lamb	Wood pigeon	Welsh lamb
Fish	Mackerel John Dory Salmon Sea bass Rainbow trout Wild brown trout * Wild salmon * Wild sea trout *	Brill Cornish sardines (Pilchards) Cromer crab Dover sole Halibut John Dory Lemon sole Salmon Sea bream Turbot Whiting Wild brown trout * Wild salmon * Wild sea trout *	Brill Cornish sea bass Mackerel Sardines Turbot Scottish mussels Wild brown trout * Wild salmon * Wild sea trout *
Vegetables	Asparagus Bay Broccoli Chervil Carrots Cucumber Radishes Rocket Sorrel Spinach Thyme Wild garlic	Asparagus Aubergines Broad beans Broccoli Carrots Cauliflower Chard Chervil Jersey royals New potatoes Salad onions Radishes Samphire Sorrel Spinach Watercress	Artichokes Asparagus Aubergines Chicory Courgettes Cucumber Florence fennel Garden peas Iceberg lettuce Lamb's lettuce New potatoes Pak choi Romaine lettuce Summer cabbage Sweet peppers Tomatoes Turnips Watercress
Fruit	Strawberries Summer rhubarb	Rhubarb Raspberries	Raspberries Strawberries

	July	August	September
Meat	Salt marsh lamb	Grouse	Goose
	Scottish venison	Hare	Mallard
	Wood pigeon	Venison	Partridge
		Wood pigeon	Venison
			Welsh lamb
			Wood pigeon
Fish	Brill	Atlantic salmon	Anchovies
	Monkfish	Brown crab	Brown crab
	Plaice	Brown shrimp	Cockles
	Sea bass	Brown trout	King scallops
	Turbot	Dover sole	Lemon sole
	Wild brown trout *	Haddock	Native oysters
	Wild salmon *	Monkfish	Red gurnard
	Wild sea trout *	Sardines/Pilchards	Turbot
		Sea bass	Wild brown trout *
		Spider crab	Wild salmon *
		Red mullet	Wild sea trout *
		Wild brown trout *	
		Wild salmon *	
		Wild sea trout *	
Vegetables	Beetroot	Aubergines	Beetroot
	Broad beans	French beans	Broad beans
	Celery	Green celery	Carrots
	Chantenay carrots	Leeks	Cauliflower
	Courgettes	Lettuce	Celeriac
	French beans	Marrows	Courgettes
	Helda beans	Onions	Maincrop potatoes
	Lettuces	Parsnips	Peas
	Onions	Runner beans	Spinach
	Pak choi	Salad leaves	Sweetcorn
	Parsnips	Sweetcorn	Tomatoes
	Radishes	Tomatoes	
	Red chicory	Turnips	
	Runner beans	Watercress	
	Tomatoes		
Fruit	Blackberries	Apples	Apples
	Blackcurrants	Blackberries	Pears
	Cherries	Currants	Plums
	Gooseberries	Plums	Quince
	Raspberries	Raspberries	
	Strawberries	Rhubarb	
		Strawberries	

	October	November	December
Meat	Goose	Goose	British grass-fed beef
	Guinea fowl	Partridge	Goose
	Partridge	Pheasant	Partridge
	Pheasant	Venison	Pheasant
	Rabbit		Suckling pig
	Venison		Turkey
	Welsh lamb		Venison
	Wood pigeon		
Fish	Brill	Plaice	
	Brown crab	Whiting	
	Langoustines		
	Lemon sole		
	Oysters		
	Prawns		
	Turbot		
Vegetables	Beetroot	Beetroot	Broccoli
	Broccoli	Broccoli	Brussels sprouts
	Cauliflower	Carrots	Cavolo nero
	Cavolo nero	Celeriac	Chestnuts
	Cucumber	Endive	Kale
	Jerusalem artichokes	Leeks	Leeks
	Kale	Parsnips	Parsnips
	Leeks	Pumpkins	Potatoes
	Maincrop potatoes	Purple sprouting broccoli	Winter cabbages
	Mushrooms	Salsify	
	Onions	Savoy cabbage	
	Pumpkins	Squashes	
	Squash	Swedes	
	Sweetcorn	Turnips	
	Tomatoes	Winter cabbage	
	Turnips	Winter celery	
	Walnuts	Winter spinach	
	Watercress		
Fruit	Apples	Apples	Apples
	Figs	Pears	Pears
	Pears		
	Quince		

UK food festivals

JANUARY

Hampshire Potato Day
www.potatoday.org

Farmhouse Breakfast Week
www.hgca.com/breakfast

FEBRUARY

National Dairy Week
www.foodloversbritain.com

National Bramley Apple Week
www.farma.org.uk

Rye Bay Scallop Festival
www.ryebayscallops.co.uk

Wakefield Festival of Food, Drink and Rhubarb
www.experiencewakefield.co.uk

Fairtrade Fortnight
www.fairtrade.org.uk

MARCH

The Great Hampshire Sausage, Pie & Ready Meal Competition
www.foodloversbritain.com

APRIL

Chester Food and Drink Festival
www.chesterfoodanddrink.com

Mid-Wales Mouthful Food Festival
www.visitmidwales.co.uk

East Anglian Game and Country Fair
www.ukgamefair.co.uk

APRIL–JUNE

British Asparagus Festival
www.britishasparagusfestival.org

MAY

Real Food Festival
www.realfoodfestival.co.uk

Tewkesbury Food and Drink Festival
www.tewkesburyfoodfestival.co.uk

Dales Festival of Food and Drink
www.dalesfestivaloffood.org

Derbyshire Food and Drink Festival
www.derbyshirefoodfestival.co.uk

Henley Food Festival
www.henleyfoodfestival.co.uk

Streatham Food Festival
www.streathamfoodfestival.com

Wholly Herbs
www.westdean.org.uk

JUNE

BBC Good Food Summer Festival
www.bbcgoodfoodshow.com

The Children's Food Festival
www.childrensfoodfestival.co.uk

Bridport Food Festival
www.bridportfoodfestival.co.uk

JUNE–JULY

Pembrokeshire Fish Week
www.pembrokeshirefishweek.co.uk

JULY

Hampshire Food Festival
www.hampshirefare.co.uk

AUGUST

Huddersfield Food and Drink Festival
www.huddersfield-htpl.co.uk/foodanddrinkfestival

River and Food Festival
www.visitcardigan.com

The Lakes Chilli Fest
www.chillifest.co.uk

Isle of Wight Garlic Festival
www.garlicfestival.co.uk

Newlyn Fish Festival
www.newlynfishfestival.org.uk

SEPTEMBER

Broadstairs Food Festival
www.broadstairsfoodfestival.org.uk

Really Wild Food and Countryside Festival
www.reallywildfestival.co.uk

Ludlow Food Festival
www.foodfestival.co.uk

Tavistock Food and Drink Festival
www.tavistockfoodfestival.co.uk

Aldeburgh Food and Drink Festival
www.aldeburghfoodanddrink.co.uk

Cornwall Food and Drink Festival
www.cornwallfoodanddrink
festival.com

York Food and Drink Festival
www.yorkfoodfestival.com

Abergavenny Food Festival
www.abergavennyfoodfestival.com

Hastings Seafood and Wine Festival
www.visit1066country.com

Great British Cheese Festival
www.thecheeseweb.com

Narberth Food Festival
www.narberthfoodfestival.com

Mold Food and Drink Festival
www.moldfoodfestival.co.uk

Feast of Dorset
www.feastofdorsetl.com

SEPTEMBER–OCTOBER

British Food Fortnight
www.lovebritishfood.co.uk

Norfolk Food Festival
www.norfolkfoodfestival.co.uk

Croydon Food Festival
www.croydonfoodfestival.com

OCTOBER

Manchester Food and Drink Festival
www.foodanddrinkfestival.com

Mendip Food and Drink Festival
www.mendipfoodfestival.co.uk

East Midlands Food and Drink Festival
www.eastmidlandsfoodfestival.
co.uk

Emsworth Seafood Week
www.emsworthseasons.org

Countryside Live – Food & Farming Fair
www.countrysidelive.co.uk

BBC Good Food Show Scotland
www.bbcgoodfoodshow.com

Exmoor Food Festival
www.exmoorfoodfestival.co.uk

Llangollen Food and Drink Festival
www.llangollenfoodfestival.co.uk

Yorkshire Food and Drink Festival
www.theyorkshirefoodanddrink
festival.co.uk

NOVEMBER

Clovelly Herring Festival
www.clovelly.co.uk

BBC Good Food Show Birmingham
www.bbcgoodfoodshow.com

Taste of Lincolnshire Christmas Food and Drink Fair
www.visitlincolnshire.com

Winchester Christmas Family Fayre
www.winchester.gov.uk

DECEMBER

Lincoln Christmas Market
www.christmasmarket.lincoln.
gov.uk

Fowey Christmas Market
www.foweymarket.co.uk

Slow Food Market at Southbank
www.slowfood.org.uk

Useful organisations

British Pig Executive (BPEX)
✉ Agriculture and Horticulture Development Board, Stoneleigh Park, Kenilworth, Warwickshire CV8 2TL
www.bpex.org.uk
☎ 02476 692051

Campaign for Real Bread
✉ c/o Sustain, 94 White Lion Street, London N1 9PF
www.realbreadcampaign.org
☎ 020 7837 1228

Country Markets (WI)
✉ Dunston House, Dunston Road, Sheepbridge, Chesterfield, Derbyshire S41 9QD
www.country-markets.co.uk
☎ 01246 261508

Department for Environment, Food and Rural Affairs (DEFRA)
✉ Customer Contact Unit, Eastbury House, 30–34 Albert Embankment, London SE1 7TL
www.defra.gov.uk
☎ 08459 335577

English Beef and Lamb Executive (EBLEX)
✉ Agriculture and Horticulture Development Board, Stoneleigh Park, Kenilworth, Warwickshire CV8 2TL
www.eblex.org.uk
☎ 08702 421394

Functional Food Centre
✉ School of Life Sciences, Oxford Brookes University, Gipsy Lane, Headington, Oxford OX3 0BP
http://functionalfood.brookes.ac.uk
☎ 01865 483297

London Farmers' Markets
✉ 11 O'Donnell Court, Brunswick Centre, London WC1N 1NY
www.lfm.org.uk
☎ 020 7833 0338

Marine Conservation Society
✉ Unit 3, Wolf Business Park, Alton Road, Ross-on-Wye, Herefordshire HR9 5NB
www.mcsuk.org
☎ 01989 566017

National Farmers' Retail & Markets Association (FARMA) and National Association of Farmers' Markets
✉ 12 Southgate Street, Winchester, Hampshire SO23 9EF
www.farma.org.uk
☎ 08454 588420

Organic Farmers and Growers
✉ The Old Estate Yard, Albrighton, Shrewsbury, Shropshire SY4 3AG
www.organicfarmers.org.uk
☎ 08453 305122

Slow Food UK
✉ 6 Neal's Yard, Covent Garden, London WC2H 9DP
www.slowfood.org.uk
☎ 020 7099 1132

Specialist Cheesemakers Association
✉ 17 Clerkenwell Green, London EC1R 0DP
www.specialistcheesemakers.co.uk
☎ 020 7253 2114

Sustain
✉ 94 White Lion Street, London N1 9PF
www.sustainweb.org
☎ 020 7837 1228

The Biodynamic Agricultural Association (BDAA)
✉ Painswick Inn Project, Gloucester Street, Stroud, Gloucestershire GL5 1QG
www.biodynamic.org.uk
☎ 01453 759501

The Guild of Fine Food
✉ Station Road, Wincanton, Somerset BA9 9FE
www.finefoodworld.co.uk
☎ 01963 824464

The Fairtrade Foundation
✉ 3rd Floor, Ibex House, 42–47 Minories. London EC3N 1DY
www.fairtrade.org.uk
☎ 020 7405 5942

Useful publications

**The Food Magazine /
The Food Commission**
✉ 94 White Lion Street, London
N1 9PF
www.foodmagazine.org.uk
☎ 020 7837 2250

**The Food Standards
Agency**
✉ Aviation House,
125 Kingsway, London
WC2B 6NH
www.food.gov.uk
☎ 020 7276 8829

The Soil Association
✉ South Plaza, Marlborough
Street, Bristol BS1 3NX
www.soilassociation.org
☎ 01173 145000

**Waste & Resources Action
Programme (WRAP)**
✉ The Old Academy, 21 Horse
Fair, Banbury OX16 0AH
www.wrap.org.uk
☎ 01295 819900

Which?
✉ Castlemead, Gascoyne Way,
Hertford SG14 1LH
www.which.co.uk
☎ 01992 822800

*Behind the Label; Eat Your
Heart Out* (2008)
by Felicity Lawrence

*British Regional Food;
British Seasonal Food* (2008)
by Mark Hix

Food in England (2009)
by Dorothy Hartley

North Atlantic Seafood
(2003) by Alan Davidson

Kitchenella
(2010) by Rose Prince

River Cottage Meat Book
(2004) by Hugh Fearnley
Whittingstall

*Shopped, The Shocking
Power of British
Supermarkets; Bad Food
Britain* (2005)
by Joanna Blythman

*Slow Food Nation, Why Our
Food Should Be Good,
Clean and Fair* (2007)
by Carlo Petrini

Tescopoly (2007)
by Andrew Simms

The Carbon Fields (2008)
by Graham Harvey

The Good Food Guide
(2011) by Elizabeth Carter

The End of the Line (2005)
by Charles Clover

*The New English Kitchen,
Changing the Way You
Shop, Cook and Eat*
(2005) by Rose Prince

The New English Table
(2008) by Rose Prince

The Savvy Shoppper
(2006) by Rose Prince

We Want Real Food (2006)
by Graham Harvey

Index of trades

Index of producers by trading name

Y

Author's acknowledgements

Grateful thanks are due to Kate Pollard, Stephen King, Clare Brenton and Jane Beaton of Hardie Grant for all their enthusiasm for the new edition of the guide. Working with them has been a real pleasure. I could not have managed without the support of other members in the team, who include hardworking researchers Caroline Tecks and Phoebe Robinson, and also my husband Dominic Prince. Additional suggestions for entries were very helpfully provided by Julia Moore, Mark Hix, Northern Ireland Tourism, True Taste Wales and of course readers who have sent in their nominations. I would also like to thank my editors at the *Daily Telegraph* for their continuing support.

The Foodies' Diary 2012

by Alan Campion and Michele Curtis

PUBLICATION DATE June 2011
PRICE £9.99 Paperback

This stunning diary for food lovers provides inspiration
on what to eat and cook based on the best fresh
produce available each month of the year. It includes
all the features of a good diary as well as beautiful
colour photography, over 60 delicious recipes, wine tips
and a guide to food and wine festivals around the UK.

ISBN 9781742701592

Feedback form

Thank you for purchasing *The Good Produce Guide 2011*. We pride ourselves on providing a comprehensive list of the best food produce in the country. If you liked, loved or hated any of the producers listed, or would like to suggest entries for next year's Guide, we'd love to hear from you.

Please send us your details along with your feedback, so that you can be entered into our seasonal prize draw where you could win a special prize courtesy of Hardie Grant Books.

You can get in touch with us in two ways:

▼ POST

Producer's Name:

Producer's Address:

Include in the Guide / Don't Include in the Guide *(Delete as appropriate)*

Please give reasons and descriptive comments:

Your Name:

Your Address:

Your E-mail:

Having completed this form, please tear it out and send it to:
Hardie Grant Books London, Dudley House, North Suite 34–35 Southampton Street, London WC2E 7HF

▼ E-MAIL

Alternatively, you can e-mail your suggestions to **info@roseprince.co.uk**

Please write '**Good Produce Guide 2011**' in the subject box of your email, and remember to include your name and address in the message.

Many thanks